Selected Writings of Victoria Woodhull

# *Acknowledgments*

Just as women's suffrage was not won by any single individual, this project owes its completion to the efforts of many people. First and foremost, I credit Sharon Harris's enthusiasm for the book, and her long-standing commitment to recovering the work of nineteenth-century American women writers. My colleagues at West Virginia University have assisted me in countless ways; Jane Donovan, John Ernest, Michael Germana, Kirk Hazen, David Krech, Carolyn Nelson, and Alyssa Wright have been particularly generous with their time. A Senate Grant from the Eberly College of Arts and Sciences at West Virginia University enabled me to do research at the Boston Public Library, Harvard University, and the New York Public Library, and a Riggle Fellowship afforded me a visit to the Southern Illinois University at Carbondale Special Collections. A book subvention grant from West Virginia University fostered the completion of this project. And I thank Kristen A. Elias Rowley, Ladette Randolph, Ann Baker, Lona Dearmont, and the others at the University of Nebraska Press who have helped bring this book to its readers.

I have also been aided by colleagues from other institutions: a Dartmouth summer seminar in July 2007 was helpful early in the book's compilation, and Bruce Mills of Kalamazoo College offered his guidance along the way.

This collection would not have been possible without earlier, foundational scholarship: Madeleine B. Stern's reader, biographies by Mary Gabriel, Barbara Goldsmith, Lois Beachy Underhill, and new critical studies like *Victoria Woodhull's Sexual Revolution* by Amanda Frisken. The Woodhull Presidential Library, http://www.victoria-woodhull.com/library.htm, has been another useful resource. Finally, I thank my students, whose surprise in learning about Woodhull for the first time helped convince me of the importance of this project.

Special acknowledgment is due to graduate students Molly Hatcher and Beth Staley, whose diligence and dedication to this project would make any nineteenth-century suffragist proud. I also thank undergraduate Brittney Warnick for her editorial assistance.

I extend my appreciation to all of those suffragists who endured countless insults and injury so that women could vote.

I thank my parents for their unvarying support of this and all my projects. And finally, Eric Bowen's patience and kindness sustains my every day.

## *Note on the Text*

Texts not intended for publication, including private letters and miscellaneous notes in Victoria Woodhull's handwriting, are presented exactly as they appear in the original. These documents were found in various archives. Nineteenth and early twentieth-century style is thus retained.

Texts intended for publication, including Woodhull's speeches and newspaper items, raise a more complicated question of authorship and intention. Scholars agree that these materials were written and edited at least in part by Stephen Pearl Andrews and Colonel James Harvey Blood. A comparison between her handwritten documents and the published texts reveals that the latter are far more polished, a fact that may reflect their status as published works more than it clearly indicates authorship. It remains difficult and perhaps not altogether desirable to determine exactly who wrote what; like any politician, Woodhull borrowed from others' words in crafting her public image. Any speech that exists in multiple versions has been edited to reflect, as much as possible, Woodhull's intentions. See individual texts for specific sources.

The only silent emendations are the following: obvious printer errors have been corrected, and variable font sizes and styles have been standardized. Anachronistic spellings and punctuation are maintained unless they would create confusion for the reader. Notes are the editor's. Woodhull's original footnotes are retained. Ellipses are used to represent the editor's textual omissions.

# Introduction

To the extent that anyone's life reflects the time in which she lives, Victoria Claflin Woodhull embodied hers. Born shortly after Samuel Morse developed the electric telegraph in the United States, she died not long after promising five thousand dollars to the first person to fly across the Atlantic. Like the inventions her life witnessed, she crossed what others deemed uncrossable. First and foremost a performer, her most extravagant crossovers occurred on stage, as she delivered speeches perhaps even more shocking by today's standards: speeches that espoused free love, a more equal distribution of wealth, and women's legal rights. In Amanda Frisken's words, Victoria Woodhull was "one of the most powerful speakers of the time. Her contribution was to act out the period's most extreme positions on a public stage" (5).

This collection offers a glimpse into the life of this complicated figure, affording us a sense not only of Woodhull's circumstances and accomplishments but of how they inform late nineteenth-century suffragism, reproductive rights, sexual politics, and spiritualism. While scholars tend to divide her life into two distinct phases—her early, progressive commitment to free love and her later conservative eugenics—I hope to show that the two are more connected than previously imagined, and that they need to be refigured in order to understand both her and her context.

Woodhull tends to be a marginal figure in many accounts of nineteenth-century women's rights, in part because of the disdain most suffragists ultimately felt toward her. Reformers like Susan B. Anthony, after a brief fascination with Woodhull, came to view her radicalism as a threat to the movement. Anthony and Elizabeth Cady Stanton's voluminous record of the women's movement only mentions Woodhull's memorial to Congress, and an early biography of Anthony ignores deemed masturbation as dangerous in part because it wasted critical bodily resources. Consider *A Lecture to Young Men* (1837), a book by Sylvester Graham—a man now best known as the namesake of the graham cracker: "therefore that the emission of semen enfeebles the body more than the loss of twenty times the same quantity of blood,— more than violent cathartics and emetics:—and hence the frequent and excessive loss of it cannot fail to produce the most extreme debility, and disorder, and wretchedness, of both body and mind" (Graham 51–52). Woodhull's "The Elixir of Life" (1873) expresses a similar sentiment: "With this knowledge [of masturbation], added to the stifled but still growing passion, they decline into a morbid sexual condition which, running into years, carries them beyond the possibility of a return to natural and healthy action to maturity, utterly ruined, sexually and physically" (chap. 19, this vol.).

While Graham and Woodhull ultimately reached different conclusions, both were preoccupied by what they saw as improper sexuality. Marshalling various medical and religious literature, Woodhull, not unlike the hygienists, sketched a vision of sexual health that seems rather draconian today. It is not difficult to draw a connection between such writing and a later eugenic preoccupation with the "fit" and "unfit." Given these parameters on sexuality, "free love" becomes something else indeed.

Woodhull was, like anyone, a product of her surroundings, which in her case were those of a profound and transformative religious and spiritual revival. Victoria Claflin was born in Homer, Ohio, in 1838, a decade before the celebrated Seneca Falls Convention. It was a time when the Second Great Awakening held sway, dotting the landscape with revival tents and bringing people like Victoria's mother, Rose, to their feet—and knees. It was a time when people had a fine (or perhaps an obtuse) sense of spectacle: the Fox sisters, two young girls who claimed to hear the rappings of a murdered salesman in Hydesville, New York, were soon exhibited by P. T. Barnum. It was a time when people knew both too much and too little: in this case, the ghost claimed to be Charles B. Rosma, who had been killed and buried in the cellar. Indeed, a skeleton was found in the cellar wall in 1904, long before DNA tests could have confirmed the ghost's story.

Victoria's father, Buck Claflin, always looking for a get-rich scheme, took advantage of the spiritualist rage and installed Victoria and her sister Tennie as mediums from a young age. Well versed as a charlatan, he led them on exhibits throughout the country. Their departures were sometimes determined by customer dissatisfaction; in the most damaging case, an Illinois cancer patient claimed in 1864 that Tennie had sold her an ineffective treatment. Tennie left the state immediately to evade authorities. For Victoria, it was a seamless slide at age fifteen from such schemes to a hasty marriage with Dr. Channing Woodhull, a Civil War veteran more devoted to drink than to his new wife. Victoria's son, Byron, was born at home in 1854 with the assistance of his intoxicated father. Victoria would always blame Byron's mental disability on the fact that he was conceived and delivered in a dysfunctional marriage. Later writings like "Stirpiculture" and "The Rapid Multiplication of the Unfit" argue that loveless matches result in "undesirable" offspring. Although such theories are repugnant today, in her time they offered women like Woodhull a compelling defense against unsatisfying marriages and restrictive gender roles. Her theory did not hold out with her daughter, Zula Maud, however, who was born under similar circumstances in 1861. Zula would become Victoria's most devoted companion.

It was Zula's birth, and Channing Woodhull's continuing intoxication, that convinced Victoria to secure a divorce. She met Colonel James Harvey Blood in St. Louis in 1864 when he consulted her as a spiritualist. They applied for a marriage license two years later in Ohio. In 1868 she reported being called to New York City by the spirit of the Greek orator Demosthenes. Woodhull thus became one of the millions who were drawn to a city by its promises of financial and political opportunities during the last three decades of the nineteenth century.

Along with Tennie, Woodhull opened a stockbroking office in New York in early 1870. It was a time of many firsts for the burgeoning city; work on the Brooklyn Bridge began that month. The sisters made much of their money through an alliance with tycoon Cornelius (Commodore) Vanderbilt, who at one point asked Tennie to marry him. She declined, apparently satisfied with their extramarital relationship. Victoria and Tennie credited their spiritualist powers for their ability to advise investors. They established their newspaper, *Woodhull and Claflin's Weekly*, with stockmarket funds. Despite its claim to be the "only Paper in the World conducted, absolutely, upon the Principles of a Free Press," it was forever linked both to their financial status and the sexualized image they acquired: men, who dominated the financial scene, could see these first lady stockbrokers in no other terms. As Amanda Frisken has shown, sporting newspapers contributed to their sexualization; *The Days' Doings*, for example, presented a suggestive image of the sisters surrounded by men (2–3). In another cartoon, Victoria and her sister Tennie, riding in a carriage on Wall Street, whip the submissive men who pull the carriage (4, 6).[3] This cartoon indicates the anxiety their public positions aroused as they crossed into a male stronghold. On February 6, 1870, the *New York Times* expressed skepticism about the brokers' future: "The place was thronged from early morning until late at night by a crowd of curiosity hunters, who gazed at the females and besieged them with questions. The older and more respectable dealers of the street remained at their offices, discussing the advent of the female financiers in the street, and there was a strong popular feeling against the persons.... A short, speedy winding up of the firm of WOODHULL, CLAFLIN & Co. is predicted" (8). The *New York Herald* was far more laudatory: "Their extraordinary coolness and self-possession, and evident knowledge of the difficult rôle they have undertaken, is far more remarkable than their personal beauty and graces of manner, and these are considerable. They are evidently women of remarkable coolness and tact, and are capable of extraordinary endurance" (quoted in *The Human Body* 296). Likewise, the *New York Courier* agreed that they were "perfectly capable of taking care of themselves" (quoted in *The Human Body* 297).

Despite these votes of confidence, the financial world Victoria and Tennie entered as the "First Lady Stockbrokers" in 1870 was a tumultuous one. On one hand, with growing opportunities in oil and steel investments, Gilded Age fortunes were made overnight; on the other, speculation and shifting government monetary policies rendered such fortunes ever fragile. The market was just recovering from Black Friday of 1869, when thousands lost money after President Ulysses S. Grant released gold into the market, thus lowering the value of gold held by private investors. The Woodhull sisters were initially able to survive market fluctuations because of their close relationship with Vanderbilt. By 1872, when that relationship came to an end following Victoria's criticism of him in speeches like "The Impending Revolution," they were more vulnerable. At that point, Victoria became dependent on income from her lectures. The newspaper and the brokerage fell into debt; *Woodhull and Claflin's Weekly* briefly ceased circulation in 1872, and when landlords refused to rent to her, Woodhull was forced to move from a regal home to her office. Her financial situation was further impeded by the size of her large and often unharmonious household: her parents, ex-husband, and various other relatives lived with her. In May 1871 her mother, notoriously mercurial, sued Colonel Blood for alienating her from Victoria's affections and threatening her with bodily harm. The very public case did not help Woodhull's reputation. The *New York Times* records Woodhull's financial decline: in 1871 she offered ten thousand dollars to the struggling women's rights movement (an amount she did not in fact deliver), while the *Times* of August 28, 1872, recorded her testimony that she did not even own "the clothes on her back" (2).

In 1871 the woman who would offer thousands to the women's suffrage movement became the first woman to speak before a U.S. congressional committee. Her memorial made an argument, known as the "new departure," that she had heard at the women's suffrage convention in 1869: the Constitution already grants women, as citizens, suffrage. Her goal was "to show that *to vote is not a privilege* conferred by a State upon its citizens, but a CONSTITUTIONAL RIGHT of every citizen of the United States, of which they cannot be deprived" (*The Origin, Tendencies, and Principles of Government*, 37). She goes on to assert that "[t]he male citizen has no more right to deprive the female citizen of the free, public, political expression of opinion than the female citizen has to deprive the male citizen thereof." Woodhull argued that women have a race, and therefore are enfranchised thanks to the Fifteenth Amendment. The argument that women's suffrage is a constitutional right was made by suffragists with words and action as they attempted to vote on a number of occasions. The majority of the committee was not convinced by Woodhull's argument, however, responding that the question of suffrage should be left up to the states. Woodhull and other suffragists were heartened by the minority opinion, which was penned by Representatives William Loughridge and Benjamin Butler.

One of Woodhull's first public statements on suffrage appeared in the *New York Herald* of April 2, 1870. The *Herald*, a major publication of the nineteenth century, was an interesting choice; its publisher was James Gordon Bennett, who has been called the father of yellow journalism. As Erika Falk notes, the paper's extensive coverage of Woodhull can be explained in part by its focus on financial matters (103). As New York's first female stockbroker, Woodhull was of obvious interest to such a publication. She begins her editorial by asserting that her actions to date have earned her the right to speak on women's behalf, while others have merely given lip service to equality: "I boldly entered the arena of politics and business and exercised the rights I already possessed" ("The Woodhull Manifesto," chap. 1, this vol.). The first part of the piece is filled with active verbs: she "asserted," "worked," and "proved," and she ends with words popular among politicians: "courage, energy and strength." After establishing her right to speak, she turns to the frequent argument of white women that if blacks (black *men*, that is) have the vote, of course "woman" should. The immensely complicated status of sectionalism and Reconstruction is here reduced to a single sentence: "The simple issue whether woman should not have this complete political equality with the negro is the only one to be tried, and none more important is likely to arise before the Presidential election." In this statement "woman" is implicitly white and "negro" is implicitly male. The alignment of women with whites and "negros" with men is also evident in Woodhull's later speech "The Scare-Crows of Sexual Slavery": "Tell me that wives are not slaves! As well might you have done the same of the negroes, who, as the women do not, did not realize their condition!" (chap. 20, this vol.). Such comments emerged within the Reconstruction era when tensions between whites and African Americans, northerners and southerners, Democrats and Republicans festered. The Fourteenth Amendment, ratified in 1868, assured citizenship for former slaves, reversing the earlier decision of *Dred Scott v. Sandford*, while the Fifteenth Amendment of 1870 banned the prohibition of suffrage based on race, color, or previous servitude. The Enforcement Act of 1870 attempted to combat rising violence and discrimination against African Americans in the South. But by 1872, reconstruction efforts were waning; President Grant, who had begun to shy away from such policies, won another term. It was in this context that Woodhull argued that "women," who were implicitly white, should be able to vote. This argument was unsuccessful in securing a sixteenth amendment for women's suffrage; it was not until 1920 that they won the vote.

Woodhull's racism took a number of forms, from claims that black men did not deserve the right to vote before white women to more subtle associations with whiteness. One of her most egregious statements comes in "The Scare-Crows of Sexual Slavery": in response to the claim that free love would result in women's unrestrained passion, she asks, "Did you not say that all the women would immediately rush into the arms of every man they should meet, let it be in the street, in the car or wherever else; that even negroes would not escape the mad debauch of white women?" Woodhull employs miscegenation, a primary fear of the time, as evidence for her own racist argument, suggesting how preposterous it would be that white women would desire black men. Her famous speech "Tried as by Fire" includes a more subtle call for women to embrace "their white-robed purity" (chap. 21, this vol.). These were powerful words, given that "pure white women" were "one of the central fictions of the antebellum southern aristocracy" (Frisken 58). In turn, the popular press produced several images suggesting that Woodhull's ticket promoted a distasteful mingling of the races (Frisken 62–84). Again, we are faced with an apparent contradiction: Woodhull ran on the equal rights ticket even as she took advantage of her white privilege and depended on racist figures like George Francis Train, who offered her financial and emotional support during her battles with anti-obscenity crusader Anthony Comstock.[4]

The Equal Rights Party, whose main goal was to secure women's suffrage, was credited with a July 4th letter of nomination that Woodhull actually wrote. The letter and Woodhull's response appeared in the *Weekly* in June 1872. At the May 1872 meeting, the 668 delegates nominated abolitionist Frederick Douglass as her running mate. For reasons that remain unknown, he never responded.[5] As Frisken argues, the party's nomination of a white woman and an African American man in this period of extensive racial violence was, if nothing else, a symbolic testament to the equal rights it claimed to pursue. The fact that Woodhull could run on this ticket even when espousing such beliefs indicates the depth and complexity of the period's racism. Most sources indicate that Woodhull received some popular votes in the presidential election, but no electoral votes. She ran again, with much less fanfare, in the 1884 and 1892 races.

The height of Woodhull's speaking career was in the 1870s; according to Amanda Frisken, "By 1872, none of the suffrage lecturers could command an audience that compared to Woodhull's" (119).[6] Even when—or perhaps because—her reputation was tainted by scandal, she made successful lectures across the country. Spectators often commented on her appearance, noting her magnetism, beauty, and the single rose that she often wore at her neck. In 1872 audience member Austin Kent described her as "[a] woman, small in stature, of good countenance, and feminine in manner, [who] took the liberty to think freely, write her thought, and read it to six thousand people,—six thousand more returning to their homes—not finding standing room in the Hall" (1). Accounts of her nervousness in her first lectures are rendered with a note of approval, suggesting that she was viewed as feminine enough to avoid outright censure. At the same time, in keeping with a larger move among suffragists to challenge the restrictive women's fashions of the day, Woodhull often wore men's clothing. Descriptions of her physical appearance indicate that at least at the height of her popularity, she was able to walk a fine line between being adequately feminine and, in wearing masculine dress, avoiding a debilitating sexualization. As a reporter from the *New York World* noted, she combined "a singular masculine grasp with the most gentle and womanly attraction" (quoted in *The Human Body* 272). Frisken notes that Woodhull was especially gifted at winning over hostile audiences, a valuable talent as she continued to battle public opinion. She did so using a variety of tactics, appearing with a Bible to deliver "The Human Body the Temple of God" in the South; speaking directly to the mothers in the audience; and beginning lectures with a shaky voice (Frisken 137–41). Her rhetorical strategies, then, were as varied as the audiences she faced.

Key to Woodhull's prominence—and her fall from the good graces of many other suffrage leaders—was her fierce adherence to free love. As she said at a dramatic moment in "The Principles of Social Freedom," "Yes, I am a Free Lover. I have an *inalienable, constitutional,* and *natural* right to love whom I may, to love as *long* or as *short* a period as I can; to *change* that love *every day* if I please, and with *that* right neither *you* nor any *law* you can frame have *any* right to interfere" (chap. 10, this vol.). Free lovers disagreed, however, on how "free" one should be; some varietists, to the displeasure of monogamists, argued for multiple lovers. Joanne E. Passet captures the term's ambiguity:

> Mainstream newspaper editors and clergy, free love's most vocal critics, called anyone who deviated from customary ideals of proper behavior a "free lover." Nineteenth-century sex radicals further confused matters because they could not agree on the term's application in daily life: for some it meant a lifelong and monogamous commitment to a member of the opposite sex, others envisioned it as serial monogamy, a few advocated chaste heterosexual relationships except when children were mutually desired, and a smaller number defined it as variety (multiple partners, simultaneously) in sexual relationships. Many who called themselves free lovers were married yet denounced marriage as an institution requiring women's subordination to men. Yet no matter what their practical interpretation of free love, they shared two core convictions: opposition the idea of coercion in sexual relationships and advocacy of a woman's right to determine the uses of her body. (2)

Indeed, Woodhull regarded sex within loveless marriages as coercive to women, and held that wives who remained in such relationships simply for the sake of convention were more "impure" than prostitutes. In turn, as Tennie argued in the *Weekly* on September 23, 1871, abortion indicated that conception occurred not in love but in the shackles of institutionalized marriage: "Abortion is only a symptom of a more deep-seated disorder of the social state. It cannot be put down by law. Normally the mother of ten children is as healthy, and may be as youthful and beautiful, as a healthy maiden. Child-bearing is not a disease, but a beautiful office of nature. But to our faded-out, sickly, exhausted type of women, it is a fearful ordeal. Nearly every child born is an unwelcome guest. Abortion is the choice of evils for such women" (9).

For reformers like Tennie Claflin and Victoria Woodhull, abortion was one inevitable result of a society in which children were conceived in loveless unions without proper support. Thus abortion itself was not the primary crime, but the social system that made it necessary.

In contrast to opponents who equated "free love" with promiscuity, some who adopted the label urged abstinence. Woodhull made a number of attempts in her speeches to distinguish "free love" from "free lust," at times preferring the more neutral term "social freedom." Such attempts were not always successful. Thomas Nast's infamous cartoon in *Harper's Weekly* sports the caption "Get thee behind me, (Mrs.) Satan!" and features a sinister Woodhull with batlike wings clutching a sign that reads "Be Saved By Free Love." Behind her a sickly woman is bent over with the weight of two infants and a whiskey-guzzling man. Nast emphasizes Woodhull's full lips and eyebrows, characteristics that seem both sensual and dangerous. Inserting the title "Mrs." here, the artists reminds readers that Woodhull's sex is of vital importance; this is not just Satan, but his wife. So the very "free love" that Woodhull espoused, with its critique of institutional marriage, is erased in this title: she is effectively married off, stripped of her name in the usual patriarchal tradition.

An understanding of Woodhull's conception of free love requires a consideration of Stephen Pearl Andrews (1812–1886), her most important mentor besides James Blood. Through lectures and writing, Andrews helped popularize Josiah Warren's notion of "Individual Sovereignty," the belief that each person was the only authority on his or her true sexual relations. Warren and Andrews had created the social experiment Modern Times at Long Island in 1851. Andrews wrote and distributed

Thomas Nast, "Get Thee Behind Me, (Mrs.) Satan!" *Harper's Weekly*, February 17, 1872. Courtesy of the American Antiquarian Society.

the 1853 pamphlet *Love, Marriage, and Divorce*, an argument for social freedom. He was an eccentric man with a long list of preoccupations: he developed a system of phonographic recording, learned thirty languages (even developing one of his own), and in 1843 proposed an unsuccessful plan to end slavery by having English abolitionists purchase and then free Texan slaves. One of his most famous inventions was "The Pantarchy," a somewhat mystical free-love organization. *Woodhull and Claflin's Weekly* was, at least initially, its organ (Stern 109). In Helen Lefkowitz Horowitz's words, it was his "odd combination of anarchic liberalism and economic radicalism" that most influenced Woodhull (349). Andrews's fingerprint is visible on Woodhull's involvement in labor rights and antimonopoly work. Both were members of Section 12 of the International Workingmen's Association, a socialist organization founded in 1864 and relocated to New York City in 1872. The *Weekly* ran regular updates on the association during this time, and its prospectus declares its commitment to a new land, economic, and industrial system "in which each individual will remain possessed of all his or her productions." Victoria and Tennie received much press attention for their participation in a parade in December of 1871 on behalf of Louis-Nathaniel Rossel and other leaders who had been executed after the failure of the Paris Commune, a short-lived socialist rule of Paris. Woodhull also held an honorary post in the American Labor Reform League. Her interest in labor issues is evident in "A Page of American History: Constitution of the United States of the World" (1870), a revision of the U.S. Constitution that gives Congress the power of the "abolition of Pauperism and Beggary" and calls for a system in which "the producer is entitled to the total proceeds of labor, which shall prevent the accumulation of wealth in the hands of non-producers" (chap. 3, this vol.). Woodhull's views on labor were shaped not only by Andrews but by political economists like Henry George, who argued that poverty resulted from the concentration of large amounts of land and natural resources in the hands of monopolies. Woodhull's commitment to free love and women's suffrage conflicted with the larger communist platform, however, and in 1872 her chapter was expelled from the International Workingmen's Association.

Woodhull's vision of free love drew in part from the tenets of the Oneida Community, which she once described as "the best order of society now on the earth" ("Tried as by Fire," chap. 21, this vol.). Founded by John Humphrey Noyes in 1848, the community held that its highest purpose was the worship of God, and that "worship," in what today seems like a generous definition of the term, included polygamous sexual relations. Indeed, within his borders, monogamy was not allowed; in its place was "complex marriage," promiscuous sexual relationships. Young men had sex with postmenopausal women in order to learn the withdrawal method that was required of all men (unless they were given permission to reproduce). Jealousy among spouses was strongly discouraged. In keeping with a communist ethos, children were raised not by their parents—indeed, parental ownership of any kind was frowned upon—but by the community at large. If women could tolerate the lack of privacy and the autocratic rule of the commune, they enjoyed a freedom from the kinds of control that existed in the larger society: they could determine when, and even if, they wanted children; they were not limited to particular kinds of labor; and they escaped the patriarchal control of a husband (although this control was handed over, in many cases, to Noyes himself). When we try to fit Oneida into contemporary models of sexuality we are inevitably stymied: its progressive spirit was stunted by Noyes's rigid control, and the proto-eugenist selection of "desirable" partnerships is likely to make anyone uncomfortable.

The structure of the Oneida Community, for better or worse, had a conclusive answer to one of the central questions posed to free lovers: what is the fate of the children of open relationships? In works like "The Scare-Crows of Sexual Slavery" (chap. 20, this vol.), Woodhull envisions a somewhat similar arrangement, but knowing that the Oneida arrangement was at once too local and too sweeping for the masses, she struggled to find a suitable answer. Stephen Pearl Andrews's letter in the *Weekly* of August 26, 1871, takes up this issue: "The third and last grand objection to Amorous Liberty relates to the maintenance and culture of Children. This objection assumes that the isolated family offers the only mode of properly caring for offspring. The family, as now constituted, is, in fact, a very hot-bed of selfishness, which, while it provides for one's own children badly enough, permits the children of others, equally good, to starve at one's door, with the comfortable assurance that the responsibility belongs with somebody else. A grand social revolution is soon to occur" (11). The nursery imagined here is "scientifically organized and adapted to the new social state" (11). This nursery would thus be a cradle, so to speak, of the communist civilization Andrews envisioned.

One of the speeches included in this volume is Woodhull's most famous articulation of free love. According to Frisken, "A Speech on the Principles of Social Freedom" (chap. 10), first delivered in 1871, is "probably the most frank defense of social freedom before a public audience in American history" (37). When Woodhull gave "Social Freedom" (also called "The True and the False") to a St. Paul audience in 1874, a reporter declared that she spoke with "considerable fierceness, and with a degree of elocution that indicates no small amount of study and labor. As a speaker she irresistibly attracts attention, both on account of the matter and the manner, and one listens continually, wondering what will come next" (quoted in Frisken 124). Others echoed this sense of her "electrifying" words (quoted in Frisken 124). Such reviews indicate that the success of Woodhull's message was due in no small part to her masterful delivery, with her speeches amounting to a kind of seduction: as one noted, "her face and form present a spectacle of bewildering loveliness such as Praxiteles might worship" (quoted in *The Human Body* 272). Given Woodhull's starring role in discussions of sex and marriage in the late nineteenth century, it is little wonder that she took center stage in one of the biggest scandals of the time, the Beecher-Tilton trial. In September 1872, after hearing rumors of the affair of fabulously popular minister Henry Ward Beecher and his parishioner Elizabeth Tilton, Woodhull detailed their infidelity in her address at the meeting of the American Association of Spiritualists. On November 2 she published it in her newly resuscitated newspaper. Woodhull was driven to expose Beecher not only because of her commitment to free love but a balder need for money. Throughout the controversy and later trial, she maintained that Beecher's crime was not his adultery but his failure to acknowledge it publicly. He was, in other words, practicing free love in private while publicly denouncing its followers. The newspaper was an immediate bestseller; copies went for as much as forty dollars each. As Horowitz details, public response to Woodhull was mixed: some defended her while others believed she had crossed the line into indecency. Woodhull's involvement in the scandal was complicated by her personal and professional relationship with Tilton, her biographer and possible lover.[7] Tilton and Beecher never fully reconciled; Beecher's trial in 1875 ended in a hung jury.

The Beecher-Tilton scandal coincided with both Woodhull's presidential ambitions and her battle with the reformer Andrew Comstock. Comstock was appalled by the "foul stories and criminal deeds" that he saw as a direct threat to innocence (*Traps for the Young* 8). Yet as historians have shown, Comstock's crusade was not as easy as one might expect. In an urban setting like New York City, prostitution was big business; at one point, there were 621 brothels (Gabriel 33). As early as the 1830s, periodicals ostensibly protesting vice delighted in publishing titillating details of prostitution and engaged, on occasion, in blackmail. According to Horowitz, opposition to "vice" was less organized at this time than it would be in later decades. Even when anti-obscenity organizations became more prevalent later in the century, Comstock was subject to judicial decisions like that of Samuel Blatchford, who ruled in 1873 that Comstock's law did not apply to newspapers. Such moments allowed Woodhull and her associates the delicious treat of lampooning him, as with their editorial "Poor Comstock." Consider Woodhull's depiction of the infamous figure in the *Weekly* on March 8, 1873: "Now, we commiserate what we know must be the feelings of so sensitive of a soul as this one is, and we hope the Christian ministry will instantly call a series of prayer meetings, lest under the extreme affliction he may fall from grace. . . . Poor Comstock! We trust your Christian hope and faith will prove sufficient in this your hour of trial, and that Christ, upon whom you so confidently lean for support, may not even now think you a heavy load to carry" (10).

On November 2, 1872, Woodhull, Tennie, and Colonel Blood were arrested on obscenity charges for the Beecher-Tilton article and sent to the Ludlow Street Jail, where they would spend Election Day. They were bailed out only to be arrested again soon after on charges of libeling Luther Challis, a man they had accused of seducing two young women. The sisters were acquitted of libel in 1874. Despite Comstock's efforts, the obscenity charges were dismissed in the summer of 1873 when the judge ruled that the 1872 law did not apply to newspapers. A more stringent law, including a special agent position that Comstock would occupy, was signed by President Grant on March 3, 1873. Molly McGarry notes that although it passed without much public notice, it "would police sexuality and govern traffic in sexual literature and information for nearly a century afterward" (9). In another momentary victory, upon hearing in January 1873 of Comstock's plans to arrest her once again, Woodhull disguised herself in order to speak at the Cooper Institute. In an editorial in the *Weekly* on February 8, 1873, she boasts of her success:

> It would be impossible for me to secrete myself in the building and to appear upon the rostrum at the proper time. Therefore I resolved to assume a disguise. Some willing friends assisted, and I soon presented the appearance of an old and decrepit Quaker lady. In this costume I confidently entered the hall, passing a half-dozen or more United States marshals, who stood guarding the entrances and warning the people that there was to be no lecture there that night—so certain they were of arresting me. But I passed them all safely, one of them even essaying to assist me on through the crowd. (9)

Her effect was momentous; as one observer wrote, "[T]here, with an energy and excitement never to be forgotten, [she] threw off her disguise, pushed her fingers through her disheveled hair with tremulous rapidity, and stood before her audience as Mrs. V. C. Woodhull" (quoted in Frisken 106). She would not, it seems, be easily silenced. The agents waited until the conclusion of the speech to make the arrest.

Woodhull's life was shaped not only by free love ideology and the anti-obscenity movement, but by spiritualism. Spiritualism and sexuality, McGarry has argued, were intimately related. According to McGarry, claims to materialization—the embodiment of spirits—who could pass over literary and abstract boundaries of space and morality, even kissing séance participants, related to the fears that the postal service could transmit vice from public to private space, urban setting to the home. Spiritualism, with its own crossings, threatened to unsettle rigid conventions, just as the "obscene" mailing could corrupt the innocent. Famous for her own crossings of public and private space, Woodhull provoked similar awe and unease. At the same time, Woodhull's spiritualism was occasionally used to defend her morality:

> In this Lecture, Mrs. Woodhull used no language touching "social freedom" which had not been often used by the best minds, in relation to mental and religious freedom,—yet a host of human hornets were ready to sting her. It was not strange, and was no "disgrace" that many Spiritualists should demur to her positions, and closely, if kindly criticize them. Some Spiritualists are and have been life-long conservatives. But how could any *Spiritualist* condemn free thought and free speech, no matter where they may have led an honest soul! At this we have a right to marvel. (Kent 1)

American spiritualism found its origins in the mystic Emanuel Swedenborg and the French socialist Charles Fourier. Swedenborgism enjoyed tremendous popularity in the United States beginning in the 1840s. It differed markedly from traditional Christian beliefs, endorsing "spiritual affinities" that might occur outside traditional marriage. Fourier's commitment to women's rights and cooperative living communities had obvious appeal to people like Noyes. Despite spiritualist departures from Christian tradition, the two beliefs often coexisted. Spiritualism became all the more popular during and after the Civil War, when a nation of mourners sought connection to the dead.

The connection between spiritualists, abolitionists, and advocates of women's rights was an intricate one: William Lloyd Garrison and the Grimké sisters, for example, were early adherents. As Ann Braude writes, "Not all feminists were Spiritualists, but all Spiritualists advocated women's rights" (3). In the first decades of the movement, a time when women speakers were still quite rare, spiritualism offered them a public position as mediums. Braude notes that mediums were most often women and girls because the position of medium was thought to require the passivity associated with females. In this capacity women thus enjoyed an authority they had not previously known. Indeed, the African American author-turned-spiritualist Harriet Wilson was able to support herself in Boston in the 1860s as "the colored medium."[8] In the spiritualist tradition, Woodhull performs passivity as a means of asserting her voice: "Do not, however, receive this as coming from me; but accept it as coming from the wisest and best of ascended Spirits—those whom you have learned to honor and love for the good done while on the earthly plane" ("The Elixir of Life," chap. 19, this vol.). Woodhull continued to refer to the spirits as inspiration on stage even in the 1870s, when women speakers were more common: in an 1873 letter to the *Pittsburgh Leader*, she wrote, "I should feel that all the blessings that make life worth having would be lost to me, were I now commanded to testify of my life, to attempt to arrogate to myself, what has been done through me by spirits."[9]

The development of spiritualism was often likened to the telegraph, which was seen as a metaphorical tie to God: a kind of spiritualist strand of pearls linking the individual and the divine. Noted authors from Margaret Fuller to James Fenimore Cooper subscribed to spiritualist tenets. With its emphasis on the individual connection to the divine and its commitment to reform, spiritualism differed markedly from Calvinism. As evident in Woodhull's mother's frequent "trances," it overlapped well with the fervency of the Second Great Awakening. For many Americans a direct connection to God was more important than precise adherence to the tenets of any one faith. In the words of historian Nathan O. Hatch, "[W]hether they came to fix their identity as Methodist or Baptist, Universalist or Disciple, Mormon or Millerite, [religious leaders] all shared a passion for expansion, a hostility to orthodox belief and style, a zeal for religious reconstruction, and a systematic plan to labor on behalf of that ideal" (56). Thus Woodhull came of age in a time when people were relatively receptive to multiple expressions of faith.

The fact that Victoria Woodhull was elected president of the American Association of Spiritualists in 1871 suggests her prominence in the field; however, Braude notes that many spiritualists felt alienated by Woodhull's view of marriage as legalized prostitution. Braude describes Woodhull as an opportunist who rose rather rapidly in the ranks of the spiritualist society as the movement was beginning to wane; mediums, once considered respectable channels to deceased loved ones, were increasingly dismissed as charlatans. Woodhull herself critiqued the "barefaced frauds" in a letter to the editor of the *Pittsburgh Leader* in 1873. It was at this point that Christian Scientists, who denounced mediums, were able to gain the esteem that spiritualists had once enjoyed. Notwithstanding her rich history of spiritualism in the United States, Braude's rather swift dismissal of Woodhull as an opportunist fails to account for Woodhull's success on stage, even as spiritualism was generally declining. The collection in the present book, by including Woodhull's speeches, aims to account for that influence.

Braude offers a useful distinction between feminist abolitionists and feminist spiritualists, the latter of whom tended to view anarchy favorably and were less likely to prioritize the end of slavery. Braude notes that some seemed preoccupied with arguing that (white) women were slaves, and in doing so neglected the position of African American men and women. She locates both Woodhull and Andrews in the latter category. Even feminist abolitionists, however, held problematic positions on slavery and race; as Karen Sánchez-Eppler has shown, in identifying with slaves on the basis of oppression through difference, white women were "inextricably bound to a process of absorption not unlike the one that they expose" (31). In other words, the particularities of black women's experiences were erased as white women abolitionists ended up reproducing, or at least appropriating, the oppressive relationships of slavery. And while one might think that Woodhull's free love, with her vow to "love whomever I choose whenever I choose," would challenge laws and mores against miscegenation, she demonstrated racist beliefs not unlike that of many white women of the time.

Although they might at first seem at odds, an important connection exists between Woodhull's attachment to free love and her eventual adoption of "sexual science." Motherhood is the crucial link between the two. Braude notes that spiritualists like Alice Stockham espoused sex education as part of the voluntary motherhood (contraceptive) movement (127). Woodhull was no doubt influenced by such reformers in her call for frank discussions of sexuality. In the maternalism of sexual science, Woodhull found a solution to the children of free love: "Nor should one-half of all the children born continue to die before reaching the age of five years, sacrificed, as they now are, to the inexcusable ignorance of mothers—murdered, it ought rather to be said, by the popular barbarity which condones ignorance of sexual matters" ("Tried as by Fire," chap. 21, this vol.). Unsatisfying marriages made for "unfit" offspring; thus, it was for the good of the children that more egalitarian relationships were pursued. In a time when anti-obscenity efforts became more prevalent and anarchists were increasingly feared, Woodhull found in motherhood an effective defense of her ideals.[10]

In a post-Holocaust world it is difficult to untangle eugenics from its most horrific twentieth-century products, yet to properly understand Woodhull's relationship to the emerging movement we must attempt to do so. Because *On the Origin of Species* was published in the midst of the Civil War, Darwinism was initially ignored by most Americans. In the last three decades of the nineteenth century, however, it gained what Richard Hofstadter calls "an unusually quick and sympathetic reception" (4). Evolutionary theory complemented certain beliefs of the time, forming what he refers to as "conservatism almost without religion" (7). Of course, religious figures were not completely disconnected from the movement; some voiced their disapproval while others, like Henry Ward Beecher, were vocal adherents to both Darwin and Spencer: "Beecher publicly acknowledged Spencer as his intellectual foster father" (Hofstadter 30). For his part, Lyman Abbott challenged conventional constructions of original sin, seeing it as a (natural) "lapse into animality" (Hofstadter 29). Figures like Beecher and Abbott enabled Woodhull to see evolution not in conflict with religion but as its partner.

Woodhull's attachment to eugenics grew stronger once she moved to Great Britain, the birthplace of the ideology. Francis Galton, Darwin's cousin and the inventor of eugenics, propagated his ideas through a number of books: *Hereditary Genius* (1869), *Inquiries into Human*

*Faculty* (1883), and *Natural Inheritance* (1889). The Oneida Community, under Noyes's stewardship, was already practicing stirpiculture when Galton's first book appeared; Noyes viewed it as further legitimation of the practice. It was Noyes, in fact, who coined the term "stirpiculture." Not surprisingly, Noyes's criteria for the "most fit" most often included himself; he fathered a number of Oneida children. Hofstadter notes that eugenicists subscribed to a belief in the "fit," who were usually of the upper classes, and the "unfit," those of a lower socioeconomic status. Eugenicists "were also in large part responsible for the emphasis upon preserving the 'racial stock' as a means of national salvation—an emphasis so congenial to militant nationalists like Theodore Roosevelt" (Hofstadter 163–64). Woodhull's calls for institutional eugenics reflect the larger social shift from laissez-faire Darwinism to an active state role and illustrate some of the race and class distinctions that Hofstadter notes.

It was at one of her eugenics speeches in London that Woodhull met the wealthy businessman John Martin. (Citing adultery, an ironic and likely arbitrary charge, she had divorced Blood in 1876).[11] Her courtship with Martin was hampered by her scandalous record, and it was only after she publicly denounced free love that they married in 1883. Their correspondence indicates a deep and anguished love as Martin was frequently absent from home, conducting the business of a late–nineteenth century British millionaire. His letters are written on a host of hotel and office stationery, from the British Association for the Advancement of Science to Overbury Court, Tewkesbury. He frequently begs Victoria either to stay home or meet him. In an odd mix of loving desperation and passive aggression, he writes, "Dearest little wife, If you knew how much I think of you all day, you would not let anything be done that would will make me unhappy when I am at my work, & have to think that you are left alone. So pray believe that I am only thinking of your happiness, & do not do anything to mar it."[12] The fact that he changes the subjunctive "would" to "will" makes his message more emphatic, transforming the letter from a request to a command. Martin emerges in these letters as an overprotective, anxious husband; as he says, "I don't like your going [illegible] by yourself, I don't see what you have to say to him." In another letter, he urges her to join him and demands to know where she has disappeared: "I asked every hour yesterday for your promised telegram, but none came, & I could not write for want of your address. At last I was obliged to telegraph to Clarke (!!!) to know what has become of you. . . . I hope that you will telegraph . . . me early this morning: don't leave me uncertain where you are." Yet her responses seem equally anguished about their separation; as she writes in one letter, "I only heard yesterday morning that you were ill—it has broken my heart to think of you so far off and suffering and I cannot go to you[.] Oh my husband *I* am so weary of life since you left I have not been well a day and I have aged so. You would not care to see *me*." Common to these letters is her sense that the entire world, including his family, is against her and that only he can protect her. In this sense, her letters correspond to the common theme of victimhood that appears in much of her later writing, as she reflected on her waning public career. "I know your family do not *love* me—and I do not trust them[;] they did not care for us when we were well. How is it possible that they should *now*." Shortly before Martin's premature death of pneumonia in 1897, she wrote him, "[I]n this world of treachery and hollowness there is still one who cares if I am suffering or in despair." Her late writings portray a woman who saw herself as a tragic, misunderstood victim of the public's whims. One who had always tried to negotiate her public image, she spent many of her last years rewriting her past, disowning many of her writings, lambasting people like Blood and Andrews, and even attempting to change her name to "Woodhall." Such efforts muddle her biographical record and leave a trace of uncertainty, making the title of one of her late essays "The Unsolved Riddle," an apt description of her life itself.

Victoria Woodhull-Martin would survive her husband by thirty years, dying in England on June 9, 1927. A document she wrote in 1918 offers us a window into her late psyche: "They have struck me down with the deepest insult they could find Entering my private home with all the brutality of Ignorant Insolence having the seal of goverment in thier hands I had to submit alas it broke me down dazed and Horified."[13] A will dated June 24, 1920, indicates her concern over her daughter's fate: "I hope that *none* of what the *world calls family* will in any way make [Zula] any trouble or annoyance."¹⁴ Despite this private despair, she posed the face of a confident, fantastically wealthy matriarch: she hosted the Ladies' Automobile Club and the Women's Aerial League of Great Britain. Clippings included in her collection at the Boston Public Library suggest she remained interested in women's rights and labor issues: one is entitled "Control of US Wealth; 41 Per. in the Hands of Women," another is "Wealth Concentrated in the Hands of the Few," and a story from the *Charlotte News* of November 26, 1928, is entitled "The Rich and the Poor."¹⁵ As a testament to her mother's influence, Zula Maud left her fortune to a eugenics society with which Margaret Sanger was also affiliated. This gesture ensured that the complicated relationship between eugenics and the women's movement would continue.

## VICTORIA WOODHULL'S WORKS

The bridge between Woodhull's free love ideology and her commitment to "sexual science" and eugenics is most evident in speeches like "The Elixir of Life" (chap. 19, this vol.), which she gave to the American Association of Spiritualists in 1873. At first glance, the speech seems consistent with many feminist beliefs today: Woodhull defines free love in contrast to the "brutal lust" to which married women are regularly subjected by their husbands, women's stifled sexual desire, and the hypocrisy of men who preach of purity and yet pursue extramarital affairs. Woodhull declares, "Is it not foolish then—aye, is it not more than this, is it not criminal, longer to attempt to place limits upon this heaven ordained passion?" In her endorsement of consensual sexual relations based on love, even and especially outside the "despotism" of marriage, she raises astonishingly modern questions about whether sexuality might exist outside patriarchal oppression.

Yet embedded within "The Elixir of Life" is an artful rhetoric that depends on a more conservative moral/immoral binary. As she states, "I indeed thank heaven for giving me the moral strength to utter the plain, unvarnished truth." In describing this as a "heaven-ordained passion," Woodhull imbues it with a sense of Christian morality, implicitly challenging those who called her ideas obscene. She also uses shame, which inevitably invokes authority: "Are we indeed so impure that to us all sexual things are impure?" This rhetorical question works on two levels, suggesting people are ashamed only if they have reason to be. She indicates that it is her duty to reveal the truth, so that the crime becomes not telling, but refusing to do so. As she says, "Standing, however, as I do, somewhat representative of the immense issue of sexual freedom that is now agitating the public mind, I have a duty to fulfill, to which I should be recreant did I withhold a single sentence that I propose to utter." This statement recalls the reference to patriotic duty in the Declaration of Independence as well as in Elizabeth Cady Stanton's Declaration of Sentiments. Woodhull thus reverses the binary in which she is "Mrs. Satan" and associates herself with truth, health, "white[ness] and pur[ity]," "perfected unity," happiness and humanity, freedom, "heaven-ordained passion," and God. On the other side is "falsity," "sickly sentimentalism," disease, slavery, and immodesty. She gets braver as she goes along, at one point describing a mirror held up to the audience to show its imperfections: "You are afraid that I may hold up a glass in which you will see your secret deformities; and you scarcely dare to look upon them." The literary trope of the looking glass also appeared in a contemporary conduct manual that discouraged women's anger. *Miss Leslie's Behaviour Book* (1856) warns that an angry woman who makes "herself a frightful spectacle, by turning white with rage, rolling up her eyes, drawing in her lips, gritting her teeth, clenching her hands, and stamping her feet, depend on it, she is not of a nervous, but of a furious temperament. A looking-glass held before her, to let her see what a shocking object she has made herself, would, we think, have an excellent effect. We have seen but few females in this revolting state, and only three of them were ladies—but we have heard of many" (209-10). In Woodhull's speech, she has the authority to hold the mirror and show others' "deformities": a word consistent with proto-eugenic discourse of the time.

In such speeches, Woodhull calls for an honest discussion of sexuality, what she calls sexual science. She authorizes her voice not only by aligning herself with morality and motherhood but by directing herself to women, whom she knew risked their reputations to attend her lectures. In the piece "To Women Who Have an Interest in Humanity, Present and Future," published in the *Weekly* on October 31, 1874, she notes, "But women are so frightened at the idea of hearing these matters talked about before the men who have demoralized them so badly, and I have had to guard my speech so carefully, lest those who had the courage to come out to hear me should be scared away, that I have finally concluded to give way to these considerations and include in my lectures one address to women alone in each place I may visit" (9). Such tactics worked, at least for a time; while her presence remained controversial, she enjoyed tremendous popularity and fierce defenders.

Woodhull's preoccupation with maternalism was accompanied by an increasing use of Christianity. "The Garden of Eden" (1876) is a symbolic tour de force that figures the human body as Eden. In this sense, the body becomes a place of purity, of "the highest and divinest functions" (chap. 22, this vol.). Each body part and function corresponds to a divine geography: "How is the body watered and fed? Is it not by a stream which is the extension of the mouth, and that changes constantly as it encircles the system? Does not the support of the body enter it by the mouth, and by the river which is the extension of the mouth, run to the stomach?" She notes that as the River Pison branches, so does the body branch into the heart and lungs. "A river, to water the land of pleasure and delight, enters by the mouth, and extending by the way of the stomach, intestines, heart, lungs, arteries and veins, waters the whole land that suffers pain and brings forth." The process of excretion becomes "a process of grace . . . of natural and involuntary purification." Thus one of the most "vulgar" aspects of the human body, and one that at the time was of great concern to urban dwellers, is sanctified. She does not shirk from explicit images, remarking that the description of the "swift current" of the river Hiddekel is the precise sound of urination. The second-to-last paragraph is crowded with exclamation marks that give the piece a sense of the religious exultation appropriate to Woodhull's mother's experience with revivals during the Great Awakening: "Welcome! Thrice welcome!!

Thou messenger of God!" Biblical scripture becomes a compelling way for Woodhull, increasingly dependent on public approval, to discuss sexuality. As Altina Waller has argued in her analysis of Elizabeth Tilton, Beecher's "Gospel of Love" held that women were of a "higher sensitive nature," which made them closer to God and at the same time more vulnerable to victimization (147). In these terms, religious affect is akin to—and perhaps a safer vehicle for—sexual passion. As Joann Passet notes, Woodhull began to infuse her speeches with biblical scripture in 1874, using her Bible and her daughter, who often read a religious piece, as props (103). This Christian ethos was adopted even before this, however; an article from the *Detroit Union* of 1873 notes her regret that her words "might be construed into a lack of veneration for Christ. She was a religious woman, and revered Him and His doctrines" (quoted in *The Human Body* 388). And as Mary Gabriel notes, beginning in 1875 the *Weekly* ran stories endorsing Catholicism, a trend that irked some spiritualists (236). In some sense, however, the Christian thread had been there all along: "But while her critics condemned her decision to embrace Christianity as hollow and opportunistic, it was not, in fact, a radical departure for her. Much of the theory of social freedom she had previously preached was founded in the Paulist socialism of the 1850s" (Gabriel 240).[16] Woodhull mined Christian rhetoric throughout her life, whether speaking of sexual science, eugenics, or free love.

Even Woodhull's early writing on suffrage contains occasional, if veiled, references to a kind of eugenics mentality. In "Qualification for the Franchise," published in the *Washington Chronicle* in 1894, she notes that a man who has reached age twenty-one is allowed to vote "though he may have no capacity to judge who should be put into office."[17] As she asks, "What liberty have we in the majority vote of the uneducated, the unfit or defective individuals?" She then makes an odd antipopulist turn in arguing that laws should be made by "scientific authorities" or "experts" who are more qualified—more, in the parlance of the time, "fit." We need those "who will free us from pernicious habits and depraved appetites."

A tension emerges between her concept of individual freedom and moral codes that is symptomatic of a larger strain between the influences of Andrews, the anti-obscenity movement, and eugenics. Woodhull's essay "Marriage and Maternity," which was published in the *Weekly Times and Echo* on June 3, 1893, features a dialogue between a man who has proposed marriage and the woman whose affection he seeks. At one point the female speaker claims, "Instinct can tell us whether we are attracted to, or repulsed from one another; but it can't reason for us, it can't draw conclusions concerning the consequences of this or that act. Education ought to do this. But, instead, love between a man and a woman is treated as if it were something to be ashamed of, to be kept out of sight, degrading when it ought to be the incentive to moral and physical perfection" (4). Woodhull goes on to say that open communication between partners about what she calls "hereditary characteristics" like intemperance would enable them to acknowledge their duties owed "to the future members of society" (4). For Woodhull, "right marriage" is the "first step towards the improvement of the race" (4). Here is a striking conflation between a call for free choice in sexuality and the coerciveness of eugenics, in which individuals are obligated to sacrifice individual needs to the "greater good," which is of course a racialized, gendered, and nationalist entity.

The front cover of Woodhull's *Humanitarian*, "A Monthly Magazine of Sociology," indicates its interest in eugenics: "The children of to-day are the citizens of to-morrow, and their value will depend on their inherited qualities no less than on their education and environment." Not surprisingly, her most explicit references to eugenics are in the essays "Stirpiculture" and "The Rapid Multiplication of the Unfit" (chaps. 23 and 24, this vol.). The former essay marvels that while progress has been made in livestock and agriculture, such human "improvement" is considered vulgar: "We build institutions in order to incarcerate the insane, the idiots, the epileptics, the drunkards, the criminals, &c. If the lower organism of animals were subject to such infirmities and propensities, we should exterminate them; and yet we have not thought it needful to take measures to eradicate them from the highest organism, man." Again, Woodhull uses the powerful imagery of maternal love and influence to advance her argument, noting that in the future people will marvel at the mothers who "looked on" as their own or other children were incarcerated for inevitable, hereditary criminal behavior. Stirpiculture thus becomes a means of "protection," of "progress," of "education." The focus has shifted from woman as free lover to mother, a focus that requires explicitly moral terms. "The truth should be brought home to every woman, and she should be made to feel that she is criminally responsible for all the misery from which the human race is suffering through her ignorance of the vital subject of proper generation." And yet at the same time, she suggests that not to follow stirpiculture is to degrade and oppress women, who alone have "the power to regenerate humanity." She employs sentimentality, describing the "unsympathetic, pitiless world" in which women are left "to weep tears of blood over the dying embers of a misspent life!" The essay demonstrates, then, her efforts to meld women's rights with eugenics.

Woodhull's late writings reflect the period's attitudes about race, including classification efforts, Anglo fears of immigration, and imperialism. Curiously, Woodhull includes what is today recognized as key evidence for the social construction of race: "There are often greater differences between individuals of the same race than between individuals of different races" ("The Rapid Multiplication of the Unfit," chap. 24, this vol.). While this statement is for modern scholars a means of chipping away at biological notions of hard-wired, genetic races, Woodhull follows this with a physiologically based discussion of individual "inferiority." Here she draws from Michael Foster's *Text Book on Physiology*, which would become a classic in the subject. She combines a Marxist critique of working conditions with the hygiene movement's concern with activities that "sap" individuals' energy. For many devotees of the hygiene movement, it was masturbation or other "impure" activities that drained one's bodily fluids and energy; here it is also the "crowded enclosed workrooms [that] supplant work in the open air.... [T]he energy of the workers is gradually sapped by artificial life in cities, and they become the progenitors of a class physically enfeebled, spiritless, incapable of sustained effort" ("The Rapid Multiplication of the Unfit," chap. 24, this vol.). In one sense, her view is more progressive than those theories that located individuals in rigid, biologically based categories; presumably, it is an argument for improved working conditions. But a more rigid classification system also emerges in her account of the "unfit hordes" from China in "The Rapid Multiplication of the Unfit" (1891). Reflecting the nativism that would only grow with the increase in immigration in the late nineteenth century, the essay sounds eerily similar to twenty-first-century rhetoric about the dangers of Latino immigration: "We have an example of this in the rapid multiplication of the negroes in America, who at some not far distant day will outnumber and outrun the whites if the rapid increase be not checked" (chap. 24, this vol.).

Such nativism coexisted with the imperialism of the late nineteenth century, which also appears in Woodhull's work. "Constitution of the United States of the World" imagines an ostensibly benevolent imperializing nation, as evident in the title itself. "We, the people," as the first paragraph contends, "to erect a government which shall be the center around which the nations may aggregate, until ours shall become a Universal Republic, do ordain and establish this Constitution of the United States of the World; which shall be the Supreme Law wherever it shall have, or acquire, jurisdiction" (chap. 3, this vol.). Although Madeleine Stern reads this document as a precursor to the interdependence ethos of the League of Nations, it also demonstrates the fine line between a benevolent interdependence and a more insidious imperialism that entities like the United Nations still struggle with today. Although imperialism was certainly not a new development at the time, Woodhull seems to anticipate the United States' involvement in places like the Philippines and Puerto Rico. Article X imagines an internal and external movement, promising that "[t]he Congress shall grant to any adult citizen of the United States, applying for the same, any desired and unoccupied part of the public land, excepting mineral, coal, oil and salt lands, not to exceed one hundred and sixty acres, so long as such citizens shall pay regularly to the Government the yearly tax required, and to be ascertained by law for such occupancy" (17). This language is strikingly similar to that of the Dawes Act of 1887, which initiated the allotment of Native American lands;

it conveniently depends on a racialist concept of an "empty" land that would have disastrous consequences for its indigenous inhabitants. Although Woodhull does not specify white landowners, her failure to account for the racial particularities of the time renders the owner white by default. Borrowing from both the Declaration and the Constitution, and adding land grants and other imperialist impulses, Woodhull's document is a telling commentary on her time.

Despite the richness of Woodhull's commentary, no comparable collection of her writing remains in print; Madeleine B. Stern's reader, published in 1974, is the most recent. Scholars' reticence to publish such a collection may be due in part to the historic amnesia surrounding her as well as a lingering question about the extent of her authorship; some have claimed that Stephen Pearl Andrews wrote all of her speeches. I am most satisfied with Frisken's explanation:

> Her own personal papers are fragmentary and heavily edited. We will never know for certain who really wrote the lectures, speeches, letters, and articles attributed to her. They were almost never written in her own hand, and she later repudiated many, saying they had been written without her knowledge or consent. Some contemporary observers said that Woodhull could barely write, and that she did not have the education, breadth of knowledge, or grasp of the language necessary to produce the writings that appeared over her name. On the other hand, many others credited her with a powerful gift for extemporaneous speech on a wide variety of subjects. Whether these conflicting assertions are accurate or an indication of contemporary prejudice remains unknowable and, perhaps, unimportant. (10)

We can conclude that Andrews and Blood contributed to her famous lectures and editorials. But the reality of politics is that such speeches were, and remain, commonly produced in collaboration. We must be cognizant of the tendency, even of Woodhull herself, to deny her authorship, and we should question any individualistic, stable construct of "the author." Further, we must not neglect the fact that Woodhull was the public voice of these controversial ideas and that she rose and fell by these, her words.

Woodhull's impassioned defense of her unorthodox lifestyle helps us understand that the early women's movement was marked by particular tensions, even between its two most famous leaders, Susan B. Anthony and Elizabeth Cady Stanton. While Anthony ultimately sought to distance herself from Woodhull's "dangerous" views, Stanton's support indicates her flexibility. A letter from Stanton to Woodhull in 1901, in which Stanton asks Woodhull to consider two of her essays for publication in the *Humanitarian*, demonstrates her enduring interest in collaborating with Woodhull.[18] In neglecting Victoria Woodhull, we create a simpler—and more limited—view of the nineteenth-century women's rights movement: one that does not include "The Manifesto," Wall Street, or free love. Nearly a century after her death, Woodhull calls attention to our assumptions about what feminism—and America itself—is and might be.

Selected Writings of Victoria Woodhull

# Chapter One

## *The Woodhull Manifesto*

*Victoria Woodhull's announcement of her candidacy for president was originally published in the* New York Herald *in April of 1870. It also appeared in Woodhull's* Argument for Women's Electoral Rights. *A revised version was published in* The Origin, Tendencies and Principles of Government *as "First Pronunciamento." The following comes from the version that appeared in the* Herald.

The disorganized condition of parties in the United States at the present time affords a favourable opportunity for a review of the political situation and for comment on the issues which are likely to come up for settlement in the Presidential election in 1872. As I happen to be the most prominent representative of the only unrepresented class in the republic, and perhaps the most practical exponent of the principles of equality, I request the favour of being permitted to address the public through the medium of the *Herald*. While others of my sex devoted themselves to a crusade against the laws that shackle the women of the country, I asserted my individual independence; while others prayed for the good time coming, I worked for it; while others argued the equality of woman with man, I proved it by successfully engaging in business; while others sought to show that there was no valid reason why women should not be treated, socially and politically, as being inferior to man, I boldly entered the arena of politics and business and exercised the rights I already possessed. I therefore claim the right to speak for the unenfranchised women of the country, and believing as

I do that the prejudices which still exist in the popular mind against women in public life will soon disappear, I now announce myself as candidate for the Presidency.

I am well aware that in assuming this position I shall evoke more ridicule than enthusiasm at the outset. But this is an epoch of sudden changes and startling surprises. What may appear absurd to-day will assume a serious aspect to-morrow. I am content to wait until my claim for recognition as a candidate shall receive the calm consideration of the press and the public. The blacks were cattle in 1860; a negro now sits in Jeff Davis's seat in the United States Senate.[1] The sentiment of the country was, even in 1863, against negro suffrage; now the negro's right to vote is acknowledged by the Constitution of the United States. Let those, therefore, who ridiculed the negro's claim to exercise the right to "life, liberty and the pursuit of happiness," and who lived to see him vote and hold high public office, ridicule the aspirations of the women of the country for complete political equality as much as they please. They cannot roll back the rising tide of reform. The world moves.

That great governmental changes were to follow the enfranchisement of the negro I have long foreseen. While the curse of slavery covered the land progress was enchained, but when it was swept away in the torrent of war, the voice of justice was heard, and it became evident that the last weak barrier against complete political and social equality must soon give way. All that has been said and written hitherto in support of equality for woman has had its proper effect on the public mind, just as the anti-slavery speeches before secession were effective; but a candidate and a policy are required to prove it. Lincoln's election showed the strength of the feeling against the peculiar institution; my candidature for the Presidency will, I confidently expect, develop the fact that the principles of equal rights for all have taken deep root. The advocates of political equality for women have, besides a respectable known strength, a great undercurrent of unexpressed power, which is only awaiting a fit opportunity to show itself. By the general and decided test I propose, we shall be able to understand the woman question aright, or at least have done much towards presenting the issue involved in proper shape. I claim to possess the strength and courage to be the subject of that test, and look forward confidently to a triumphant issue of the canvass.

The present position of political parties is anomalous. They are not inspired by any great principles of policy or economy; there is no live issue up for discussion.

A great national question is wanted, to prevent a descent into pure sectionalism. That question exists in the issue, whether woman shall remain sunk below the right granted to the negro, or be elevated to all the political rights enjoyed by man. The simple issue whether woman should not have this complete political equality with the negro is the only one to be tried, and none more important is likely to arise before the Presidential election. But besides the question of equality others of great magnitude are necessarily included. The platform that is to succeed in the coming election must enunciate the *general* principles of enlightened justice and economy.

A complete reform in our system of prison discipline, having specially in view the welfare of the families of criminals, whose labour should not be lost to them; the rearrangement of the system and control of internal improvements; the adoption of some better means for caring for the helpless and indigent; the establishment of strictly neutral and reciprocal relations with all foreign Powers who will unite to better the condition of the productive class, and the adoption of such principles as shall recognize this class as the true wealth of the country, and give it a just position beside capital, thus introducing a practical plan for universal government upon the most enlightened basis, for the actual, not the imaginary benefit of mankind.[2]

These important changes can only be expected to follow a complete departure from the beaten tracks of political parties and their machinery; and this, I believe my canvass of 1872 will effect.

With the view of spreading to the people ideas which hitherto have not been placed before them, and which they may, by reflection, carefully amplify for their own benefit, I have written several papers on governmental questions of importance and will submit them in due order. For the present the foregoing must suffice. I anticipate criticism; but however unfavourable the comment this letter may evoke I trust that my sincerity will not be called in question. I have deliberately and of my own accord placed myself before the people as a candidate for the Presidency of the United States, and having the means, courage, energy and strength necessary for the race, intend to contest it to the close.

Victoria C. Woodhull

# Chapter Two

## *Killing No Murder*

*The following item appeared in* Woodhull and Claflin's Weekly *on June 11, 1870 (8). Like many women's rights advocates of the time, Woodhull used temperance arguments to advance her cause. At this time, wives were often considered the property of their husbands, subject to their rule under the law. A North Carolina Supreme Court case of 1864 overturned a lower verdict and declared a husband's beating of his wife as allowable. It was not until 1882 that Maryland became the first state to make "wife-beating" a crime. This piece reflects the common strategy of using temperance arguments to make a case against domestic violence. The final paragraph is omitted here.*

A man in Brooklyn . . . has been killing his wife. The occurrence is so commonplace—it happens every week in Brooklyn, or Boston or some other good place—that it is hardly worth mentioning as news. But we should like it better understood that when a man is insane, or when a man is drunk, the law holds him harmless. If he beats or shoots or knife[s] another man it seems objectionable, though not surprising. But if he brutalizes his wife it is the most natural thing in life; it is just what we expect from a drunken man. If he comes home in the dead of night, and because his wretched slave is asleep, or his supper is not ready at an impossible hour, or, being ready, is not cooked to his liking; or if, for any reason, or for no reason, he should beat and kick and pound that slave, why, of course, nobody interferes—it is only a man licking his wife, and as he is drunk he is not to blame, and the laws of domicile, the home and the castle, and so on, are so sacred that even a policeman may not interfere. Perhaps after a long night, dragging her about by the hair of her head, beating, throwing her round, stamping on her and otherwise giving the devilish brutalism of his nature full swing, he succeeds in torturing the wretched life out of the wretched body. Then, but not till then, a policeman feels justified in making his appearance (the law may punish, it may not prevent), and with the remark that the man was drunk, the monster's hellish cruelty is wiped out. He was drunk! She is dead, it is true, she died of torture so brutally outraged that Indian torture would have been a mercy; but then the man was drunk! Mind you it is the fault of the party stabbed, shot or tortured that he or she should get in the way of a drunken madman. Why does a woman live with a drunken man? Why, indeed? What else can she expect.

# Chapter Three

## *A Page of American History*
Constitution of the United States of the World

*This speech, described on the title page as "The First Suggestion of its kind made in America, and commented on widely by the Press," was given at Washington's Lincoln Hall in 1870. It was also published as* A New Constitution for the United States of the World Proposed for the Consideration of the Constructors of Our Future Government *(1872). Notice how it departs from the U.S. Constitution in its emphasis on social welfare and the nationalization of resources. Madeleine Stern notes that its attention to global interdependence makes it a forerunner of the League of Nations. Sections that differ most significantly from the U.S. Constitution have been excerpted.*

DECLARATION OF PURPOSE

We, the people of the United States—a National Union—and of the several States as its component parts, proceeding upon the Natural Right inherent in humanity, and in order to secure a perfect and enduring Union; to establish equality as a birth-right; to administer common justice; to secure peace, tranquility and prosperity; to provide for the common defense; to promote the general welfare; to secure the blessings of freedom, and protection for the exercise of individual capacities to ourselves and our posterity; and to erect a government which shall be the center around which the nations may aggregate, until ours shall become a Universal Republic, do ordain and establish this Constitution of the United States of the World; which shall be the Supreme Law wherever it shall have, or acquire, jurisdiction.

DECLARATION OF INDEPENDENCE

All persons are born free and equal, in a political sense (in every sense except heredity), and are entitled to the right to life, which is inalienable; and to liberty and the pursuit of happiness; and these shall be absolutely unabridged, except when limited in the individual for the security of the community against crime or other human diseases.

DECLARATION OF THE RIGHTS OF PERSONS

All persons are entitled to the full and unrestrained use of all their natural and acquired powers and capacities; but such use by the individual, or by aggregations of individuals, shall never extend to infringement upon; or abridgment of, the same use in other persons.

DECLARATION OF THE RIGHTS OF THE COMMUNITY

The community has the right, under this Constitution, to organize and maintain government, by which every individual shall be protected in the exercise of rights, and prevented from interfering with those of others. But by organizing government the people shall surrender no rights.

DECLARATION OF THE SPHERE OF GOVERNMENT

It shall be the sphere of the government to perform the duties required of it by the people under the guidance of this Constitution; and the government shall be vested with the power to perform them, and be limited to such performance....

Article IV

Sec. 1.—The Congress of the United States shall, as soon as practicable, and in the order prescribed, enact laws and prescribe rules and regulations, to provide for the government of the people, in accordance with the tenor and provisions of this Constitution, and as set forth in the Principles of its Declarations.

Sec. 2.—The Congress shall prescribe a form for a Constitution which shall be common to, and adopted by, each State now constituting one of the United States; as well adopted by every State that may hereafter be admitted into the Union.

Sec. 3.—

1. The Congress shall provide uniform laws to raise a revenue to maintain the Government of the United States as organised under this Constitution. But no means shall be resorted to, which shall fall unequally, either upon citizens or upon States, except as hereinafter provided.

2. To maintain the equality of all citizens before the laws.

3. To secure the equal right to the exercise of all common rights.

4. To establish a general system of Criminal Jurisprudence.

5. To establish a general system of Common Law.

6. To regulate the naturalization of foreigners; commerce between the States, and with other nations; Marriage; Divorce; and Education; each according to the principles of the Declarations.

7. To fix the standards of weight and measures.

8. To establish Post Offices, Post Roads, Post Railroads, Post Telegraphs; and a Postal Money Order System to meet all the demands of exchange; and affix such Postal Rates for the same as shall be deemed necessary to maintain them; or to provide for their maintenance for the public benefit.

9. To provide for the maintenance of an Army of, not to exceed ten maximum Regiments, in time of peace; and a Navy; and to regulate and govern the same.

10. To provide at once for the admission, free of duty, of every article of commerce not produced in the United States; and to provide for the free admission of all commodities classed as the necessities of life, when the general system of Revenue shall have been inaugurated.

11. To provide a regular reduction in the existing Tariff, which

shall entirely abolish the system in its application to all foreign importations from countries opening their Ports to the commerce of the United States free.

Sec. 2.—The Congress shall have power:

1. To provide for organising the Militia of States, and in time of war, for calling it into the service of the United States.

2. To provide for the promotion of the Arts and Sciences; and for that purpose may secure for limited times, not to exceed twenty years, to Authors and Inventors, the exclusive right to their respective writings, discoveries and inventions; or at their discretion to purchase the same for the general benefit of the people.

3. To establish a National Money System, and to provide for loaning the money to the people, either as a means of Revenue, or at the cost of maintaining the system; and to regulate and affix the value of the same by providing for its conversion into United States Bonds, drawing a rate of interest not to exceed the established rate in the increase of the general wealth of the country; or, when less than that rate, the rate of the taxation laid on loans of money made to the people; the Bonds also to be convertible into money at the option of the holder; and to order the payment of any part of the public debt at any time at par in the National Money.

4. To inaugurate a system of surveillance over, and care for, the destitute classes, looking to their utilization as members of society, and to the abolition of Pauperism and Beggary, upon the principle that if people cannot obtain employment government should supply it to them; if they will not labor, government should compel them sufficiently to support themselves; if they cannot labor, government should maintain them.

5. To inaugurate and provide for the maintenance of a system of Industrial Education, which may be made general for all children, based upon the proposition that they belong to society as a whole, in a still more general and important sense, than to the individuals of it who are their parents; and especially that

it is the duty of the Government to become the guardian and protector of all children whose interests are not maintained and protected by their parents; and provide for and adopt all children relinquished to society by their parents.

6. To inaugurate a new system of Prison Discipline, based upon the proposition that to be restrained of liberty is not as punishment for crime, since all rewards and punishments are administered by the immutable laws of the universe; but that it is a necessary precaution for the safety of the community; and which shall secure to every person restrained, or to the family, if dependent, the entire net proceeds of all labor performed.

7. To inaugurate a system of justice and equality as to property rights, based upon the proposition that the producer is entitled to the total proceeds of labor, which shall prevent the accumulation of wealth in the hands of non-producers; and to provide for the gradual return to the People of all monopolies of land by individuals, based upon the principle that the soil is, or should be, as common property as the air is, or the water, by requiring that upon the decease of persons seized of personal property to a greater amount than a sum to be ascertained by law, or of landed estate, such property and estate shall revert to the Government, for the benefit of the People; and when such system shall be inaugurated, then to forbid all sales and transfers of land, as well as gifts and nominal sales of other property, and to establish rules and regulations for its use, of all such property and estate, by the people for the public benefit, all of which looks to the practical recognition of the greatest of all human facts, the unity of the human race, having common interests and purposes, and to the perfect practice of the theory of equality, upon which this Constitution is founded.

8. To increase the rate of taxation on accumulations of wealth in excess of one hundred thousand dollars in the following manner, to wit: If the tax on one hundred thousand dollars be one-half of one per cent., on over one hundred thousand dollars it shall be

one per cent.; on over two hundred thousand dollars it shall be two per cent.; on over three hundred thousand dollars it shall be three per cent.; on over four hundred thousand dollars it shall be four per cent.; on over five hundred thousand dollars it shall be five per cent.; on over seven hundred and fifty thousand dollars it shall be ten per cent.; on over one million dollars it shall be fifteen per cent.; on over one million five hundred thousand dollars it shall be twenty per cent.; on over two million dollars it shall be twenty-five per cent.; and in the same proportions upon any other basic rate than upon one-half of one per cent. upon $100,000.

9. To inaugurate and provide for a system of National Railways, based upon the proposition that whatever involves the direct interests of the public should be in the hands and under the control of the people, for the public welfare, and to that end may purchase existing railways, at a price to be ascertained by law, but not greater than the same could be constructed for, or construct new roads, as the circumstances shall seem to require; and the system shall be operated either at the cost of maintenance or for the public benefit from the public funds.

10. To inaugurate a system of Public Markets for all the products of the world, having in view the abolition of the system of middlemen or hucksters, and which shall secure to producers the entire amount paid by consumers, less only the cost of transportation and distribution.

11. To abolish the Tariff, and provide for the control of the importation of foreign goods, in such quantities only as the demands of the country shall require; and to determine the price at which such imports shall be sold to the people by general law, except as is herein otherwise provided for free admission.

12. To inaugurate a system that shall give employees, equally with employers, a direct interest in the results of their co-operation for production; which shall, after the payment to the employer of the same rate of interest for the money invested by him as is paid for

the use of the National Money; and the payment of salaries to the employees and the employers, and all other legitimate expenses, divide the net profits in an equitable manner among them.

13. To provide for the return to the people of all mineral, coal, oil and salt lands, and for their operation for the public benefit.

14. And to propose to the several Nations of the world a plan for an International Tribunal to which all disputes of Nations shall be referred for arbitration and settlement; which plan shall also include provisions for an International Army and Navy to enforce the edicts of the Tribunal and to maintain the peace of the world.

*Article V*

Sec. 1.—

1. No taxes shall be levied by any legislative body in the United States, except for the legitimate purposes of government in protecting the rights of persons and nationality. Neither shall any legislative body have power to exempt any property whatever from taxation; or to discriminate in favour of any property as to rate, except as is herein otherwise provided; and there shall be no methods of taxation that shall, in any manner, protect certain classes of the people at the expense of certain other classes, except as herein otherwise provided in Article IV, Section II, Par. 8 and 11. And no special taxes of any kind shall be levied, upon any pretext or for any purpose whatever.

2. All taxes, whether for National, State, County or Municipal purposes, shall be laid and collected by one Revenue System, with the exceptions to which reference is made in the preceding paragraph.

Sec. 2.—No legislative body in the United States shall have power to give or loan the public property or credit to individuals, or to corporations, to promote any enterprise, or for any purpose whatever.

Sec. 3.—No money shall be drawn from any Treasury of the

people, in the United States, unless in consequence of appropriations made by law; and a regular detailed account of receipts and expenditures, giving each separate item in the accounts, of all public moneys, shall be published; those arising in the accounts of the United States and the several States, weekly; and those upon the accounts of other subdivisions, weekly or monthly; and the accounts of the United States and of the States shall be published in a periodical issued for the purpose, at the expense of the public, in a manner to be determined by law....

*Article IX*

Sec. 1.—

1. No incorporated company existing in the United States, or under the authority of any law of the United States, shall, upon any pretext, issue stock certificates to represent a greater sum than the actual amount of money paid in; nor shall any incorporated company make any stock or scrip dividends, nor money dividends to exceed four per cent., for any current year, upon its entire stock; nor shall any such company be permitted to, in any manner whatever, evade the letter or the spirit of these provisions; but whenever the earnings shall produce a sum in excess of the operating expenses, and four per cent. upon the capital stock, then the rate of charges shall be changed so as to reduce the earnings to the standard of four per cent. Any net earnings in excess of four per cent. for any current year, shall be paid over to the General Government.

2. Any company or corporation which shall evade or attempt to evade any of the provisions of this Article, shall upon proof of the same forfeit their charter to the people; and the Government, for and in the name of the people, shall assume the conduct of the affairs of such company, either paying to the stockholders the original amount of their investment, or the net earnings up to four per cent. per annum.

3. The provisions of Article IV, Section 8, for taxation, shall apply

to the individuals comprising stock companies; but the taxes shall be collected from the companies.

4. The Congress shall have power to enforce and carry out the provisions of this Article by appropriate legislation.

## Article X

**Sec. 1.—**

1. New States may be admitted into the Union whenever the people living within the limits of the proposed jurisdiction shall, by vote of the majority, decide to organize as a State under the General State Constitution; provided, however, that such proposed State shall contain a sufficient population to entitle it to at least one Representative in Congress.

2. The Congress shall have power to make all needed rules and regulations for all the Territorial and other public property, provided, however, that they shall have no power to in any manner dispose by sale of any property whatever, except as provided by law for property other than land.

3. The Congress shall grant to any adult citizen of the United States, applying for the same, any desired and unoccupied part of the public land, excepting mineral, coal, oil and salt lands, not to exceed one hundred and sixty acres, so long as such citizens shall pay regularly to the Government the yearly tax required, and to be ascertained by law for such occupancy; but such tax shall not exceed the general rate for other property elsewhere in the Union.

4. Whenever the inhabitants of any Territory not already included in the Union shall have signified, by a vote of the majority, their desire to be admitted, they shall be admitted, after organizing as a State, under the General State Constitution, and when not having sufficient population to be admitted as a State, then as a Territory under the General Law established by Congress for the government of Territories.

5. All Territories shall be entitled to one Representative to

Congress, who shall be entitled to vote upon all questions which do not specially refer to the Government of the States, or to the States as such....

*Article XII*

The United States shall guarantee equality of rights, privileges and duties to all the States as States; to all the citizens of the several States as individuals, and shall see to it that no State shall enforce any law which shall trespass upon individual rights as declared to be such by this Constitution.

*Article XIII*

Sec. 1.—

1. All persons born, or who shall have been, or shall hereafter be, naturalized in the United States, and subject to the jurisdiction thereof, are citizens of the United States, and of the State wherein they reside.

2. The citizens of the United States shall consist of two classes, to wit: Adult citizens and Minor citizens.

3. Adult citizens shall consist of all citizens who shall have attained to the age of eighteen years and upward.

4. Minor citizens shall consist of all citizens who shall not have attained the age of eighteen years.

5. All adult citizens except Idiots and the Insane shall exercise the Elective Franchise at their pleasure, for all purposes, subject to the following regulation only:—

For all United States officers, without reservations;

For all State officers and Representatives to Congress, after a residence in the State for three months;

For all other officers, after a residence within the limits of their jurisdiction for one month;

When not restrained of their liberty, being charged with, or after conviction of and restraint for, some crime. In all other cases the elective franchise shall be absolutely unabridged.

6. All citizens, while serving in the Army or Navy of the United States, or as officers of the United States, shall be entitled to vote for United States officers only, except as may be provided by Congress for officers within their respective organizations.

*Article XIV*

Sec. 1.—

1. All elections in all the States shall be held simultaneously on the first Monday in November of each year, beginning at six o'clock in the morning and closing at six o'clock in the evening.

2. All judicial officers, all legislative officers, except United States Senators, and all executive officers provided by or under the authority of this Constitution to officiate as heads of departments, divisions, and sub-divisions, shall be elected by the votes of the people among whom they are to have jurisdiction; and all other officers in such jurisdiction shall be appointed by them, and hold their offices during good behavior; and shall be removed for cause only and in such manner as shall be ascertained by law.

3. Representatives to Congress, Representatives and Senators to the several State Legislatures, by Congressional districts, and all lesser legislative bodies, and all Judges of all Courts, shall be elected in the same manner by which it is provided that the Electoral College shall be elected, except that the districts having the largest fractional remainder of votes shall be taken to complete the quota of officers, and that the officers elected shall be those who shall have received the largest vote instead of in the order of numbered districts or divisions on each ticket.

4. All executive officers not otherwise provided, whether of the United States or the States, may be elected by a majority or plurality vote, or by minority representation, as may be provided by law.

5. No officer elected by the people shall ever be required to take an oath of office or to give bond for the performance of the duties of the office; the fact of election being *prima facie* evidence that the people accept the officer as capable and honest.

6. No officer elected by the people shall be removed from office during the term for which the election was had, except by a vote of the people in the same manner as in the election of the officer.

Article XV

Sec. 1.—

1. The Congress shall have power to pass no law that shall in any manner deny, abridge, or interfere with the most complete exercise of every power, capacity, and talent possessed by the individual; but shall guarantee every individual peaceful pursuit therein, as against all other individuals.

2. That shall in any manner deny, abridge, or interfere with the right of two or more individuals to contract together in whatever manner, but shall guarantee protection to all contracting parties as against all interference.

Sec. 2.—

1. All contracts between individuals shall stand upon their own merits and upon the integrity and capacity of the parties involved, without appeal by them to any power for redress; provided, however, that when contracting parties, at the time of making a contract, shall declare in the contract that they, not having mutual confidence in their ability and integrity to faithfully perform the same, desire the guarantee of other parties, or that Government shall enforce them, then the Government may have the power to take cognizance of an appeal to it, through proper forms, to be prescribed by law, but not otherwise.

2. Laws may be made to compel the enforcement of pecuniary contracts on the part of incorporated companies organized under the authority of law; since their integrity and capacity may depend upon the perfectness of the laws by which they exist, which are the people's provisions, and not upon the honor and integrity of the individuals composing the company; and to require the record or publication of such contracts as may affect and indirectly involve the community.

3. No oath or affirmation shall be required by law of any person upon any pretext, or for any purpose whatever. But in any processes of law where evidence is required or given, if it be established that such evidence is false testimony, the person giving it may be held accountable in a manner to be ascertained by law.

*Article XVI*

**Sec. 1.—**

1. It is expressly understood that the Government thus organized has no power conferred upon it except that which is necessary to carry out the instructions of the people, as expressed through the laws framed by their representatives, and approved by themselves, according to the provisions of this Constitution.

2. The people may, by direct vote at any time, instruct their chosen representatives in regard to any issue before them, and all legislative bodies are to be held to be the representatives of the people, and not of their own ideas as opposed to the will of the people.

*Article XVII*

The United States shall compel every State to maintain within its limits a Republican form of government upon all matters in all its legislation and administration; and such a form is pronounced to be one in which the rights of all adult citizens to participate is absolutely unabridged except by forfeiture; and in which the equal interests of all minor citizens are secured.

*Article XVIII*

This Constitution may be amended in the same manner in which all laws are required to be passed, by the Congress of the United States and the approval of the people; provided, however, that all such amendments shall be approved by a vote of three-fifths of the entire vote cast.

*Article XIX*

Sec. 1.—

1. The House of Representatives shall have the power, whenever in the judgment of three-fifths of its members it shall be proper to do so, to submit to the people an Amendment to this Constitution abolishing all Senatorial bodies, which shall become the law when approved by the requisite vote of the people.

2. The people may, at any time, without the initiative on the part of the Congress, amend, or abolish parts of this Constitution by a vote of three-fifths of the adult citizens, and the people shall have the right to vote upon any proposition of this kind at any General Election; and all such votes shall have the same force and effect as though made upon subjects submitted to them by the Congress.

3. This Constitution shall be held to be adopted by the people whenever three-fifths of the whole number of adult citizens of the United States, according to the last census, shall have given it their approval; and they may then constitutionally proceed to organize the government as herein provided; but all other and previous legislation under the old Constitution shall continue in full force and effect, until the necessary legislation supplementary to, and in place of it, shall have been provided.

4. Nothing in this Constitution or in the legislation authorized under it shall be held as invalidating contracts existing at the time of its adoption, except in cases herein otherwise expressly provided.

# Chapter Four

## *The Memorial of Victoria C. Woodhull*

On January 11, 1871, Victoria Woodhull became the first woman to address a U.S. congressional committee. One witness recalled that "her voice trembled with emotion and she started hesitantly almost gasping for breath" until she gained confidence (quoted in Underhill, The Woman Who Ran for President, 102). The memorial appeared in several publications, including Woodhull and Claflin's The Human Body the Temple of God (1890).

*To the Honorable the Senate and House of Representatives of the United States in Congress assembled, respectfully showeth*:

That she was born in the State of Ohio, and is above the age of twenty-one years; that she has resided in the State of New York during the past three years; that she is still a resident thereof, and that she is a citizen of the United States, as declared by the XIV Article of Amendments to the Constitution of the United States.

That since the adoption of the XV Article of Amendments to the Constitution, neither the State of New York nor any other State, nor any Territory, has passed any law to abridge the right of any citizen of the United States to vote, as established by said article, neither on account of sex or otherwise:

That, nevertheless, the right to vote is denied to women citizens of the United States, by the operation of Election Laws in the several States and Territories, which laws were enacted prior to the adoption of the said XV Article, and which are inconsistent with the Constitution as amended, and therefore, are void and of no effect; but which, being still enforced by the said States and Territories, render the Constitution inoperative as regards the right of women citizens to vote:

And whereas, Article VI, Section 2, declares that "this Constitution, and the laws of the United States which shall be made in pursuance thereof, and all treaties made, or which shall be made under the authority of the United States, shall be the supreme law of the land; and all judges in every State shall be bound thereby, anything in the Constitution and laws of any State to the contrary notwithstanding":

And whereas, no distinction between citizens is made in the Constitution of the United States on account of sex; but the XV article of Amendments to it provides that "No State shall make or enforce any law which shall abridge the privileges and immunities of citizens of the United States, nor deny to any person within its jurisdiction the equal protection of the laws."

And whereas, Congress has power to make laws which shall be necessary and proper for carrying into execution all powers vested by the Constitution in the Government of the United States, and to make or alter all regulations in relation to holding elections for senators or representatives, and especially to enforce, by appropriate legislation, the provisions of the said XIV Article:

And whereas, the continuance of the enforcement of said local election laws, denying and abridging the right of citizens to vote on account of sex, is a grievance to your memorialist and to various other persons, citizens of the United States, being women—

Therefore, your memorialist would most respectfully petition your Honorable Bodies to make such laws as in the wisdom of Congress shall be necessary and proper for carrying into execution the right vested by the Constitution in the Citizens of the United States to vote, without regard to sex.

And your memorialist will ever pray.

Victoria C. Woodhull
Dated New York City, December 19, 1870

# Chapter Five

*Constitutional Equality*

*This essay is included in Victoria Woodhull's* Congressional Reports on Woman Suffrage *(1871). A modified version, entitled "A Legal and Moral View of Constitutional Equality," was given at Lincoln Hall in Washington on February 16, 1871. Lois Beachy Underhill reports that Woodhull was joined by a number of suffrage leaders (a ticket includes Isabella Beecher Hooker's name alongside Woodhull's), and "newspapers reported the audience to be the largest ever at Lincoln Hall" (*The Woman Who Ran for President, *110). Newspaper reviews of the speech were quite positive. Another version appears in "Second Pronunciamento" in* The Origin, Tendencies, and Principles of Government *(1871) and in* Woodhull and Claflin's Weekly *(January 14, 1871). The speech was published in book form as* Constitutional Equality the Logical Result of the XIV and XV Amendments *(1871). It was also published in* The Human Body the Temple of God *(1890).*

*To the Hon. the Judiciary Committees of the Senate and the House of Representatives of the Congress of the United States:*

The undersigned, Victoria C. Woodhull, having most respectfully memorialized Congress for the passage of such laws as in its wisdom shall seem necessary and proper to carry into effect the rights vested by the Constitution of the United States in the citizens to vote, without regard to sex, begs leave to submit to your honorable body the following in favor of her prayer in said Memorial which has been referred to your Committee:

The public law of the world is founded upon the conceded fact that sovereignty cannot be forfeited or renounced. The sovereign power of this country is perpetual in the politically-organized people of the United States, and can neither be relinquished nor abandoned by any portion of them. The people in this Republic who confer sovereignty are its citizens: in a monarchy the people are the subjects of sovereignty. All citizens of a republic by rightful act or implication confer sovereign power. All people of a monarchy are subjects who exist under its supreme shield and enjoy its immunities.

The subject of a monarch takes municipal immunities from the sovereign as a gracious favor; but the woman citizen of this country has the inalienable "sovereign" right of self-government in *her own proper person*. Those who look upon woman's status by the dim light of the common law, which unfolded itself under the feudal and military institutions that establish right upon physical power, cannot find any analogy in the status of the woman citizen of this country, *where the broad sunshine of our Constitution has enfranchised all.*

As sovereignty cannot be forfeited, relinquished or abandoned, those from whom it flows—the citizens—are equal in conferring the power, and should be equal in the enjoyment of its benefits and in the exercise of its rights and privileges.

One portion of citizens have no power to deprive another portion of rights and privileges such as are possessed and exercised by themselves. The male citizen has no more right to deprive the female citizen of the free, public, political expression of opinion than the female citizen has to deprive the male citizen thereof.

The sovereign will of the people is expressed in our written Constitution, which is the supreme law of the land. The Constitution makes no distinction of sex. The Constitution defines a woman born or naturalized in the United States, and subject to the jurisdiction thereof, to be a citizen. It recognizes the right of citizens to vote. It declares that the right of citizens of the United States to vote shall not be denied or abridged by the United States or by any State on account of "race, color or previous condition of servitude."

Women, white and black, belong to races; although to different races. A race of people comprises all the people, male and female. The right to vote cannot be denied on account of race. All people included in the term race have the right to vote, unless otherwise prohibited.

Women of all races are white, black or some intermediate color. Color comprises all people, of all races and both sexes. The right to vote cannot be denied on account of color. All people included in the term color have the right to vote unless otherwise prohibited.

With the right to vote sex has nothing to do. Race and color include all people of both sexes. All people of both sexes have the right to vote, unless prohibited by special limiting terms less comprehensive than race or color. No such limiting terms exist in the Constitution.

Women, white and black, have from time immemorial groaned under what is properly termed in the Constitution "previous condition of servitude."

Women are the equals of men before the law, and are equal in all their rights as citizens.

Women are debarred from voting in some parts of the United States, although they are allowed to exercise that right elsewhere.

Women were formerly permitted to vote in places where they are now debarred therefrom.

The Naturalization Laws[1] of the United States expressly provide for the naturalization of women.

But the right to vote has only lately been distinctly declared by the Constitution to be inalienable, under three distinct conditions—in all of which woman is distinctly embraced.

The citizen who is taxed should also have a voice in the subject matter of taxation. "No taxation without representation" is a right which was fundamentally established at the very birth of our country's independence; and by what ethics does any free government impose taxes on women without giving them a voice upon the subject or a participation in the public declaration as to how and by whom these taxes shall be applied for common public use?

CONSTITUTIONAL EQUALITY

Women are free to own and to control property, separate and apart from males, and they are held responsible in their own proper persons, in every particular, as well as men, in and out of court.[2]

Women have the same inalienable right to life, liberty and the *pursuit of* happiness that men have. Why have they not this right politically, as well as men?

Women constitute a majority of the people of this country—they hold vast portions of the nation's wealth and pay a proportionate share of the taxes. They are intrusted with the most holy duties and the most vital responsibilities of society; they bear, rear and educate men; they train and mould their characters; they inspire the noblest impulses in men; they often hold the accumulated fortunes of a man's life for the safety of the family and as guardians of the infants, and yet they are debarred from uttering any opinion, by public vote, as to the management by public servants of these interests; they are the secret counsellors, the best advisers, the most devoted aids in the most trying periods of men's lives, and yet men shrink from trusting them in the common questions of ordinary politics. Men trust women in the market, in the shop, on the highway and the railroad, and in all other public places and assemblies, but when they propose to carry a slip of paper with a name upon it to the polls, they fear them. Nevertheless, as citizens women have the right to vote; they are part and parcel of that great element in which the sovereign power of the land had birth: and it is by usurpation only that men debar them from their right to vote. The American nation, in its march onward and upward, cannot publicly choke the intellectual and political activity of half its citizens by narrow statutes. The will of the entire people is the true basis of republican government, and a free expression of that will by the public vote of all citizens, without distinctions of race, color, occupation or sex, is the only means by which that will can be ascertained. As the world has advanced in civilization and culture; as mind has risen in its dominion over matter; as the principle of justice and moral right has gained sway, and merely physically organized power has yielded thereto; as the might of right has supplanted the right of might, so have the rights of women become more fully recognized, and that recognition is the result of the development of the minds of men, which through the ages she has polished, and thereby heightened the lustre of civilization.

It was reserved for our great country to recognize by constitutional enactment that political equality of all citizens which religion, affection and common sense should have long since accorded; it was reserved for America to sweep away the mist of prejudice and ignorance, and that chivalric condescension of a darker age, for in the language of Holy Writ, "The night is far spent, the day is at hand, let us therefore cast off the work of darkness, and let us put on the armor of light. Let us walk honestly as in the day."[3]

It may be argued against the proposition that there still remains upon the statute books of some States the word "male" to an exclusion, but as the Constitution in its paramount character can only be read by the light of the established principle, *ita lex Scripta est*;[4] and as the subject of sex is not mentioned and the Constitution is not limited either in terms or by necessary implication in the general rights of citizens to vote, this right cannot be limited on account of anything in the spirit of inferior or previous enactments upon a subject which is not mentioned in the supreme law. A different construction would destroy a vested right in a portion of the citizens, and this no legislature has a right to do without compensation, and nothing can compensate a citizen for the loss of his or her suffrage—its value is equal to the value of life. Neither can it be presumed that women are to be kept from the polls as a mere police regulation: it is to be hoped, at least, that police regulations in their case need not be very active. The effect of the amendments to the Constitution must be to annul the power over this subject in the States whether past, present or future, which is contrary to the amendments. The amendments would even arrest the action of the Supreme Court in cases pending before it prior to their adoption, and operate as an absolute prohibition to the exercise of any other jurisdiction than merely to dismiss the suit.

3 Dall., 382; 6 Wheaton, 405; 9 Id., 868; 3d Cure., Pa., 1832.[5]

And if the restrictions contained in the Constitution as to color, race or servitude, were designed to limit the State governments in reference to their own citizens, and were intended to operate also as restrictions on the Federal power, and to prevent interference with the rights of the State and its citizens, how then can the State restrict citizens of the United States in the exercise of rights not mentioned in any restrictive clause in reference to actions on the part of those citizens having reference solely to the necessary functions of the General Government, such as the election of representatives and senators to Congress, whose election the Constitution expressly gives Congress the power to regulate?

S.C., 1847: Fox vs. Ohio, 5 Howard, 410.[6]

Your memorialist complains of the existence of State Laws, and prays Congress, by appropriate legislation, to declare them, as they are, annulled, and to give vitality to the Constitution under its power to make and alter the regulations of the States contravening the same.

It may be urged in opposition that the Courts have power, and should declare upon this subject.

The Supreme Court has the power, and it would be its duty so to declare the law; but the Court will not do so unless a determination of such point as shall arise make it necessary to the determination of a controversy, and hence a case must be presented in which there can be no rational doubt. All this would subject the aggrieved parties to much dilatory, expensive and needless litigation, which your memorialist prays your Honorable Body to dispense with by appropriate legislation, as there can be no purpose in special arguments "ad inconvenienti,"[7] enlarging or contracting the import of the language of the Constitution.

*Therefore*, Believing firmly in the right of citizens to freely approach those in whose hands their destiny is placed, under the Providence of God, your memorialist has frankly, but humbly, appealed to you, and prays that the wisdom of Congress may be moved to action in this matter for the benefit and the increased happiness of our beloved country.

Most respectfully submitted,

Victoria C. Woodhull
Dated New York, January 2, 1871

# Chapter Six

## *The New Rebellion*
The Great Secession Speech of Victoria C. Woodhull

*Victoria Woodhull gave this speech at the National Woman Suffrage Convention in New York's Apollo Hall on May 11, 1871. Notice how she uses ultimatums and the language of slavery, both tactics of previous suffragists, to make her argument. At this time she still enjoyed the respect of most women suffragists; she had the honor of being seated between Lucretia Mott and Elizabeth Cady Stanton. Her speech was received with enthusiasm; even the* New York Tribune *noted, "This is a spirit to respect, perhaps to fear, certainly not to be laughed at" (quoted in Gabriel,* Notorious Victoria, *97). At the same time, the competing American Woman Suffrage Convention denounced Stephen Pearl Andrews's free love resolution introduced at the National Woman Suffrage Convention. It was Woodhull's association with free love that would ultimately distance her from even the National Woman Suffrage Association.*

Since this is not a convention for the consideration of general political questions, I am not certain that I have any thing to say which will prove of interest or profit to you. But with your permission I will endeavor to state the position which the movement for political equality now occupies, and attempt to show therefrom the duties which devolve upon those who advocate it.

Whatever there may have been spoken, written or thought in

reference to the constitutional rights of women citizens of the United States, as defined by the XIV and XV Articles of Amendments to the Supreme Law of the Land, the first practical movement under it to secure their exercise was made in the Congress of the United States during the past winter. A memorial setting forth the grievances of a woman citizen, who was denied the right of citizenship, was introduced into both Houses of Congress, and by them referred to their Judiciary Committees. Upon this memorial the House Judiciary Committee made two reports; that of the majority while admitting the validity of the foundation upon which the memorial was based, was adverse to congressional action thereon, naively attempts to ignore the force of the argument by thrusting the responsibility back upon the States, which have acted upon the point in question by the adoption of said Amendments. That of the minority, than whom there is no more conclusive judiciary authority in the United States, took issue with the entire pleading of the majority, and fortified their position by such an array of authority, judicial decisions and logic, as to fully establish the fact of the right of women to the elective franchise in every unprejudiced mind.

So forcible was the conviction which this report carried wherever analyzed, that even Democrats who, everybody well knows, are constitutionally predisposed against the extension of suffrage, acknowledged it as unanswerable. Besides this, there has been so much high judicial authority also expressing itself in the same terms of approbation, there can be no question whatever about the fact that women, equally with men, are entitled to vote. This conclusion, though at first received with great skepticism by very many who wished it were really so, is gradually spreading among the people, and settling into a well defined conviction in their hearts. Many of your own journals even ridiculed the matter, more I presume from dislike to the movers in it than from convictions of its incapacity to meet the required demand.

I am glad, however, to now announce that most of these journals have reconsidered the subject, since there has been such enthusiasm and action raised all over the country by it, resulting in bringing women forward to demand their rights which have been accorded to them in a sufficient number of cases to finally decide the true value of the movement. If I mistake not[,] some of those who were instrumental in preventing the exercise of these claimed rights will have the pleasure of paying for their presumption in money, if not by imprisonment, both of which may be meted to them under the [Enforcement] act which it seems was almost providentially passed by Congress in May, 1870, to meet just such cases as are now required to be met.

There are two ways by which the success already gained may be pushed on to ultimate and complete victory, both of which I count as legitimate and justifiable. One is to continue the appeals to the courts, until by a final decision of the Supreme Court, it shall be fully determined. The other is for Congress to pass an act declaring the equal rights of all citizens to the elective franchise. To this method some object that it stultifies the position that the Constitution already grants every thing we ask. But these objectors forget that by Par. 17, Sec. VIII, Article 1 of this same Constitution it is made one of the duties of Congress to make all laws which shall be necessary and proper for carrying into execution all powers vested by the constitution in the Government of the United States, and that one of the special powers vested in Congress is the right to make *all* laws necessary for enforcing the provisions of the XIV and XV Amendments. It seems to me that petitioning Congress to enforce the provisions of these Amendments is eminently proper, and that any who object thereto either do not understand the powers and duties of Congress or do not wish so easy a solution of the franchise question, which solution cannot be expected from the courts, as a decision therein may be deferred for years.

A Washington correspondent of the *Tribune* of May 2d, speaking of this matter, says: "There is no probability that the women of this District will vote by the next Presidential election, if they depend on a decision of the Courts in their favor for the privilege. The action is brought in the Circuit Court of the District, which will adjourn before reaching the case. It cannot, then, be decided until the October term; but, no matter what the decision may be, the case will be appealed to the United States Supreme Court, which, judging from the present condition of its docket, will not be able to render an opinion in less than two or three years."

The matter of time is an important element in this issue. I am aware that women do not yet fully appreciate the terrible power of the ballot, and that they have made no calculations what they will do should the right to vote be accorded them the next session of Congress. I hold that when women are fully decided in their minds that they are entitled by law to the elective franchise, it is their solemn duty to determine how they shall use this new power.

The enfranchisement of ten millions of women, is a revolution such as the world has never seen, and effects will follow it commensurate with its magnitude and importance. Whatever the women of the country shall determine, to do that will be done. It seems to me that nothing could be more wise and judicious than for them even now to begin to consider what they will do.

I have had ample occasion to learn the trite worth of present political parties, and I unhesitatingly pronounce it as my firm conviction if they rule this country twenty years to come as badly as they have for twenty years past, that our liberties will be lost, or that the parties will be washed out by such rivers of blood as the late war never produced. I do not speak this unadvisedly. I know there are men in Congress—great men—who know that unless change for the better come this will.

What do the Republican leaders care for the interests of the people if they do not contribute to their strength. They have prostituted and are prostituting the whole power of the government to their own selfish purposes. They have wrung the very last possible dollar from the industries of the country and are now hoarding it in the vaults of the Treasury. One hundred and thirty millions of dollars in actual cash is a great power, a dangerous power it might be made by unscrupulous men, and I do not think but that there are those near the head of the government who are ambitious and unscrupulous enough to take advantage of any favorable opportunity in which to make use of this power.

True the Republican party did a mighty work to which all future ages will look back with reverence. True that they opened the door, unwittingly though it was done, to our enfranchisement. True that they have made the name of slavery odious, and added new lustre to that of freedom.

But having delivered us from one damnation shall they be permitted to sell us to another, compared to which the first is but a cipher? They have told us that the Southern slave oligarchy had virtual control of the government for many years, and that the terrible war which we waged was the only means by which this power could be humbled.

But do they tell us of a still more formidable oligarchy which is now fastening upon the vitals of the country? Do they tell us that they have given four hundred millions of acres of the public domain, millions of dollars and tens of millions of credit to build up this new tyrant? Do they tell us that this tyrant is even now sufficiently powerful to buy up the whole legislation of the country, to secure the confirmation of any nomination which it desires made, and to bribe officials everywhere to the non-performance of their duty? Do they tell us matters have been so arranged that all the revenue they can extract from the people is turned over to this power, by which process the vitality of the country is being gradually absorbed? No, not a bit of it. This they will leave us to learn through bitter experience as we were left to learn what were the fruits of forty years['] plotting by the slave oligarchy. This new oligarchy has plotted less than ten years and it has already attained the most threatening and alarming proportions.

Shall we turn to the Democratic party with the hope that they may prove the necessary salvation from the wrath to come. To do this would indeed be to show the dire extremity to which we are driven. I hold that the Democratic party is directly responsible for the late war. The Democratic party South would not have rebelled had not the Democratic party North promised them their support. Can we expect anything better from them than from the Republican party? They are not now making themselves so antagonistic to the true interests of the country as are the Republicans, simply because they have not got the power so to do. But where they have the power, their leaders do not hesitate to make the most use of it to their own aggrandisement.

Therefore, it is my conviction, arrived at after the most serious and careful consideration, that it will be equally suicidal for the Woman Suffragists to attach themselves to either of these parties. They must not—cannot afford to—be a mere negative element in the political strife which is sure to ensue in the next Presidential election. They must assume a positive attitude upon a basis compatible with the principles of freedom, equality and justice which their enfranchisement would so gloriously demonstrate as the true principles of a republican form of government. I do not assume to speak for any one. I know I speak in direct opposition to the wishes of many by whom I am surrounded. Nevertheless, I should fail to do my duty, did I conceal what I feel to be the true interests of my sex, and through them, those of humanity; for the interests of humanity will never be understood or appreciated until women are permitted to demonstrate what they are, and how they shall be subserved. I have thus as briefly as possible given what I conceive to be the position which the Woman's Rights Party occupies at this time, their prospective power, importance and duties, and the dangers by which this country is threatened, from which they may save it.

If Congress refuse to listen to and grant what women ask, there is but one course left them to pursue. Women have no government. Men have organized a government, and they maintain it to the utter exclusion of women. Women are as much members of the nation as men are, and they have the same human right to govern themselves which men have. Men have none but an usurped right to the arbitrary control of women. Shall free, intelligent, reasoning, thinking women longer submit to being robbed of their common rights. Men fashioned a government based on their own *enunciation* of principles: that taxation without representation is tyranny; and that all just government exists by the consent of the governed. Proceeding upon *these* axioms, they formed a Constitution declaring all persons to be citizens, that one of the rights of a citizen is the right to vote, and that no power within the nation shall either make or enforce laws interfering with the citizen's rights. And yet men deny women the first and greatest of all the rights of citizenship, the right to vote.

Under such glaring inconsistencies, such unwarrantable tyranny, such unscrupulous despotism, what is there left women to do but to become the mothers of the future government.

*We will have* our rights. We say no longer by your leave. We have besought, argued and convinced, but we have failed; *and we will not fail.*

We will try you *just once more*. If the very next Congress refuse women all the legitimate results of citizenship; if they indeed merely so much as fail by a proper declaratory act to withdraw every obstacle to the most ample exercise of the franchise, then we give here and now, deliberate notification of what we will do next.

There is one alternative left, and we have resolved on that. This convention is for the purpose of this declaration. As surely as one year passes, from this day, and this right is not fully, frankly and unequivocally considered, we shall proceed to call another convention expressly to frame a new constitution and to erect a new government, complete in all its parts, and to take measures to maintain it as effectually as men do theirs.

If for people to govern themselves is so unimportant a matter as men now assert it to be, they could not justify themselves in interfering.

If, on the contrary, it is the important thing we conceive it to be, they can but applaud us for exercising our right.

We mean treason; we mean secession, and on a thousand times grander scale than was that of the South. We are plotting revolution; we will overslough[1] this bogus republic and plant a government of righteousness in its stead, which shall not only profess to derive its power from the consent of the governed, but shall do so in reality.

We rebel against, denounce and defy this arbitrary, usurping and tyrannical government which has been framed and imposed on us without our consent, and even without so much as entertaining the idea that it was or could be of the slightest consequence what we should think of it, or how our interests should be affected by it, or even that we existed at all, except in the simple case in which we might be found guilty of some offense against its behests, when it has not failed to visit on us its sanctions with as much rigor as if we owed rightful allegiance to it; which we do not, and which, in the future, we will not even pretend to do.

This new government, if we are compelled to form it, shall be in principles largely like that government which the better inspirations of our fathers compelled them to indite in terms in the Constitution, but from which they and their sons have so scandalously departed in their legal constructions and actual practice. It shall be applicable, not to women alone, but to all persons who shall transfer their allegiance to it, and shall be in every practicable way a higher and more scientific development of the governmental idea.

We have learned the imperfections of men's government, by lessons of bitter injustice, and hope to build so well that men will desert from the less to the more perfect. And when, by our receiving justice, or by our own actions, the old and false shall be replaced by the new and true; when for tyranny and exclusiveness shall be inaugurated equality and fraternity, and the way prepared for the rapid development of social reconstruction throughout.

Because I have taken this bold and positive position; because I have advocated radical political action; because I have announced a new party and myself as a candidate for the next Presidency, I am charged with being influenced by an unwarrantable ambition. Though this is scarcely the place for the introduction of a privileged question, I will, however, take this occasion to, once and for all time, state I have no personal ambition whatever. All that I have done, I did because I believed the interests of humanity would be advanced thereby.

Had I been ambitious to become the next president I should have proceeded very differently to accomplish it. I did announce myself as a candidate, and this simple fact has done a great work in compelling people to ask: and why not? This service I have rendered women at the expense of any ambition I might have had, which is apparent if the matter be but candidly considered.

In conclusion, permit me again to recur to the importance of following up the advantages we have already gained, by rapid and decisive blows for complete victory. Let us do this through the courts wherever possible, and by direct appeals to Congress during the next session. And I again declare it as my candid belief that if women will do one-half their duty until Congress meets, that they will be compelled to pass such laws as are necessary to enforce the provisions of the XIV and XV Articles of Amendments to the Constitution, one of which is equal political right for all citizens.

But should they fail, then for the alternative.

# Chapter Seven

## *My Dear Mrs. Bladen*

*This letter was written to fellow suffragist Elizabeth Bladen. In 1872 Bladen, Isabella Hooker, Elizabeth Cady Stanton, Susan B. Anthony, and others presented a memorial to the Senate. Original misspellings are retained. The original letter is located in the Garrison Family Papers, Sophia Smith Collection, Smith College, Northampton, Massachusetts.*

New York, June 22nd, 1871.

My Dear Mrs. Bladen,

    I assure you I rec'd your letter with very much satisfaction. Placed as I have been before the world maligned by those whom I could not defend myself against I appreciate the confidence which a very large circle of friends have reposed in me. I confess to much surprise that the world at large has been as just as it has. I did not give them credit for so much perception as is really possessed.

    I know that the right will come uppermost in the end. All the experiences of my life teach me there is a divine compensation and an exact justice which none may hope to escape, and I had learned the lesson too deeply and well long before the present outbreak to be broken by it or to lose confidence in it, though all the world were set against me. Already the reaction has set in and brought me new and valuable friends, beside strengthening all my old ones. My faith is firm that I shall not be harmed one *single hair* when the account shall be balanced.

In regard to the Christian Union Libel[1] I would answer that I shall be very sorry to be obliged to defend myself *in that* direction. But Mrs. Stowe has been so outrageously bitter an[d] denunciatory of me and all I have attempted to do that some of my warmest friends insist that a lesson be taught her. I personally prefer to leave her to her conscience and her God, and my defence and exculpation also to Him.

I am much misunderstood because I choose to adopt the term "Free Love" to indicate what I conceive one of the holiest things of life. If thieves have stolen the lining of heaven in which to serve the devil I do not see why I should despise the word which it is called. Approbrious epithets in all ages have been accepted and made respectable by their acceptors, so also will it be with "Free Love." To the pure in heart all things are pure and per contra.[2] If vile and sensual people use the holy term to mean something it does not why should I discard it, when it means what I wish to use it for. I intend to live or die by that term. I have no fear but that time will wash it of all impure connections. I may be a low debased woman. If I am I must abide the consequences. I am, at least, just what I appear to be to those to whom I appear at all. I will not accept the judgement of those who never saw me and who do not know anything about me except hearsay: nor will I permit them to direct others against me when I can prevent. My opinions and convictions are not so widely different from the general public. I am only different in daring to speak and live what they know to be truth, but have not the courage to live it, except subrosa.[3] These people who are the most strenous advocates of Capital punishment are just those who most need the fear of the law to controle them in respect for life. The inference in regard to all other things is plain. I have this satisfaction: I know that in many instances my defamers are really as black as they have the world think I am. The time will come when I shall permit every incident of my life—good, bad & indifferent—to be published. To this and to my public and private life hereafter I am perfectly satisfied to entrust my justification for my friends' sake: for myself I have it always in my own soul.

MY DEAR MRS. BLADEN

I should be very glad to have "Cape May"⁴ correspondence, especially from you. I hope you may find it agreeable to write me occaisionly and rest assured I prize your friendship very highly.

Yours affectionately,
[signed] Victoria C. Woodhull

# Chapter Eight

## *Correspondence between the Victoria League and Victoria C. Woodhull*
The First Candidate for the Next Presidency

*The precise origins and membership of the Victoria League remain mysterious; Lois Beachy Underhill claims Woodhull actually wrote the July 4 letter that is attributed to her supporters (The Woman Who Ran for President, 164). Whatever its origins, the Victoria League soon evolved into the Equal Rights Party.*

### THE LETTER OF NOMINATION

New York, July 4, 1871

Mrs. Victoria C. Woodhull:

 *Madam*—A number of your fellow-citizens, both men and women, have formed themselves into a working committee, borrowing its title from your name, and calling itself the Victoria League.

 Our object is to form a new national political organization, composed of the progressive elements in the existing Republican and Democratic parties, together with the Women of the Republic, who have been hitherto disfranchised, but to whom the Fourteenth and Fifteenth Amendments of the Constitution, properly interpreted, guarantee, equally with men, the right of suffrage.

 This new political organization will be called the Equal Rights Party, and its platform will consist solely and only of a declaration of the equal civil and political rights of all American citizens, without distinction of sex.

We shall ask Congress at its next session to pass an act, founded on this interpretation of the Constitution, protecting women in the immediate exercise of the elective franchise in all parts of the United States, subject only to the same restrictions and regulations which are imposed by local laws on other classes of citizens.

We shall urge all women who possess the political qualifications of other citizens, in the respective States in which they reside, to assume and exercise the right of suffrage without further hesitation or delay.

We ask you to become the standard-bearer of this idea before the people and for this purpose nominate you as our candidate for President of the United States, to be voted for in 1872 by the combined suffrages of both sexes.

If our plans merit your approval, and our nomination meet your acceptance, we trust that you will take occasion in your reply to this letter, to express your views in full concerning the political rights of women under the Fourteenth and Fifteenth Amendments.

Offering to you, Madam, the assurance of our great esteem, and harboring in our minds the cheerful prescience of victory which your name inspires, we remain,

Cordially yours,
The Victoria League

THE LETTER OF ACCEPTANCE

New York, July 20, 1871

Fellows Citizens of the Victoria League:

I beg you not to regard my delay in replying to your flattering invitation to become the candidate of the Equal Rights party for the Presidency as evincing indifference on my part. The delay has, in fact, been occasioned by just the opposite cause; the state of mingled emotion, anxiety and reflection into which the serious proposition from a responsible source that I should accept such a nomination has thrown me. It is true that I have, now nearly a year ago, *announced myself* as a candidate for the high office in question, but that was rather for the mere purpose of lifting a banner, of provoking agitation and for giving emphasis to an opinion, and a rallying point for the great unorganized party of progress.

But the case is now different. Things have progressed to an astonishing degree during this year past. I may have been qualified to raise an excitement, to inaugurate a definite movement, to seize an outpost, and even, perhaps, to project a programme. But does it follow that I am the proper person to become the permanent "standard bearer," as you phrase it, of a great political party, and actually to guide the State.

Little as the public think it, a woman who is now nominated may be elected next year. Less change of opinion than has occurred already, in the same direction, will place her in the White House. The American people are generous and noble, and when their hearts are touched they are susceptible of a grand enthusiasm. They are also—the *men* of the nation I mean now—capable of a gallantry toward my sex, which would rival the devotion of the age of chivalry. They are also essentially just; and when the thought shall really come home to them, with the cogency of conviction, that they have, through thoughtlessness, been all along acting unjustly to their mothers and wives and daughters, by depriving them of political rights, it may happen that there will come up a great swelling-tide of reactionary sentiment which will make a sudden revolution.

I feel that I *know* that just the right woman to touch the right chord of the public sympathy and confidence—if the right woman could be found—would arouse such a tempest of popularity as the country has never seen, and as a consequence should ride triumphantly on the tide of a joyous popular tumult to the supreme political position.

Just at this moment, also, the two great political parties of the past are positively without any issue. General Washington's popularity extinguished for the moment all partizan opposition, and made of the whole nation one grand fraternizing party. The advent of the first woman to the Presidential chair may be the occasion of the next great national fraternization—of the jubilee of the whole people; and this grand event may be, and, to say more, to my prophetic vision, is, at this very moment, actually impending.

It is possible, therefore, that if I am your candidate, I may be elected. And the question recurs, am I the woman, among all the noble women of the land, who can either touch the true chord of sympathy in the national heart to secure the first result, or to manifest that high grade of feminine wisdom which should characterize the first Woman President of the United States?

It is this momentous question which gives me pause; and, after even this long delay, I find it no easy matter calmly to assume the responsibilities to which you invite me.

But there has been another cause of delay. You ask me to state the argument in full for the political rights of women, under the Fourteenth and Fifteenth Amendments, and I have tried to comply with your request. I have returned repeatedly to the task. But, gentlemen and ladies, *I have lost all inspiration for that work.* "Let the dead bury their dead."* I made my argument on that subject, last winter, before the Judiciary Committee of the House of Representatives,—aided by these noble auxiliaries, Mrs. Paulina Wright Davis and Mrs. Isabella Beecher Hooker. I had the good fortune, also, to call out from that committee that unanswerable minority report signed by Benjamin F. Butler and Judge William Loughridge—an instrument which constitutes a Gibraltar of woman's political rights against which all opposition is vain, and which has already grown to be the settled constitutional law in both the judicial and the popular opinion on that whole subject....

The only shadow of an adverse argument which survives is based on the assumption that the amendments did not explicitly contemplate the case of women. The framers and adopters of these provisions did not intend, it is said, to confer rights on us, but only on the negro. That perhaps may be true; but it is equally true that they just as little intended *to exclude* or *except* women. The probable truth is that these law-makers did not at the time so much as think of the existence of women—so completely has woman been unconsciously ignored, until the last winter, at Washington, by these male politicians, as being in any way entitled to political rights.

How, then, does the matter stand? Why, just in this way. That, the legislators having had no intention whatsoever, for or against, in respect to this application of the law, the intention of the legislators, apart from the words used, cannot be appealed to on either side; and we are driven to fall back on the naked interpretation of the words themselves, and to gather all that we have any right to presume of *intention*, from the strict legal interpretation of the language employed.

If we have got the concession of our rights from the mere fact that those who were in the exercise of power had so little respect for or so little thought even of our rights that *they forgot to take steps to defraud us out of them*, shall we be called upon to carry courtesy so far as to decline to take advantage of their forgetfulness? Some may think we ought to do that way; but we propose to do otherwise, and to avail ourselves of all which the indifference or the unconscious contempt of men in power may carelessly have thrown in our way. If they have left down the bars, we shall quietly walk in; especially as it is only coming home to our own pasture.

I propose to *rendezvous*, again, at Washington the coming winter. No Representative or Senator will be more punctual than I. But I do not go there *to argue* the question of our rights. The argument is concluded. I shall go, accompanied by a corps of the representative women of the land, *to insist* on the *practical recognition* of rights which are already, by the public verdict, *theoretically established* and conceded. We shall demand that that be made existent *de facto* which already exists *de jure*.[1] We shall claim the passage of a Declaratory Act, merely the signing of the judgment basis of the verdict already rendered in our favor; and wo[e] to the political trickster or pettifogger who shall dare to hinder our rights by any motion in arrest of judgment or otherwise for delay.

I expect to succeed. I do not expect that the women will leave Washington this very winter until after such Declaratory Act[2] shall form part of the statutes of the country. It is simply scandalous that a nation whose very existence rose out of the axioms, *no taxation without representation*, and who fought for that principle to the death, should persist for a single year, after the subject is fairly broached, to impose on us taxation and to refuse us representation; or that a people whose fundamental political idea in opposition to all class-legislation should disfranchise, by the act of a minority, the very largest *class* of its citizens.

The early coming of female participation in the business of legislation is inevitable; and from now on, destruction will await the politician who does not heed the rising tide. The action of every public *man on this question is noted, and the* Nemesis of political destiny will overtake every recreant to the true principles of a real republic, which involves the equality of woman. Republicanism *shall have* its fair trial, which it never has had hitherto. If female suffrage is an experiment, so was republicanism itself; and this is the next experiment to be tried in the order of governmental evolution. And as it absolutely has to be tried, those who would prolong the crisis of its inauguration are mere obstructionists, and enemies of the public peace. In many a revolution the real disturbers are, when the matter is looked at deeply, those who oppose it. If a thing is in accordance with the spirit of the age, it cannot be successfully resisted; and who does not know that the spirit of this age is unbounded emancipation?

It is the merest waste of time, therefore, to fight any longer over this dead issue. Let both the old effete and dying-out political parties be wise at once. Let them "accept the situation," and inaugurate from now the still greater "new departure." Slavery has been abolished. The world waits for this other and more hidden, but no less real, slavery of restrictions on woman to be, likewise, hustled out of existence and relegated to the limbo of the dead past.

My countrymen, do not regard this concession as a defeat! But noble, gallant and loving men do not shrink from defeat even at the hands of a woman. They sometimes say that they *love to be conquered*. How noble the vanquishment, which will be only the surrender to your sisters and lovers of rights which have been unjustly—but thoughtlessly, on our part as much as on yours—withheld.

Moreover, do not fear the nature of woman! Let it be your glory and your choice to make her free to the uttermost—to expand into her most glorious possible womanhood. Do not think that you must prescribe the law of her being. Perhaps even now you are *needing something* in your own culture, something for the development of your own higher manhood, which can only be derived from the environment of a truly enfranchised womanhood, such as the world has never yet seen. Among the Quakers or Friends women, though not wholly free, have, for more than a century stood, in many respects, side by side with and as the equal helpers of men; and no such disaster has resulted to the characters of either men or women as is feared from the admission of women into politics; but quite the reverse.

My brothers! we are not, and cannot be, your enemies. It is among you, on the contrary, that we look to find our lovers and dearest friends—our protectors and our chosen co-operators in the responsible business of life. We have no interests which are not intimately linked with your interests and with the interests of your children. We want nothing which is not right, and as right for you and for them as for us.

We know, too, that this strife between women and men, this partial elicitation of the two hemispheres of humanity in this age, is working most deleterious results, and especially upon the characters of the next immediate generation. Children have no fathers and no mothers while men and women distrust and repel each other, even in that mild sense which this struggle implies. And yet the struggle cannot end, because it *ought not* to end—and because we cannot consent that it *should end*—until our perfectly equal rights and freedom, socially and politically, are completely established.

Whosoever obstructs or hinders the earliest possible concession of what we ask is therefore, either ignorantly or intentionally, perverse.

So far from wishing to degrade you, my brother, we would be so glad that we would rejoice with exceeding great joy if we could find you manly and god-like enough to command our worship. The greatest misfortune of women is that there are so few great and truly noble men; and it is the greatest misfortune of men, and perhaps, as yet, a greater misfortune on their part—for women have been hitherto cramped and degraded—that there are so few great and truly noble women. I am saddened when I think of the weary waste of commonplace and inferior natures.

We need, my brothers and sisters, all our conjoint exertions to found and rear the grand edifice of future society. Every day used in simply removing restrictions and obstructions, and still worse, in maintaining them, is a day lost from the nobler occupation. This bondage of women is the last withe[3] that binds us to the dead past. Sever it, and we rise into the freedom of a new future.

Perhaps I should also mention in this connection the oppressive weight which capital, in its greedy ignorance, still lays upon labor. The freedom of woman and the freedom of the laborer are conjointly the cause of humanity. Industry, finance and the home must all be rightly adjusted, as transitional to the higher order. Democrats and Republicans must make haste to take up these great new issues, or the fusion of the women and the workingmen and the Internationalists will render their further existence, as parties, unnecessary. The National Labor Union,[4] just now convening at St. Louis, has, for the first time, invited women upon equal terms to that convention. It is, of course, noticed that neither Republicans nor Democrats have, with some exceptions in Massachusetts, invited us yet into their political assemblages.

It may be thought that my demands are too urgent, and my expectations too immediate and too large. But that has been thought before now; and yet the realization has exceeded the hope.

At the last meeting of Congress my Memorial set forth that since the adoption of the Fifteenth Article of the Amendments to the Constitution, no State or Territory either has abridged, or has the right to abridge, the right of the citizens to vote; and that the *status* of women as citizens is completely established. At that time it was only a small but bold wing of either party that dared to express sympathy with this new announcement. At this day, however, only eight or nine months later, the real leaders of both the Republican and Democratic parties stand squarely upon this platform of doctrine, and are lending their influence to mold the action of their parties in that direction. The names of Sumner, Wade, Morton, Trumbull, Wilson, Carpenter, Sprague, Nye, Pomeroy, Stearns, Harris, Arnell, Maynard, Banks, Julian, Burdett, Lynch, Woodward, Ela, Morrill, Vallandigham, Kerr, Chase, and Black, with a host or others that might be mentioned, fill the list of great politicians—and there are none greater—who have given in their allegiance to woman's suffrage.

Indeed, I stand almost appalled at the success of what has been already attempted. And it is not alone the statesmen. The public press also is already virtually converted. It is everywhere admitted that it is only a question of time. Why not then shorten the time to the utmost? The work of a single day in Congress may end the agitation and quietly begin the new *regime*. The change will be far less than has occurred within the twelvemonth. Revolutions are often completed at the time from which chronology dates their commencement; and this revolution has, in fact, definitively ended. Nobody sneers now at woman's suffrage. Everybody has already "in thought accepted the new situation;" and the real revolution is always that which takes place *in the thoughts* of the people. All else is merely the recording of the verdict and the incidentals of the execution.

I cannot speak of pride, for that is not the feeling; but I cannot repress a sense of solemn joy and lofty exultation—something like that, perhaps, of Miriam upon the shore of the Red Sea,[5] celebrating the rescue of her people under the guidance of the marvelous cloud by day and pillar of fire by night—when I reflect on what the spirits in heaven, aided by devoted spirits in the flesh, are so rapidly and so marvelously accomplishing for the complete enfranchisement of my sex, and, through them, of all humanity.

If, fellow-citizens, with these views, with this faith and this hope, under God, and with such powers as I have, dedicated to their service, you still think that I am the fitting woman to represent this movement—to be, as you say, its "standard bearer"—I cannot and will not decline such nomination as you may see fit to make of me to the public.

Perhaps I ought not to pass unnoticed your courteous and graceful allusion to what you deem the favoring omen of my name. It is true that a Victoria rules the great rival nation opposite to us on the other shore of the Atlantic, and it might grace the amity just scaled between the two notions, and be a new security of peace, if a twin sisterhood of Victorias were to preside over the two nations. It is true, also, that in its mere etymology the name signifies *Victory!* and the victory for the right is what we are bent on securing. It is again true, also, that to some minds there is a consonant harmony between the idea and the word, so that its euphonious utterance seem to their imaginations to be itself a genius of success. However this may be, I have sometimes thought, myself, that there is, perhaps, something providential and prophetic in the fact that my parents were prompted to confer on me a name which forbids the very thought of failure; and, as the great Napoleon believed the star of his destiny, you will at least excuse me, and charge it to the credulity of the woman, if I believe also in fatality of triumph as somehow inhering in my name.

With profound esteem, your obedient servant,

Victoria C. Woodhull

*Instead of making the argument in question a part of this reply as requested by you I enclose it herewith as a separate document.

# Chapter Nine

*My Dear Mrs. Mott*

This letter was written to Lucretia Mott on July 13, 1871. The original letter is located in the Garrison Family Papers, Sophia Smith Collection, Smith College, Northampton, Massachusetts.

Mrs. Woodhull to L. Mott

July 13____1871

My dear Mrs. Mott

    I scarcely know how to tell you how much I bless your dear self for the nobleness kindness & love you have shown to me. Whatever those who do not know me may say, I feel I may say to you that I never will prove unworthy of your esteem. I love the truth, for the sake of the truth; the right for the sake of the right, & if people willfully misunderstand me, because it is politic to do so, I cannot afford to let it ~~damage~~ annoy me again. I bless you for yr. sustaining love and comforting assurances wh. come so timely to my heart, which scarcely knows what a mother's love is. Yr. affec. daughter in truth

Victoria C. Woodhull

# Chapter Ten

## *"And the Truth Shall Make You Free"*
A Speech on the Principles of Social Freedom

*This speech was given at New York's Steinway Hall on November 20, 1871, to a diverse audience of three thousand people. According to Amanda Frisken, it was Woodhull's "first free love lecture to northeast audiences ranging from 2,500 to 4,000" (Frisken, Victoria Woodhull's Sexual Revolution, 126). The version that was published in London (1894) begins with James Russell Lowell's poem "The Present Crisis," a statement by writer Edward Bulwer-Lytton, and quotes by Cicero, "Hermes," and Euripides. These quoted passages, along with Woodhull's introductory paragraphs, are omitted here.*

It can now be asked: What is the legitimate sequence of Social Freedom? To which I unhesitatingly reply: Free Love, or freedom of the affections. "And are you a Free Lover?" is the almost incredulous query.

I repeat a frequent reply: "I am; and I can honestly, in the fulness of my soul, raise my voice to my Maker, and thank Him that *I am*, and that I have had the strength and the devotion to truth to stand before this traducing and vilifying community in a manner representative of that which shall come with healing on its wings for the bruised hearts and crushed affections of humanity."

And to those who denounce me for this I reply: "Yes, I am a Free Lover. I have an *inalienable, constitutional,* and *natural* right to love whom I may, to love as *long* or as *short* a period as I can; to *change* that love *every day* if I please, and with *that* right neither *you* nor any *law* you can frame have *any* right to interfere. And I have the *further* right to demand a free and unrestricted exercise of that right, and it is *your duty* not only to *accord* it, but as a community, to see that I am protected in it. I trust that I am fully understood, for I mean *just* that, and nothing less!

To speak thus plainly and pointedly is a *duty I owe* to myself. The press have stigmatized me to the world as an advocate, theoretically and practically, of the doctrine of Free Love, upon which they have placed their stamp of moral deformity; the vulgar and inconsequent definition which they hold makes the theory an abomination. And though this conclusion is a no more legitimate and reasonable one than that would be which should call the Golden Rule a general license to all sorts of debauch, since Free Love bears the *same* relations to the moral deformities of which it stands accused as does the Golden Rule to the Law of the Despot, yet it obtains among many intelligent people. But they claim, in the language of one of these exponents, that "Words belong to the people; they are the common property of the mob. Now the common use, among the mob, of the term Free Love, is a synonym for promiscuity." Against this absurd proposition I oppose the assertion that words *do not* belong to the mob, but to that which they represent. Words are the exponents and interpretations of ideas. If I use a word which exactly interprets and represents what I would be understood to mean, shall I go to the *mob* and *ask* of *them* what interpretation *they* choose to place upon it? If lexicographers, when they prepare their dictionaries, were to go to the mob for the rendition of words, what kind of language would we have?

I claim that freedom means *to be free*, let the mob claim to the contrary as strenuously as they may. And I claim that love means an exhibition of the affections, let the mob claim what they may. And therefore, in compounding these words into Free Love, I claim that united they mean, and should be used to convey, their united definitions, the mob to the contrary notwithstanding. And when the term Free Love finds a place in dictionaries, it will prove my claim to have been correct, and that the mob have not received the attention of the lexicographers, since it will not be set down to signify sexual debauchery, and that only, or in any governing sense.

It is not only usual but also just, when people adopt a new theory, or promulgate a new doctrine, that they give it a name significant of its character. There are, however, exceptional cases to be found in all ages. The Jews coined the name of Christians, and, with withering contempt, hurled it upon the early followers of Christ. It was the most opprobrious epithet they could invent to express their detestation of those humble but honest and brave people. That name has now come to be considered as a synonym of all that is good, true and beautiful in the highest departments of our natures, and is revered in all civilized nations.

In precisely the same manner the Pharisees[1] of to-day, who hold themselves to be representative of all there is that is good and pure, as did the Pharisees of old, have coined the word Free Love, and flung it upon all who believe not alone in Religious and Political Freedom, but in that larger Freedom, which includes both these, Social Freedom.

For my part, I am extremely obliged to our thoughtful Pharisaical neighbours for the kindness shown us in the invention of so appropriate a name. If there is a more beautiful word in the English language than *love*, that word is *freedom*, and that *these two* words, which, with us, attach or belong to *everything* that is pure and good, should have been *joined* by our enemies, and *handed* over to us *already* coined, is certainly a high consideration, for which we should never cease to be thankful. And when we shall be accused of all sorts of wickedness and vileness by our enemies, who in this have been so just, may I not hope that, remembering how much they have done for us, we may be able to say, "Father, forgive them, for they know not what they do,"[2] and to forgive them ourselves with our whole hearts....

Will any of you dare to stand up and assert that Religious Freedom ever produced a *single bad* result? or that Political Freedom *ever* injured a *single* soul who embraced and practiced it? If you can do so, then you may legitimately assert that Social Freedom *may* also produce *equally* bad results, but you cannot do otherwise, and be either conscientious or honest.

It is *too late* in the age for intelligent people to cry out *thief*, unless they have first been robbed, and it is equally late for them to succeed in crying down *anything* as of the devil to which a name attaches that angels love. It may be very proper and legitimate, and withal perfectly consistent, for philosophers of the *Tribune* school[3] to bundle all the murderers, robbers and rascals together, and hand them over to our camp, labelled as Free Lovers. We will only object that they ought to hand the whole of humanity over, good, bad and indifferent, and not assort its worst representatives.

My friends, you see this thing we call Freedom is a large word, implying a deal more than people have ever yet been able to recognize. It reaches out its all-embracing arms, and while encircling our good friends and neighbours, does not neglect to also include their less worthy brothers and sisters, every one of whom is just as much entitled to the use of his freedom as is either one of us.

But objectors tell us that freedom is a dangerous thing to have, and that they must be its conservators, dealing it out to such people, and upon such matters, as they shall appoint. Having coined our name, they straightway proceed to define it, and to give force to their definition, set about citing illustrations to prove not only their definition to be a true one, but also that its application is just.

Among the cases cited as evidences of the evil tendencies of Free Love are those of Richardson and Crittenden. The celebrated McFarland-Richardson case was heralded world-wide as a case of this sort.[4] So far as Richardson and Mrs. McFarland were concerned, I have every reason to believe it was a genuine one, in so far as the preventing obstacles framed by the "conservators" would permit. But when they assert that the murder of Richardson by McFarland was the *legitimate result* of Free Love, then I deny it *in toto*. McFarland murdered Richardson because he believed that the law had sold Abby Sage *soul* and *body* to him, and, consequently, that he *owned* her, and that *no* other person had *any* right to her favour, and that she had *no* right to bestow her love upon any other person, unless *that ownership* was first satisfied. The murder of Richardson, then, is not chargeable to his love or her love, but to the fact of the supposed ownership, which right of possession the law of marriage conferred on McFarland.

If anything further is needed to make the refutation of that charge clear, I will give it by illustration. Suppose that a pagan should be converted to Christianity through the efforts of some Christian minister, and that the remaining pagans should *kill* that minister for what he had done, would the crime be chargeable upon the Christian religion? Will any of you make that assertion? If not, neither can you charge that the death of Richardson should be charged to Free Love. But a more *recent* case is a still *clearer* proof of the correctness of my position. Mrs. Fair killed Crittenden. Why? Because she believed in the spirit of the marriage law; that she had a *better right* to him than had Mrs. Crittenden, to whom the law had granted him; and rather than to give him up to her, to whom he evidently desired to go, and where, following his right to freedom, he *did* go, she killed him. Could a more *perfect* case of the *spirit* of the marriage law be formulated? Most assuredly, no!

Now, from the standpoint of marriage, reverse this case to that of Free Love, and see what would have been the result had all those parties been believers in and practisers of that theory. When Mr. Crittenden evinced a desire to return to Mrs. Crittenden, Mrs. Fair, in practising the doctrine of Free Love, would have said, "I have no right to you, other than you freely give; you loved me and exercised your right of freedom in so doing. You now desire to return to Mrs. Crittenden, which is equally your right, and which I must respect and in peace, and my blessing shall follow, and if it can return you to happiness, then will you be happy."

Would not *that* have been the *better*, the *Christian* course, and would not every soul in the broad land capable of a noble impulse, and having knowledge of all the relevant facts, have *honored* Mrs. Fair for it? Instead of a murder, with the probability of another to complement it, would not *all* parties have been *happy* in having done right? Would not Mrs. Crittenden have even *loved* Mrs. Fair for such an example of nobility; and could she not *safely* have received her even into her own heart and home, and have been a *sister* to her, instead of the means of her conviction of murder?

I tell you, my friends and my foes, that you have taken hold of the *wrong* end of this business. You are shouldering upon Free Love the results that flow from precisely its antithesis, which is the spirit, if not the letter, of your marriage theory, which is slavery, and not freedom.

I have a better right to speak, as one having authority in this matter, than most of you have, since it has been my province to study it in all its various lights and shades. When I practiced clairvoyance, *hundreds*, aye thousands, of desolate, heart-broken men, as well as women, have come to me for advice. And they were from all walks of life, from the humblest daily labourer to the haughtiest dame of wealth. The tales of horror, of wrongs inflicted and endured, which were poured into my ears, first awakened me to a realization of the hollowness and the rottenness, of society, and compelled me to consider whether laws which were prolific of so *much* crime and misery as I found to exist should be continued; and to ask the question whether it were not *better* to let the bond go free. In time I was fully convinced that marriage laws were productive of precisely the *reverse* of that for which they are supposed to have been framed, and I came to recommend the grant of entire freedom to those who were complained of as inconstant; and the frank asking for it by those who desired it. My *invariable* advice was: "Withdraw lovingly, but completely, all claim and all complaint as an injured and deserted husband or wife. You need not perhaps disguise the fact that you suffer keenly from it, but take on yourself all the fault that you have not been able to command a more continuous love; that you have not proved to be *all* that you once seemed to be. Show magnanimity, and in order to *show* it, try to *feel* it. Cultivate that kind of love which loves the happiness and well-being of your partner *most*, his or her person next, and yourself last. Be kind to, and sympathize with, the new attraction rather than waspish and indignant. Know for a certainty that love *cannot* be clutched or gained by being *fought* for; while it is not *impossible* that it may be won back by the nobility of one's own deportment. If it cannot be, then it is gone forever, and you must make the best of it and reconcile yourself to it, and do the next best thing—you may perhaps continue to *hold on* to a slave, but you have *lost* a lover."

Some may indeed think if I can keep the *semblance* of a husband or wife, even if it be not a lover, *better still* that it be so. Such is not my philosophy or my faith, and for such I have no advice to give. I address myself to such as have *souls*, and whose souls are in question; if you belong to the other sort, take advice of a Tombs[5] lawyer and not of me. I have seen a *few* instances of the most magnanimous action among the persons involved in a knot of love, and with the most angelic results. I believe that the love which goes forth to bless, and if it be to *surrender* in order to bless, is love in the *true* sense, and that it tends greatly to beget love, and that the love which is demanding, thinking only of self, is not love.

I have learned that the first *great* error most married people commit is in endeavouring to *hide* from each other the little irregularities into which all are liable to fall. *Nothing* is so conducive to continuous happiness as mutual confidence. In *whom*, if not in the husband or the wife, should one confide? Should they not be each other's *best* friends, *never* failing in time of anxiety, trouble, and temptation to give disinterested and unselfish counsel? From such a perfect confidence as I would have men and women cultivate, it is *impossible* that bad or wrong should flow. On the contrary, it is the *only* condition in which love and happiness can go hand in hand. It is the *only* practice that can insure continuous respect, without which love withers and dies out. Can you not see that in mutual confidence and freedom the very *strongest* bonds of love are forged? It is more blessed to grant favours than to demand them, and the blessing is large and prolific of happiness; or small and insignificant in results, just in proportion as the favour granted is large or small. Tried by this rule, the greater the *blessing* or happiness you can confer on your partners, in which your own selfish feelings are not consulted, the greater the satisfaction that will redound to yourself. Think of this mode of adjusting your difficulties, and see what a clear way opens before you. There are none who have once felt the influence of a high order of love, so *callous*, but that they *intuitively* recognise the true grandeur and nobility of such a line of conduct. It must always be remembered that you can never do *right* until you are first free to do *wrong*; since the doing of a thing under *compulsion* is evidence *neither* of good nor bad intent; and if under compulsion, who shall decide what would be the substituted rule of action under full freedom?

AND THE TRUTH SHALL MAKE YOU FREE

In freedom *alone* is there safety and happiness, and when people learn this great fact, they will have just begun to know how to live. Instead then of being the destroying angel of the household, I would become the angel of purification to purge out all insincerity, all deception, all baseness and all vice, and to replace them by honor, confidence, and truth....

If our sisters who inhabit Greene Street[6] and other filthy localities *choose* to remain in debauch, and if our brothers *choose* to visit them there, they are only exercising the *same* right that we exercise in remaining away, and we have no *more right* to abuse and condemn *them* for exercising their rights that way, than they have to abuse and condemn us for exercising our rights our way. But we have a *duty*, and that is by our love, kindness, and sympathy, to endeavor to prevail upon them to desert those ways which we feel are so damaging to all that is high and pure and true in the relations of the sexes.

If these are the *stray sheep* from the fold of truth and purity, should we not go out and gather them in, rather than remain within the fold and hold the door shut, lest they should enter in and defile the fold? Nay, my friends, we have only an assumed right to thus sit in judgment over our unfortunate sisters, which is the same right of which men have made use to prevent women from participation in government....

But the public press, either in real or affected ignorance of what they speak, denounce Free Love as the justification of, and apologist for, all manner and kind of sexual debauchery, and thus, instead of being the *teachers* of the people, as they *should* be, are the power which inculcates falsehood and wrong. The teachings of Christ, whom so many now profess to imitate, were *direct* and simple upon this point. He was not too good to acknowledge all men as brothers and all women as sisters; it mattered not whether they were highly advanced in knowledge and morals, or if they were of low intellectual and moral culture.

It is seriously to be doubted if any of Christ's disciples, or men equally as good as were they, could gain fellowship in *any* of your Fifth Avenue Church palaces, since they were nothing more than the *humblest* of fishermen of no social or mental standing. Nevertheless, they were *quite* good enough for *Christ* to associate with, and *fit* to be appointed by Him to be "fishers of men."[7] The Church seems to have forgotten that good *does* sometimes come out of the Nazareths of the world, and that wisdom *may* fall from the "mouths of babes and sucklings."[8] Quite *too much* of the old pharisaical spirit exists in society to-day to warrant its members' claims, that they are the representatives and followers of Christ. For they are the I-am-holier-than-thou kind of people, who affect to, and to a great extent do, prescribe the standards of public opinion; and who ostracise *everybody* who will not bow to their mandates.

Talk of Freedom, of equality, of justice! I tell you there is scarcely a *thought* put in practice that is *worthy* to be the offspring of those noble words. The *veriest systems of despotism* still reign in *all* matters pertaining to social life. Caste stands as boldly out in this country as it does in political life in the kingdoms of Europe.

It is true that we are obliged to accept the situation *just as it is*. If we accord freedom to all persons we must expect them to make their own best use thereof, and, as I have already said, must protect them in such use until they learn to put it to better uses. But in our predication we must be consistent, and now ask who among you would be *worse* men and women were *all* social laws repealed?

Would you *necessarily* dissolve your present relations, *desert* your dependent husbands—for there are even some of them—and wives and children simply because you have the *right* so to do? You are all trying to deceive yourselves about this matter. Let me ask of husbands if they think there would be fifty thousand women of the town supported by them if their wives were ambitious to have an *equal* number of men of the town, to support, and for the same purposes? I tell you, nay! It is because men are held *innocent* of this support, and all the vengeance is visited upon the *victims*, that they have come to have an immunity in their practices.

Until women come to hold men to equal account as they do the women with whom they consort; or until they regard these women as just as respectable as the men who support them, society will remain in its present scale of moral excellence. A man who is well known to have been the constant visitor to these women is accepted into society, and if he be *rich* is eagerly *sought* both by mothers having marriageable daughters and by the daughters themselves. But the women with whom they have consorted are *too vile* to be even acknowledged as worthy of Christian burial, to say nothing of common Christian treatment. I have heard women reply when this difficulty was pressed upon them, "We cannot ostracise *men* as we are compelled to *women*, since we are *dependent* on them for *support*." Ah! here's the rub. But do you not see that these *other* sisters are *also* dependent upon men for *their* support, and *mainly* so because you render it next to impossible for them to follow any *legitimate* means of livelihood? And are only those who have been fortunate enough to secure *legal* support entitled to live?

When I hear *that* argument advanced, my heart sinks within me at the degraded condition of my sisters. They submit to a degradation simply because they *see no alternative* except self-support, and they see no means for that. To put on the semblance of holiness they cry out against those who, for like reasons, submit to like degradation; the only difference between the two being in a licensed ceremony, and a slip of printed paper costing twenty-five cents and upward.

The good women of one of the interior cities of New York some two years since organized a movement to put down prostitution. They were, by stratagem, to find out who visited houses of prostitution, and then were to ostracise them. They pushed the matter until they found their own husbands, brothers, and sons involved, and then suddenly desisted, and nothing has since been heard of the eradication of prostitution in that city. If the same experiment were to be tried in New York, the result would be the same. The supporters of prostitution would be found to be those whom women cannot ostracise. The same disability excuses the presence of women in the very home, and I need not tell you that Mormonism is practised in *other* places beside Utah.[9] But what is the logic of these things? Why, simply this: A woman, be she wife or mistress, who consorts with a man who consorts with *other* women, is equally, with *them and him*, morally responsible, since the receiver is held to be as culpable as the thief.

The false and hollow relations of the sexes are thus resolved into the mere question of the *dependence* of women upon men for support, and women, whether married or single, are supported *by* men because they *are* women and their opposites in sex. I can see no moral difference between a woman who marries and lives with a man because he can provide for her wants, and the woman who is *not* married, but who is provided for at the same price. There is a *legal* difference, to be sure, upon one side of which is set the seal of respectability, but there is no virtue in law. In the *fact* of law, however, is the evidence of the lack of virtue, since if the law be *required* to enforce virtue, its real presence is wanting; and women need to comprehend this truth.

The sexual relation must be rescued from this *insidious* form of slavery. Women must rise from their position as *ministers* to the passions of men to be their equals. Their entire system of education must be changed. They must be trained to be *like* men, permanent and independent individualities, and not their mere appendages or adjuncts, with them forming but one member of society. They must be the companions of men from *choice, never* from necessity....

Free Love, then, is the law by which men and women of all grades and kinds are attracted to or repelled from each other, and does not describe the results accomplished by either; these results depend upon the condition and development of the individual subjects. It is the *natural* operation of the *affectional* motives of the sexes, unbiased by *any* enacted law or *standard* of public opinion. It is the opportunity which gives the opposites in sex the conditions in which the law of chemical affinities raised into the domain of the affections can have unrestricted sway, as it has in *all* departments of nature *except* in enforced sexual relations among men and women.

It is an impossibility to compel incompatible elements of *matter* to unite. So also is it impossible to compel incompatible elements of *human nature* to unite. The sphere of chemical science is to bring together such elements as will produce harmonious compounds. The sphere of social science is to accomplish the same thing in humanity. Anything that stands in the way of this accomplishment in either department is an *obstruction* to the natural order of the universe. There would be just as much common sense for the chemist to write a law *commanding* that two incompatible elements should unite, or that two, once united, should so remain, even if a third, having a stronger affinity for one of them than they have for each other, should be introduced, as it is for chemists of society to attempt to do the same by individuals; for both are impossible. If in chemistry two properties are united by which the environment is not profited, it is the same law of affinity which operates as where a compound is made that is of the greatest service to society. This law holds in social chemistry; the results obtained from social compounds will be just such as their respective properties determine.

Thus I might go on almost infinitely to illustrate the difference which *must* be recognized between the operations of a law and the *law itself*. Now the whole difficulty in marriage law is that it endeavours to *compel* unity between elements in which it is impossible; consequently there is an attempt made to subvert not only the general order of the universe, but also the special intentions of nature, which are those of God. The results, then, flowing from operations of the law of Free Love will be *high, pure*, and *lasting*, or *low, debauched and promiscuous, just in the degree* that those loving, are high or low in the scale of sexual progress; while each and all are strictly natural, and therefore legitimate in their respective spheres.

Promiscuity in sexuality is simply the *anarchical stage of development*[10] wherein the passions rule supreme. When spirituality comes in and rescues the real man or woman from the domain of the purely material, promiscuity is simply impossible. As promiscuity is the analogue to anarchy, so is spirituality to scientific selection and adjustment. Therefore I am fully persuaded that the very highest sexual unions are those that are monogamic, and that these are perfect in proportion as they are lasting. Now if to this be added the fact that the highest kind of love is that which is utterly freed from and devoid of *selfishness*, and whose *highest* gratification comes from rendering its object the *greatest* amount of happiness, let that happiness depend upon whatever it may, then you have my ideal of the highest order of love and the most perfect degree of order to which humanity can attain. An affection that does not desire to bless its object, instead of appropriating it by a selfish possession to its own uses, is not worthy the name of love.

AND THE TRUTH SHALL MAKE YOU FREE

Love is that which exists to *do* good, not merely to *get good*, which is constantly giving instead of desiring. ...

The general test of love to-day is entirely different from that which Christ gave. That is now deemed the greatest love which has the strongest and most uncontrollable wish to be made happy, by the appropriation, and if need be the sacrifice, of all the preferences of its object. It says: "Be mine. Whatever may be your wish, yield it up to me." How different would the world be were this sort of selfishness supplanted by the Christ love, which says: Let this cup pass from me. Nevertheless, not my will but Thine be done.[11] Were the relations of the sexes thus regulated, misery, crime and vice would be banished, and the pale, wan face of female humanity replaced by one glowing with radiant delight and healthful bloom, and the heart of humanity beat with a heightened vigour and renewed strength, and its intellect cleared of all shadows, sorrows and blights. Contemplate this, and then denounce me for advocating Freedom if you can, and I will bear your curse with a better resignation.

Oh! my brothers and sisters, let me entreat you to have more faith in the self-regulating efficacy of freedom. Do you not see how beautifully it works among us in other respects? In America everybody is free to worship God according to the dictates of his own conscience, or even not to worship anything, notwithstanding you or I may think that very wicked or wrong. The respect for freedom we make paramount over our individual opinions, and the result is peace and harmony, when the people of other countries are still throttling and destroying each other to enforce their individual opinions on others. Free Love is only the appreciation of this beautiful principle of freedom. One step further I entreat you to trust it still, and though you may see a thousand dangers, I see peace and happiness and steady improvement as the result.

To more specifically define Free Love I would say that I prefer to use the word *love* with *lust* as its antithesis, *love* representing the spiritual and *lust* the animal; the perfect and harmonious interrelations of the two being the perfected human. This use has its justification in other pairs of words; as good and evil; heat and cold; light and dark; up and down; north and south; which in *principle* are the same, but in *practice* we are obliged to judge of them as *relatively* different. The point from which judgment is made is that which we occupy, or are related to, individually, at any given time. Thus what would be up to one person might be down to another differently situated, along the line which up and down describe. So also is it of good and evil. What is good to one low down the ladder may not only be, but actually is, evil to one further ascended; nevertheless it is the same ladder up which both climb. It is the comprehension of this scientific fact that guarantees the *best* religion. And it is the *non-comprehension* of it that sets us as judges of our brothers and sisters, who are below us in the scale of development, to whom we should reach down the kind and loving hand of assistance, rather than force them to retreat farther away from us by unkindness, denunciation and hate....

I know full well how strong is the appeal that can be made in behalf of marriage, an appeal based on the sanctions of usage and inherited respect, and on the sanctions of religion reinforced by the sanctions of law. I know how much can be said, and how forcibly it can be said, on the ground that women, and especially that the children born of the union of the sexes, must be protected and must, therefore, have the solemn contract of the husband and father to that effect. I know how long and how powerfully the ideality and sentiment of mankind have clustered, as it were in a halo, around this time-honoured institution of marriage. And yet I solemnly believe that *all that* belongs to a dispensation of force and contract, and of a low and unworthy sense of mutual ownership, which is passing, and which is destined rapidly to pass, completely away; not to leave us without love, nor without the happiness and beauty of the most tender relation of human souls; nor without security for woman, and ample protection for children; but to lift us to a higher level in the enjoyment of every blessing. I believe in *love with liberty*; in *protection without slavery*; in *the care and culture of offspring by new and better methods, and without the tragedy of self-immolation on the part of parents*. I believe in the family, *spiritually constituted*, expanded, amplified, and scientifically and artistically organized, as a unitary home. I believe in the most wonderful transformation of human society as about to come, as even now at the very door, through general progress, science and the influential intervention of the spirit world. I believe in more than all that the millennium has ever signified to the most religious mind; and I believe that in order to prepare minds to contemplate and desire and enact the new and better life, it is necessary that the old and still prevalent superstitious veneration for the legal marriage tie be relaxed and weakened; not to pander to immorality, but as introductory to a nobler manhood and a more glorified womanhood; as, indeed, the veritable gateway to a paradise regained....

I prize dearly the good opinion of my fellow-beings. I would, *so gladly*, have you think well of me, and not ill. It is because I love you all, and love your well-being still more than I love you, that I tell you my vision of the future, and that I would willingly disturb your confidence, so long cherished, in the old dead or dying-out past. Believe me honest, my dear friends, and so forgive and think of me lovingly in turn, even if you are compelled still to regard me as deceived. I repeat, that I love you all; that I love every human creature, and their well-being; and that I believe, with the profoundest conviction, that what I have urged in this discourse is conducive to that end.

Thus have I explained to you what Social Freedom or, as some choose to denominate it, Free Love, is, and what its advocates demand. Society says, to grant it is to precipitate itself into anarchy. I oppose to this arbitrary assumption the logic of general freedom, and aver that order and harmony will be secured where anarchy now reigns. The order of nature will soon determine whether society is or I am right. Let that be as it may, I repeat: "The love that I cannot command is not mine; let me not disturb myself about it, nor attempt to filch it from its rightful owner. A heart that I supposed mine has drifted and gone. Shall I go in pursuit? Shall I forcibly capture the truant and transfix it with the barb of my selfish affection, and pin it to the wall of my chamber? Rather let me leave my doors and windows open, intent only on living so nobly that the best cannot fail to be drawn to me by an irresistible attraction."

# Chapter Eleven

## *A Speech on the Impending Revolution*

*This speech was given at Boston's Music Hall on February 1, 1872, to a standing-room-only crowd. Critiquing wealthy men like Cornelius Vanderbilt, the speech "helped widen the breach between herself and the women who had lent her their support" (Shaplen,* Free Love and Heavenly Sinners, *156). When she gave it again in March, eight thousand people attended, "with an additional 10,000 denied admittance" (Frisken,* Victoria Woodhull's Sexual Revolution, *126). "Even the critical* New York Herald *reported that six thousand attended, with as many more turned away for lack of seats. Woodhull's revolutionary message, and the audience's enthusiastic response to her calls for an uprising of the disenfranchised workers, generated extraordinarily negative commentary in the commercial press" (Frisken 45). She gave the speech throughout 1872 in places like Chicago and Cincinnati. It was reprinted in* Woodhull and Claflin's Weekly *on November 1, 1873. Introductory and concluding remarks are omitted here.*

Now, individual freedom in its true sense means just the same thing for the people that freedom for the air and water means to them. It means freedom to obey the natural condition of the individual, modified only by the various external forces which are brought to bear upon, and which induce action in, the individual. What that action will be, must be determined solely by the individual and the operating causes, and in no two cases can they be precisely alike; since no two human beings are precisely alike. Now, is it not plain that freedom means that individuals having the right to it, are subject only to the laws of their own being, and to the relations they sustain to the laws of other things by which they are surrounded?

If, then, freedom mean anything, it means that no individual is subject to any rule or law to be arbitrarily imposed by other individuals. But several individuals may agree among themselves to be governed by certain rules, since that is their freedom to do so. And here is the primal foundation and the only authoritative source or government. No individual can be said to be free and be held accountable to a law to which he or she did not consent.

In the light of that analysis, have the people of this country got freedom? But should it be objected that such freedom would be liable to abuse, we reply that that is impossible. Since the moment one individual abuses his or her freedom, that moment he or she is encroaching upon the freedom of some one else who is equally who entitled to the same right. And the law of the association must protect against such encroachment. And, so far as restraint is concerned, this is the province—the sole province—of law, to protect the rights of individual freedom.

But what is equality, which must be maintained in freedom? A good illustration of what equality among the people means, may be drawn from the equality among the children of a family in the case of an equal division of the property of the deceased father. If the property is divided among them according to their respective merits, that would not be equality.

Now, equality for the people means the equality of the family, extended to all families. It means that no personal merit or demerit can interfere between individuals, so that one may, by arbitration or laws, be placed unequally with another. It means that every individual is entitled to all the natural wealth that he or she requires to minister to the various wants of the body, and to an equal share of all accumulated, artificial wealth—which will appear self-evident when we shall have analyzed wealth. It also means that every person is entitled to equal opportunity for intellectual acquirements, recreation and rest, since the first is necessary to make the performance of the individual's share of duty possible; while the second and third are the natural requirements of the body, independent of the individuality of the person, and which was not self-created but inherited.

Under this analysis have we any such thing as equality in this country? And yet it should be the duty of government, since it is a fundamental portion of its theory, to maintain equality among the people; otherwise the word is but a mere catch, without the slightest signification in fact.

What, then, should be the sphere of justice in maintaining equality in freedom? Clearly to maintain equal conditions among free individuals. But this will appear the more evident as we proceed. The impending revolution, then, will be the strife for the mastery between the authority, despotism, inequalities and injustices of the present, and freedom, equality and justice in their broad and perfect sense, based on the proposition that humanity is one, having a common origin, common interests and purposes, and inheriting a common destiny, which is the complete statement of the religion of Jesus Christ, unadulterated by his professed followers.

But does the impending revolution imply a peaceful change or a bloody struggle?

No person who will take the trouble to carefully observe the conditions of the various departments of society can fail to discern the terrible earthquakes just ready to burst out upon every side, and which are only now restrained by the thick incrustations with which customs, prejudices and authorities have incased humanity. Indeed, the whole surface of humanity is surging like the billows of the stormy ocean, and it only escapes general and destructive rupture because its composition, like the consciences of its constituent members, is so elastic. But, anon, the restrained furies will overcome the temper of their fastenings, and, rending them asunder, will sweep over the people, submerging them or cleansing them of their gathered debris, as they shall have located themselves, with regard to its coming. . . .

It is a crime for a single person to steal a dollar, but a corporation may steal a million dollars, and be canonized as saints.

Oh, the stupid blindness of this people! Swindled every day before their very eyes, and yet they don't seem to know that there is everything wrong, simply because no *law* has been violated. In their eyes everything that is lawful is right, and this has become the curse of the nation. But the opposite—that everything which is right is lawful—don't follow as a part of their philosophy.

No matter what a person does if it is not actionable under the law; he is an honest man and a good church member. But heaven defend us from being truthful, natural beings, unless the law says we may—since that is to be an infamous scoundrel.

A Vanderbilt[1] may sit in his office and manipulate stocks, or make dividends, by which, in a few years, he amasses fifty million dollars from the industries of the country, and he is one of the remarkable men of the age. But if a poor, half-starved child were to take a loaf of bread from his cupboard, to prevent starvation, she would be sent first to the Tombs, and thence to Blackwell's Island.[2]

An Astor may sit in his sumptuous apartments, and watch the property bequeathed him by his father, rise in value from one to fifty millions, and everybody bows before his immense power, and worships his business capacity. But if a tenant of his, whose employer had discharged him because he did not vote the Republican ticket, and thereby fails to pay his month's rent to Mr. Astor, the law sets him and his family into the street in midwinter; and, whether he dies of cold or starvation, neither Mr. Astor or anybody else stops to ask, since that is nobody's business but the man's. This is a free country, you know, and why should I trouble myself about that person, because he happens to be so unfortunate as not to be able to pay Mr. Astor his rent?

Mr. Stewart, by business tact, and the various practices known to trade, succeeds, in twenty years, in obtaining from customers whom he has entrapped into purchasing from him fifty millions dollars, and with his gains he builds costly public beneficiaries, and straightway the world makes him a philanthropist. But a poor devil who should come along with a bolt of cloth, which he had succeeded in smuggling into the country, and which, consequently, he could sell at a lower price than Mr. Stewart, who paid the tariff, and is thereby authorized by law to add that sum to the piece, would be cast into prison.

Now these individuals represent three of the principal methods that the privileged classes have invented by which to monopolize the accumulated wealth of the country. But let us analyze the processes, and see if it is wholly by their personal efforts that they gain this end.

Nobody pretends that Mr. Stewart ever produced a single dollar of his vast fortune. He accumulated it by dealing in the productions of others, which he first obtained at low rates, and then sold at a sufficient advance over the cost of handling to make in the aggregate a sum amounting to millions.

Now, I want to ask if all this is not arriving at the same result, by another method, at which the slaveholders of the South arrived, by owning negroes? In the case of the latter, the slaveholder reaped all the benefits of the labors of the negroes. In the former case the merchant princes, together with the various other privileged classes, reap the benefit of the labors of all the working-classes of the country. Every year the excess of the produced wealth of the country finds final lodgment in the pockets of these classes, and they grow richer at each succeeding harvest, while the laborers toil their lives away; and when all their strength and vigor have been transformed into wealth, which has been legally transferred to the capitalists, they are heavy with age, and as destitute as when they began their life of servitude. Did ever Southern slave have meaner end than this?

In all seriousness, is there any common justice in such a state of things? Is it right that the millions should toil all their lives long, scarcely having comfortable food and clothes, while the few manage to control all the benefits? People may pretend that it is justice, and good Christians may excuse it upon that ground, but Christ would never have called it by that name. He would even give him that labored but an hour as much as he that had labored all the day, but to him who labored not at all he would take away even that which he hath. And yet we hear loud professions of Christianity ascending from the pulpit throughout the length and breadth of the land. And when I listen, I cannot help exclaiming, "O, ye hypocrites, how can ye hope to escape the damnation of hell?"

Am I asked, How are these things to be amended? I will tell you in the first place, that they must be remedied; and this particular case of dealing in the labor of the people is to be remedied by abolishing huckstering, or the system of middle-men, and substituting therefor a general system of public markets, conducted by the people through their paid agents, as all other public business is performed. In these markets the products of the country should be received, in first hands, direct from the producers, who should realize their entire proceeds. In this manner the immense fortunes realized by middle-men, and the profits made by the half-dozen different hands through which merchandise travels on its way to consumers, would be saved to the producer. A bushel of apples, purchased in the orchard at twenty-five cents, is finally sold to the consumer at a dollar. Now, either the consumer has paid at least a half dollar too much, or the producer has received a half dollar too little, for the apples; since, under a perfect system, the apples would go direct from the orchard to the market, and thence direct to the consumer.

We are forever talking of political economy, but it appears to me that the most vital points—one of which is our system of huckstery—is entirely overlooked.

Suppose Mr. Stewart, instead of having labored all these years for his own selfish interests, had labored in the interests of the people? Is it not clear that the half-a-hundred million dollars he has accumulated would have remained with the people who have consumed his goods? Place all other kinds of traffic upon the same proposed basis, and do you not see that the system which makes merchant-princes would be abolished? Neither would it require one-half the people to conduct a general system of markets who are now employed speculating in the results of labor.

In short, every person should either be a producer or a paid agent or officer of consumers and producers, and our entire system of shop keeping reduced to a magnificent system of immense public markets. In this way there could also be a perfect control exercised over the quality of perishable goods, the want of which is now felt so severely in summer in all large cities, and a thousand unthought of remedies would necessarily suggest themselves as the system should develop.

But let us pass to one of the other branches of this same system. We have in our midst thousands of people of immense wealth who have never even done so much to justify its possession as the merchant-princes have done to justify themselves. I refer to our land monopolists, and to Mr. Astor as their representative. Mr. Astor inherited a large landed estate, which has risen in value to be worth millions of dollars, to which advance Mr. Astor never contributed even a day's labor. He has done nothing except to watch the rise and gather in the rents, while the whole laboring country has been constantly engaged in promoting that advance. What would Mr. Astor have been without the City of New York? And what would the City of New York have been without the United States? You see, my friends, it will not do to view this matter superficially. We live in too analytic an age to permit these things to go on in the way they have been going. There is too much poverty, too much suffering, too much hard work, too many hours of labor for individuals, too many sleepless nights, too many starving poor, too many hungry children, too many in helpless old age, to permit these villanous abuses to continue sheltered under the name of respectability and public order.

But again, and upon a still worse swindle of the people. A person having money goes out into the public domain and acquires an immense tract of land. Shortly a railroad is projected and built, which runs through that tract. It offers a fine location for a station. A city springs up, and that which cost in some instances as little as a shilling per acre, is divided into town lots, and these are reluctantly parted with at five hundred dollars each.

Again, I wish to inquire, in the name of Justice, to whom does that advance belong? To the person who nominally holds the land? What has he done to entitle him to receive dollars for what he only paid cents? Is there any equality—is there any justice—in such a condition? He profits by the action of others; in fact at the public expense, since in its last analysis it is the common public who are the basis of all advance in the value of property.

Now, I say, that that common public is entitled to all the benefits accruing from common efforts; and it is an infamous wrong that makes it accrue to the benefit of a special few. And a system of society which permits such arbitrary distributions of wealth is a disgrace to Christian civilization, whose Author and his Disciples had all things in common. Let professing Christians who, for a pretense, make long prayers, think of that, and then denounce Communism, if they can; and denounce me as a Revolutionist for advocating it, if they dare.

But, is it asked, how is this to be remedied? I answer, very easily! Since those who possess the accumulated wealth of the country have filched it by legal means from those to whom it justly belongs—the people—it must be returned to them, by legal means if possible, but it must be returned to them in any event. When a person worth millions, dies, instead of leaving it to his children, who have no more title to it than anybody else's children have, it must revert to the people, who really produced it. Do you say that is injustice to the children? I say, No! And if you ask me how the rich man's children are going to live after his death, I answer, by the same means as the poor man's children live. Let it be remembered that we have had simple freedom quite long enough. By setting all our hopes on freedom we have been robbed of our rights. What we want now is more than freedom—we want equality! And by the Heaven above us, earth's growing children are going to have it! What right have the children of the rich to be born to luxurious idleness, while the children of the poor are born to, all their lives long, further contribute to their ease? Do they not in common belong to God's human family? If I mistake not, Christ told us so. You will not dispute his authority, I am sure. If, instead of preaching Christ and him crucified quite so much, we should practice his teaching a little more, my word for it, we should all be better Christians.

And when by this process all the land shall have been returned to the people, there will be just as much of it, and it will be equally as productive, and just as much room on it as there is now. But instead of a few people owning the whole of it, and farming it out to all the rest at the best possible prices, the people will possess it themselves in their own right, through just laws, paying for its possession to the government such moderate rates of taxes as shall be necessary to maintain the government.

But I may as well conclude what I have to say regarding railroads, which must also revert back to the people, and be conducted by them for the public benefit, as our common highways are now conducted. Vanderbilt, Scott & Co. are demonstrating it better and better every day that all the railroads of the country can be much more economically and advantageously conducted under one management than under a thousand different managements. They imagine that very soon they will have accomplished a complete consolidation of the entire system, and that by the power of that consolidation they will be able to control the government of this country....

And I will tell you another benefit that will follow the nationalization of our railroads. You have all heard of the dealing in stocks, of the "bulls" and the "bears," and the "longs" and the "shorts," and the "lame ducks" of Wall street. Well, they will all be abolished. There will be no stocks in which to deal. That sort of speculation, by which gigantic swindlers corner a stock and take it in at their own figures, will, to use a vulgar phrase, be "played out." And if you were to see their customers, as I have seen them, rushing about Broad street to catch sight of the last per cent. of their margins as they disappear in the hungry maw of the complacent brokers, you would agree with me that it ought to be "played out."

Under the system which I propose, not only will stock gambling be abolished, but also all other gambling, and the hundreds of thousands of able-bodied people who are now engaged in it, living from the products of others, will be compelled to go to producing themselves.

But, says the objector, take riches away from people and there will be no incentive to accumulate. But, my dear sir, we don't propose to do anything of the kind, nor to destroy any wealth. There will never be any less wealth than now, but a constant increase upon it. We only propose that the people shall hold it in their own right, instead of its being held in trust for them by a self-appointed few. Instead of having a few millionaires, and millions on the verge of starvation, we propose that all shall possess a comfortable competence—that is, shall possess the results of their own labors.

I can't see where there is a chance for a lack of motive to come in.

It seems to me that everybody will have a better and a more certain chance, as well as a better incentive to accumulate. Will the certainty of accumulation destroy the desire to accumulate? Nobody but the most stupid would attempt to maintain that. It is not great wealth in a few individuals that proves a country prosperous, but great general wealth evenly distributed among the people. That country must be the most prosperous and happy where the people are most generally comfortably and happily circumstanced. And in this country, instead of a hundredth part of the people living in palaces and riding in coaches, while the balance live in huts and travel on foot, every person may live in a palace and ride in a coach. I leave it to you to decide which is the preferable condition and which the more Christian.

And why should the rich object to this? If everybody has enough and to spare, should that be a subject of complaint? What more do people want, except it be for the purpose of tyrannizing over others dependent upon them? But no objections that may be raised will be potent enough to crush out the demand for equality now rising from an oppressed people. This demand the possessors of wealth cannot afford to ignore. It comes from a patiently-enduring people, who have waited already too long for the realization of the beautiful pictures of freedom which have been painted for them to admire; for the realization of the songs which poets have sung to its praise. Let me warn, nay, let me implore them not to be deaf to this demand, since they do not know so well as I know what temper there is behind it. I have tested it, and I know it is one that will not much longer brook the denial of justice....

These privileged classes of the people have an enduring hatred for me, and I am glad they have. I am the friend not only of freedom in all things, and in every form, but also for equality and justice as well. These cannot be inaugurated except through revolution. I am denounced as desiring to precipitate revolution. I acknowledge it. I am for revolution, if to get equality and justice it is required. I only want the people to have what it is their right to have—what the religion of humanity, what Christ, were he the arbiter, would give them. If, in getting that, the people find bayonets opposing them, it will not be their fault if they make their way through them by the aid of bayonets. And these persons who possess the monopolies and who guard them by bayonets, need not comfort themselves with the idea that the people won't fight for their rights. Did they not spring to arms from every quarter to fight for the negro? And will you say they will not do the same against this other slavery, compared to which the former is as an gentle shower to a raging tempest?

Don't flatter yourselves, gentlemen despots, that you are going to escape under that assumption. You will have to yield, and it will be best for you to do it gracefully. You are but as one to seven against them. Numbers will win. It will be your own obduracy if they are goaded on to madness. Do not rely upon their ignorance of the true condition. Upon that you have anchored your hopes as long as it is safe. There are too many reform newspapers in circulation. And though the columns of all our great dailies are shut to their truths, still there are channels through which they flow to the people—aye, even to those who delve in the coal mines of Pennsylvania, seldom seeing the joyous sunshine. And this education shall continue until every person who contributes to the maintenance of another in luxurious idleness shall know how such a result is rendered possible.

Hence, I say, it lies in the hands of those who have maintained this despotism over the common people to yield it up to them and recognize their just relations.

And remember what I say to you to-night: If this that is claimed is not granted—if, beside freedom, equality is not made possible by your giving up this power, by which the laborer is robbed of the results of his labor, before our next centennial birthday, July 4th, 1876, you will have precipitated the most terrible war that the earth has yet known.

For three years before the breaking out of the slavery rebellion I saw and heard with my spiritual senses the marching of armies, the rattle of musketry, and the roar of cannon; and I already hear and see the approach of this more terrible contest. I know it is coming. There is but one way in which it can be averted. There was one way by which the slave war could have been avoided—the abolition of slavery. But the slave oligarchy would not listen to our Garrisons, Sumners,[3] Tiltons and

Douglasses. They tried the arbitration of war, but they lost their slaves at last. Now, will not these later oligarchies—the land, the railroad, the money aristocracies—learn a lesson from their terrible fate? Will they not listen to the abolitionists—to the Garrisons, the Sumners, the Tiltons and the Douglasses—of to-day? Will they try the arbitration of war, which will result as did the last, in the loss of that for which they fight? I would that they should learn wisdom by experience. The slaveholders could have obtained compensation for their negroes. They refused it and lost all. Ponder that lesson well, and do not neglect to give it its true application. You can compromise now, and the same general end be arrived at without the baptism of blood. It shall not be my fault if that baptism comes. Nevertheless, equality and justice are on the march, and they cannot be hindered. They must and will attain their journey's end. The people shall be delivered.

# Chapter Twelve

## *The Correspondence of the Equal Rights Party*

This correspondence was published in Woodhull and Claflin's Weekly on June 15, 1872. The Equal Rights Party convention itself took place in May, and over six hundred people attended, "representing 22 states and 4 territories" (Underhill, The Woman Who Ran for President, 208). The Equal Rights Party primarily consisted of spiritualists and self-described free lovers.

LETTER OF NOTIFICATION

New York, June 3, 1872

Victoria C. Woodhull—Dear Madam:

    The National Convention of the Equal Rights Party who recently assembled in Apollo Hall in this city, has instructed the undersigned officers of the Convention to inform you that you have been nominated by acclamation as its candidate for the Presidency of the United States. The Platform and Resolutions unanimously adopted by the Convention we also submit to your consideration, and request your acceptance of the same as well as of the nomination.

J. D. Reymert, *President*
Anna M. Middlebrook,
John T. Elliot,
Isaac Frazier,     } *Vice Presidents*
Lavinia C. Dundore,
John M. Spear,

Harriet B. Burton,  
George R. Allen, } *Secretaries*  
Ruth W.S. Briggs, *Treasurer*

LETTER OF ACCEPTANCE

New York, June 5, 1872

*Hon. J. D. Reymert, President of the Nominating Convention of the Equal Rights Party, and Associates:*
Gentlemen and Ladies:
  Your communication received this day, conveying the formal statement to me of the simple fact that the Equal Rights Party, recently represented in convention in this city, has nominated me as the chief standard-bearer of the party in the coming conflict, recalls the vivid sensations of gratitude, renewed responsibility and profound humility with which I was overwhelmed on that memorable evening when the spontaneous acclaim of a great, enthusiastic and admirable assembly of male and female citizens, gave me the same information without waiting for the formalities of announcement. You speak almost as if this simple fact were one of the ordinary events of polities. But to my apprehension it is far more than that. It is not even a common-place historical event. The joint assemblage of all the reformers, of all schools, for the first time in the history of the great transition which human society is undergoing, blended and fused into the same spirit, coming to agree to stand upon the same platform of ideas and measures, and nominating by an outburst of inspiration a woman known to be representative of the most advanced and unmitigated radicalism, and because she was so known: and a negro, one of the boldest of the champions and defenders of human rights, a representative man and a representative woman of the two oppressed and repressed classes, for the two highest offices in the gift of a great people—such an occurrence rises in my mind into the sublimity and pregnant significance of the grander class of the events of history. It is an event which marks in various senses the climacteric; and more than that, even; the reversal of the current of human affairs, from the drift towards selfish absorption and class interests, towards

magnanimity and justice; from the disposition to impose wrong, to a generous readiness to make reparation: from the low, semi-barbarous greed for the exercise of an authority, to the gallant and truly civilized impulses of well-bred gentlemen and ladies, to cede the place of honor to those whom brute force might otherwise repress. It is the first redemption in politics of the pledge given in the prophecy, that "the first shall be last, and the last first."[1] In a word, it is the appropriate inauguration of the Equal Rights Party; which, in its larger aspect, contemplates not American polities merely, or alone; but the establishment of justice throughout the world. It is also the subordination of party strife, among reformers themselves to the unity of a common cause.

This last aspect of the subject cannot be too much insisted on. The reformers in the world are the strongest party in the world; the mightiest political power in the world the moment they unite. The conservative world knows that fact better, even than the reformers themselves; knows the meaning of such a union and trembles in the prospect or the presence of its actual occurrence.

The reformers have been kept asunder by various causes; and divided and weakened, they have been conquered. Their intensity in the perception of particular and different evils, and of their remedies, has tended to divide them. But they are coming now to perceive that the greatest of all evils, relatively to their conflict with the common enemy the organized injustice of society, is the diversity in their own views, carried to the extent of defeating their common action. The higher truth is unity in the midst of their diversity, the unity of a combined phalanx[2] for action; with the freedom of absolute toleration. The organization of the Equal Rights Party is the expression of the fact that the cohorts of reform have at length arrived at this solid center of united activity.

Another cause for the division of the ranks of reformers has been the different degrees of radicalism, by which they have been severally characterized. These a little behind have feared to trust those a little in advance; until at length it is clearly seen that they are all travelling along the same road, and destined to reach the same goal—the absolute dissolution of the old order of social managements, and the erection of a totally new order, on the two bases of freedom and justice.

This point once gained, everything is gained. Reformers, instead of falling asunder like a rope of sand, at every strain will be consolidated, by their co-operation, into a mighty strength, from the moment that they can no longer be frightened by any other degree of radicalism beyond where they severally stand. *They have evidently reached that point when they nominate me.* It has been the purpose of my life to administer to them *that test.* I have uttered as radical thoughts in behalf of social and individual freedom (short of encroachment), as I could find the power to frame into words; and you have called me to the front, not, I presume, in spite of the fact, but *in virtue* of the fact, as that I have been so plainspoken. At all events, I stand by all that I have uttered. If by retracting one word I have written or spoken in behalf of human emancipation *from all the slaveries,* except merely to remove misapprehensions, I could be proclaimed, to-morrow, Empress of the World, I would not retract. What I have said stands; and, by your nomination, I understand you to mean that you stand with it; not in the details, nor necessarily, in the form of utterance, but in the general spirit of ultra devotion to human rights.

Nor is it to be understood, that in accepting your generous and enthusiastic nomination of me, a woman, I resign one iota of my right to be equally free-spoken in the future. The Presidential chair could be no bribe for my silence, and I am glad that you do not so intend it. It has been the cause of this country and of the political arena, and in some sense the vice of republican institutions, that the promise and the attainment of office are alike a padlock upon the lips of honest expression; but, I pledge you my honor, that I will make one exception, if there be no other, to that rule. By accepting my course in the past, and by conceding me your confidence for the future, you aid me in my determination to utter still grander truths hereafter. My work for the reorganization of society will never cease until social, industrial, political and educational liberty and equality, be achieved for all.

No one understands better than I do that all those great results cannot be attained through merely political means. Disruptive agitation is only a way for the achievement of freedom; and freedom itself, when achieved, is no more than opportunity. What we must come to in the end is the scientific organization of society, under the leadership of, and in devoted allegiance to, the best thought in the world, consecrated to the highest uses. Politics, in the ordinary or vulgar sense of the term will, in preponderance, give way to social science. Knowledge will take the place of merely blind experiment, and, in a great measure, of inspirational guidance itself. The actual establishment of the Social and Industrial Palace at Guise, as detailed in the April number of *Harper's Monthly Magazine*, and as one of the solutions of the labor and capital question, is a greater event than the outcome of any war that ever was fought.

Still wars have been, and, perhaps, still are a necessity, and so of the violent affirmation of rights, until rights are conceded and peace inaugurated upon a right basis. The uses of political movements, and more especially this one of them, are to wipe away hindrances. It is chiefly in breaking down the old and ushering in the new, that I know that I have a special function to perform; and in doing this humanitarian work, my inspirations and my spiritual previsions reveal to me views which I look upon with dread. I do not hold my life dear, except for its value to this cause, but an ordinary courage might shrink from what I foresee will oppose itself to this movement. I know not that I understand, myself, the full meaning of scenes which open to my inner vision. Is it possible that the wealthy and well to do in our midst, who have fattened from the country's industries will be blinded to the signs of the times, and refuse justice to those who have reaped down their fields,[3] until, as with the slaveholders of the South, calamity overtakes them? Is it possible they can believe that the working men and the women are not in earnest in their demands, and that nothing but a bloody commune will convince them?

I did intend to make some comment on the utterly trivial and foolish character of the platforms of the other political parties in the face of the tremendous issues which are really rising on this nation; but I will restrain myself to a single point. Horace Greeley,[4] in his letter of acceptance of the nomination made of him at Cincinnati, prates of "solemn constitutional obligations to maintain the equal rights of all citizens," meaning thereby the equal rights of all *male* citizens, ignoring completely and contemptuously the rights of more than a full half of the citizens of the United States; with, in a word, the same superciliousness with which the slaveholders spoke, a few years since, of the rights of the people, never meaning or including the rights of the slave. Mr. Greeley does this not by oversight or thoughtlessness, which would be sufficiently insulting; but with deliberate insult; for no one knows better than he, or is more awake to the fact, that the women of the country are earnestly and persistently insisting that they shall go for something in the civil constitution of the State. He repeats, that there should "henceforth be no privileged class, and no disfranchised caste within the limit of our union"; referring to the disfranchised *slaveholders*, but never in the least to the *women*. So, again, his "impartial suffrage," and his being "President not only of a party, but of the whole people," if elected, means President of his own "caste" and "class", and the self-appointed ruler of all others.

It may be expected that I shall make some reference to our own platform, some exposition of my own views of its principles. But this is scarcely necessary, since it is well known that everything which is legitimately a deduction from the principles of freedom, equality and justice, finds a hearty response in my heart, a cordial reception in my mind. However, the pride I feel for that grand enunciation of human rights, will not permit me to pass it by in utter silence. The scope of its application, the comprehensiveness of its theories, the supreme devotion to principle of its construction, are of themselves sufficiently soul-inspiring to demand the undivided sympathy of the best humanitarians; but when to these considerations are added the causes which at this time demand such a construction of such principles, and the results to be attained when they shall have found form in law, glorious visions of the future rise in resplendent grandeur in my soul, lifting it from the temporary and transitional things of the present into a comprehension of humanity redeemed from all its arbitrary conditions relieved of all its heavy yokes of bondage, and ushered into millennial perfections prophesied and promised by all prophets since the world began.

The Equal Rights Party in constructing this platform has not attempted to evade even a single issue that presents itself, nor to envelop in mist and doubt the methods by which it proposes to meet it. By the use of the plainest words, in the tersest language and with the most startling directness, has it announced both its purposes and its methods. It did not seek to find a way to avoid the prejudices of gaunt, fossilized conservatism, nor yet the cowardice of respectable, time-serving radicalism; but, in the vulgar sense of the terms, ignoring all policy and all expediency, it struck directly at the heart of the system that has borne the bitter fruits upon which so large a proportion of the people feed, proposing its utter overthrow.

In all this I most heartily concur. I do not believe in hoodwinking the people in order that they may be deceived into giving their support to any movement. I believe the cause which commands our zeal and devotion to be in itself sufficiently potent to guarantee for itself a successful issue. I know there are those who condemn our methods; but I feel that the people are greater than any individuals, and that they *do* understand the issues now rising into form and demanding solution; in fact that even now they are anxiously awaiting the more forcible and direct presentation, of the issues so that there may be a more tangible, and at the same time a more substantial point around which to rally. All this is provided for and presented in this platform. The principles of the various reformatory movements are there gathered and formulated into a single structure, offering to their respective advocates a more forcible enunciation of their several propositions than they have ever before obtained.

I said the platform strikes directly at the heart of the system under which we live. By this I mean very much more than the present governmental structure. I mean the much farther reaching theory of the uses of government. Heretofore governments have been maintained almost wholly upon the idea that they are for the protection of property; hitherto legislation has altogether overlooked humanity, and proceeded as if there were no such thing as human rights, which were entitled to respect. It is now proposed to reverse completely this order of things and to make human rights the pivotal center around which legislation shall cluster the rights of property ever remaining of secondary importance, or as the means only to greater and better ends. Under our present system people are, perhaps it may be, almost unconsciously compelled to make property the chief end and aim of life; are compelled to live, as if with death, all existence ceases. The reversal of all this will [lead to] the reversal of the causes which compel it, and the people instead of living the theory of individual selfishness, will come up to the realization of the fact that each one is but a part of one perfect whole, which includes all; and that the interests and well being of every individual member of the whole are best promoted when the interests and well being of the whole are made the governing motives.

Thus to set forth completely its purposes and methods, the Equal Rights Party declares its intention to construct, from the principles it enunciates, a new organic law, which will admit the full possession and the free exercise of every human right for all individuals. Trampling the theories vitalized by present constitutions, National and State, under its feet, it boldly pushes on, announcing that all criminal and civil laws shall be National in application, and uniform in execution. I am thus proposing to administer a death-blow to the system by which vast hordes of the officials of so-called justice live and grow fat upon the dimensions among the people, and thus restoring to the people their long-lost right to self-government, of which they have, in their blind devotion to the mere outward semblance of freedom, permitted themselves to be deprived.

Not only has it claimed the sacred right of self-government, but also the almost equally important measure, that the people themselves shall be their own law-makers; and that our Congress and Legislatures shall be restricted to their legitimate duties as working committees, whose acts must be approved by, before becoming binding upon, the people. This single plank in this platform will, when carried out in practice, do more to abolish corrupt legislation than all the measures ever proposed by legislative bodies. All well informed persons know that the people have nothing to do with present legislation; know that it is capital—wealth—in one form or another, that controls not only the law-making, but the law-executing power, as well. The people no longer require rings, lobbies and cliques to attend to their business, and in adopting the *referendum* as one of the demanded reforms they propose to wipe them out of existence.

Again, the people are becoming sick of legalized monopolies. They know of no reason why the government should grant chartered privileges to any man or any set of men which permit him or them to absorb all surplus earnings, while they toil on year after year eating the hard crusts of industrial dependence, their legalized masters rolling in luxuries they have not earned. Into this condition it is proposed to introduce a little of the leaven of equality and equity, so that every man, aye, and every woman also, shall be confirmed and protected in the possession of all the results of their labors.

But in abolishing monopolies they do not intend also to abolish the systems that have grown up under them. These they propose to wrest from the hands of the powerful corporations which now possess them, and to whom all the benefits accrue, and take them into their own hands and reap all their advantages. The one thousand millions of dollars in excess of costs of maintenance which our present system of internal improvements makes it possible for railroad corporations to wring yearly from the industries of the country, the people propose to retain in their own hands; and also to assume their management, so that it shall be impossible to compel the public to pay seven dollars per ton for the transportation of coal less than two hundred miles, to satisfy the insatiable maw of the Dividends Takers.[5]

Neither do they propose longer to quietly submit to the loss of their interest in the public domain. This is a heritage inalienably vouchsafed to them by the fact of its being natural inheritance. No person can ever acquire title—a just title—an absolute ownership—to any of the wealth which, upon coming into existence, they found awaiting them. Not only do they intend that there shall be no more land-grabbing, but they farther intend that the hundreds of millions of acres of land that have already been "grabbed" shall be reclaimed and hereafter held for free occupancy by actual settlers.

The Equal Rights Party further proposes that the innumerable leeches called money-lenders, now fastened upon the vitals of the productive classes, shall be choked off and compelled to give up their profession, and from filching their support from the people, to turn to supporting themselves by productive industry. The people are sick of paying to capitalists annually thirty millions of dollars for the exclusive privilege which they possess of furnishing a circulating medium, when the public can furnish its own circulating medium at the mere cost of the paper and printing.

The Equal Rights Party also proposes that so long as government is maintained wholly upon the theory that it is for the protection of property instead of individual human rights, that property shall pay the expenses of its maintenance, and upon the proposition that the more wealth an individual possesses the larger should be his proportion of the expense incurred for its protection; and also during the transition from the wages, to an equitable system of industry, that the laborer shall be legally protected against the exactions made upon his physical strength, and that the National and State eight hour law shall be enforced, if not by the Government, then, rising in their sovereign capacity, by the people themselves; and also that the laborer shall be guaranteed a just compensation for his toil; and still further that every person who desires to do so, shall have the opportunity to labor without being under the necessity of begging for employment, and, failing to obtain it, of seeing his family grow gaunt and weak from the pinching effects of unsatisfied hunger.

If it be a duty of Government to secure to individuals the rights which the Declaration pronounces to be inalienable, this duty is not performed, when hundreds, thousands, aye, millions of human beings, men, women and children, wander the streets of our cities and the highways of our country, hungry, ragged and cold, vainly seeking in this land of plenty, where physical want should be unknown, for the honorable means of support; and if, perchance, to save themselves from actual starvation, they take a portion of what, perhaps, they themselves produced, then they are hurried to the station before their own hands have builded.[6] Instead of the continuation of such impeachments of our civilization, the Government *must* become the paternal guardian of these classes of its citizens, guaranteeing them the employment they require.

The Equal Rights Party declares against the present system of criminal jurisprudence, denies the right of government to assume a jurisdiction which belongs to the immutable government of the Universe, and proposes to transform the instruments of punishment into methods of reformation.

It also agrees with the propositions of Horace Greeley as to universal amnesty and impartial suffrage, but differs entirely from him in his applications of them. Universal amnesty, it holds, should include not only those who once rebelled against the Government, but also all of that sex which, though never rebellious *de facto*, is equally under the ban, and that impartial suffrage should be something more than a cheat, used for the purpose of beguiling the people; in fact, that it should be considered as applying to all citizens, which he denies. The Equal Rights Party also proposes that the people shall resume the appointing power, and reduce all Executive officials, including even the President, to be their servants instead of investing them with a power that virtually transforms them into masters.

It also maintains that every son and daughter of the nation is entitled to equal opportunities for acquiring an education, which shall be, not only intellectual, but also industrial. In so doing it strikes a fatal blow at the most insidious of all existing despotisms, and the most demoralizing of all monopolies, viz.: that of educational superiority; and it furthermore demands that the Government shall supervise, and be held responsible for the methods by which such National education shall be conducted.

The Equal Rights Party also recognizes the destiny of nations, and affirms its purpose to be, to work in consonance therewith. It accepts the prophecy of all ages, that the time shall come when, instead of a multitude of constantly opposing nations, the whole world shall be united under a single paternal government, whose citizens shall become a common brotherhood owning a common origin and inheriting a common destiny.

I return, in conclusion, to what I have said of the transitional nature of the impending political revolution. When this conflict shall be concluded, either with or without actual bloodshed; when the spirit of conceding justice shall have been secured, either by convincement or force; the call will be made on all sides for constructive science and wisdom. Sociology is the rising science of the day. The writings and living thoughts of the great students of social phenomena of all ages, in the strictly scientific point of view, will become the common property of the whole people. In the mean time let us do well the preliminary work. Let there be, first, a *whole people*; let there be freedom; let there be the universal desire for the reign of justice; then there will be a fitting preparation for the final grand organization of all human affairs.

Finally, I gratefully accept the nomination made of me, and pledge myself to every honorable means to secure, at the earliest possible day, the triumph of the principles enunciated in the platform, which being those of justice, and for the welfare of humanity, I know they must shortly succeed.

Your obedient servant,
Victoria C. Woodhull

# Chapter Thirteen

## *Speech of Victoria C. Woodhull*

*This speech, given at the ratification meeting of the Equal Rights Party, was published in* Woodhull and Claflin's Weekly *on June 22, 1872. The meeting, intended as the nomination of the party ticket, was beset by difficulties: Frederick Douglass did not appear in what was supposed to be Woodhull's formal announcement of his place on the ticket, and the event had to be moved to the Cooper Institute after the Grand Opera House cancelled it. Regardless, the hall was full and Woodhull appeared triumphant (Underhill,* The Woman Who Ran for President, *212).*

It is an unusual—I may, perhaps, say, an unprecedented—thing for a person bearing a nomination for the highest office in the gift of the people, to appear before them as an advocate of the cause represented by such nomination. But the movement which the Equal Rights party has inaugurated is itself also unprecedented; and this fact is sufficient apology, if, indeed, apology be needed at all, for my appearance before you to-night. Besides, as you well know, I am not much given to the habit of conforming to conventionalities. In fact, if there be one thing that I hold more lightly in esteem than any other, it is the doing, or the refraining from doing, anything, simply because it is in accordance with an established custom so to do. The greater question with me is, is it right, and if the answer be in the affirmative, or the negative, it is the final arbitrator. The grand effort which is about to be put forth in the interest of humanity, demands the best and most self-sacrificing devotion of every living soul which can feel and appreciate its great need; and to promote such a cause I am willing to depart widely, if it need be, from the well-beaten track of all my predecessors and contemporaries, and stand boldly before you, advocating the cause which is equally dear to all our hearts, and urging upon you all to lose no opportunity to help on the glorious work.

But what is this work? What is humanity suffering, from which it needs to be redeemed?

I do not know that it can be more succinctly, and at the same time, so comprehensively set forth, as it has been done in the platform constructed by the People's Convention in Apollo Hall, on the 10th of May. It is true, however, that this platform relates more specifically to methods than to the reasons for them, or to the results to be gained by them. Therefore, we ought perhaps to inquire into the diseases by which we are afflicted; and also into the conditions to which our methods look forward. The theory of our government justifies the position that every human being is in the eyes of the theory, equal in life. Admitting this, there is no escaping the fact, that the uses of government should be to foster, protect and promote the possession of equality. How does the condition of society reply to this standard for government? Is there anything that even approaches to equality in any of the various phases of life? I unhesitatingly answer, no! Look where we may, to whatever class of people or condition, and in place of equality, we find the greatest, gravest, aye, the most terrible distinctions, existing in every thing with which law has ought to do. Everything is made to turn upon the rights of property, and nothing upon the rights of humanity.

The monarch was once the point around which all legislation evolved. In this country, this has been so far changed, that, for the man king, is substituted the king, capital; while we all remember that, not many years ago, cotton, through slavery, was king. But we also remember that this king was dethroned, and the throne itself washed away by a torrent of human blood. But behind the place where its gaunt form stood, stands another, now revealed by its destruction, with still more subtle grasp upon the vital life of this country, and that king is wealth. To its demands the entire industry of the country is compelled to pay tribute; to its decrees, every industrial knee is compelled to bow; at its beck and nod, every busy hand stays its task and trembles lest its task shall be completed. This king, though so newly installed, already thinks itself so firmly seated upon the throne, that it even goes to the length of ignoring all law, which the politicians enacted, by which to catch the votes of the laborers.

The Legislature of the State of New York, on the 20th day of May, 1870, passed the following law:

"Section 1. On and after the passage of this act, eight hours shall constitute a legal day's work, for all classes of mechanics, workingmen and laborers, excepting those engaged in farm and domestic labor; but overwork, for an extra compensation, by agreement between employer and employee, is hereby permitted."[1]

Now this stands to-day the law in this State. But are its decrees respected by king wealth? But this, even, is not all the law held in contempt. The Congress of the United States passed a law similar in its provisions to this one of this State. Nothing, however, is sufficiently authoritative to commend itself to this despot that is attempting to ride rough shod over every right of the workingman, which interferes with the immense revenues it is accustomed to toll from them.

But this superiority to law is even surpassed in insolence by the bravado with which it is assumed that you, and not it, are the law breakers and defiers. When workingmen come together and jointly agree to demand that the law shall be respected, in their behalf, this presuming tyrant prates to you in the most approved style of hypocritical cant, of your obligations as peaceable, law-abiding citizens.

When I consider what the working people of this country have endured, I am lost in wonder and astonishment at their patience and forbearance; not that they have simply remained thus patient and forbearing, but that they have not long since risen in their sovereign might, to do and redress their own wrong in the most summary and thorough manner. But has their forbearance earned them any consideration? No! but on the contrary it has encouraged the despot to attempt still greater demands, to make still more extensive exactions year after year. If he wants more rent, larger profits, greater discounts, more mortgages, more costly residences, more sumptuous equipages, more servants to answer its call, in a word, more of every thing that by your labor you can furnish them, for you do furnish and pay for them all in the end; and this fact should be borne more in mind when this despot is to be approached by you.

You should know that instead of this power being your master, it should be your servant. Since all it is it owes to you. Let this fact permeate every thought of your souls, and never again permit yourselves to approach this king with doffed hats or upon bended knee. I would have every workman or workwoman feel that he or she is equal in all respects to any wealthy person who lives upon the alms of industry; upon which every one who does not labor does live. Such are in no wise a whit better than your meanest paupers.

But to return to the demands of labor. In this city there have been perhaps, as many as fifty thousand men upon strike, to compel the enforcement of the law which I have quoted. Some trades have succeeded, others have not as yet; while others still are being caught by compromises. Now, I say, if it is right to compromise, it is wrong to strike. They who having struck in consent with the general movement, compromise without the consent of the movement are traitors, just as much traitors as if they had sold themselves to the enemy upon the eve of a great battle. It is the right of those who do not wish to strike, to remain quietly at their work, and no man has any right forcibly to interfere with them; but a deserter is not entitled to any consideration.

But this King offers compromises to be accepted in lieu of full justice. When the law says a pound of flesh and not a drop of blood, it wants to take a portion of blood; when the law says, eight hours, it proffers you nine hours. Do you know, that in admitting the nine hours, where it has until now exacted ten, it admits the justice of all that is claimed. If it be not right for the King to exact ten hours, when the bond provides but eight, how can it be just to attempt to reply to this, but I trust their logic may fall upon already convinced ears.

I know all the hardships it may be necessary for some to endure. I know how cruel it is to see those dependent upon the weekly wages for the comforts of life, deprived of them. But we should remember that unless we have the courage to endure even to death, we are not worthy to count ourselves the sons and daughters of the men and women, who barefooted trod the wintry roads of Valley Forge, blood marking their way. It would have been easy for those heroes of the revolution to have sold themselves for British gold and thereby obtained relief: it is easy now for you to sell yourselves for the gold of this King. But had they sold out, or deserted to their foe, you, of to-day, would not have had even the blessings you now enjoy. Even so it is with you. If you do not now show the same determined devotion to freedom and justice, you will not be able to bequeath to your children that for which they will look back to you as now we look back to our fathers. Stand firm, then, in your demands. Yield not a single inch: and even [if] it require you to walk the streets of this opulent city without shoes, remember that you but imitate your noble, your valiant fathers; and that as they by their steadfastness won their cause, so also will you, by similar steadfastness win your cause.

I would not be understood as advocating violence to gain your ends. I would have every conceivable method tried, and proven a failure before resorting to the final one. I would have every laborer in the country demand that eight hours should constitute a day's work, and stick to the demand, until this proud king is willing to do them justice. But if, after doing everything, you still fail to compel it to respect the law, why then, take the execution of it into your own hands: and such being your right may also become even your duty.

But for a moment, laying aside this part of the subject, permit me to tell you that for all the wrongs that working people suffer, they are themselves *chiefly* at fault. You should not lay all the blame upon the shoulders of this king. It is all your own work. You have created this king, placed it upon the throne, and more even than that, it is you who maintain the throne. Every year at every election you vote that this king shall continue to rule over you; shall continue to rule over you; shall continue to euchre[2] you out of all you earn. It was, as it were, but yesterday, when you shouted "Long live this king!"—and to-morrow you will again resume the old cry; to-morrow you will march to the polls and cast your votes as this king commands, and the next day again cry out against his despotism.

In this city there are one hundred and twenty-five thousand workingmen's votes; but is there a workingmen sent to Albany? or to Washington? No; you have sent the satellites of this king up and down there; who; after getting there, turn upon and laugh at your foolishness. You may not like these things; they may not be palatable, but nevertheless they are true, and if they are bitter pills, it would do you good to swallow them and permit them to cleanse your system of this capacity for truckling to this king.

To-day you cry "down with this king!" I advise you upon the next election day to not only utter the same cry, but to also by your votes re-echo it until its resoundings shall shake the throne upon which it sits. But I desire to call your attention to a fact of which perhaps you have not seriously thought. Who, let me ask you, have produced all the wealth which this country possesses? Have they who hold and call it theirs? You know better than that. *You* know that all our Vanderbilts, Stewarts and Astors have never earned as much as the weakest man among you. Have they, then, an equitable title to what they possess?

I will admit, if it please them, that it is possible they may have a legal title, though there may be good reasons to question even that; but an equitable title, never! The wealth that these persons hold, in equity, belongs to those who produced it. Who has done this? Why, the people have done it, and it belongs to the people, and to them, in good time, it must be surrendered. All these people know all this, and the wiser of them are forestalling public judgment by expending large sums in investments made in the interests of the so-called lower classes. They also are aware that the time is near at hand when their accumulations will be taxed out of their hands. If a person owning ten thousand dollars in property, which he produced, is taxed one per cent., Mr. Stewart, who has his half a hundred millions, must be taxed, says, twenty-five per cent—under such a system how long would his wealth last? But it is not the Stewarts alone, nor chiefly, who rob the industries. They may take their thousands of dollars annually, but there is another class which takes its millions. I mean the bondholders. For the twenty-five hundred million dollars that the people are said to owe this class, it is demanded, that there shall in interest and principal, be returned nearly five thousand millions. Now how do we propose to escape this extortion? In this way: The people owe this debt in interest-bearing bonds; these they propose to pay at once in National currency, and thus stop the yearly drain upon the producing classes of one hundred and fifty million dollars. Will this do one any injustice? No! The money lenders will have received the face of their loan; while the people will have transformed an interest bearing debt into a non interest bearing debt; a redeemable indebtedness into a permanent circulating medium, which the faith and credit of the people will always make current. Thus, at one stroke, will the gold and interest despots be forever dethroned.

These are but portions of the work that the people must perform, before there will be any such thing as industrial equity possible; but they are important portions. Now the question arises, what will the people do to help this their redemption along, toward consummation? We all know that all political movements require a money support. This one, looking to Equal Rights for the people cannot expect, especially in its early stage, any aid from wealth. This will not come until it shall be a necessity for wealth to enlist in the cause to save itself; that time will come; but until it does come, the movement must look to those, in the direct interest of whom it is inaugurated. Is the end to be gained worthy of this support? For years those of you who are now called upon have given up your all, in the demand made by the means of the systems that this movement will overturn. When *this* is accomplished, the millions are paid into the roads of Wealth, will remain in the pockets of industrial people; and instead of there being the *very rich few* and the *very poor many*, all will be rich enough to have all the comforts that wealth and enjoyment demand. I say, that to attain to such a condition should enlist the aid of every laborer in this country; and I further add that if the industrial classes come to the support of this movement in the manner it deserves to be supported, the entire revolution can be peaceably accomplished by the next election; and I know they will come to its support. I know that the true policy of their redemption has been felt in many a heart, and spreading from these, all the noble hearts in the country, which have been borne down by toil, will catch up the glad inspiration, and, bearing it along its path as it proceeds, shall grow broader and wider, until it shall have swept over the whole land; and when its course shall have been ended, not so much as a single arbitrary inequality, not a single injustice, shall be left in power to prey upon the laboring masses.

# Chapter Fourteen

## *The Beecher-Tilton Scandal Case*

Victoria Woodhull first went public with her account of the scandal at the American Association of Spiritualists Convention in September 1872. When the response was muted, she resuscitated her newspaper to print the story in its November 2 issue. Sales of this issue were unprecedented; copies went for as much as forty dollars each. This version is excerpted from Victoria C. Woodhull's Complete and Detailed Version of the Beecher-Tilton Affair *(1876)*. The final paragraph, along with Woodhull's correspondence with fellow suffragist Laura Cuppy Smith, is omitted here.

I propose, as the commencement of a series of aggressive moral warfare on the social question, to begin in this article with ventilating one of the most stupendous scandals which has ever occurred in any community. I refer to that which has been whispered broad-cast for the last two or three years through the cities of New York and Brooklyn, touching the character and conduct of the Rev. Henry Ward Beecher in his relations with the family of Theodore Tilton. I intend that this article shall burst like a bomb-shell into the ranks of the moralistic social camp.

I am engaged in officering, and in some sense conducting, a social revolution on the marriage question. I have strong convictions to the effect that this institution, as a *bond* or *promise* to love one another to the end of life, and forego all other loves or passional gratifications, has outlived its day of usefulness; that the most intelligent and really virtuous of our citizens, especially in the large cities of Christendom, have outgrown it; are constantly and systematically unfaithful to it; despise and revolt against it, as a slavery, in their hearts; and only submit to the semblance of fidelity to it from the dread of a sham public opinion, based on the ideas of the past, and which no longer really represent the convictions of any body. The doctrines of scientific socialism have profoundly penetrated and permeated public opinion. No thought has so rapidly and completely carried the conviction of the thinking portions of the community as stirpiculture. The absurdity is too palpable, when it is pointed out, that we give a hundred times more attention to the laws of breeding as applied to horses and cattle and pigs, and even to our barn-yard fowls, than we do to the same laws as applied to human beings. It is equally obvious, on a little reflection, that stirpiculture, or the scientific propagation and cultivation of the human animal, demands free love, or freedom of the varied union of the sexes under the dictates of the highest and best knowledge on the subject, as an essential and precedent condition. These considerations are too palpable to be ignored, and they look to the complete and early supercedure of the old and traditional institution of marriage, by the substitution of some better system for the maintenance of women as mothers, and of children as progeny. All intelligent people know these facts and look for the coming of some wiser and better system of social life. The supercedure of marriage in the near future, by some kind of socialistic arrangement, is as much a foregone conclusion with all the best thinkers of to-day as was the approaching dissolution of slavery no more than five or ten years before its actual abolition in the late war....

But, in the meantime, the question came to press itself upon my consideration: Had I any right, having assumed the championship of social freedom, to forego the use of half the weapons which the facts no less than the philosophy of the subject placed at my command for conducting the war—through any mere tenderness to those who were virtual traitors to the truth which they knew and were surreptitiously acting upon? Had not the sacred cause of human rights and human well-being a paramount claim over my own conduct? Was I not, in withholding the facts and conniving at a putrid mass of seething falsehood and hypocrisy, in some sense a partaker in these crimes; and was I not, in fact, shrinking from the responsibility of making the exposure more through regard for my own sensitiveness and dislike to be hurt than from any true sympathy with those who would be called upon to suffer?

These questions once before my mind would never be disposed of until they were fairly settled upon their own merits, and apart, so far as I could separate them, from my own feelings or the feelings of those who were more directly involved. I have come slowly, deliberately, and I may add reluctantly, to my conclusions. I went back to and studied the history of other reforms. I found that Garrison[1] not only denounced slavery in the abstract, but that he attacked it in the concrete. It was not only "the sum of all villainies," but it was the particular villainy of this and that and the other great and influential man, North and South, in the community. Reputations had to suffer. He bravely and persistently called things by their right names. He pointed out and depicted the individual instances of cruelty. He dragged to the light and scathed and stigmatized the individual offenders. He made them a hissing and a by-word, so far as in him lay. He shocked the public sensibilities by actual and vivid pictures of slaveholding atrocities, and sent spies into the enemies' camp to search out the instances. The world cried shame! and said it was scandalous, and stopped their ears and blinded their eyes, that their own sensibilities might not be hurt by these horrid revelations. They cast the blanket of their charities and sympathies around the real offenders for their misfortune in being brought to the light, and denounced the informer as a malignant and cruel wretch for not covering up scenes too dreadful to be thought upon; as if it were not a thousand times more dreadful that they should be enacted. But the brave old cyclops ignored alike their criticisms, their protests, and their real and their mock sensibilities, and hammered away at his anvil, forging thunderbolts of the gods; and nobody now says he was wrong. A new public opinion had to be created, and he knew that people had to be shocked, and that individual personal feelings had to be hurt. As Bismarck is reported to have said: "If an omelet has to be made some eggs have to be broken."[2] Every revolution has its terrible cost, if not in blood and treasure, then still in the less tangible but alike real sentimental injury of thousands of sufferers. The preliminary and paramount question is: Ought the revolution to be made, cost what it may? Is the cost to humanity greater of permitting the standing evil to exist? and if so, then let the cost be incurred, fall where it must. If justice to humanity demand the given expenditure, then accepting the particular enterprise of reform, we accept all its necessary consequences, and enter upon our work, fraught, it may be, with repugnance to ourselves as it is necessarily with repugnance to others.

I have said that I came slowly, deliberately and reluctantly to the adoption of this method of warfare. I was also hindered and delayed by the fact that if I entered upon it at all I saw no way of avoiding making the first onslaught in the most distinguished quarters. It would be cowardice in me to unearth the peccadillos of little men, and to leave untouched the derelictions and offences of the magnates of social and intellectual power and position. How slowly I have moved in this matter, and how reluctantly it may be inferred, will appear from these little points of history....

In June, 1876, *Woodhull & Claflin's Weekly* published an article in reply to Henry C. Bowen's attack on myself in the columns of *The Independent*, the editorship of which had just been vacated by Theodore Tilton. In this article the following paragraph occurred: "At this very moment awful and herculean efforts are being made in a neighboring city to suppress the most terrific scandal which has ever astonished and convulsed any community. Clergy, congregation and community will be alike hurled into more than all the consternation which the great explosion in Paris[3] carried to that unfortunate city, if this effort at suppression fail."

Subsequently I published a letter in both *World* and *Times* in which was the following sentence: "I know a clergyman of eminence in Brooklyn who lives in concubinage with the wife of another clergyman of equal eminence."

It was generally and well understood among the people of the press especially, that both of these references were to this case of Mr. Beecher's, and it came to be generally suspected that I was better informed regarding the facts of the case than others, and was reserving publicity of my knowledge to a more convenient season. This suspicion was heightened nearly into conviction when it transpired that Theodore Tilton was an earnest and apparently conscientious advocate of many of my radical theories, as appeared in his far-famed biography of me, and in numerous other publications in *The Golden Age* and elsewhere. Mr. Tilton's warmest friends were shocked at his course, and when he added to his remarkable proceedings his brilliant advocacy of my Fourteenth Amendment theory, in his letters to Horace Greeley, Chas. Sumner and Matt. Carpenter, they considered him irremediably committed to the most radical of all radicals. Assurance was made doubly sure when he presided at Steinway Hall, when I, for the first time, fully and boldly advanced my free-love doctrines. It was noted, however, that this man who stood before the world so fully committed to the broadest principles of liberty, made it convenient to be conspicuously absent from the convention of the Woman Suffragists at Washington last January. All sorts of rumors were thereupon rife. Some said he had "gone back" on his advocacy of free love; some said a rupture had taken place between him and the leaders of the suffrage movement, and many were the theories brought forward to explain the facts. But the real cause did not transpire until Mr. Tilton was found at Cincinnati urging as a candidate the very man whom he had recently so severely castigated with his most caustic pen. It was then wisely surmised that political ambition, and the editorial chair of the *Tribune*, and his lifelong personal devotion to Mr. Greeley, were the inducements which had sufficed to turn his head and heart away, temporarily at least, from our movement.

About this time rumors floated out that Mrs. Woodhull, disgusted at the recent conduct of Mr. Tilton and the advice given him by certain of his friends, was animadverting[4] in not very measured terms upon their conduct. An article specifying matters involving several of these persons, obtained considerable circulation, and with other circumstances, such as the definite statement of facts, with names and places, indicated that the time was at hand, nigh even unto the door, when the things that had remained hidden should he brought to light, and the whole affair be made public.

Sometime in August last there appeared in the *Evening Telegram* a paragraph which hinted broadly at the nature of the impending *expose*. About this time, a gentleman from abroad, to whom I had related some of the facts in my possession, repeated them to a member of Mr. Beecher's church, who denounced the whole story as an infamous libel; but some days later he acknowledged both to his friend and me that he had inquired into the matter, and learned that it was a "damning fact." This gentleman occupies a responsible position, and his word is good for all that he utters. Such was the facility with which confirmations were obtained when sought for. When, therefore, those who were conversant with the case, saw in the *Boston Herald* and other papers that I had made a public statement regarding the whole matter, they were not in the least surprised. It shows that the press had concluded that it was time to recognise the sensation which, whether they would or not, was destined soon to shake the social structure from its foundation.

A reporter was then specially detailed to interview me in order, as be said, that the matter might be published in certain of the New York papers. Why that interview has been suppressed is not possible to affirm with certainty, but it be easy to guess. An impecunious reporter can be bought off with a few hundred dollars. And there are those would readily pay thousands to shut the columns of the press against this exposure. Fortunately I have a nearly verbatim copy of the report, as the interviewer prepared it, and in this shape I shall now present it to the public.

But before proceeding to the main matter, let me relate, more in detail, the facts which finally determined me to enter upon this adventurous and responsible method of agitation.

In September, 1871, I was elected, at the annual convention at Troy, President of the National Association of Spiritualists. I had never consociated with the Spiritualists, although for many years both a Spiritualist and a medium myself, with rare and wonderful experiences of my own from my childhood up. I went to this convention merely as a spectator, with no previous concert or machinery of any kind, and was myself as absolutely taken by surprise by my nomination and election as could have been any one present. It was said editorially in our paper, September 30, 1871, and said truly: "Her surprise at her reception, and her nomination to the Presidency of the Society was equaled only by the gratitude which she felt, and will ever feel, at the unexpected and tumultuous kindness with which she was then and there honored beyond her desert."

In *Woodhull & Claflin's Weekly*, of Nov. 11. 1871, I addressed a President's message to the American Association of Spiritualists. In that document I made use of these words: "A new and mightier power than all the rings and caucuses, than all the venal legislatures and congresses, has already entered the arena. Not only are all the reform parties coalescent in the reform plane, but they have *already* coalesced in spirit, under the new lead, and 'a nation will be born in a day.' They have already taken possession of the public conviction. Somewhat unconsciously, but really, all the people look to the coming of a new era; but all of them are not so well aware as we are that the spirit world has always exerted a great and diversified influence over this, while it is not till quite recently that the spiritual development of this world has made it possible for the other to maintain real and continuous relations with it.

"Your enthusiastic acceptance of me, and your election of me as your President, was, in a sense, hardly your act. It was an event prepared for you, and to which you were impelled by the superior powers to which both you and I are subject. It was only one step in a series of rapid and astounding events, which will, in a marvellously short time, change the entire face of the social world...."

At a large and enthusiastic National Convention of the reformers of all schools, held in Apollo Hall, New York, the 11th and 12th of May, 1872, I was put in nomination as the candidate of the Equal Rights Party for the presidency of the United States. Despite the brilliant promise of appearances at the inception of this movement, a counter current of fatality seemed from that time to attend both it and me. The press, suddenly divided between the other two great parties, refused all notice of the new reformatory movement; a series of pecuniary disasters stripped us, for the time being, of the means of continuing our own weekly publication, and forced us into a desperate struggle for mere existence. I had not even the means of communicating my condition to my own circle of friends. At the same time my health failed from mere exhaustion.[5] The inauguration of the new party, and my nomination, seemed to fall dead upon the country; and, to cap the climax, a new batch of slanders and injurious innuendos permeated the community in respect to my condition and character.

Circumstances being in this state, the year rolled round, and the next annual convention of the National Association of Spiritualists occurred in September, 1872, at Boston. I went there—dragged by the sense of duty—tired, sick and discouraged, as to my own future, to surrender my charge as President of the Association, feeling as if I were distrusted and unpopular, and with no consolation but the consciousness of having striven to do right, and my abiding faith in the wisdom and help of the spirit world.

Arrived at the great assemblage, I felt around me everywhere, not indeed a positive hostility, not even a fixed spirit of unfriendliness, but one of painful uncertainty and doubt. I listened to the speeches of others and tried to gather the sentiment of the great meeting. I rose finally to my feet to render an account of my stewardship, to surrender the charge, and retire. Standing there before that audience, I was seized by one of those overwhelming gusts of inspiration which sometimes come upon me, from I know not where; taken out of myself; hurried away from the immediate question of discussion, and made, by some power stronger than I, to pour out into the ears of that assembly, and, as I was told subsequently, in a rhapsody of indignant eloquence, with circumstantial detail, the whole history of the Beecher and Tilton scandal in Plymouth Church, and to announce in prophetic terms something of the bearing of those events upon the future of Spiritualism. I know perhaps less than any of those present, all that I did actually say. They tell me that I used some naughty words upon that occasion. All that I know is, that if I swore, *I did not swear profanely*. Some said, with the tears streaming from their eyes, *that I swore divinely*. That I could not have shocked or horrified the audience was shown by the fact that in the immense hall, packed to the ceiling, and as absolutely to my own surprise as at my first election of Troy, I was re-elected President of the Association. Still impressed by my own previous convictions, that my labors in that connection were ended, I promptly declined the office. The convention, however, refused to accept my declinature.

The public press of Boston professed holy horror at the freedom of my speech, and restricted their reports to the narrowest limits, carefully suppressing what I had said of the conduct of the great clergyman. The report went forward, however, through various channels, in a muffled and mutilated form, the general conclusion being, probably, with the uninformed, simply that Mrs. Woodhull had publicly slandered Mr. Beecher.

Added, therefore, to all other considerations, I am now placed in the situation that I must either endure unjustly the imputation of being a slanderer, or I must resume my previously formed purpose, and relate in formal terms, for the whole public, the simple facts of the case as they have come to my knowledge, and so justify, in cool deliberation, the words I uttered, almost unintentionally, and by a sudden impulse, at Boston.

I accept the situation, and enter advisedly upon the task I have undertaken, knowing the responsibilities of the act and its possible consequences. I am impelled by no hostility whatever to Mr. Beecher, nor by any personal pique toward him or any other person. I recognize in the facts a fixed determination in the Spirit world to bring this subject to the light of day for high and important uses to the world. They demand of me my co-operation, and they shall have it, no matter what the consequences may be to me personally.

The following is the re-statement from notes, aided by my recollection, of the interviewing upon this subject by the press reporter already alluded to:[6]

**Reporter.**—Mrs. Woodhull, I have called to ask if you are prepared and willing to furnish a full statement of the Beecher-Tilton scandal for publication in the city papers?

**Mrs. Woodhull.**—I do not know that I ought to object to repeating whatever I know in relation to it. You understand, of course, that I take a different view of such matters from those usually avowed by other people. Still I have good reason to think that far more people entertain views corresponding to mine than dare to assert them or openly live up to them.

**Reporter.**—How, Mrs. Woodhull, would you state in the most condensed way your opinions on this subject, as they differ from those avowed and ostensibly lived by the public at large?

**Mrs. Woodhull.**—I believe that the marriage institution, like slavery and monarchy, and many other things which have been good or necessary in their day, is now *effete*, and in a general sense injurious, instead of being beneficial to the community, although of course it must continue to linger until better institutions can be formed. I mean by marriage, in this connection, any *forced* or *obligatory tie* between the sexes, *any legal intervention* or *constraint* to prevent people from adjusting their love relations precisely as they do their religious affairs in this country, in complete personal freedom; changing and improving them from time to time, and according to circumstances.

**Reporter.**—I confess, then, I cannot understand why you of all persons should have any fault to find with Mr. Beecher, even assuming everything to be true of him which I have hitherto heard only vaguely hinted at.

**Mrs. Woodhull.**—*I* have no fault to find with him in any such sense as you mean, nor in any such sense as that in which the world will condemn him. I have no doubt that he has done the very best which he could do under all the circumstances—with his demanding physical nature, and with the terrible restrictions upon a clergyman's life, imposed by that ignorant public opinion about physiological laws, which they, nevertheless, more, perhaps, than any other class, do their best to perpetuate. The fault I find with Mr. Beecher is of a wholly different character, as I have told him repeatedly and frankly, and as he knows very well. It is, indeed, the exact opposite to that for which the world will condemn him. I condemn him because I know, and have had every opportunity to know, that he entertains, on conviction, substantially the same views which I entertain on the social question; that, under the influence of these convictions, he has lived for many years, perhaps for his whole adult life, in a manner which the religious and moralistic public ostensibly, and to some extent really, condemn; that he has permitted himself, nevertheless, to be over-awed by public opinion, to profess to believe otherwise than as he does believe, to help, persistently, to maintain, for these many years that very social slavery under which he was chafing, and against which he was secretly revolting both in thought and practice; and that he has, in a word, consented, and still consents to be a hypocrite. The fault with which I, therefore, charge him, is not infidelity to the old ideas, but unfaithfulness to the new. He is in heart, in conviction and in life, an ultra socialist reformer; while in seeming and pretension he is the upholder of the old social slavery, and, therefore, does what he can to crush out and oppose me and those who act and believe with me in forwarding the great social revolution. I know, myself, so little of the sentiment of fear, I have so little respect for an ignorant and prejudiced public opinion, I am so accustomed to say the thing that I think and do the thing that I believe to be right, that I doubt not I am in danger of having far too little sympathy with the real difficulties of a man situated as Mr. Beecher has been, and is, when he contemplates the idea of facing social opprobrium. Speaking from my feelings, I am prone to denounce him as a poltroon, a coward and a sneak; not, as I tell you, for anything that he has done, and for which the world would condemn him, but for failing to do what it seems to me so clear he ought to do; for failing, in a word, to stand shoulder to shoulder with me and others who are endeavoring to hasten a social regeneration which he believes in.

**Reporter.**—You speak very confidently, Mrs. Woodhull, of Mr. Beecher's opinions and life. Will you now please to resume that subject, and tell me exactly what you know of both.

**Mrs. Woodhull.**—I had vaguely heard rumors of some scandal in regard to Mr. Beecher, which I put aside as mere rumor and idle gossip of the hour, and gave to them no attention whatever. The first serious intimation I had that there was something more than mere gossip in the matter came to me in the committee room at Washington, where the suffrage women congregated during the winter of 1870, when I was there to urge my views on the Fourteenth Amendment. It was hinted in the room that some of the women, Mrs. Isabella Beecher Hooker, a sister of Mr. Beecher, among the number, would snub Mrs. Woodhull on account of her social opinions and antecedents. Instantly a gentleman, a stranger to me, stepped forward and said: "It would ill become these women, and especially a Beecher, to talk of antecedents or to cast any smirch upon Mrs. Woodhull, for I am reliably assured that Henry Ward Beecher preaches to at least twenty of his mistresses every Sunday."

I paid no special attention to the remark at the time, as I was very intensely engaged in the business which had called me there; but it afterward forcibly recurred to me, with the thought also that it was strange that such a remark, made in such a presence, had seemed to have a subduing effect instead of arousing indignation. The women who were there could not have treated me better than they did. Whether this strange remark had any influence in overcoming their objections to me I do not know; but it is certain they were not set against me by it; and, all of them, Mrs. Hooker included, subsequently professed the warmest friendship for me.

**Reporter.**—After this, I presume you sought for the solution of the gentleman's remark.

**Mrs. Woodhull.**—No, I did not. It was brought up subsequently, in an intimate conversation between her and me, by Mrs. Pauline Wright Davis, without any seeking on my part, and to my very great surprise. Mrs. Davis had been, it seems, a frequent visitor at Mr. Tilton's house in Brooklyn—they having long been associated in the Woman's Rights movement—and she stood upon certain terms of intimacy in the family. Almost at the same time to which I have referred, when I was in Washington, she called, as she told me, at Mr. Tilton's. Mrs. Tilton met her at the door and burst into tears, exclaiming: "Oh, Mrs. Davis! have you come to see me? For six months I have been shut up from the world, and I thought no one ever would come again to visit me." In the interview that followed, Mrs. Tilton spoke freely of a long series of intimate, and so-called criminal relations, on her part, with the Rev. Henry Ward

Beecher; of the discovery of the facts by Mr. Tilton; of the abuse she had suffered from him in consequence, and of her heart-broken condition. She seemed to allude to the whole thing as to something already generally known, or known in a considerable circle, and impossible to be concealed; and attributed the long absence of Mrs. Davis from the house to her knowledge of the facts. She was, as she stated at the time, recovering from the effects of a miscarriage of a child of six months. The miscarriage was induced by the ill-treatment of Mr. Tilton in his rage at the discovery of her criminal intimacy with Mr. Beecher, and, as he believed, the great probability that she was *enceinte*[7] by Mr. Beecher instead of himself. Mrs. Tilton confessed to Mrs. Davis the intimacy with Mr. Beecher, and that it had been of years' standing. She also said that she had loved Mr. Beecher before she married Mr. Tilton, and that now the burden of her sorrow was greatly augmented by the knowledge that Mr. Beecher was untrue to her. She had not only to endure the rupture with her husband, but also the certainty that, notwithstanding his repeated assurance of his faithfulness to her; he had recently had illicit intercourse, under most extraordinary circumstances, with another person. Said Mrs. Davis: "I came away from that house, my soul bowed down with grief at the heartbroken condition of that poor woman, and I felt that I ought not to leave Brooklyn until I had stripped the mask from that infamous, hypocritical scoundrel, Beecher." In May, after returning home, Mrs. Davis wrote me a letter, from which I will read a paragraph to show that we conversed on this subject.

Extract from a Letter

Dear Victoria: I thought of you half of last night, dreamed of you and prayed for you.

I believe you are raised up of God to do a wonderful work, and I believe that you will unmask the hypocrisy of a class that none others dare touch. God help you and save you. The more I think of that *mass of Beecher corruption* the more I desire its opening.

Ever yours, lovingly,

Paulina Wright Davis
Providence, R.I., May, 1871

**Reporter.**—Did you inform Mrs. Davis of your intention to expose this matter, as she intimates in the letter?

**Mrs. Woodhull.**—I said in effect to her, that the matter would become public, and that I felt that I should be instrumental in making it so. But I was not decided about the course I should pursue. I next heard the whole story from Mrs. Elizabeth Cady Stanton.

**Reporter.**—Indeed! Is Mrs. Stanton also mixed up in this affair? Does she know the facts? How could the matter have been kept so long quiet when so many people are cognizant of it?

**Mrs. Woodhull.**—The existence of the skeleton in the closet may be very widely known, and many people may have the key to the terrible secret, but still hesitate to open the door for the great outside world to gaze in upon it. This grand woman did indeed know the same facts, and from Mr. Tilton himself. I shall never forget the occasion of her first rehearsal of it to me at my residence, 15 East Thirty-eighth street, in a visit made to me during the Apollo Hall Convention in May, 1871. It seems that Mr. Tilton, in agony at the discovery of what he deemed his wife's perfidy and his pastor's treachery, retreated to Mrs. Stanton's residence at Tenafly, where he detailed to her the entire story. Said Mrs. Stanton, "I never saw such a manifestation of mental agony: He raved and tore his hair, and seemed upon the very verge of insanity. 'Oh!' said he, 'that that damned lecherous scoundrel should have defiled my bed for ten years, and at the same time have professed to be my best friend! Had he come like a man to me and confessed his guilt, I could perhaps have endured it, but to have him creep like a snake into my house leaving his pollution behind him, and I so blind as not to see, and esteeming him all the while as a saint—oh! it is too much. And when I think how for years she, upon whom I had bestowed all my heart's love, could have lied and deceived me so, I lose all faith in humanity. I do not believe there is any honor, any truth left in anybody in the world.'" Mrs. Stanton continued and repeated to me the sad story, which it is unnecessary to recite, as I prefer giving it as Mr. Tilton himself told it me, subsequently, with his own lips.

**Reporter.**—Is it possible that Mr. Tilton confided this story to you? It seems too monstrous to be believed!

**Mrs. Woodhull.**—He certainly did, and what is more, I am persuaded that in his inmost mind he will not be otherwise than glad when the skeleton in his closet is revealed to the world, if thereby the abuses which lurk like vipers under the cloak of social conservatism may be exposed and the causes removed. Mr. Tilton looks deeper into the soul of things than most men, and is braver than most.

**Reporter.**—How did your acquaintance with Mr. Tilton begin?

**Mrs. Woodhull.**—Upon the information received from Mrs. Davis and Mrs. Stanton I based what I said in the *Weekly*, and in the letters in the *Times* and *World*, referring to the matter, I was nearly determined—though still not quite so—that what I, equally with those who gave me the information, believed, but for wholly other reasons, to be a most important social circumstance, should be exposed, my reasons being, as I have explained to you, not those of the world; and I took that method to cause inquiry and create agitation regarding it. The day that the letter appeared in the *World* Mr. Tilton came to my office, No. 44 Broad street, and, showing me the letter, asked: "Whom do you mean by that?" "Mr. Tilton," said I. "I mean you and Mr. Beecher." I then told him what I knew, what I thought of it, and that I felt that I had a mission to bring it to the knowledge of the world, and that I had nearly determined to do so.

I said to him much else on the subject; and he said: "Mrs. Woodhull, you are the first person I have ever met who has dared to, or else who could, tell me the truth." He acknowledged that the facts, as I had heard them, were true, but declared that I did not yet know the extent of the depravity of that man—meaning Mr. Beecher. "But," said he, "do not take any steps now. I have carried my heart as a stone in my breast for months, for the sake of Elizabeth, my wife, who is broken-hearted as I am. I have had courage to endure rather than to add more to her weight of sorrow. For her sake I have allowed that rascal to go unscathed. I have curbed my feelings when every impulse urged me to throttle and strangle him. Let me take you over to Elizabeth, and you will find her in no condition to be dragged before the public; and I know you will have compassion on her." And I went and saw her, and I agreed with him on the propriety of delay.

THE BEECHER-TILTON SCANDAL CASE

**Reporter.**—Was it during this interview that Mr. Tilton explained to you all that you know of the matter?

**Mrs. Woodhull.**—Oh, no. His revelations were made subsequently at sundry times, and during months of friendly intercourse, as occasion brought the subject up. I will, however, condense his statements to me, and state the facts as he related them, as consecutively as possible. I kept notes of the conversation as they occurred from time to time, but the matter is so much impressed on my mind that I have no hesitation in relating them from memory.

**Reporter.**—Do you not fear that by taking the responsibility of this *expose* you may involve yourself in trouble? Even if all you relate should be true, may not those involved deny it *in toto*, even the fact of their having made the statements?

**Mrs. Woodhull.**—I do not fear anything of the sort. I know this thing must come out, and the statement of the plain ungarnished truth will outweigh all the perjuries that can be invented, if it come to that pass. I have been charged with attempts at blackmailing, but I tell you, there is not money enough in these two cities to purchase my silence in this matter. I believe it is my duty and my mission to carry the torch to light up and destroy the heap of rottenness, which, in the name of religion, marital sanctity, and social purity, now passes as the social system. I know there are other churches just as false, other pastors just as recreant to their professed ideas of morality—by their immorality you know I mean their hypocrisy. I am glad that just this one case comes to me to be exposed. This is a great congregation. He is a most eminent man. When a beacon is fired on the mountain, the little hills are lighted up. This exposition will send inquisition through all the churches and what is termed conservative society.

**Reporter.**—You speak like some weird prophetess, madam.

**Mrs. Woodhull.**—I am a prophetess—I am an evangel—I am a Saviour, if you would but see it; but I, too, come not to bring peace, but a sword....

Mr. Tilton first began to have suspicions of Mr. Beecher on his own return from a long lecturing tour through the West. He questioned his little daughter, privately, in his study, regarding what had transpired in his absence. "The tale of iniquitous horror that was revealed to me was," he said, "enough to turn the heart of a stranger to stone, to say nothing of a husband and father." It was not the fact of the intimacy alone, but in addition to that, the terrible orgies—so he said—of which his house had been made the scene, and the boldness with which matters had been carried on in the presence of his children. "These things drove me mad," said he, "and I went to Elizabeth and confronted her with the child and the damning tale she had told me. My wife did not deny the charge nor attempt any palliation. She was then *enceinte*, and I felt sure that the child would not be my child. I stripped the wedding ring from her finger. I tore the picture of Mr. Beecher from my wall and stamped it in pieces. Indeed I do not know what I did not do. I only look back to it as a time too horrible to retain any exact remembrance of. She miscarried the child and it was buried. For two weeks, night and day, I might have been found walking to and from that grave, in a state bordering on distraction. I could not realize the fact that I was what I was. I stamped the ring with which we had plighted our troth deep into the soil that covered the fruit of my wife's infidelity. I had friends, many and firm and good, but I could not go to them with this grief, and I suppose I should have remained silent through life, had not an occasion arisen which demanded that I should seek counsel. Mr. Beecher learned that I had discovered the fact, and what had transpired between Elizabeth and myself, and when I was absent, he called at my house and compelled or induced his victim to sign a statement he had prepared, declaring, that so far as he, Mr. Beecher, was concerned, there was no truth in my charges, and that there had never been any criminal intimacy between them. Upon learning this, as I did, I felt, of course, again outraged, and could endure secrecy no longer. I had one friend who was like a brother, Mr. Frank Moulton.[8] I went to him and stated the case fully. We were both members of Plymouth Church. My friend took a pistol, went to Mr. Beecher and demanded the letter of Mrs. Tilton, under penalty of instant death.

[Mrs. Woodhull here remarked that Mr. Moulton had himself, also, since described to her this interview, with all the piteous and abject beseeching of Mr. Beecher not to be exposed to the public.]

Mr. Moulton obtained the letter... and told me that he had it in his safe, where he should keep it until required for further use. After this, Mr. Tilton's house was no house for him, and he seldom slept or [ate] there, but frequented the house of his friend Moulton, who sympathized deeply with him. Mrs. Tilton was also absent days at a time, and, as Mr. Tilton informed me, seemed bent on destroying her life. I went, as I have said, to see her, and found her, indeed, a wretched wreck of a woman, whose troubles were greater than she could bear. She made no secret of the facts before me. Mr. Beecher's selfish, cowardly cruelty in endeavoring to shield himself and create public opinion against Tilton, added poignancy to her anxieties. She seemed indifferent as to what should become of herself, but labored under fear that murder might be done on her account.

This was the condition of affairs at the time that Mr. Tilton came to me. I attempted to show him the true solution of the imbroglio, and the folly that it was for a man like him, a representative man of the ideas of the future, to stand whining over inevitable events connected with this transition age and the social revolution of which we are in the midst. I told him that the fault and the wrong were neither in Mr. Beecher, nor in Mrs. Tilton, nor in himself; but that it was in the false social institutions under which we still live, while the more advanced men and women of the world have outgrown them in spirit; and that, practically everybody is living a false life, by professing a conformity which they do not feel and do not live, and which they cannot feel and live any more than the grown boy can re-enter the clothes of his early childhood. I recalled to his attention splendid passages of his own rhetoric, in which he had unconsciously justified all the freedom that he was now condemning, when it came home to his own door, and was endeavoring, in the spirit of a tyrant, to repress.

I ridiculed the *maudlin sentiment* and *mock heroics* and "*dreadful suzz*"[9] he was exhibiting over an event the most natural in the world, and the most intrinsically innocent; having in it not a bit more of real criminality than the awful wickedness of "negro-stealing" formerly charged, in perfect good faith, by the slaveholders, on every one who helped the escape of a slave. I assumed at once, and got a sufficient admission, as I always do in such cases, that he was not exactly a vestal virgin himself; that his real life was something very different from the "awful virtue" he was preaching, especially for women, as if women could "sin" in this matter without men, and men without women, and which, he *pretended*, even to himself, to believe in the face and eyes of his own life, and the lives of nearly all the greatest and best men and women that he knew: that the dreadful "suzz" was merely a *bogus sentimentality, pumped* in his imagination, because our sickly religious literature, and Sunday-school morality, and pulpit pharaseeism had humbugged him all his life into the belief that *he ought to feel and act* in this harlequin and absurd way on such an occasion—that, in a word, neither Mr. Beecher nor Mrs. Tilton had done any wrong, but that it was he who was playing the part of a fool and a tyrant; that it was he and the factitious or manufactured public opinion back of him, that was wrong; that this babyish whining and stage-acting were the real absurdity and disgrace—the unmanly part of the whole transaction, and that we only needed another Cervantes to satirize such stuff as it deserves, to squelch it instantly and forever. I tried to show him that a true manliness would protect and love to protect, would glory in protecting the absolute freedom of the woman who was loved, whether called wife, mistress, or by any other name, and that the true sense of honor in the future will be, *not to know even* what relations our lovers have with any and all other persons than ourselves—as true courtesy never seeks to spy over or to pry into other people's private affairs.

I believe I succeeded in pointing out to him that his own life was essentially no better than Mr. Beecher's, and that he stood in no position to throw the first stone at Mrs. Tilton or her reverend paramour. I showed him again and again that the wrong point, and the radically wrong thing, if not indeed, quite the only wrong thing in the matter, was the barbarous idea of ownership in human beings, which was essentially the same in the two institutions of slavery and marriage. Mrs. Tilton had in turn grown increasedly unhappy when she found that Mr. Beecher had turned some part of his exuberant affections upon some other object. There was, in her, therefore, the same sentiment of the real slaveholder. Let it be once understood that whosoever is true to himself or herself is thereby, and necessarily, true to all others, and the whole social question will be solved. The barter and sale of wives stands on the same moral footing as the barter and sale of slaves. The god-implanted human affections cannot, and will not, be any longer subordinated to these external, legal restrictions and conventional engagements. Every human being belongs to himself or herself by a higher title than any which, by surrenders or arrangements or promises, he or she can confer upon any other human being. Self-ownership is inalienable. These truths are the latest and greatest discoveries in true science.

Perhaps Mr. Beecher knows and feels all this, and if so, in that knowledge consists his sole and his real justification; only the world around him has not yet grown to it; institutions are not yet adapted to it; and he is not brave enough to bear his open testimony to the truth he knows.

All this I said to Mr. Tilton; and I urged upon him to make this providential circumstance in his life the occasion upon which he should, himself, come forward to the front and stand with the true champions of social freedom.

**Reporter.**—Then Mr. Tilton became, as it were, your pupil, and you instructed him in your theories.

**Mrs. Woodhull.**—Yes, I suppose that is a correct statement; and the verification of my views, springing up before my eyes on this occasion, out of the very midst of religion and moral prejudices, was, I assure you, an interesting study for me, and a profound corroboration of the righteousness of what you call "my theories." Mr. Tilton's conduct toward Mr. Beecher and toward his wife began from that time to be so magnanimous and grand—by which I mean simply just and right—so unlike that which most other men's would have been, that it stamped him, in my mind, as one of the noblest souls that lived, and one capable of playing a great *role* in the social revolution, which is now so rapidly progressing.

I never could, however, induce him to stand wholly, and unreservedly, and on principle, upon the free-love platform; and I always, therefore, feared that he might for a time vacillate or go backward. But he opened his house to Mr. Beecher, saying to him, in the presence of Mrs. Tilton: "You love each other. Mr. Beecher, this is a distressed woman; if it be in your power to alleviate her condition and make her life less a burden than it now is, be yours the part to do it. You have nothing to fear from me." From that time Mr. Beecher was, so to speak, the slave of Mr. Tilton and Mr. Moulton. He consulted them in every matter of any importance. It was at this time that Mr. Tilton introduced Mr. Beecher to me, and I met him frequently both at Mr. Tilton's and at Mr. Moulton's. We discussed the social problem freely in all its varied bearings, and I found that Mr. Beecher agreed with nearly all my views upon the question.

**Reporter.**—Do you mean to say that Mr. Beecher disapproves of the present marriage system?

**Mrs. Woodhull.**—I mean to say just this—that Mr. Beecher told me that marriage is the grave of love, and that he never married a couple that he did not feel condemned.

**Reporter.**—What excuse did Mr. Beecher give for not avowing these sentiments publicly?

**Mrs. Woodhull.**—Oh, the moral coward's inevitable excuse—that of inexpediency. He said he was twenty years ahead of his church; that he preached the truth just as fast as he thought his people could bear it. I said to him, "Then, Mr. Beecher, you are defrauding your people. You confess that you do not preach the truth as you know it, while they pay for and persuade themselves you are giving them your best thought." He replied: "I know that our whole social system is corrupt. I know that marriage, as it exists to-day, is the curse of society. We shall never have a better state until children are begotten and bred on the scientific plan. Stirpiculture is what we need." "Then," said I, "Mr. Beecher, why do you not go into your pulpit and preach that science?" He replied: "If I were to do so I should preach to empty seats. It would be the ruin of my church." "Then," said I, "you are as big a fraud as any time-serving preacher, and I now believe you are all frauds. I gave you credit for ignorant honesty, but I find you are all alike—all trying to hide, or afraid to speak the truth. A sorry pass has this Christian country come to, paying 40,000 ministers to lie to it from Sunday to Sunday, to hide from them the truth that has been given them to promulgate."

**Reporter.**—It seems you took a good deal of pains to draw Mr. Beecher out.

**Mrs. Woodhull.**—I did. I thought him a man who would dare a good deal for the truth, and that, having lived the life he had, and entertaining the private convictions he did, I could perhaps persuade him that it was his true policy to come out and openly avow his principles, and be a thorough consistent radical, and thus justify his life in some measure, if not wholly, to the public.

**Reporter.**—Was Mr. Beecher aware that you knew his relations to Mrs. Tilton?

**Mrs. Woodhull.**—Of course he was. It was because that I knew of them that he first consented to meet me. He could never receive me until he knew that I was aware of the real character he wore under the mask of his reputation. Is it not remarkable how a little knowledge of this sort brings down the most top-lofty from the stilts on which they lift themselves above the common level.

**Reporter.**—Do you still regard Mr. Beecher as a moral coward?

**Mrs. Woodhull.**—I have found him destitute of moral courage enough to meet this tremendous demand upon him. In minor things, I know that he has manifested courage. He could not be induced to take the bold step I demanded of him, simply for the sake of truth and righteousness. I did not entirely despair of him until about a year ago. I was then contemplating my Steinway Hall speech on Social Freedom, and prepared it in the hope of being able to persuade Mr. Beecher to preside for me, and thus make a way for himself into a consistent life on the radical platform. I made my speech as soft as I conscientiously could. I toned it down in order that it might not frighten him. When it was in type, I went to his study and gave him a copy, and asked him to read it carefully and give me his candid opinion concerning it. Meantime, I had told Mr. Tilton and Mr. Moulton that I was going to ask Mr. Beecher to preside, and they agreed to press the matter with him. I explained to them that the only safety he had was in coming out as soon as possible an advocate of social freedom, and thus palliate, if he could not completely justify, his practices, by founding them at least on principle. I told them that this introduction of me would bridge the way. Both the gentlemen agreed with me in the view, and I was for a time almost sure that my desire would be accomplished. A few days before the lecture, I sent a note to Mr. Beecher asking him to preside for me. This alarmed him. He went with it to Messrs. Tilton and Moulton asking advice. They gave it in the affirmative, telling him they considered it eminently fitting that he should pursue the course indicated by me as his only safety; but it was not urged in such a way as to indicate that they had known the request was to have been made. Matters remained undecided until the day of the lecture, when I went over again to press Mr. Beecher to a decision. I had then a long private interview with him, urging all the arguments I could to induce him to consent. He said he agreed perfectly with what I was to say, but that he could not stand on the platform at Steinway Hall and introduce me. He said, "I should sink through the floor. I am a moral coward on this subject, and I know it, and I am not fit to stand by you, who go there to speak what you know to be the truth; I should stand there a living lie." He got upon the sofa on his knees beside me, and taking my face between his hands, while the tears streamed down his cheeks, begged me to let him off. Becoming thoroughly disgusted with what seemed to me pusillanimity, I left the room under the control of a feeling of contempt for the man, and reported to my friends what he had said. They then took me again with them and endeavored to persuade him. Mr. Tilton said to him: "Mr. Beecher, some day you have got to fall; go and introduce this woman and win the radicals of the country, and it will break your fall." "Do you think," said Beecher, "that this thing will come out to the world?" Mr. Tilton replied: "Nothing is more certain in earth or heaven, Mr. Beecher; and this may be your last chance to save yourself from complete ruin."

Mr. Beecher replied: "I can never endure such a terror. Oh! if it must come, let me know of it twenty-four hours in advance, that I may take my own life. I cannot, cannot face this thing!"

Thoroughly out of all patience, I turned on my heel and said: "Mr. Beecher, if I am compelled to go upon that platform alone, I shall begin by telling the audience why I am alone, and why you are not with me," and I again left the room. I afterward learned that Mr. Beecher, frightened at what I had said, promised, before parting with Mr. Tilton, that he would preside if he could bring his courage up to the terrible ordeal.

It was four minutes of the time for me to go forward to the platform at Steinway Hall when Mr. Tilton and Mr. Moulton came into the anteroom asking for Mr. Beecher. When I told them he had not come, they expressed astonishment. I told them I should faithfully keep my word, let the consequences be what they might. At that moment word was sent me that there was an organized attempt to break up the meeting, and that threats were being made against my life if I dared to speak what it was understood I intended to speak. Mr. Tilton then insisted on going on the platform with me and presiding, to which I finally agreed, and that I should not at that time mention Mr. Beecher. I shall never forget the brave words he uttered in introducing me. They had a magic influence on the audience, and drew the sting of those who intended to harm me. However much Tilton may have since regretted his course regarding me, and whatever he may say about it, I shall always admire the moral courage that enabled him to stand with me on that platform, and face that, in part, defiant audience. It is hard to bear the criticisms of vulgar minds, who can see in social freedom nothing but licentiousness and debauchery, and the inevitable misrepresentation of the entire press, which is as perfectly subsidized against reason and common sense, when social subjects are discussed, as is the religious press when any other science is discussed which is supposed to militate against the Bible as the direct word of God to man. The editors are equally bigots, or else as dishonest as the clergy. The nightmare of public opinion, which they are still professionally engaged in making, enslaves and condemns them both.

[Mrs. Woodhull concluded by saying that since her Steinway Hall speech she had surrendered all hope of easing the fall of Mr. Beecher, that she had not attempted to see him, and had not in fact seen him. She only added one other fact, which was that Mr. Beecher endeavored to induce Mr. Tilton to withdraw from his membership in Plymouth Church, to leave him, Mr. Beecher, free from the embarrassment of his presence there; and that Mr. Tilton had indignantly rejected the proposition, determined to hold the position with a view to such contingencies as might subsequently occur.]

So much for the interviewing which was to have been published some months ago; but when it failed or was suppressed, I was still so far undecided that I took no steps in the matter, and had no definite plan for the future in respect to it, until the events, as I have recited them, which occurred at Boston. Since then I have not doubted that I must make up my mind definitely to act aggressively in this matter, and to use the facts in my knowledge to compel a more widespread discussion of the social question. I take the step deliberately, as an agitator and social revolutionist, which is my profession. I commit no breach of confidence, as no confidences have been made to me, except as I have compelled them, with a full knowledge that I was endeavoring to induce or to force the parties to come to the front along with me in the announcement and advocacy of the principles of social revolution. Messrs. Beecher and Tilton, and other half-way reformers, are to me like the border States in the great rebellion. They are liable to fall, with the great weight of their influence, on either side in the contest, and I hold it to be legitimate generalship *to compel* them to declare on the side of truth and progress.

My position is justly analagous with that of warfare. The public, Mr. Beecher included, would gladly crush me if they could—will do so if they can—to prevent me from forcing on them considerations of the utmost importance. My mission is, on the other hand, to utter the unpopular truth, and make it efficient by whatsoever legitimate means; and means are legitimate as a war measure which would be highly reprehensible in a state of peace. I believe, as the law of peace, *in the right of privacy*, in the sanctity of individual relations. It is nobody's business but their own, in the absolute view, what Mr. Beecher and Mrs. Tilton have done, or may choose at any time to do, as between themselves. And the world needs, too, to be taught just that lesson. I am the champion of that very right of privacy and of individual sovereignty. But that is only one side of the case. I need, and the world needs, Mr. Beecher's powerful championship of this very right. The world is on the very crisis of its final fight for liberty. The victory may fall on the wrong side, and his own liberty and mine, and the world's, be again crushed out, or repressed for another century, for the want of fidelity in him to the new truth. It is not, therefore, Mr. Beecher as the individual that I pursue, but Mr. Beecher as the representative man; Mr. Beecher as a power in the world; and Mr. Beecher as my auxiliary in a great war for freedom, or Mr. Beecher as a violent enemy and a powerful hindrance to all that I am bent on accomplishing.

To Mr. Beecher, as the individual citizen, I tender, therefore, my humble apology, meaning and deeply feeling what I say, for this or any interference on my part with his private conduct. I hold that Mr. Tilton himself, that Mrs. Beecher herself, have no more right to inquire, or to know, or to spy over with a view to knowing, what has transpired between Mr. Beecher and Mrs. Tilton than they have to know what I ate for breakfast or where I shall spend my next evening; and that Mr. Beecher's congregation and the public at large have just as little right to know or to inquire. I hold that the so-called morality of society is a complicated mass of sheer impertinence, and a scandal on the civilization of this advanced century; that the system of social espionage under which we live is damnable, and that the very first axiom of a true morality is for the people *to mind their own business*, and learn to respect, religiously, the social freedom and the sacred social privacy of all others; but it was the paradox of Christ, that as the Prince of Peace, he still brought on earth, not *peace*, but *a sword*. It is the paradox of life that, in order to have peace, we must first have war; and it is the paradox of my position that, believing in the right of privacy and in the perfect right of Mr. Beecher socially, morally, and divinely, to have sought the embraces of Mrs. Tilton, or of any other woman or women whom he loved and who loved him, and being a promulgator and a public champion of those very rights, I still invade the most secret and sacred affairs of his life, and drag them to the light, and expose him to the opprobrium and vilification of the public. I do again, and with deep sincerity, ask his forgiveness. But the case is exceptional, and what I do I do for a great purpose. The social world is in the very agony of its new birth, or, to resume the warlike simile, the leaders of progress are in the very act of storming the last act of bigotry and error. Somebody must be hurled forward into the gap. I have the power, I think, to compel Mr. Beecher to go forward and to do the duty for humanity from which he shrinks; and I should, myself, be false to the truth if I were to shrink from compelling him. Whether he sinks or swims in the fiery trial, the agitation by which truth is evolved will have been promoted. And I believe that he will not only survive, but that when forced to the encounter he will rise to the full height of the great enterprise, and will astound and convince the world of the new gospel of freedom, by the depth of his experiences and the force of his argument....

The evil and the whole evil in this whole matter, then, lies elsewhere. It lies in a false and artificial or manufactured opinion, in respect to this very question of what is good or what is evil in such matters. It lies in the belief that society has the right to prohibit, to prescribe and regulate, or in any manner to interfere with the private love manifestations of its members, any more than it has to prescribe their food and their drink. It lies in the belief consequent upon this, that lovers own their lovers, husbands their wives and wives their husbands, and that they have the right to complain of, to spy over, and to interfere, even to the extent of murder, with every other or outside manifestation of love. It lies in the *compulsory hypocrisy and systematic falsehood* which is thus enforced and inwrought into the very structure of society, and in the consequent and wide-spread injury to the whole community. ...

Still, in conclusion, let me add, that in my view, and in the view of others who think with me, and of all, as I believe, who think rightly on the subject, Mr. Beecher is to-day, and after all that I have felt called upon to reveal of his life, as good, as pure, and as noble a man as he ever was in the past, or as the world has held him to be, and that Mrs. Tilton is still the pure, charming, cultured woman. It is, then, the public opinion that is wrong, and not the individuals, who must, nevertheless, for a time suffer its persecution.

# Chapter Fifteen

*The Naked Truth;*
or, the Situation Reviewed!

*This speech was delivered at New York City's Cooper Institute on January 9, 1873. It was reproduced in* Woodhull and Claflin's Weekly *on January 25, 1873. Warned beforehand that federal authorities planned to come to the lecture hall and arrest her on obscenity charges, Woodhull disguised herself as an elderly Quaker woman. She eluded authorities until she reached the stage, at which point she removed the disguise. Agents waited until the conclusion of her speech to arrest her. In an enthusiastic review, a reporter from the* New York Evening Post *described her as "the bravest and truest of her sex" (quoted in Woodhull and Claflin,* The Human Body the Temple of God, *374). She was arrested immediately after the speech. She gave it to large audiences throughout the country.*

My Friends and Fellow-Citizens:

I come into your presence from a cell in the American Bastille,[1] to which I was consigned by the cowardly servility of the age. I am still held under heavy bonds to return to that cell, or to meet my trial in a United States Court, upon a scandalous charge trumped up by the ignorant or the corrupt officers of the law, conspiring with others to deprive me, under the falsest and shallowest pretences, of my inherited privileges as an American citizen. In my person, the freedom of the press is assailed, and stricken down, and such has been the adverse concurrence of circumstances that the press itself has tacitly consented, almost with unanimity, to this sacrilegious invasion of one of the most sacred of civil rights. Public opinion too has been abused into concurring for a moment with this outrage.

But I have no intention of entering upon a specific defense of myself to-night. I was not unaware of what would be done when the method of social agitation, which furnished the grounds for the tyrannous exercise of power, was begun, and I am not disappointed. I was informed of the old United States statute, regarding the transmission of obscene literature through the mails, and also of the law as amended last June[2] to specially meet this case. To suppress our paper was the only method of precedure[3] by which the old *regime* could meet our argumentation; but its representatives, though wise in their own conceit, have unwittingly played directly into my hands, and for the benefit and ultimate triumph of the very thing they sought to crush.

In this, which to me, is the higher and truer sense, instead of being my enemies and persecutors, as they are in spirit and purpose, they are my active, most efficient and most effective allies; and I wish it to be distinctly understood at the very outset, that whatever I may feel called upon to say in arguing the subject upon the plane, and for the more complete understanding of the people, I here and now claim that Mr. Comstock,[4] the characteristic agent of the Young Men's Christian Association, acting under the inspiration of Messrs. Bowen, Claflin & Co., members of Plymouth Church; that District Attorney Noah Davis, and his assistant, General Davies, and Mr. Commissioner Osborne, backed up by those who are determined, as was stated in the *Tribune*, "to run her to the earth if it took every hour of his life and every dollar of his fortune," and the United States Grand Jury; that Mr. Challis, with his hundred thousand dollars, and Mr. Justice Fowler; in a word, that all and every one of them who have had any active or passive hand in what, in the common acceptance, is personal and vindictive persecution, though personally enemies to me, are, indeed, my most esteemed friends, without whom and their recent active and well-calculated interference, no such vantage as the present revolution has attained could possibly have been gained.

THE NAKED TRUTH

Therefore, without further argument, I hold that I am justified in claiming them all as my faithful though unwilling allies in the social revolution in which I am engaged; and to whatever length their ire, their hate, their vindictiveness, their bitter foolishness, their stupidity or ignorance may push them on in their line of action, they inevitably proceed just so much the further to secure the rapid and complete success of the latest, greatest and grandest revolution of the centuries, to the inauguration and completion which I am thoroughly and entirely devoted and consecrated. . . .

My sister and myself are now indicted in the United States Court on the preposterous charge of sending obscene literature through the United States mail—a charge which the officers of the Government will never dare to bring to a trial, as they cannot afford themselves to be brought into complete ridicule. If anything which I can say in this address, or which I can say or write at any time, can provoke or sting them into the folly and madness of exposing the weakness and the damnable outrage of this unhallowed proceeding against peaceable and law-abiding citizens, by bringing the case to trial, I shall consider that success the most fortunate event of my life. But I now predict before you, and make my formal record of that prediction for future reference and use, that I shall fail, utterly fail in the attempt. The District Attorney, and everybody concerned in this nefarious matter have either already accomplished all they aimed at, by covering my sister and me with the odium of being prisoners and accused of a scandalous offense, or they have had enough of the whole matter, seeing that it was a blunder from the start, and wish themselves fairly rid of it.

I repeat my prediction, and make it as marked and distinct as possible: the United States Government will never proceed to trial, in the case now on their court docket in the Southern District of New York, against Victoria C. Woodhull and Tennie C. Claflin, for violating the statute of Congress against transmitting obscene literature through the mails. They will never dare to do it. On the other hand, I predict that the Government will not enter a *nolle prosequi*,[5] and make thereby the only honorable reparation, to some slight extent, which it would be in their power to make, for the outrage they have committed on our individual rights. And, my friends, you must not forget that, when an individual is wronged, by the superaction of law officers, the whole people is thereby outraged. I predict, however, that the course they will pursue will be to hold the case over our heads, as a threat, to delay and postpone it from time to time, to pretend that they intend to bring us to trial, and yet never to do so in fact; in the hope that fortune will favor them in getting them out of the scrape, through our death or poverty, or virtual surrender to the force of a long-continued persecution.

But they reckon without their host. The cards of fate are shuffled for a different deal. I give notice here and now, I hope the occasion is a sufficiently public one, that the publication office of *Woodhull & Claflin's Weekly* is at 48 Broad street, New York city, and that from that office there will soon be issued and sold to all applicants a revised edition of the suppressed number of *Woodhull & Claflin's Weekly*, containing the "Beecher-Tilton Scandal," and that within a few weeks there will probably have been sent a million copies of it to every part of the world, so that the whole public shall be my jury and decide whether there is anything obscene in that earnest and all-important statement....

The issue of our paper in question, that of Nov. 2, 1872, is, undoubtedly, one of the boldest we have ever issued in the war we are conducting in behalf of progress, free thought and untrammeled lives; breaking the way for future generations; but throughout all its fifty closely printed columns, there is only one passage, and that of only three lines, to be found in the article now known as the Challis article,[6] which the most fastidious literary critic, who was honest, could by any possibility construe into obscenity; and that is not half so bad as a hundred isolated passages which might be selected from the bible, and which pious fathers and mothers and moral teachers, and perhaps they who belong to the Young Men's Christian Association, read in the family before prayers, to youth of both sexes, morning and evening, all over the land.

But neither the zealot Comstock, nor the District Attorney, nor the Grand Jury had, as yet, got their eye on this dreadful three-line paragraph when they had my sister and me arrested and, with unseemly haste, indicted for obscenity. Their procedure was based entirely on the "Beecher-Tilton Scandal," and it was an after-thought altogether when the Assistant District Attorney said in court that he "meant the whole paper"—an after-thought for which I am greatly obliged to him, as it puts him in my power in ways of which he is, as yet, totally unconscious.

Their action was, as they then avowed, entirely for the purpose of "protecting the reputation of revered citizens," as if it were any part of their business to protect the reputation of anybody by instituting an arbitrary censorship of the press in this free country, or except in an action for libel which had not been instituted nor even thought of; as if Americans were under the paternal wing of self-constituted legal protectors, self-constituted tyrants, otherwise speaking; and finally, as if the charge of obscenity was in any way related to that of the attack on, or the defense of, "revered citizens."

The law was open to Mr. Beecher and others for any wrong done them, and they did not move in the matter, for reasons which were alike satisfactory to them, and to us, at the time, and which are now rapidly becoming satisfactory to the whole public. What right, then, had the District Attorney, and through his agency and solicitation, the Grand Jury—the United States, in other words—through their representatives to interfere, and still, without charging any libel, to trump up another factitious and scandalous, flimsy and ridiculous, irrelevant and preposterous charge, to get, by indirection, at the result they wished to achieve—that, in a word, of simply stopping our mouths at any cost, to protect the reputations of "revered citizens," and entirely irrespective of the question whether we were telling the truth or not, or of the other question, whether our motives were good or bad? As in the case of the slave-holders and Garrison, it was not a question of the truth, nor of the motive, but of the absolute necessity for their keeping us hush on the subject.

Now, it so happens that in another case, that of Challis against Col. Blood, entirely apart from that of the United States against my sister and me, the whole Challis article came before the public and was published in full, or, as the lawyers say, verbatim, *literatim et punctatim*,[7] in the *New York Herald*, and various other newspapers: has been, in a word, pretty extensively circulated over the country in other newspaper columns than our own, and Mr. Comstock has not informed upon, and Mr. District Attorney Noah Davis has not presented, and the Grand Jury have not indicted the publishers of the *Herald* and the other papers.

Is it that men are so generally accustomed to say and print obscenity that these paragons of purity and protectors of pious and revered citizens don't mind that? Is it that the masculine sex has the monopoly of obscenity as they have of tobacco and bad whisky? Is it that obscenity is any less obscenity when it appears in the *Tribune* or the *Times* or the *Herald*? Or is it that those publishers are known to be rich and powerful, while we were supposed, from our recent misfortunes, to be poor, and possibly friendless? Or is it, after all, that the whole world knows that these respectable and well-to-do publishers and editors don't mean anything by it, except merely to make money in the ordinary course of business, while it feels instinctively that we are in earnest, and mean to do what we can to put an end to the vicious conditions of society, obscenity among the rest of them? Is it, then, the old story that the craft is in danger, that practices and habits and modes of life exist, and are held to be respectable, and must be protected, which are so obscene in their character, that we cannot even mention them without seeming to be, ourselves, guilty of obscenity? Is it the old cry of "stop thief," merely to turn away attention? Is it the old fear that the temple of the great goddess Diana should be despised,[8] and her magnificence should be destroyed, whom all Asia and the world worshipeth? Finish out the reading of the nineteenth chapter of the Acts of the Apostles, when you go home to your houses, and inwardly reflect on it and digest the old story, and you will understand the whole subject better than by the reading of all the newspapers....

I have told you that the *New York Herald* has boldly and unhesitatingly reprinted the most objectionable matter which was contained in the number of our paper which was suppressed by violent and illegal seizures, and for which we were arrested. Not only this, but, in our very next issue, we deliberately reprinted the language of that terrible three-line sentence, the same as contained in the *Herald*, repeating it several times; and we have not been complained of for doing so.

But that is not all. George Francis Train, like a true knight-errant as he is, flew to our side as a champion, when we were in prison, and, treating the matter with his peculiar idiosyncrasy, he published and had circulated broadcast through the city and sent through the mails, several numbers of a newspaper sheet which he styled the *Train Ligue*.[9] In it, he repeated and paraded and rang the changes in every possible way, upon every one of the possible objectionable passages in our whole paper, being purposely, if we were obscene in a direct, simple statement of facts, ten times more audaciously obscene in reproducing us, flaunting his utterances in the very faces of those distinguished legal authorities who had arrested us, "stumping them," as the boys say, with every insulting circumstance of provocation to arrest him on the same charge.

But the heroes of the United States law had become wary in conducting the warfare. They saw that they had already, so to speak, "put their foot in it"; or, permit me still to be homely in my expressions, and "not to put too fine a point upon it," they "smelt a rat," after the District Attorney found that revered citizens could not be brought into court. *They couldn't afford to become utterly ridiculous*, and there was something in the atmosphere, that warned them that they were becoming, *just a little ridiculous, just a little odious*, and *just a little contemptible* already; *contemptible* for their ignorance of the law and of the literature they assumed to judge of; *contemptible* for their ignorance of the American principle of the freedom of the citizen and the press; *contemptible* for their unconscionable usurpation of authority, and contemptible, above all, for their ungallant and ungentlemanly discrimination against women, in their exercise of their judicial functions when there were so many men who could be charged as we were charged.

You now see why the District Attorney will not have me arrested again for repeating my offense against "revered citizens"—offense, forsooth!—for exercising my simple and unquestionable rights as an editor and an advocate of social reform. He can't arrest all the James Gordon Bennetts,[10] all the George Francis Trains and all the Victoria C. Woodhulls; and he can't, in the face and eyes of this exposure, arrest Tennie and me and throw us again into Ludlow-street Jail, for publishing precisely the same things which they publish, and which Train published, purposely exaggerated, to show that they dare not trouble him. He cannot arrest us unless he is ready to arrest us all, or along with us, all the other editors in the city.

The District Attorney can't afford to arrest everybody who says a naughty word, not even to carry out his assumed new office of protector of the reputation of "revered citizens." Pushed one step too far, his procedure in that direction incurs ridicule. "Come shortly off," not impartially carried out; not applied even to those who flaunt their offenses and try to get arrested, in order to bring out the absurdity, it will at a certain point provoke universal indignation. The United States District Attorney cannot afford either to have a ridiculous cognomen annexed to his name. That would swamp him in this community. "A hasty plate of soup" tacked, to the reputation of even a great man, and in good-natured jocosity, haunted and annoyed him to his grave. The District Attorney is not even a great man, and *his* nickname may have real meaning in it. I warn him not to defy the stab of a steel pen! Inventive genius sometimes displays itself in other ways than in devising new offenses against the law or new offices as public protectors of the reputation of revered citizens.

Another reason why the Government cannot, very well, proceed to trial, is this: Since our arrest, Attorney-General Williams,[11] of President Grant's Cabinet, has, at the instance and by request of Postmaster-General Creswell,[12] rendered an opinion having a direct bearing upon this case, as follows: "Post-office officials have no right to open or detain letters or other matter transmitted through the Post-office, though they may know they contain obscene matter. And Postmasters have no more authority to open letters, other than those addressed to themselves, than have other citizens of the United States."[13]

Coupled with this, we have the denial of the officials of the New York Post-office, as to their complicity in the outrage committed upon the mails. Mr. Knapp, the special agent of the Post-office Department, said he read the paper of November 2 from beginning to end, and he would not take any responsibility, such as the District Attorney desired him to take, to hold the entire mail on account of alleged obscenity.

Therefore, under the opinion of the Attorney-General, and the disclaimer of Mr. Knapp, the District Attorney stands in the position of having, with the cognizance of somebody, robbed the mail of the package of papers upon which the charge was based. Do you not see, then, that Mr. District Attorney Davis or Mr. Assistant District Attorney Davies cannot afford to move further in this matter?

The fellow Comstock is, I think, too conceitedly egotistic to realize the position into which his action has placed him. He is also, I think, just enough fool and knave combined, to believe he can himself "put up a job" and then make others responsible for it. He it was instead of ourselves who procured the placing in the Post-office of the package complained of, by buying the papers and having them addressed and sent to the Post-office on his own account, by a person having neither right or authority to act for my sister and me....

I tell you, Mr. District Attorney, very frankly, I have your head "in chancery,"[14] and I intend to punch it. I believe this is a correct use of the language of the ring, although I am not, literally, a pugilist; and I may make a mistake in the thing said, but not in the thing meant. That you may rest assured of, unless you mend your manners, and then I may have larger game to fly at and may forget my little appointment with you. In the meantime please don't have me arrested,—forgetting my sex—for this unfortunate allusion, to the prize ring, *on a charge of being a prize-fighter*; for I perceive, now I have said it, that this verbal expression holds precisely the same relation to an offense against the laws prohibiting pugilistic encounters, by professional bruisers, as what we published in our paper, holds to an offense against the laws prohibiting obscene literature....

Again: This affair with Mr. Train is, to me, utterly incomprehensible. I can very well understand why the youthful zeal of the Christian Young Men should stand horrified at the doctrines of the *Weekly*, especially when they are accompanied by personal illustrations of the mysteries of godliness; but that their reverential piety should pretend to be shocked because Mr. Train, in his zeal to expound the Bible to the understanding of those who are not as familiar with it as they should be, considering that they account themselves as good Christians, is, as I said, simply incomprehensible. Can it be possible that he is a better Biblical scholar than are the representatives of the Young Men's Christian Association, that he should have found a ph[r]ase of religion in their Holy Book of which they knew nothing? It seems that this must be so, since there is no other explanation for their conduct in arresting him for quoting the Bible on them, except that they are themselves actually ashamed to have the attention of the world called to the true character of the Book which they claim to be the infallible word of their God.

I speak with no feeling of disrespect for this venerable Book, or of Him whom they claim as its Author; but what must we think of a God who speaks language to his people that, when used by others than by those of their own household, even His Elect feel called upon to prosecute the intruder upon what is all their own, for obscenity? If Mr. Train is guilty of obscenity for printing extracts from the Bible, is not the American Bible Society equally guilty for printing the same in the Bible as a whole? Nor can they dodge the issue they themselves have evoked, by saying that the charge is not based upon the Bible quotations, since those quotations form, by far, the most objectionable part of the *Train Ligue*; and I am free to confess that, if any language can be called obscene, the extracts in question must be so considered; and it is clear that Mr. Train so considered them, since his nice sense of honor would not permit him to plead "not guilty" to the charge of obscenity....

I speak of myself as conducting a warfare on the present impacted mass of love and hate, of confidence and jealousy, of prudery and flippancy, of deceit and hypocrisy, marital infidelity, sexual debauchery, seduction, abortion and consequent general moral degradation, all mingled in frightful confusion, and labeled the social system. Then I think of this as being the foundation of morality, as it is called, I wonder if to the label it ought not to be added, "to be well shaken before taken." Unfortunately, however, it *is* a warfare, because the world will insist on making war on me and my ideas. For myself, I love *everybody*; *every human being*, and have no desire in my soul to fight or contest with anybody; I would far rather be engaged in teaching what I know, and in learning of others who are wiser than I am, what they know.

Least of all, have I any piques to gratify, or any personal hostilities to wage with any one....

In accordance with this determination, and for reasons which are more elaborately set forth in the article itself, we published in our issue of November 2d, the Beecher-Tilton Scandal. In that article I stated what I happened very well to know to be true, by means therein fully stated, that Henry Ward Beecher is, on conviction, a free-lover, as I am, and as many of the noblest and wisest of the representative men and women of the land, and of the world, really are, whether they have or have not the moral courage—by which I mean fidelity to their convictions—to avow it; and, to make good my assertions in respect to his theory—derived, probably, as many as fifteen or twenty years ago, from the writings and counsels of Fourier, Warren, Andrews and other great socialistic thinkers—I stated, with detail and circumstances, facts which were also in my knowledge, derived in a great part from Mr. Beecher himself, in a way which dispensed me from any obligation of confidence, to the effect that he had not hesitated to live his own life of social freedom in his own way, and I added, that these facts were well known to a considerable circle of Mr. Beecher's church and congregation, and that I had been taken into this circle socially and intimately, because they learned that I had become possessed of these facts (in the first instance through Paulina Davis and Elizabeth Cady Stanton, and subsequently through Mr. Tilton himself, and others), and because they feared that I would publish them, and because by communicating them unreservedly, they hoped to divert me from my purpose to use them in behalf of the interests of social emancipation, and the great principle of human freedom....

Free love means nothing more and nothing less, in kind, than free worship, freedom of the press, freedom of conscience, free trade, free thought, freedom of locomotion (without a passport system), free schools, free government, and the hundred other precious, special systems of social freedom, which the great heroes of thought have fought for, and partially secured for the world, during this last period of the world's growth and expansion. It is all one and the same thing, it is just freedom and nothing else. It is simply impossible that any great thinker like Mr. Beecher, if the subject is once fairly brought before his mind, can see the matter in any other light; and, if he is on the side of freedom at all, if he believes in the American principle, in the Declaration of Independence, in anything distinctly American, that he should come to any other conclusion, than that the compulsory regulation of our love affairs by statute law, is a remnant, as slavery was, of an old and opposite order of things, is simply ridiculous.

Mr. Beecher believes in free worship, that is to say, in the freedom of every individual to worship God as he sees fit, or not to worship him at all; he believes also in freedom of conscience, and also, doubtless, that every act of his life should be made a matter of conscience; how then can he or could he be anything else than a free lover? How can I regulate my life by my conscience, in the most secret and sacred things, if it has already been regulated for me by the hurried and ignorant legislation of a set of crude and corrupt legislators at Albany? It is the question whether our virtue, if we have any, shall be something vital and self regulating, or whether it shall be something dead, formal and legal, merely.

But what, in the next place, is freedom? Folks talk and think—I fear, my dear hearers, that you yourselves still think—that freedom means merely the license to do something bad. Is there, then, no need of freedom equally to do good things and right things? How easily you understand all this subject if we take it into any other sphere than just this one of love. We Americans believe in the freedom of worship, which is eminently an American doctrine. It is already secured, for at least this country. Does it follow that all Americans rush at once into devil worship? Do they as a matter of fact, erect altars and churches to the devil? Is it true, even, of the majority, that they do so? You know it is not; and yet anybody is perfectly free here—anywhere from the broad Atlantic to the broader Pacific—to erect altars and churches to the devil; and if they did so, you and I, Mr. Beecher, and the utmost conservative and orthodox divines, all over the land, would stand staunchly up together, as one man, in defense of their perfect (civic) right to do so; for if anybody can say, arbitrarily, that anybody else, shall not worship the devil, that same somebody may next say, in the same arbitrary way, that nobody shall worship God.

If anybody have the right to prohibit the erection of a Chinese Joss temple[15] on our shores, he must have equally the right to prohibit baptism by immersion or by sprinkling, or the elevation of the host, or the saying of mass.

As the condition of our freedom, therefore, we as Americans, *insist on the freedom of others, on the right of others*, to do even that, and just that, which we, as individuals, *believe to be wrong*. Nay, more, I hope that the doctrine reaches far deeper; that it is not *because it is the condition of our own freedom*, that we assent to all this, but that it is that THAT *itself is our religion*; not merely or chiefly that, in certain times, it favors and secures us, which is still a selfish and insecure basis for freedom, but that we *penetrate to the divine essence of the idea*, and see and know that this ultra, radical idea of freedom *is the profoundest of moral truths and of sound solutions*; and hence that we are devotees for its maintenance and defense, because it is intrinsically true, and whether it works well or ill for our individual predictions at the time.

I know that this is a fearful and tremendous doctrine. I know that it is the most searching and testing of all doctrines, of the fidelity and honesty of our own love of truth. I doubt if one in a million of this great American people, who have nevertheless founded their institutions on the idea, have yet penetrated to the full significance of the idea. I doubt whether you, any of you, fully realize the profundity of the moral convictions, on which this Government was founded. And yet in this matter of worship, we have substantially realized the ideal. A hundred churches lift their spires to heaven, side by side, in the same city, dedicated to as many different orders of worship and creed, and all the congregations, peacefully and with mutual respect, pursue, from Sabbath to Sabbath, their various attractions and convictions; and all this, simply because we have wisely concluded (after thousands of years or bloodshed and strife over the subject) to say "hands off"; and to remit the whole subject to the conscience, to the judgment, to the good taste (or the bad taste), in a word, to the individuality of the individual—which is freedom.

Now let us return to the matter of love. The real thinkers believe, that this same principle will work the same harmonious and beautiful results, in this sphere also, and will completely and divinely regulate in the end, and, coupled with all other good influences, all our social disharmonies. They believe that our social disharmonies, those, I mean, of the family, are prolonged and aggravated, by the futile attempts of legislation to regulate them, just as the religious strifes of the past were fomented by a similar outside interference; and that, left entirely to themselves, they will regulate themselves....

But now see, again, how you, and the people at large, misunderstand us on this subject. I have said sometimes and often, that I live my own free life in accordance with my doctrine; and I said in my Steinway Hall speech, something to the effect, that I have the right to change my love every day or every night if I choose to do so; and the public press, and the public itself, cry out in chorus, Mrs. Woodhull confesses that she lives an utterly abandoned life; she lives and sleeps with two or three or five hundred or some other egregious number of men.

Now all this is very absurd, and the public will come, at some early day, to be very much ashamed of it. Let us return to the matter of worship; and suppose I had been engaged in fighting the battle for that freedom; and suppose I said, I go to church or not, as I please, and I have a right to go to a different church, and worship God in a different way, every Sunday of my life, and suppose on the strength of this, the public said, Mrs. Woodhull confesses that she has no religious convictions whatever, and that she is an out-and-out infidel, or that one church is no better than another, and all are equally bad, etc. Why, the merest tyro in reasoning would see how utterly inconsequential were these conclusions, and would set down their holders as the stupidest of asses.

Now, probably there are not ten in this audience—in many an audience that I address there is not one—who know or have any right to assume to know, from anything I ever said, or from anything they know of my life, whether I live the life of a nun, or whether I live as the exclusive wife of one man, or whether I am what the cry indicates. Mrs. Hooker and several other of my anxious female friends, who have had the opportunity to know most about my life, have on various occasions, taken the pains to assure the public that I am one of the most exclusive and monogamic of matrons. For my own part I have been perfectly willing that the world should think just the other way, if that same public choose to humbug itself into whatsoever preposterous idea—both to accustom the world to accept the idea of freedom for others, who might want a broader social sphere than I do, and also to give the world just this lesson—that it is none of its business (except for very special occasions) what my private life is, as it is none of my business (except for very special occasions) what the private life of anybody else is.

Do you not now begin to understand, that whosoever believes in the better policy, for society, of leaving the love affairs of the community to regulate themselves, instead of trusting to legislation to regulate them, is a free lover; and that being a free lover no more determines that one is low or promiscuous in one's habits, than believing that people shall have the right to choose their own food, determines that the person who believes so, has the personal habit of living on rotten meat or bad eggs. . . .

Our old habits, under the marriage *regime*, now happily coming to an end, have made us all intolerably impertinent; until our social order is an impacted conspiracy of mutual spies and informers, so dense, so tyrannous, so awful, that if it were political, no civilized community would or could endure it; and such that the socially enfranchised communities of the future will look back upon it, with the same horror with which we regard the atrocious despotisms of Commodus or Caligula.[16] Mrs. Grundy[17] has a despotism, a million times more overwhelming and degrading, over the entire populations of England and New England, and generally, of all other countries, than ever any Nero or Tarquin[18] had over Rome. Like slavery, hers is a despotism, which reaches every homestead, and is all pervading, and utterly terrific, to all but the stoutest hearted heroes and heroines; and religion, which seldom establishes anything, but only consecrates what is, has consecrated this severe despotism. Better, a thousand times say, with nonchalance, like Cain, "Am I my brother's keeper?"[19] than to belong to this hellish conspiracy to keep our brothers and sisters, so hugged by the iron arms of false morality and custom, that the life and spontaneity is all pressed out of them. Anybody, with half an ear, who knew the meaning of logic, who has listened to Mr. Beecher's stirring sermons on individuality, interspersed along through the last twenty years, would have heard in them the whisperings of social emancipation.

If, therefore, Mr. Beecher, in being true to the new doctrine of freedom, has been infidel and false to the old, that is none of our business, except to rejoice, if it come incidentally to our knowledge; and if he has on any grounds been unwise, he is the one to learn the fact, and to improve in the use of freedom, by availing himself of the privileges which it alone confers, to improve. And if we had any business to know, yet, how could we know? Solomon says, "The heart of man knoweth its own bitterness." Are any of us competent to tell what domestic sufferings have been endured by the man and the woman in the two involved households; or by the men and the women in any households; and what consolations must come, or the heart must break! I know nothing of promiscuity by Mr. Beecher. I suppose variety is not necessarily promiscuity, any more upon the social keyboard, than it is upon the keyboard of the piano; and every soul must find for itself, the harmony of its own chords....

The public has stood aghast, with anxious expectation, for some denial from some quarter, of the truth of these allegations; but days passed into weeks and weeks rolled into months, and not a word of denial, nor even of explanation had been volunteered from any source; until the conviction has now gradually settled down upon the public mind, that there is no answer or explanation which can possibly be made. The whole case has been suffered to go by default. The admission has virtually been made; or, in any event, has been assumed by the people to have been made, that what I stated, and all that I stated was a simple narrative of the truth, which both pastor and congregation, have been compelled, in this tacit way, to admit....

They have said to him almost unanimously: Whether these allegations be true or not, we do not feel bound even to inquire; whether they be true or not, we believe in *you*, Henry Ward Beecher; we accept you as our teacher, and you as our instructor, in any new and higher truth; and if there be any truth, which you have felt bound to withhold from us, and yet, which you have not felt required to forego in your own life, we wait in confidence—we abide in faith, until the circumstances, and the growth in public opinion, shall enable us to come to a better understanding of that which you have already learned.

The scene has been, from the first, sublime. Mr. Beecher has gone forth, preaching, praying and pouring forth his great soul of inspiration, as if nothing had happened. His elders and deacons have gathered around him as a solid phalanx, saying: "Make no explanation—not even to us; we ask none; we will see that the church and congregation accept and maintain the same tacit league of acquiescence." And they have done so; and church, and congregation, and the public—to a large extent—have quietly subsided into the acceptance of his position, whatsoever it may be.

By this magnanimous system of tactics, which could not have been carried out at any former period of the world's history—which could not have been carried out, probably, in any other church and congregation in the world—which marks grandly and sublimely the exalted influence which the great preacher has rightly acquired, during all these years, over the minds of his people—what otherwise would have been a disastrous fall, has been broken, opinion has been modified, adverse judgment of the conduct itself, mollified, and the way prepared for the ulterior acceptance, by the whole world, of that which, but a few weeks before, it would have been deemed impossible to have projected, in any form, into the public thought, in such a way, as to secure acceptance....

Socialism, the belief that just as great changes are impending, and must be effected for the ultimate good of mankind, in the relation of the sexes—in the more widespread influence of love—in the elevation of love out of its lower forms of mere passional excitement, of its purification, without repression or destruction of any part, however, of the sentiment; the belief that the construction of our homes must be radically changed, to accommodate these new ideas; that industry must be organized around the great composite home or hive of people; that women must be cared for and sustained, not in domestic bondage, but in complete freedom, and all that stands connected and related with these beliefs—in a word, Socialism is no longer confined to the few agitators and radical thinkers—is no longer to be traced home to French infidelity or free-thinking, but is widely diffused, even in the most religious circles, and where the sentiments of piety most profoundly prevail.

John H. Noyes and the Oneida Community, with their system of complex marriage or practical Free Love, were the outbirth, not of French Socialism, but of New England Revivalism, and of the more vital interpretation of the spirit and letter of the New Testament. Prof. Upham, who has recently died, and who stood for fifty years at the head of New England theology, a vital pietist of the Madame Guion school,[20] was for many years a full convert, through his study of the Scripture, to the belief that unlimited freedom in the relations of the sexes would, in the Millennial order,[21] supersede our present marital restrictions. These doctrines were taught by him, in a subdued and partial sense, to the hundreds of young men who have gone forth from Bowdoin College to preach, and to pursue the various professions, during the past generation.

During the last twenty years Prof. Upham has steadily visited, from year to year, and communed with Noyes and Andrews and all the other leaders of the most advanced social doctrines. He has encouraged and upheld them by his great words, filled with religious auction and sound philosophy. He has believed that men and women were to be lifted to higher and still higher excellencies, through the deepest and most varied experiences of the heart, and that the doctrine of Love divine, as promulgated by Christ, meant nothing less, and nothing else, than the ultimate introduction upon the earth of a complete social emancipation.

I have heard Mr. Andrews say that he has been closeted, at his own house, with no less than five or six of the leading Doctors of Divinity of the country, during a single year, in the closest and most confidential consultation in respect to these great subjects; and I might occupy the remaining portion of my hour in detailing to you the simple evidences of what I can now only reaffirm as the fact: and which is, that the whole public sentiment of the great Republic is permeated and honey-combed with the belief in, and expectation of, an early and complete overturn of the existing social order, and the introduction of a higher type of morality and social truth....

But let us consider for a moment, what it is which constitutes obscenity or indecency or indelicacy. Where is the line to be drawn between what it is proper to discuss, or speak of, or put in type, and what ought to be, or may rightly be suppressed by the law? And in reply, I would say, that nothing said with an earnest purpose and for a good end, is or can be obscene. If any other standard than this be erected the very first book to be condemned and burned for obscenity is the Bible itself. The next books will be the law books. Not a book on medical jurisprudence can be permitted to be printed or sent through the mails. The next will be the medical books. I have in my library an anatomical atlas and other works of the kind which must be instantly repressed.

I am having, at this time, an exhaustive collection made of all the passages in the Bible which may be considered, by this mode of interpretation, obscenity; and I am having, through counsel, a similar collection made, of the prints, discussions and expositions to be found in the legal and medical books. I am having a similar research made throughout the literature of the world; although, in this respect, I have been nearly saved from the necessity of labor, by a remarkable work which has already performed this service.

Near the end of the war, Mr. Secretary Harlan, of the Department of the Interior at Washington, moved by spasm of piety, removed the distinguished poet and philanthropist, Walt Whitman, from an office which he held in his department, on the ground of the obscenity of his poems. Having no appreciation of the legitimate license of genius to deal with the most delicate subjects, and reading the sublimest passages of inspiration, with the bleared ignorance of uncultured stupidity, he thought it belonged to him, as the Young Men's Christian Association, through its pious agent, think it belongs to them to oversee the morals of the community, and he removed Whitman from office. Unaware of the fact that Rabelais, Montaigne, Hudibras, Sterne, Burns, Byron and Shakespeare himself, and fully a thousand other great poets and philosophers, fill the libraries of the most refined people in all countries, and that their works abound in pictures and allusions which, in the mouths of vulgar people, would be vulgar and obscene, the pious Secretary made his ridiculous raid upon the most representative and characteristic of American poets.

Immediately, however, a storm of indignation arose. The Secretary of another department conferred on Whitman a higher office, and Whitman's literary friend, William O'Connor, wrote in defense, a pamphlet, called "The Good Gray Poet," which is the most exhaustive display of the freedom which has been accorded to genius, in this direction, which is to be found anywhere in literature. The work itself is a credit to the literary craft.*

My counsel have taken this whole subject in hand; and, in case the Government of the United States ever dare, which I have assured you they will not, to press the case against me and my sister for trial, the court house, the public press and the country will be flooded with such oceans of reading matter of an unusual character from all these sources, from the Bible down to the last novelette, that those who have moved in this business will, it is hoped, be fully satiated with the results.

Such are some of the great words of the great poets found in defense of the free scope and untrammeled career of genius in literature. I recur, now, for one moment, in conclusion, to the direct and far more weighty purpose of this discourse. I stand here to make my defense of the spirit of this age; of that drift toward social freedom, which is now bursting all bounds, and insisting upon the complete enfranchisement of the human affections.

The head and the hand are already free. Free-thinking and free-acting within the just limits which inhibit encroachment, are now grandly tolerated in the world, except in that one department of human affairs, which includes the sentiment of love. In that local centre of our lives we are still slaves. The land mourns with the bitterness of its bondage. The reverend clergymen who have labored earnestly and honestly to fasten still on the community their traditional ideas of morality, never permitting themselves even to ask if there is anything wrong in their methods; or if there is, perchance, some better way, have felt the reaction of the vital forces within their own persons and within the community and the age in which they live, as severely as any other class. The old fear of hell-fire has lost its repressive terrors, even over their consciences and lives. Somebody, it is said, has gathered the names of no less than seven hundred preachers of all sects and denominations, who have been driven from their pulpits within the four years, and in this country alone; their congregations and the public scandalized, and themselves and their families disgraced and socially ruined by their sexual offences against the effete and false systems of their own moral teachings.

All the other classes of society suffer no less terribly. There is a skeleton in every house. There is hardly a family of ten persons in the land which does not contain in its numbers, some one or more poor, wretched, heart-broken or tortured victim of our ill-advised laws and perverted notions of purity and prosperity; and sometimes every adult person in the entire household is such a victim of repression or compression, or else of starvation, or else, still, of gorging and satiety of their sexual nature.

Every third person of the audience I am now addressing is a conscious, and to some extent a rebellious slave under this tyrannical social system, begotten of other ideas than those that now prevail, and which was, perhaps, well enough adapted to other times, but which now has become a galling tyranny over their domestic lives; and *they* know that what I say is true. Most of the remainder of my audience, and they are simply representatives of the country at large, if not so consciously, are still unconsciously dragging out a miserable social existence of domestic wretchedness, a common lot of the homes of the people, derived from the same bad brood of pernicious causes.

Repulsions, discontent, and mutual torment, haunt the household everywhere. Brothels and social hells crowd the streets and avenues; passional starvation, enforced by law and a factitious public opinion on the one hand, and sickly and weary wives, and even husbands, on the other hand, overwrought, disgusted, and literally murdered, in their utter incompetency, to meet the legitimate demands of healthy natures, coupled with them; ten thousand forms of domestic damnation cropping and bursting out in ten thousand ways, through all the avenues of life; and everybody crying, "Peace! peace! when there is no peace"; and the few who dare to speak of these evils and to call for a remedy, hounded to the death by the same old persecuting spirit, which, from the earliest ages, has met and martyred every new and struggling reformatory idea.

But there is, nevertheless, a brighter side to the picture. The dawn of the better day is already shining over the hill-tops of the gorgeous orient. Sexual freedom, the last to be claimed for man, in the long struggle for universal emancipation—the least understood and the most feared of all the freedoms, but destined to be the most beneficent of any—will burst upon the world, through a short and sharp encounter with the forces of evil. We who are assembled in this very hall to-night, will, many of us, meet in a few months or years, to celebrate the glorious incoming of the age of a rounded-out and completed Human Freedom. The passions, instead of being regarded as we have been taught to regard them, as merely satanic or malign forces to be repressed or enslaved, will be recognized for what they are; as the *voice of God*, in the soul; as the promptings of our best nature; as the holy premonitions of a divine harmony in society, so soon as they shall be understood and adjusted under the beneficent influences of freedom.

Rising up out of our false notions of propriety and purity; coming to know that everything is proper which enhances happiness and injures no one; and that everything, *whatsoever*, is pure that is healthful and natural, we shall greet each other on that joyous occasion with smiles of a benign joy, while looking back with a touch of sadness through the past hours of the long night of social bondage; and shall prepare, from that day, for the perfect and pure blessedness of the coming millennium of the absolute liberty of the Human Heart.

*Here followed copious quotations from the Book referred to.

# Chapter Sixteen

## *Dear Lucretia Mott*

*In the split between Elizabeth Cady Stanton and Susan B. Anthony's National Woman Suffrage Association and the American Woman Suffrage Association in 1869, Lucretia Mott sided with the former, prioritizing women's suffrage as the most important goal for the movement. Like Stanton and Anthony, Mott came to feel somewhat wary of Victoria Woodhull. The original letter is located in the Garrison Family Papers, Sophia Smith Collection, Smith College, Northampton, Massachusetts.*

48 Broad St N.Y.

Feby. 27 1873

Dear Lucretia Mott

You know very well that I seldom seek personally, the favor or disfavor of any person; and that I care little for any one[']s good opinion, any further than it may ~~further~~ advance the interests of the cause I have espoused; and that I have learned patiently to bear the ill-favor of most persons, by long and continuous experiences.

You won my heart under peculiarly impressive circumstances; which have ever caused a sort of reverence to fill my soul for you. I felt that of all women who seemed to understand me somewhat, you understood me best; and I never believed you could misunderstand me.

But I have heard from several, what makes my heart sad; for I fear you would not stand on the rostrum by me as you did at Apollo Hall two years ago. I do not believe I either hold or advocate ideas, which, if understood by you as I understand them, can cause you to withdraw from me the love and confidence I have treasured so long and so well; and I beg you to offer me the opportunity to correct, as I think I can, any points, which if uncorrected, may cause you to shrink from me[.]

But in either case, I hope you may not lose sight of the issue, in the individual. The issue now is *not* Victoria Woodhull, *but* Free Speech *and* free press, to the rescue of which from their present threatened position, everyone ought to hasten. The Abolitionists used to say "It is none of our business what the Negro does with his freedom." Is it any more our business now, what people do with their freedom?

Your affectionate would-be-daughter,
Victoria

# Chapter Seventeen

## *Reformation or Revolution, Which?*
or, Behind the Political Scenes

*This speech was given on October 17, 1873, at the Cooper Institute in New York City. The title page notes that it was given "to an audience of 4,000 people, filling to its utmost capacity the Hall, to which thousands found it impossible to gain admission." Amanda Frisken reports that Democratic newspapers in the Midwest were particularly approving of the speech, which criticized Grant's administration (Frisken,* Victoria Woodhull's Sexual Revolution, *129).* Woodhull and Claflin's Weekly *includes rave reviews in its December 13 issue. A reporter from the* St. Joseph (MO) Herald *wrote, "We have it from reliable gentlemen who have heard her elsewhere that she is the best lecturer now before the public" (quoted in Woodhull and Claflin,* The Human Body the Temple of God, *365).*

It may appear presumptuous, perhaps ridiculous, for a woman to talk to an audience composed largely of men, about politics and government. Men have had the management of these questions so long, it ought at least to be presumed that what they do not know is not worth talking about. I have listened attentively to speeches from many different men—Statesmen, Legislators, Congressmen—but I failed to find in the institutions which they represented, anything that is an excuse, even, for the grandiloquent laudations that they usually indulged in. On the contrary, I find so much of which to complain, in which not only my own interests, but those of every working man and woman in the country are involved, that I cannot hold my peace and see the impending desolation—which now threatens to bring a period of woe to us all—approach unopposed. . . .

So general and oppressive has this condition become, and its injustice so evident, that on every hand the murmurings of discontent among the masses are breaking out into rebellion, in which the hope for reformation is replaced by the desire for revolution. All up and down this broad country secret meetings are held, in which the most extreme remedies are freely discussed; and yet those to whom the people have intrusted the public interests sleep on peacefully, and dream of the next job, seemingly ignorant that the day of judgment is at hand; while still another class are watching the opportunity, tiger-like, to spring upon the throat of liberty as it struggles in the strife, and strangle it in its despotic grasp, so that they may plant themselves upon its ruins. When we thus pass behind the political scenes and observe what is there going on, the heart that beats with the love of justice and freedom; which cares for its country's welfare; which has a single sentiment of the brotherhood of man born in the soul, may well cry out: Can there be Reformation, or must it be Revolution, before justice shall be done?

But what were the ends to be secured by the establishment of this government, different from those that had resulted from other governments, and wherein has it failed, and of what can it be impeached? Let us go back to the beginning, and by the words of its constructors learn what their intentions were. We can then decide by comparing them with what the results have been, whether their ideas are realized, or whether there is a failure. . . .

Furthermore, a constitution for a republic should contain no provisions that could possibly cause the popular will to be defeated. Constitutions and governments for republics should be framed; first, to protect the inalienable rights of each member of the community, and should declare these rights in language so clear that they could not be mistaken; and second, to administer the popular will, as expressed by the people themselves in their approval of all measures before they take effect. The Declaration of Independence and the text of the

Constitution were written evidently with these two ideas prominent, and the reason it was feared by some that the Constitution, as adopted, would prove a failure, was because it was not framed in consonance with these ideas. This Declaration and text were the rule by which the structure should have been erected, and had it so been erected, there would have been no need for, or danger of, revolution to-day; whereas we are standing upon its verge, without the remotest hope that it may be averted, and perhaps when the situation is inspected, it may not appear altogether as if it ought to be averted. There are times in the affairs of nations when revolutions are not only necessary, but obligatory upon a people, and it is an open question if such a time is not now impending over this country. One of two things will surely be: There must be reformation behind the political scenes, or there will be revolution outside of them.

Is it asked of what the people complain that, ignored, should call them to take back the power which the government has smuggled? If so, the reply will come back: Of almost everything that exists to-day as the result of government. There is neither freedom, equality or justice in the land, as I will shortly show. The attempt, by the British Government, to enforce a stamp act, such as the people have endured here, almost without murmur, for the last ten years, was one of the chief causes of disaffection of the colonies; while the further attempt to introduce and tax tea, was sufficiently obnoxious to rouse the people to declare that "The time of destruction, or manly opposition, has now come."[1]

And now mark the result. The action of about fifty men in destroying a cargo of tea, brought on the revolutionary war. If fifty men, out of three millions of inhabitants at that time, with the limited dissatisfaction that existed against the crown, could bring about a revolution, how many men and women out of forty millions inhabitants are required, with the wide-spread dissatisfaction now existing, to bring about revolution?

Do not misunderstand me. I am not advocating revolution; I am demanding what belongs of right to the people. I am asking for reformation; but if it be denied, I fall back upon the right of revolution, which no freeman will deny, and I will use every effort I have at my command to produce it.

The people all over the country are saying: Give us back our rights, or we will take them; and the stupid legislators and blundering officials, with their consciences and perceptions alike blunted by the array of spoils upon which their eyes are fixed, to the exclusion of everything else, don't seem to know that anything is the matter; they act as if everything was calm and quiet. And so it is, but it is the calmness that precedes the earthquake; and I forewarn them that they are sleeping over what is liable to burst forth any day, and cost them their heads for their stupid blundering.

This may be called seditious; but would you have me, knowing this, permit it to come upon them unawares? I speak for the people, the great, honest, industrial masses, who, being obliged to toil every day to obtain barely their needed sustenance, have no time to look after the persons to whom they have entrusted their interests, and who, knowing they are being robbed day after day, year after year, cannot leave their labor to counsel together as to the means of relief. Want stands at their home-door, grinning a ghastly grin at their families, and warning them to waste no time; they know there is something wrong somewhere, but they have not the opportunity to find it out.

I repeat, I speak for this class, and as against that class which devotes its time and talent to devising means to secure the results which the other class produce. As between these two I demand justice; and by the God of Justice it shall be rendered, peaceably if it can, forcibly if it must. Hunger, with its long, bony fingers, pinched cheeks and fiery eye, shall not much longer hold horrid revel in hut or hovel, in a land that trembles under the weight of its own productions, and is studded from end to end with palatial homes in which luxury abides. Not much longer shall thousands of men, women and children eke out a miserable life upon what a "sport" would disdain to feed his dogs, while the favored few wallow in superfluities.

GENERAL CHARGES

But I was about to speak of the causes for dissatisfaction that are driving this country into revolution, and had said that almost everything which exists as a result of government belongs among them. Two years ago, when I was importuning Congress to do political justice to woman, which was denied, I found that the wiser portion of Congressmen feared the country was drifting into revolution. Not less than three, whom I consider the wisest of the whole lot, confessed, when pressed to answer, that they did not believe another administration would pass without tremendous political changes; and the pulse-beats of the country indicate that they are near at hand. The immediate causes will be, as I shall shortly show, the efforts of those who have monopolized the power, the wealth and the money, to hold them, as against the growing demand for a settlement on the part of the people who have produced them.

Will they who scout the idea of revolution remember that until Fort Sumter was fired upon, there were scarcely a hundred people in the country who believed war possible; and that they were accounted as insane? But it came in spite of the wise ones, and it scourged the country as it was never scourged before. The single question of losing its negroes inspired the South to fight. Shall we repeat the blunder of that time by assuming that the people who hold the political power and the wealth of the country will not fight when they see that they are going to be taken from them?

Do not deceive yourselves. Negro slavery was not so great a cause of dissatisfaction then, as are the more subtle slaveries of to-day, now. Nor were the slave oligarchs any more alarmed about their slaves then, than are the political, financial and industrial oligarchs for their possessions, now. The public sentiment, however, had outgrown the institution of slavery, and sealed its doom. So also is the public sentiment outgrowing the despotic rule of the aristocrats of to-day, and it will seal their fate. But the latter, no less than was the former, are a part of our system of government, and as slavery proved a failure, and as such was abolished, so also are the others to follow in the same way.

The developments of the past two years—the corruptions, frauds and failures—are a sweeping condemnation of the system under which they have flourished. From Tammany down to the latest Brooklyn *expose*, first and last, one and all—they speak in unmistakable tones of the approaching culmination of the system. They prove beyond cavil that the government has degenerated into a mere machine, used by the unscrupulous to systematically plunder the people. Look where we may, confirmation stares us in the face. From the head at Washington down to the pettiest public office, it is the same story—fraud, corruption, peculation everywhere.

What else is to be expected? If Congress—in league with, probably, the Cabinet, if not the President himself—can be induced to push a Pacific Railroad scheme to obtain stock in a Credit Mobilier,[2] and, being exposed, can whitewash itself by such a farce as was enacted in Congress last winter, why, indeed, should not every official in the country go into the same business, and hope to escape in like manner? Examples like that, set in high places, will be copied in lower grades; and these again are legitimate fruit of our system of government.

Even the highest officials no longer hesitate to openly ally themselves with professional speculators, and this brings the exclamation: Can it be possible that the people's money, paid by them into the public treasury, is being used as a basis for speculation, that officials, even the President himself, should rush frantically to the rescue of the jeopardized market? Can it be true, as hinted by those who ought to know, that the large banking firms, recently suspended, were operating on government funds; and, as has been stated of a case in Washington, that drafts upon the Treasury for large amounts were made recently to bolster up their trembling ventures?

Nothing is more probable. It is a well-known fact that, on the eve of the Pennsylvania election last year, the Secretary of the Treasury went into Wall street, and manipulated the market through his pet bankers.[3] Who that knows anything about that little scheme doubts that the profits were largely used to make that election certain?

When officials near the head of the government are known to speculate *a la* Credit Mobilier; when jobbing schemes are continually bought through Congress, to say nothing about the needed approval at the White House; when men of highest respectability in the community, and very religious withal—Head-Lights in the Young Men's Christian Assassination Association—warm friends of the administration—by a method that is winked at as a mistake only, accidentally defraud the revenue of a few millions; when bank officials remove from the country and safely carry the people's deposits with them; when a Tammany Ring[4] converts millions of the public money to its own use, for charitable purposes (?), and it is accounted of little significance; when hypocrisy sits enthroned in the most popular churches, and the Christians, in a holy unity that was never known until now, seek to establish a Sectarian God, Christ and Bible in the organic law of the country, and are going to succeed; in a word, when everything that is false, corrupt and damnable runs riot at the expense of the hard-working, industrial masses, and is considered too respectable to be inquired into by anybody who comes out of a Nazareth; when all these things are, is it not time that a change come? is it not time for this Babel (which we call government, and which is growing so high as to put its occupants beyond reach of the people), to topple over and be buried in its own ruins?

I do not war upon the people as individuals who are involved in these things. To put others in their place would be a change of persons merely. It is the system that is at fault. If it were not for its glaring defects, individuals, however badly disposed, could not take advantage of the people, who elevate them to positions of honor and trust. I repeat, again, therefore, that our system of government, after a century's trial, has been proved a failure. It has ultimated in corruption and peculation in all its departments, and is rotten and ready to fall; and it ought to fall, and it will fall.

It is in vain to hope that the tide now rushing on a headlong course can be turned into safer channels. Things are going from bad to worse too fast, and with too great momentum. No mere revulsion can purify them. A system in which disease generates and spreads to involve its every part, coursing with fevered rapidity in all its veins, is as impossible of medication as rottenness itself. These things to which we have referred are the symptoms of the disease, which, itself, lies back in the vital parts of the system out of which they are evolved....

### ERRORS OF OMISSION

I have thus far discussed chiefly those evils which oppress the people by the commission of errors by the government. There is still another class of crimes, almost equally reprehensible, which may be named *Errors of Omission*. These have special reference to the dependent and unfortunate classes—the women, the children, the criminals, the maimed and the insane, which together make up a sum total of human misery almost too horrible to contemplate, and which fix a stigma of reproach, an indelible blotch of infamy, upon this pretendedly enlightened people which would merit the contempt of the most barbarous nation on the globe. This, at the first glance, may seem to be too severe an indictment of our civilization; but I say it is just, since such things as obtain here would put the savages to shame.

The people have fought for freedom, and become drunk upon the name. They have forgotten that this blessed boon cannot exist unless equality and justice also obtain. They have imprinted the former, omitting the last two, upon their banners, and have first gone mad with enthusiasm, and, secondly, have sunk into a comatose condition, in which they occasionally, when stung into temporary consciousness by some passing event, yelp out Freedom with all their might, without the least idea as to what is really going on about them in the world.

I say the dependent and unfortunate classes, and name women as among them, and they belong to both of them. And when I say they so belong, I mean that the beautiful social system that has been enforced virtually commits every woman to one or the other of these classes. I do not say that there are not any women who rise superior to the condition imposed upon them by the system. No thanks to the system, however, that they do it; but in spite of it. I say that the present social system, enforced both by law and a falsely educated public opinion, makes every woman dependent for support and comfort upon some man, and it does not give the least consideration as to whether she obtains it or not. It says to her: Here is the theory, live by it if you can; die by it if you must and the devil take the unfortunate. We, the government, we the men to whom belong all the realities of this world, can't do anything more for you except you become a social outcast, as they gracefully call unfortunate women, when we will perhaps patronize you as our demands require. I repeat again, and I wish my voice could reach the ear and the soul of every man and woman in the world, that the theory of our social system is, that women are dependent upon men, and that to secure support they must marry and merge their identity and individuality in some man, and then it leaves her unmindful and indifferent as to whether she secure it or not.

If she do not do this, however, and, following the male theory, attempts to support herself and to answer the demands of her maternal nature, she is compelled to suffer social death. Hence, I say, woman belongs to the unfortunate as well as to the dependent class. These are facts, and though you may ignore you can't dodge them however unpalatable they may be. Take them home and think about them, and see if you can come to any just and truthful conclusion except that woman is man's industrial and social slave; dependent upon her ministrations to his demands to obtain a support. Think of it, I repeat, calmly and deliberately, and then condemn those who are demanding social reform, if you can.

So long as men maintain this social theory, and so long as women are its willing slaves, I say change the law so that they shall be protected in it; so that women shall not be made dependent upon individual men. Make it a duty of the State to see that the theory which it insists on enforcing is carried out to its logical results. Let it see that woman has a support and not compel her to surrender herself to a single person, and to forever after be compelled to rely upon him for life and its comforts, when in so many instances both are denied her.

I want to ask every woman who, under this theory, has secured all the necessities and the comforts of life, how many women would frequent the haunts of vice in the Green streets of the world, if they were placed on an equality with you; and before you come to a conclusion, remember, if you had been situated in the same circumstances that have driven them there, and they in those that have surrounded you, that it is more than probable you would have been where they are while they, perhaps, would have filled your places?

Therefore, society having constructed a social system that makes it impossible that there should not be unfortunately circumstanced women, and as it afterward condemns them to social ostracism and death because they are unfortunate, it is a self-contradiction and stultification and needs to be remodeled to make it consistent with itself. The fashionable women of the day say that outcasts prefer to remain in vice rather than do the menial work they can obtain; but let them ask themselves if they were driven to the acceptance of one or the other of these alternatives, whether they would not choose the comforts that are lavished upon the mistress, with indolence and ease, rather than the drudgery to which the kitchen scrub is subjected?

A beautiful thing, this social system of yours! People sit in judgment over their brothers and sisters, when, if they were to exchange places, they would do the same thing which is condemned. Yea, verily, a beautiful, a just, a righteous system, worthy a so-called Christian civilization, but which would not be tolerated among the heathen. Let the government, let the male lords and rulers provide that women shall not be dependent upon men as individuals. So long as she conforms to the instituted theory and is therefore dependent, make her the ward of the State, of man collectively.

The same principle involved here applies with equal force to children. Under this social system children are born and made dependent upon the individual—the father—for support and proper training, without any provision whatever for a failure. If the father do not or cannot provide for them, what does the State care, except to commit them for vagrancy?

What does the City of New York, this Christian city, with its numerous churches dedicated to God and Christ, care for the thousands of children who live from its slop barrels, or the thousands more who die from partial starvation and neglect! Does your beautiful social system have any place or care whatever for them? No! none at all. The very classes which need its care and protection are utterly ignored in its provisions. Out upon such Christianity as this. It is unworthy of a barbarous age, to say worthy of this professedly Christian time.

I arraign this thing that goes by the name of Christianity, as a fraud; and its so-called teachers as imposters. They profess to be the followers of Jesus of Nazareth, while they neither teach, preach or practice the fundamental principles which He taught and practiced....

Jesus frequented the abodes of the lowly and despised of earth.

He ate with publicans, sinners and harlots; and of these last He said to the Scribes of His time, as He would to the Scribes of our times, They will enter the kingdom of heaven before you. If Jesus, with His rough-clad disciples, should make His appearance, some Sunday, near a Fifth-avenue church, and should offer to heal the sick by the laying on of hands, and to tell fortunes, as He did, these impostors would have him arrested as a blasphemer; or if he were to pass through the country and break into a field of corn and gather it for Himself and disciples, He would be charged as a thief and sent to Sing Sing; or again if Paul were to stand up in any of the churches, and discuss the social question as he did to the Corinthians, the YMCA would have him in Ludlow for obscenity; and would take care to fix his bail at so large a sum they would feel sure that none of his crowd could get him out;—and this is your boasted Christianity. How many years longer shall such a disgrace to an enlightened people rear its head in this land? I give it until 1900 to die, twenty years for every spire that now points skyward, to be leveled with the ground or changed to other uses. Remember, I say till 1900.

There are thousands of fathers in New York out of employment and out of money, with wives and from three to ten children suffering for bread. How are they to get on through the winter? Does your boasted system ask or care? No! But if they should steal a loaf of bread to keep the children from starving, or a basket of coal to keep them from freezing, it makes ample provision that they shall be sent to Sing Sing. Isn't this true? Then never again extol your social system, until you have swept it of its brutalities; nor of your beautiful government and of your Christian institutions, until those who need their protection are given consideration. I'll none of them until some of the principles and teachings of Christ are reduced to practice.

The Bible says, "Go to now ye rich men, weep and howl for the miseries that shall come upon you. Behold the hire of the laborers who have reaped down your fields, which is kept back by fraud, crieth, and the cries of them which have reaped, have entered the ears of the Lord."[5] Do the professed Christians, with their long purses and longer faces, believe this? Did the recent Evangelical Alliance have anything to say about it? No! Yet it is in the Bible, by which they profess to govern their lives! The judgment day, however, is at hand. The cries of them that have reaped down the fields of the rich; that have builded their houses; that have produced their wealth, crieth, and the cries of them have reached the ears of the Lord of Justice, and woe to the rich men. Let them weep and howl for the miseries that shall come upon them if they hearken not to the cries, while yet there is time of their own accord to do justice to the classes who have made them what they are.

So long as the government maintains a theory that compels every man to depend upon his individual exertions for a living for himself, wife and children, it should also guarantee him continuous labor at equitable wages. I said there are thousands whose families are suffering for food who cannot obtain work at any price. What shall they do? Beg, steal or starve? These are their only alternatives, and yet you will curse them if they do either.

Governmental employ for everybody who cannot obtain labor elsewhere; and governmental care for wives and children who need it must be introduced as a supplement to the present systems. Not to do this is barbarous. Already is our civilization blackened with the disgraceful accounts of the miseries that the omission to do this has caused, and if it be not done, and that at once. (I speak it in sorrow, but I know it too well), there will be riot in New York before spring.

Yes, there must be provisions for unprovided wives and uncared-for children by government, that will place them upon an equality with the best classes of society as to food, shelter and clothing, with physical and industrial, as well as intellectual education for the children; and employment must be given to every needy man and woman. Under such regulation only, is there the remotest possibility for a continuation of the present governmental and social systems. In no other way can Reformation prevent Revolution; and it ought not to be prevented by anything less.

Your criminal jurisprudence has also developed another infamous system. Your station-houses and jails are a sickening disgrace; while your prisons and penitentiaries are foul generators of misery and crime. A term in them will harden the best man or woman into confirmed degradation. In your eagerness to punish crime, you destroy the man or woman. You rush them, being merely charged with crime, into your pest-hells, where they lie pent up for months, without even an investigation, and then you hurry them through something called a trial, often without a defense, and if it possible to fix the act upon them with any degree of certainty, they are hurried to the place which seals their future career, and where they are treated worse than brutes, and as if they were not human. A "States Prison Bird" has little chance in your social system. He can practice only those things for a living which continually return him. And all this is done by your system and its executors, as I said in the case of unfortunate women, never stop to think if they had been placed in the same circumstances as under which the criminal committed his crime, that they would have undoubtedly done the same thing, or perhaps something worse.

You erect and maintain a system one of the legitimate fruits of which is crime, and then you punish the unfortunate individuals who enact the villain character of the drama prepared by you for them. Verily consistency is a jewel that is sadly wanting in all parts of this beautiful system which is palmed off upon the world as the one thing good and true and pure, but in which ignorance too frequently passes for innocence and experience is mistaken for crime.

You must, therefore, change your criminal discipline from the theory of punishment for crime, to that of reform for the man and woman. In the first place, according to your own theory of Christianity, you have no right to punish anybody. "Judge not lest ye be judged,"[6] is fundamental to the Christian theory, and how can you punish, unless you first judge? I repeat, then, that you have no right whatever to punish anybody for any crime; but you may protect yourselves from its recurrence. In doing this, however, you should use no means that of themselves will tend to make men and women worse than they are. Your Prisons must be transformed into vast Reformatory Workshops, where men and women can work and be paid equitable wages, having all the common comforts during their restraint.

Sometimes, however, when I see the utter indifference to the horrid barbarities that are practiced under these systems, I almost despair of reform. Indeed, I seem to feel to say to you that there will be no reformation except through bloody revolution. Wrongs have been heaped upon wrongs until they have reached heavenward and moved the avenging angel. Great wrongs have always been washed out by great rivers of blood, and I fear the time for this has not yet passed away from the earth.

Behind the political scenes the actors in the political drama are so busily engaged in their own personal schemes they have no time to listen to the cries that are reaching the ears of the God of Justice, and you, the people, are too much engrossed in your individual money getting, to give the necessary attention to secure any change. For the last three years, in one way and another, I have done everything that lay in my power—I have sacrificed fortune, reputation and friends—in the attempt to rouse the people to a sense of the impending danger. But they will not listen. For my efforts, however, they have branded me all over the world as the vilest of women and the most dangerous of individuals. They have robbed me of everything except my self-respect, which they could not take and with which only remaining I defied them as they made off with the rest; they have locked me up in jail when the officials who made out the order knew there was no law for it, and have pursued me without mercy on every hand.

And why? Simply because, as I told you, I have endeavored to rouse the people to a realization of the impending judgment, for long years of crime which the government has committed against the people. And they knew unless they could shut my mouth that I should succeed and they would be relieved by the people from further official duty. Yes, though I am only a little woman, the political oligarchs who are manipulating this country for a monarchy, fear me. And well they may, for I preach their doom. I sing the battle cry of freedom, equality and justice for the people, and they know that it will be caught up by them and that its re-echo from the pine forests of Maine, from the wheat fields of Minnesota, from the golden mountains of the Pacific slope, from the cotton and rice plantations of the South, will hurl from the places builded by the labors of the masses all who have been false to the trusts reposed in them.

REFORMATION OR REVOLUTION, WHICH?

Now to what does all this logically tend? Clearly, if it be correctly understood, to the redistribution among the people of the natural wealth of the world as well as the equal benefits and comforts resulting from its use, and the establishment for the present aristocracies of society, which are the chief aim of almost everybody's life, an aristocracy founded on personal worth, intellectual capacity and moral grandeur, which will become the new incentives or motives of life. *Now*, only man is compelled by the political, industrial and social systems that are enforced, to make wealth or money-getting his chief aim, while every woman's highest aim is to entrap the most successful man into marriage. *Then*, for these will be substituted in the case of both men and women, who will be equal in the wealth plane, the attainment of the highest positions in the community, not for the sake of their emoluments, for these will be equal in all grades, but for the sake of doing the most good to society, and of thus becoming its most honored and beloved members. Can any one think of any really valid objection to such a change? I think not! . . .

My mind has taken this turn in consequence of the wonderful change which I have myself experienced within the last few months in the temperature of the social atmosphere. Up to, and subsequent to the time of my imprisonment in this city, for the cause of freedom and free speech, bitterness and hostility towards me personally seemed literally to fill the air. The glacial breezes from the north pole could not be more frigid and unsympathetic than the public sentiment which surrounded me. But of late a wonderful revolution in this particular has taken place. I have of late been basking in the genial rays of public favor. In New Jersey, at the State Convention of Spiritualists, I was received after my release from prison, with an ovation. In Massachusetts, at the great camp meeting at Silver Lake and Harwich, I addressed audiences of from five to fifteen thousand people amidst acclamations of enthusiasm, and the Boston press reported fairly and without slang or abatement the substance of what I said. Now, I have just returned from the three-days' meeting of the National Convention of Spiritualists at Chicago, where, after three days of the most unrestricted discussion and with the whole issue centered on the question of indorsing or repudiating my social doctrines, I was, almost unanimously, elected for the third time President of that Association. And there also at Chicago I was treated with courtesy and high appreciation by almost the entire press. It is not alone Spiritualists, therefore, but the whole public which seems to have quietly and sincerely arrived at the determination that I and the principles which I advocate shall have fair play according to merit, and along with all other things.

It may at first seem arrogant that I should assume, that a change of treatment towards me personally and towards my ideas, indicates any great or wide-spread change in social opinion at large. But if you reflect that I stand representative for the most radical and the most opprobrious of doctrines, and that these very doctrines as I have promulgated them, have just aroused the old and seemingly dead lion of persecution into what, we may now hope, were the final agonies of a feeble death-struggle, it may not seem too much to claim that when I am tolerated *everything* is tolerated; and that the extension of courtesy, kindness and fair play to me, anew, and after all that has past, is a solemn reaffirmation of a true Americanism, and perhaps the tocsin[7] of freedom for all opinion actually achieved, and without the bloody catastrophy which my too anxious intuitions have foreseen. I am at least willing and desirous to entertain this hope, and no one will rejoice more than I to have my own prophecies thus happily disappointed. . . .

Perhaps I can look forward to the cessation at an early day of my duties as an agitator. I have a loving heart for all mankind, and I would far rather be understood and loved than to be misunderstood and hated. I would rather teach and lead into the higher philosophy and the higher life than to break up old foundations, horrifying and disturbing the minds of men. I am tired of fighting. I would rather be Hypatia than Semiramis or Boadicea.[8] I would rather know and make known the highest truth than conquer the whole earth.

Thus much at least I see. Politics and patriotism are falling into the position of relative inferiority as compared with statesmanship and publicism, and statesmanship and publicism are in turn yielding the palm to sociology, as that science which deals with every range of human affairs in their cosmical or planetary amplitude. Sociology must in time have its basis in universal science. Reformers must, therefore, I see, become scientific, when they pass from the destructive to the construction phase of their work.

I would rather help to form true institutions, and so call down the blessings of this age and of posterity on my head for positive and permanent achievements, than merely to combat old errors, or achieve negative triumphs, ever so many, or ever so brilliant. Sympathize with me my dear sisters, and my true brothers, in the effort to learn, in order that I may teach; and let us all be instant in season and out of season in the good work of the future.

Then, when we shall have accomplished this work, will begin the long-time sung and prophesied millennium, in which love instead of hate, equality in place of aristocracy, and justice where now is cruelty, shall reign with undisturbed and perpetual sway, and peace on earth and good will among men abound. Because I see this for humanity, in the near future, has made me willing and able to endure what its advocacy has cost me of personal discomfort and of public censure. Finally, in conclusion: May the God, Justice; the Christ, Love, and the Holy Ghost, Unity—the Trinity of Humanity—ascend the Universal Throne, while all nations, in acknowledging their supremacy, shall receive their blessings—their benedictions.

# Chapter Eighteen

## *The Spirit World*
A Highly Interesting Communication
from Mrs. Victoria C. Woodhull

> *This letter was published as an editorial in the* Pittsburgh Leader *in 1873. A copy is included in the Victoria Woodhull-Martin Papers, Special Collections Research Center, Morris Library, Southern Illinois University–Carbondale. Only the year is given as the date on this copy.*

During the last quarter of a century the doctrines of spiritualism have made the most wonderful progress. Never in the history of religious evolution was there anything to compare with it. Having, as it is generally conceded, made its advent in the tiny raps at Hydesville, N.Y., more commonly known as the Rochester Knockings, it has swept through all classes in society and over the whole civilized world. Some of the best men and women as well as those who occupy positions of influence, both in the social and scientific sphere, have yielded their allegiance to its evidences, and the Church, though strongly opposing it from its pulpits, has been impregnated through and through. Hundreds and thousands of those who have been "convinced" have never publicly avowed themselves, and have held aloof from the society of professed spiritualists, so that not less than one-third of the inhabitants of this country actually entertain its fundamental propositions, while a large part of the remainder hope that it may be true.

Therefore, no body will venture to deny the rapid and mighty conquests made by modern Spiritualism. In the face of facts it would be foolhardy to attempt to do so. Now if the facts be given their legitimate weight, can it be any better denied that it has been a mighty instrument for good. Had it not been for its influence over the public mind, who can tell how far it might not have by this time advanced into materialism. All the evidences of modern scientific thought turn unmistakably to such an end, and had it not found an opponent in spiritualism, it would have swept the masses who have now fallen upon the other side, irresistibly into its cold arms. Reason had had too much development to be confined to the narrow limits of a Church's creed; it could no longer be held in subjection by a faith that was in opposition to its deductions. In this situation it was waiting to fall into the scepticism of materialistic science, which was dawning upon the world in brilliancy, when modern spiritualism burst upon its logic and confounded its mathematical deductions, and caused it to halt, there were evidences of an unseen power which eluded its grasp as artfully as had the faith from which it fled; it could not lay hold of it and in the crucible of science, reduce it to understanding. If this were reality, why might not the greater unseen power to which faith had asked it to adhere, be also real? With one third of the people spiritually inclined, if not decided, who will attempt to argue that Spiritualism has not opposed the only possible barrier to the spread of infidelity? If this be conceded, then the church should find no fault with the new doctrine. It should rather welcome it as its Saviour, for such it really is. The church was powerless, is powerless, to touch the masses who have been carried away by the phenomena of the most modern development of religion, and unless it shall soon claim it as its own, it will begin to show its external evidences of the decay that are already all too evident within.

But spiritualism, like all other rapid developments, has not been wholly healthy, and is now paying the penalty for accepting, adopting and defending everything that has come in its name. In this way it has invited to its bosom a mass of frauds and conjurers whose pretensions, being now ruthlessly exposed, are stinging it to death. In their eagerness to attain to the proof of undeniable, spiritualists have laid themselves open to deception from within and to ridicule from without, and spiritualism is now floundering hopelessly in the slough between the two. Materialization, with which it thought to speedily convince the world, seems about to be the cause of its strangulation. The world could not be wholly caught with chaff. Everybody would not accept appearances as evidence, and those who were determined to test these appearances, have disclosed such barefaced frauds, that spiritualists, who have blindly accepted everything, are beginning to ask themselves, "Is it possible that we too have been deceived?" and there is danger that this great mass which have been so easily carried away will react to the other extreme, as such masses generally do when there is a cause. It therefore behooves those who are wise among this mass, to themselves shake it free from the impositions that are being practised, and not doggedly hold on to them until they are torn away by the opposition. The strongest evidence of confirmed faith in anything is to fearlessly invite investigation, and to ruthlessly slough off whatever fungi that investigation may develop, while the best evidence there can possibly be of weakness is the attempt to bolster up pretensions.

I am conscious that the time is upon us, when every one's work, especially the work of mediums, are being tried by fire of what sort they are, and in this consciousness I come to offer my evidence to the truth of spiritualism. Our lives and works (my sister's and my own), from childhood to the present, have been one chain of spiritual phenomena, nothing similar to which, either in substance or in meaning, having fallen to any other mediums. Our lives have been one purpose, directed by a single class or circle of spirits, to whom only of all spirit influences we have given allegiance. Turning neither to the right nor left, we have pursued their course amid whatever storms of oppression and disgrace it has evoked, and we now stand upon a height from which we can see in the distance the culmination of that work as it was pointed out to us before we had set out to do it. When I was scarcely more than four years of age, I was told that I should live to see and take part in the very scenes that are now transpiring, and that are about to transpire. An adult friend, a neighbour who was very fond of me, died suddenly.

A few hours thereafter her spirit came to me. I became unconscious and was taken by her to the Spirit World, and to several spirits whom I since knew to be Demosthenes, Bonaparte and Josephine.[1] They told me that I was to be in their charge, and that they were to constantly guide, guard, instruct and care for me, so that I should be, when grown, fitted to do their work on earth. I saw the spirits descending to earth and mortals ascending to the spirit world and mingling in a common unity. They said all that I saw would be realised during my life, and that to make it possible was one part of their work, in which I would bear a prominent part. The people seemed to be much engaged as people are. They were coming and going as if they were very busy, and the scenery of that world was a counterpart of this. Towards the close of the visit for such it really was, I was shown what I now know to have been a panoramic view of the future. The mountains and the valleys changed places with the seas, and the entire face of nature underwent a transformation. Cities sunk and the people fled before the appalling disaster in dismay. Then a wondrous calm settled over everything, and confusion, anarchy and destruction were replaced with a scene of beauty and of glory which is beyond the power of language to describe. The earth had been changed from what it is, into a more perfect paradise, and had become the common abode of the people of both spheres, who had been saved from destruction. When I returned to physical consciousness, I told mother as well as I could in my childish way all that had occurred to me. I had been among the angels. My body had been unconscious for two hours.

This visit to the spirit world left the more wonderful impression. From that time to this I have never doubted that I should live to see something occur in the world of which that panoramic view was the prototype; and this faith has grown stronger year by year as I have seen the events occur that must lead up to it, and my own connection with them, brought in ways which have been most marvellous. During my after-childhood, these spirits, especially Josephine, were with me constantly, assisting me in my studies and duties, and joining in my recreations. I often performed the most laborious task without fatigue, and mastered studies only by magic. Another more singular experience that when walking it seemed to me that my feet did not touch the ground; that while I saw my body going along, I was two or three feet above in the air. This phenomena has followed me all my life. From these evidences of spirit aid and influences, it can be seen now that we have been able to endure the persecutions that we have suffered and still remain alive, and how we have been also finally able to triumph over all of our persecutors, I should feel that all the blessings that make life worth having would be lost to me, were I now commanded to testify of my life, to attempt to arrogate to myself, what has been done through me by spirits. Whatever I am; whatever I have done, belongs to them, and I know that they are now preparing a surprise for the world that will soon come upon it and show just what their work has been, and to what it is to lead. But I may state that the spirits whom I have named, are themselves the agents of a still higher power and authority than their own, the same as we are for them.

I had known Josephine for many years as the spirit who had special charge over me; but I did not know Demosthenes till the following occurrence; nor Bonaparte till a still later time. I had been directed to go to New York, there to receive further instructions. I had journeyed as far as Pittsburgh, at which place I stopped and determined to go no further. Our public work had not then began, and circumstances had made me somewhat rebellious. During the night a familiar spirit appeared in my room and began to make letters on a table. They were of fire and lighted the room distinctly. When he had finished he turned away and said "Read." I read the word "Demosthenes." He then chided me for my rebellious spirit and reminded me of instances of my life and asked how I could doubt him with such evidences before me.

He said that my active work was about to begin and that it was for this that I was to go to New York; and that he had already provided a house for me, at such a number and on such a street, as well as the means with which to occupy it. All turned out as he said it would. On entering the house I walked involuntarily to a circular table upon which there were a number of books lying in confusion and taking hold of one without thinking, found I held in my hand "The Orations of Demosthenes." In that house occurred the more wonderful prophecies of my life; prophecies which when they shall all be realised, as some of them have already been, and as I believe they will all be, will be indeed the consummation of the panoramic view shown me upon my first visit to the spirit world.

# Chapter Nineteen

## *The Elixir of Life;*
or, Why Do We Die? An Oration

*This speech was given on September 18, 1873, at the tenth annual convention of the American Association of Spiritualists, which was held at Grow's Opera House in Chicago. It was published by Woodhull and Claflin in 1873.*

I appear before you to-night to speak of a subject which, more than any other, ought to command the attention of the enlightened world; but which, more than any other, receives the anathemas of its professed representatives—the so-called Christians—because, forsooth, to discuss it, is to attack, necessarily, one of the chiefest pillars of the Christian edifice. The subject involves the necessity of free speech, in plain terms. John Stuart Mill, whom all reformers have learned to love, said: "The diseases of society can, no more than corporeal maladies, be prevented or cured, without being spoken about in plain language."[1] I propose to speak about the diseases of society, and if I expect to present either a preventative or a cure, I must speak in terms so plain that none can mistake my meaning. You may affect to blush, and the papers may call me indecent and vulgar, and say I have no shame, to speak as I shall, what they do not dare to repeat. But ought not you and they rather blush with shame that such diseases as I shall mention, exist at all to be spoken about? I say shame upon the newspapers, and shame upon your preachers, teachers and doctors, that I should have cause to stand here and tell you what they should have freely discussed, years ago, and thus have saved me the present unpleasant task.

Standing however, as I do, somewhat representative of the immense issue of sexual freedom that is now agitating the public mind, I have a duty to fulfill, to which I should be recreant did I withhold a single sentence that I propose to utter. But, more than this, even: I am intrusted with a mission by those whose disapproval I would not earn, were it to gain the approval of a thousand audiences like this; therefore, though the task be not a pleasant one, I would not shirk it if I could. If, however, in performing it, instead of driving you farther away from me than you now are, I should draw you all nearer, then should I indeed thank heaven for giving me the moral strength to utter the plain, unvarnished truth, as I know it, about the most important question that has ever interested or distracted the human mind....

I think I know enough of the world at large, and of individuals specially to say, that there are not a half dozen persons present, who are not in the most abject slavery to what the world pleases to call, their secret vices. Wouldn't it be strange if these should, after all, turn out to be virtues instead. Then wouldn't their subjects be heartily ashamed of themselves for having been frightened at shadows, merely, into being liars, thieves and hypocrites so large a part of their lives!

Again and finally, let me entreat that, for once in your lives, you throw off the sickly sentimentalism about sexual love—your sham morality and mock modesty about the most common and harmless, as well as innocent and beautiful of things; and like common-sense individuals, with me, consider, specially, that department of our natures with which, though you have pretended such immaculateness, you would no sooner part than with life itself; indeed, to blot which out of life, would be to leave but a precious little worth living. For once be men and women, acting as if you were known by each other, as you are, to be men and women, possessed of all the endowments of nature, and wanting to know if there is still something to learn that will make them yet richer, more beautiful and bountiful of happiness than ever before; and willing to accept the lesson at least for consideration, to which I will proceed without further delay.

THE ELIXIR OF LIFE

I have said that this problem of sexual love is the most important one that ever engaged the human mind. It becomes so because within it is concealed the science that shall finally solve the problem of life and death, which must remain unsolved until this science is discovered to the world. When I say life and death, I mean literally what I say. I mean that within the sexual problem is concealed the law that shall enable us to solve the mystery of life by conquering death....

Do not, however, receive this as coming from me; but accept it as coming from the wisest and best of ascended Spirits—those whom you have learned to honor and love for the good done while on the earthly plane; those to whom, if they were to appear before you here, you would willingly yield implicit obedience; and who would appear here, were not the one essential element still wanting, and to whom for six years I have yielded a willing and appreciative obedience. Gladly would I name them. They are familiar to you all; but I must not presume beyond my commission; but I am commissioned, aye commended, to declare unto you, and through you to the world, that in the despised, the ignored problem of Sexuality, lies the keys that shall unlock to Spirits the doors of materiality, and show in boldest relief that of which, the most blessed, have as yet caught but faintest glimpses—Spirit Materialization.[2] ...

Not any body will deny the desirability of a perfected physical health for humanity; but many may doubt the possibility of its attainment. I, however, make the bold, bald assertion, that disease, when the new era shall be inaugurated, will be banished [from] the human body; and that too by the same means that shall make the era a new one. Almost everybody has witnessed the beneficent results of so-called magnetism in the removal of disease; as well as the further fact that not the same magnetism will produce equally beneficial results upon the same disease in different persons; and still further, that magnetic effects are the most positive and apparent when the operator and subject are of different sexes. It has also been observed that these effects may be produced, though distance separate the persons involved; but that the effects are more palpable when they are, for instance, in the same room, with their minds concentrated upon the conditions;

and still more so, when there is actual physical contact over the parts diseased.

Now what is the philosophy of this healing by magnetic power? This, simply, and it has a whole volume of meaning in it, to the analytic observer: That the operator and the subject, are positively and negatively related to each other; that the approach of the poles of the battery have been sufficiently near to make the connection, and that upon the perfectness of the connection depends the extent of the effect produced, and the consequent curative influence. That is to say, where a person positive or negative to another, afflicted with disease, is brought into magnetic relations, with this other, and the positive and negative currents are established, that disease, whatever it may be, necessarily departs, since where these currents exist, disease cannot remain.

It is safe then to assume that all diseases that have not already destroyed organs upon which life depends may and ought to be cured; and, if this method of cure were once established, no disease would be permitted to go on to the extent of vital organic destruction, and consequently that death from disease would be virtually abolished.

This is the philosophy; but upon what is this philosophy based? What is this magnetic relation that produces such wonderful results? It is called Animal Magnetism, and so indeed it is. But what is Animal Magnetism?[3] It is Sexual vitality merely; and it is nothing else. A person, whether male or female, cannot be a magnetic healer, except he have sexual vitality; and it will be found, that the most successful healers, are those who have the most of this element. Nor does the fact that those of the same sex, often relieve each other, impeach this statement; since he who has the vitality, imparts it to him who hath it not, by the law of equalization.

It is an axiom in the medical profession that the patient who experiences sexual desire is not dangerously ill; and also that the patient who has been dangerously ill is convalescent when sexual desire returns. Thus, it is held that the presence of the sexual appetite is a symptom of health; but if it turn out, as I hold that it will, this statement, to make it strictly true, will have to be reversed. That is, cause and effect have been transposed, the effect having been placed behind the cause. Sexual appetite is the basis of health, and when re-established in an invalid, health follows. This becomes clear, when it is considered upon what a cure by magnetism depends. It is the restoration of sexual vitality, or animal magnetism—the introduction of this into the system, of the patient, causing health; and not a certain condition of health, making it possible for it to be introduced. Thus in this as in almost all pretended science, the real truth reverses the existing order of things; and in this if what I say be true, you will see how nearly the whole world is bordering on promiscuous sexual intercourse, and not only this, but how much the health and happiness of the world depend upon still further, so-called promiscuousness, or, more strictly, perhaps, upon a harmonious variety or a composite and a perfected unity.

But this may not be so evident until another fact is made clear. And this fact is this: almost all disease among adults is caused by some unnatural or untimely sexual condition. Take the married classes. Show me a man or woman who is a picture of physical health and strength, and I will show you a person who has healthy sexual relations; but these may be at the expense of the other person in the partnership. Show me, however, a man and a woman who live together, who are perfectly healthy, physically, and I will show you a God-ordained marriage, which man cannot put asunder. Or again, show me men and women who are in perfect health, whether they are married according to law, or whether they live monogamically or promiscuously, and I will show you persons who are living according to the laws of nature, sexually, and, consequently, are living rightly. Dispute this who can!

It is useless to kick against facts. They are stubborn things, and the world has been butting its head against the science and facts of sexuality, already too long. Although the attempt has been made to bury it in the mud, it shall, nevertheless, be exalted white and pure, to the throne; and there it shall rule the world in peace, happiness and endless progress. If, as I tell you the fountain of health, is concealed in this great problem; shall we be so foolish as to longer ignore it, and thus deprive ourselves of its priceless boon? I say, No! A thousand times, No! Rather let every thing that is held sacred or profane, perish in a common ruin, than let this problem remain longer unsolved.

THE ELIXIR OF LIFE

If health depend upon proper sexuality, it follows that disease depends upon improper sexuality. To this general proposition I make another and a specific one: That all disease not directly to be attributed to so-called accidental causes, is the result of improper, or the want of proper, sexual conditions. And this applies to persons of all ages and both sexes. Show me the man or woman, married or single, old or young, who is suffering from any chronic complaint, and I will show you a person who has either improper or no sexual relations.

Now, just here arises the great and grave question: What are and what are not proper sexual relations. In endeavoring to answer this, I must be permitted to speak so as to be properly understood. And why should I not? Are we not endowed by nature with the sexual passion; and is it not given us for a purpose—one that should be a blessing, instead of a curse as it mostly is, to humanity? Nobody will pretend to answer, No! Then why should we not discuss it as freely as we do any other subject? Is it because our thoughts and desires about it have became so abominable, so perverted and so impure, obscene and vulgar, that any, even needed reference to the subject, brings the blush of shame to the face and a sense of degradation to the soul? Are we indeed so impure that to us all sexual things are impure? I lay it down as an axiom that he or she who blushes and is ashamed at any mention of sexual intercourse, has, at some time or other, done something sexually of which to be ashamed. I hold that every thing connected with the manner and method in which human life has its fountain, is a proper and a modest subject for either public or private discussion, and I simply pity all who say Nay! to this.

Sexual intercourse that is in accordance with nature, and therefore proper, is that which is based upon mutual love and desire, and that ultimates in reciprocal benefit. Sexual intercourse that is improper is that which is not based upon mutual love and desire, and that does not ultimate in reciprocal benefit. Of the former there is but one class of cases, since in this class, all the conditions of perfectness are present. First, Love; Second, desire based upon love; and, Third, mutual happiness as the result. Who is there that shall dare to interfere with such sexual relations? Let it be whoever it may, he is an impious wretch, and an enemy to human happiness, and consequently to humanity.

Of the latter there are several classes, which deserve to be enumerated, so that they may be understood wherever any of them may be met. First, that class where it is claimed by legal right; second, that class where the female, to please the male, submits without the proper self desire; third, that class where, for money, or any motive other than love, the female sells the use of her body to the male for his gratification; fourth, that class where mutual love and desire exist, but where there is such want of adaptation as to make mutual consummation impossible.

Now, under either of these conditions, if sexual intercourse be maintained for any considerable length of time, disease and sexual demoralization will surely follow; but the most destructive to health as well as the most numerous, are the first and the last classes, which occur almost altogether in marriage. The wife who submits to sexual intercourse against her wishes or desires, virtually commits suicide; while the husband who compels it, commits murder, and ought just as much to be punished for it, as though he strangled her to death for refusing him.

But this even is not so destructive to health as is that intercourse, carried on habitually, without regard to perfect and reciprocal consummation. And when it is known that three-fourths of all married women, who otherwise might be happily mated, suffer from this cause, the terrible and wide-spread results may be readily conceived, and the need for amelioration as readily understood. I need not explain to any woman the effects of unconsummated intercourse though she may attempt to deceive herself about it; but every man needs to have it thundered in his ears until he wakes to the fact that he is not the only party to the act, and that the other party demands a return for all that he receives; demands that he shall not be enriched at her expense;[4] demands that he shall not, either from ignorance or selfish desire, carry her impulse forward on its mission only to cast it backward with the mission unfulfilled, to prostrate the impelling power and to breed nervous debility or irritability and sexual demoralization, and to sow the seeds of disease broadcast among humanity. What is merely hinted at here involves a whole science and a fine art, incomparably the most important of all the sciences and of all the arts, hardly yet broached to the human thought, and now criminally repressed and defeated in their effort at birth by the prejudices of mankind—by your prejudices, and even, perhaps, by mine.

It is a fact terrible to contemplate, yet it is nevertheless true, and ought to be pressed upon the world for its recognition: that fully one-half of all women seldom or never experience any pleasure whatever in the sexual act. Now this is an impeachment of nature, a disgrace to our civilization—an eternal blotch upon the otherwise chivalrous conduct of men toward women. It is a standing reproach upon physiological science that this ignorance has existed so long; and upon medical science, that its dire effects have been so long concealed. I have recently had repeated interviews with a member, in high standing, of the New York College of Physicians; and he does not hesitate to acknowledge that, more than all I have yet said is true, about the sexual demoralization of the race; but the age of hypocrisy reigns as supremely in this, as in the clerical profession. Its members are waiting for the world to get ready to hear the truth, and have thus made it necessary that a weak woman should proclaim it, who, instead of being a recognized authority, competent to enforce her statements, is almost crucified, because she feels it her duty to do what they should have done, whose business it is to guard the health of humanity....

There is, however, another and a graver consideration lying back of the present demoralized sexual condition of the people; and this is the result it is producing upon the coming generation. If the present social system of compulsory marriage were all that its admirers claim for it; were it the guardian of peace, prosperity and purity; in short, were it the one thing good and true in our present civilization, yet for the curse it entails upon children, I would wash it out, if need be, by the blood of one-half of our race.

Four-fifths of all children who are conceived are undesired, and they come into the world, as it were, with the brand of Cain upon their brows; or else with the seeds of some fatal disease in their systems; which accounts for one-half of these dying off before they reach the age of five years—a commentary upon the present social system that sinks it to the lever of a horrid, aye, a brutal tragedy. And yet the world pretends to have a deep solicitude for the children. It crieth out: What will become of the children if marriage be done away?

I will tell you just what will become of the children which, if the children of to-day had inherited, should not now have had occasion to enter my protest against the awful crime that is being committed against them. In the first place, without marriage; and with women made, as they must be, independent of the individual man for support, there will be no unwelcomed children born; secondly, they will be born in health and with a lease of life beyond the adult age, and, thirdly, they will all inherit the same right to equal education—physical, mental and moral, and thus enter upon adult life having had equal preparation.

It is as much better to be the ward of society than to be dependent upon an individual, as society is greater than the individual. Who would not rather have the bond of the United States—even under present political conditions—than that of any individual? How much more to be preferred for children, then, will be the faith of the future reconstructed government, over either the legal or moral duty of the individual merely. They would do well to examine the outcome of children, who cry out against the social revolution, because of them. Of all the improved conditions possible, those of dependent women and children will be most improved. We are looking earnestly forward to a better race of men and women, and one of the means by which it will be produced, will be this condition for children.

To begin. Children must first be conceived, gestated and born in proper conditions; and afterward, properly and scientifically reared and educated; and with this neither marriage or present customs will have aught to do; indeed they have nothing to do with such matters now, except to interpose obstacles in the way of their natural development. People argue as if children are the result of marriage, while the truth is, that to them, marriage is an arbitrary incident, merely, entailing unthought-of misery.

It is also to be observed that another horrible result of the system of marriage, is sexual vice, both in children and adults, and when its terrific ravages are considered, a remedy, let it be whatever it may, should be joyfully welcomed by the whole world. I need not tell you that four-fifths of the children practice self-abuse before they are old enough, of their own wisdom to know better; nor that, finding the inroads it is making upon their health, they attempt to abandon it, and spermatorrhea[5] is substituted for the original vice; nor that almost everybody, female as well as male, when licensed, legally, to enter upon the relations of sex, are so fearfully debilitated by this vice, or this disease, as to debar them from even a medium measure of happiness; and still more to unfit them to reproduce themselves in children. Indeed does vice in childhood culminate in misery in adult life!

The repressions of law and a pretended public opinion, and the resulting enforced and unwilling relations in marriage, are already yielding natural fruit—a growing disgust sexually, between the sexes. Were I to tell you the extent to which Sodomy[6] in man and its antitype in woman have attained, I should shock you beyond measure; and if to this I were to add the beastly practices to which resort is had to revive or stimulate the depraved and demoralized sexuality in men, and women too, I should disgust you, though speaking nothing but the truth, and such truth as the world needs to know.

I am only reiterating what is known to be true, by those who have investigated the subject, medically and physiologically, when I say that a change for the better must soon be made; since if things go on for the next century as they have for the last, there will be no further reproduction possible, or even desirable. These are questions of mighty import for the consideration of the present. They come to *us*, and *we* must determine whether the race shall become extinct, or whether we will have the moral courage to inquire into the matter, and find the remedy; and when found to apply it....

Now, the remedy for all the ills to which I have called your attention is the substitution for the present rule of sexual intercourse, the rule of mutual consent based upon mutual desire, which may be temporary, or may continue during life. To prove this, permit me to ask if any person ever knew of any detrimental results following from the application of that rule; did ever any disease, or anything but happiness and peace, follow from natural, mutually desired sexuality? I tell you nay! You may search the world through and through and fail to find a single exception. It is impossible that anything but good should follow the natural expression of a natural desire; while we have found that almost all the ills of life, follow as the results of intercourse, based upon an entirely opposite rule.

Again, let me ask if any body is so blind as to imagine that the law has anything whatever to do with the begetting of good children; and, again, if children begotten under the rule of love and consent, can possibly be bad?

And here I desire to correct an error that exists regarding my theory of stirpiculture. It is supposed by many, that I contend, when a woman desires a child she should select for its parent, some person, who, from physical health and perfectness, should be something like an ideal man. I utterly repudiate all such stirpiculture as this. I do not believe it possible for a woman to produce her best child, except by the man whom she loves best and for whom she has the keenest sexual desire. If this be for the perfect physical man, why, all the better; but I have observed that even when the physical conditions of parents are not so good as they ought to be, but when they are closely allied by love, that good children follow; while I have seen the most inferior children result from parents who, from physical appearances, ought, apparently, to beget the very best; therefore I am obliged to conclude that the order of children depends not so much upon the physical perfection of parents, as it does upon the perfectness of the love upon which the sexual impulse is based, that precedes conception. The conditions for the future generation of children, then, are: 1st, Perfect love; 2d, Mutual desire; 3d, Perfect health.

Furthermore, I hold that for a woman to have sexual intercourse with a man, for any other reason than that that she loves him and has a sexual desire for him, is to degrade herself, while the opposite conditions must always produce the opposite effect of exaltation. I hope, therefore, that nobody will hereafter class me among those stirpiculturalists, who reduce the begetting of children to the level of that of cattle; and who would exalt the best merely physically endowed men to be the progenitors of the race, without regard to any natural attraction and denying sexuality to all of inferior endowments. I repeat again; and I wish emphatically to impress it upon you that, to me, love is the element by which the best children are begotten; and that when there shall be no sexual intercourse except that based upon love, then there will be no half-made-up children born to be a curse to themselves, and a burden to society.

Again it is to be observed that there is no course so safe when there is danger of any kind ahead, as to have those who are to encounter fully informed of its character, and thus prepared to meet it. But in the matter of sexuality, the world's practice is entirely different. Those who know anything about the dangers by which the sexual passion is surrounded, make the most strenuous efforts to conceal them from those who are ignorant of the perils which attend their development. It is utterly incomprehensible to me how mothers, fathers, teachers, preachers and doctors are so diligent in impressing the young under their charges against the habits of lying, cheating and stealing; while never a word is said to them about the dangers of self abuse. Children at some period of growth find a strange sensation present with them, and in their simplicity, perhaps, seek to learn what it all means; but they are met with a certain and effectual rebuff, and probably are treated to a dissertation about the awful wickedness of such thoughts, and the most positive injunction never again to entertain them. But they will come, and they will not be discarded, and thus they are left to drift almost assuredly into obtaining, surreptitiously, sufficient knowledge to teach them the manner in which gratification is had. With this knowledge, added to the stifled but still growing passion, they decline into a morbid sexual condition which, running into years, carries them beyond the possibility of a return to natural and healthy action to maturity, utterly ruined, sexually and physically.

Now, in place of this repression, children need early instructions in the uses and abuses of sexuality. They need to be taught that it is a divinely-gifted agent for human happiness, and to regard it as a capacity to be cherished equally with all other capacities. All secretiveness and false modesty and sickly sentimentalism ought to be removed, and the subject reduced to an every-day affair, and thus we shall rob it of the morbidness and mawkishness by which it is now enveloped, and by which it is cursed, and the passion itself will be permitted to develop, healthfully under the guidance of an enlightened understanding of all its possibilities.

From the day that sexual science is introduced into schools, as assuredly it will be, from that day the sexual evils that now beset the youth of both sexes will begin to vanish. Familiarity with anything robs it of the power to harm as well as of the power to demoralize. If this question of sex were as common a subject for conversation as that of diet or any other human need, many of the ills that now grow out of it would fade away, and it would be rapidly reduced to a science, and everybody come to know to whom they are and to whom they are not related by the ties of love; and knowing it for their own happiness, would be guided by this knowledge.

But what is this mystic power called love and from whence does it derive its potent power over mankind? In the first place genuine love is something beyond volition, and exists entirely independent of the will. There never was a love that was learned. A deep and sincere regard, even a pure affection, may be acquired; but love is the recognition of the relationship that exists naturally between the positive and negative conditions of matter. Wherever there are two or more elements blended, by attraction, there is the love of nature. Love, therefore, is the attraction of opposites by the inherent power of relation that exists, but can never be created. Hence in human beings, it is found exhibiting itself where it is least suspected to be possible. Moreover when the related elements exist in two persons, let them meet wherever they may it is impossible to avoid mutual recognition, and let them bound elsewhere in whatsoever manner, they must love, because they have no power to prevent it.

It is also to be observed that there are various degrees of love, all the way from the merest present exhibition, to the most complete blending. Hence there is need for freedom that the fittest may predominate, since if love at all be right, then the highest—the most perfect—should be the love that should control, and he or she who does not obey the higher love, sins against the law of love and must suffer the inexorable consequences of that law.

Therefore, from the point of present human happiness merely, the further we analyze this matter of love the more convincing the proofs become, that it must and will be free; and the more conclusive the evidence that, though the bodies of two may be kept asunder by the terrors of the law and a fearful crucifixion be thereby entailed upon them, yet their souls will mingle and the magic thrills of reciprocal feeling pass and repass whenever they come within the sphere of each other's influence. Is it not foolish then—aye; is it not more than this, is it not criminal, longer to attempt to place limits upon this heaven ordained passion? Shall we not then rather recognize the truth as stated by Pope when he says: "Love free as air at sight of human ties, / Spreads his light wings and in a moment flies."[7]

As the results of freedom for love, then, we may predicate the elevation of humanity out of the awful chasm of misery and despair into which it has been precipitated by slavery and the endeavor to escape or evade its duties, to purity, peace and happiness. We may expect from it that hypocrisy, deceit and lust will be banished from the earth, and that in their places will be enthroned a love that shall seek to bless, instead of to possess, its object.

But a great many people say Oh, yes! I believe in free love, but not in free lust, meaning thereby that they believe in free love for such as are exactly upon their planes of love, but not for those who are not yet so far ascended. Now I am striving for freedom for all conditions; for those low down in the scale of development as well as for those higher up the ladder of progress. A freedom that grants less than this is despotism. If freedom be an inherent natural right, then all individuals of whatever status are entitled to it. The only limit that can be placed upon it is the boundary of its own sphere, so that the sphere of another shall not be invaded, without first obtaining the necessary consent. All sexual love based upon consent must be free love, since there is no compulsion involved.

What then are we to understand by free lust, and what do they mean who say they are in favor of the former but not of the latter? I have already defined love to be an attraction existing between opposites in sex, independent of the volition of either party, and sexual intercourse by such opposites as proper sexual conditions. It can make no difference whether those conditions continue an hour, a day or a lifetime. It is sufficient that they exist. But lust is the perverted action of the desire for sexual love exhibiting itself in masturbations, sodomy, purchased intercourse as in prostitution, or in enforced intercourse as in marriage; and to this sort of lust I am as much opposed as anybody can be—and therefore while the people will have marriage laws, I would also have laws to protect wives from the beastly lust that now prevails so fearfully in marriage, and by which thousands of wives are annually sent to untimely graves, and the world peopled by intellectual, moral, or social dwarfs and abortions.

Yes! it exists and what is the remedy? Why, simply the freedom that will permit this lust to exhibit itself in proper sexual relations and thus become love; hence when freedom is inaugurated, lust will have lost its domain, and there will soon cease to be any such thing. But the objectors do not mean this, they mean that those who are inclined to constant change, shall not be permitted to change. But who is to decide when freedom is the rule? Surely not any individual for anybody but himself. So it matters not how promiscuously inclined anybody may be, there can be no possible right to restrain him, except through growth from his conditions. This whole matter must be remanded from the control of law to the sphere of education and growth. The person who desires promiscuous sexuality has just the same right to obtain it that he who desires pure monogamy has to obtain that. To state it differently: They who desire promiscuousness, have just as good a right to enforce it as a rule for society, as they who desire monogamy, have to enforce it as a rule. It is strange, however, how few people there are who are able to look at this question from a point of view opposite to their own.

Because I advocate the right of freedom for all classes, I am charged, as I said before, with advocating promiscuousness; but I can easily and clearly show the utter foolishness and the absurdity of that charge. I advocate the freedom for religion, to be enjoyed equally by the Christian, the Infidel, the Pagan and the Jew; but I am neither one or the other of any of these, but a Spiritualist. Now why is it not charged, because I advocate this freedom, that I advocate Paganism? Simply because I do not—and people are so well versed in religious affairs as not to make so ridiculous an assertion; but the same persons who would never think of charging me with the advocacy of fire-worship, because I advocate the right of the fire-worshiper; do not hesitate to charge me with promiscuousness because I advocate the right to that condition for those who desire it. Is there anybody here who fails to see the analogy or the inconsistency of my would be judges?

Since the manly letter of Moses Hull[8] appeared in the *Weekly*, many persons have written to ask me if that is Woodhullism. I reply, No! That is Hullism without the Wood. But if there be anything that may with propriety be called Woodhullism it is this right of everybody to their own lives. And for my part I wish that all professing spiritual teachers would be as honest as Moses and Elvira Hull have been, and tell us the results of their experiences. Should they do so, I have no doubt that many of them would excel their predecessors—the Hulls—in profitable lessons. I do not think I venture anything in saying if every person present, who has been before the people as a spiritual teacher, were to relate his or her sexual experiences truly, that from this day the revolution would be accomplished. Moses Hull writes in the last *Weekly* that more than fifty speakers have said to him privately: "I have lived the same life you have, and with the same results; but I am not a big enough fool to tell of it." A pretty lot of teachers, surely. They have lived a certain life from which they confess to having received benefit over the accepted methods, and yet they will not enlighten us by the facts of their experiences so that we may profit thereby.

Compared with such hypocrites, Moses Hull is an angel of light, and I trust the time will come, and that he will have no peace until it comes, when Moses Hull shall support his own statements by those of a similar character received from these persons who are afraid to be anything but hypocrites, so that the world may know how much of its happiness and goodly conditions depend upon such loves as it pretends to condemn; and more than this even: I hope and trust that he may be stung, if nothing else will do it, into reminding a few professing "immaculates" who have ministered to his relief, that it is not exactly in good taste to denounce those who advocate sexual freedom....

Whatever you may say of "Woodhullism," it cannot be that it is rotten at the core, of deceit; or that externally it is mildewed by hypocrisy. You may, however, if you will, slime it all over with freedom, sexual freedom if you please, for the highest as well as the lowest, for all grades and kinds, and I will still rejoice that this ism is affixed to my name. There is but one other word in which I glory more than in that of freedom, and that word is love—love, the fulfilling of the law. Love, all that we can know of God—indeed that is God. Oh! what possibilities cluster around that heavenly name, that shall be realized when, with it, is joined its needed counterpart, freedom—freedom for love—freedom in love—freedom to love; and when it shall be the highest blessing of life to love and to be loved freely—when both men and women shall be able, with pride, to proclaim it to the world that they love, instead of as now, being compelled to shrink into the dark corners of the earth with their happiness, lest it be learned of men. Then indeed shall men and women be as the angels in heaven, who neither marry or are given in marriage, and heaven and earth be merged in one. Such is to be the fulfiling of the law, "that ye love one another."

But I must pass to another and still more momentous part of my subject. I have shown you why we die, and it is not because of our false religion, our politics or our lack of them; but because of our false sexual relations. Here is the cause, and here must we look for the remedy. But how obtain it? I have told you that the inhabitants of the oldest planet, still die, and that as spirits, they are not yet resurrected; and also that the needed elements by which to arrive at this condition, must first be combined upon the earth, since here they are only to be found.

Now what does the resurrection, of which so much is said in all so-called holy, because inspired writings, mean? Simply a return to physical life, as thousands of spirits have been endeavoring to do for the last few years; and only partly and unsatisfactorily, at best, succeeding. At most, admitting all that is claimed to be true, they are able merely to make themselves known to friends. Even this is a great success, and merits all the adoration that is given it; but what is this compared with that which shall be when this return shall be complete and made at will; when they shall return, and, assuming a body of flesh, abide again with us on the earth? No spiritualist will be prepared to deny this possibility. Indeed I believe it is generally conceded, by spiritualists, that materialization will soon be perfected.

But do any consider what that means to us of earth? Do any imagine that, when, the great and good of spirit life, shall return and, in the flesh, abide with us, they will pay tribute or respect to the present order of social things? Will they, who thousands of years have been, as the angels in heaven, neither marrying nor given in marriage, conform to our laws which pretend to control sexual intercourse? Will they marry their loves on earth legally?

Perhaps some respectable Spiritualists who frown upon me for advocating an order of things that must be, before Materialization can be, had better set their faces against this new and dangerous thing, for I tell you that the spirits are coming back to tear your damned system of sexual slavery into tatters and consign its blackened remnants to the depths of everlasting hell. And would to Heaven they would come here to-night and confirm my words. You would believe them while you will not believe me, who now speak for them.

Do you not suppose that many, now on earth, are loved in heaven; and that when these spirits come again that that love will make itself manifest? Do you suppose they will care for your marriage laws? I tell you they will walk into your families and claim as their loves those who are held as slaves and carry them off before your very eyes. They will come to your daughters and inspire them with a love which, perhaps, they have never known. Will you turn your children from your doors, because forsooth, they have dared to love a resurrected spirit, without having the consent of the Parson or the Squire? Bosh! I am disgusted with such pitiful morality, and am sorry for those who have yet to be awakened to the fact that it is pitiful, who imagine that purity and virtue are lodged in a license which is granted by law, at a cost of twenty-five cents and upward, *permitting* people to consort sexually.

No! They will laugh at your professed ownership in sex, and tell you to enforce it if you can. They will snap their fingers at your officer and spit upon your laws as I have been taught by them, to do. Nor will they wait for divorces either. They will love whom they will; and in their loving, lift us of earth, to their level. I know there are thousands who have been sexually inspired of spirits; and many more whom spirits control and through whom they receive the benedictions of love. Once and for all I tell you, Oh, children of earth, that you had better put your houses in order and await the coming of the bridegroom or the bride. Accept sexual freedom while yet it can be attained, by degrees, and not wait until it shall tear your souls at its sudden coming. I know how hard it is to give up to the embrace of another the one whom you think you love, but whom you desire for selfish gratification rather than to bless. I know that it is often easier to yield life itself; and I have come to you, in time, to warn you to prepare for what is surely coming, aye, is even now at your very doors, liable to break in upon you and find you like the foolish virgins with your lamps untrimmed. . . .

There is a something abroad in the land, however, that assumes the name of freedom—in which to hide its deformities—against which I wish to declare my personal objections. It is that freedom which conceals itself behind the mask of hypocrisy; that seeks its own line of life while passing, for living something quite different; that has a make-believe love for the husband or the wife, while really loving elsewhere; that receives the caresses of the husband or wife, inwardly disgusted by them, while lavishing those which proceed from the heart, elsewhere. Once, and for all time, permit me to say, that I hold this thing—which many people at present call freedom, and which many more live, and name it respectability—is the poison Upas tree[9] of the present social condition, and the bane of freedom. Beside such damned hypocrisy as this, Moses and Elvira Hull are, in my esteem, as white as snow. People must live the lives with which they wish to stand accredited before the world. Then, and not till then, can there be freedom; since those who live a life they do not wish the world to know, are degraded slaves, as much below the negro or the legal slave, as he who wallows in bestiality for its own sake, is below her who sells her body to buy food for her starving children.

The new element that the Spirits require for the purposes of more effective and permanent materializations, is a spiritualized sexual aura, to be exhaled by the perfect blending of the sexes, in the highest and divinest relations known to humanity. The conditions, requisite to develop this element, reside, without question, in many individuals—many pairs of individuals; and without doubt, various temporary exhibitions of the perfect unity of these conditions have occurred, which, had there been unlimited freedom for their existence, might, ere this, have evolved what is required; hence, the triumph over slavery, in all its forms, must be, before these conditions can be, and continue. All things that operate as obstructions or hindrances, must be removed, so that the opposite poles of the battery may remain in undisturbed connection. Like the magnetic telegraph, the medium over or through which the positive and negative currents pass, must be unbroken and undisturbed. The foul atmosphere, arising from a diseased public opinion, must be corrected by the sanitary influence of some powerful disinfectant, so that its miasm may not blight the new-born life, nor poison its vigorous action. The child of heaven must live, even if all that is must die that it may live; but to no such extremity need things come, if the contaminating grasp of the despot be removed from the throat of freedom, and it be permitted to breathe, as if it had a right in the world. But there must be freedom before there can be life; and there must not be so much as a criticism, even, of public opinion, to prevent its full and free reception and action; nor to deter the people from seeking it with earnest desire....

Now, do you not see the solution of this whole matter? The strife in life is to be, to attain to the condition of triumph over death, and this comes only by the perfect blending of two of opposite sex. To gain this there must be, as in every other department of discovery, freedom to experiment, until the law that governs it is discovered, when everybody will be able to know who is his negative or her positive.[10]

I wish here, however, to explain what will be perhaps unwelcome to many, who think that, promiscuousness is the process through which this boon is to be gained. I am sorry to feel compelled to disappoint their anticipations; but I do not mean, if I can help it, to be misunderstood about this matter any longer.

The law by which this attainment is governed is this: the greater the number of failures made by people in seeking their sexual mates, the greater the difficulty will be in mating when they are found. This will become evident when it is considered that every sexual act which is not the legitimate expression of sexual unity, has a deleterious effect on the sexual organs and impulse. This may be illustrated by the stomach. A hungry person may, in the absence of the most proper food, eat that which, not being best adapted to his condition, will produce derangement of the stomach; but which, nevertheless, serves to prevent starvation for the time. A sufficient continuance of this food will cause chronic dyspepsia, which will yield only when that which was needed at the outset to prevent the disease, is procured.

So also is it with Sexuality. Pure and perfect conditions and uses are as necessary to its health, as is proper food for the stomach. In the absence of perfect conditions, imperfect relations are maintained, which, continued indefinitely, produce chronic derangement—demoralization—of the organs, and through them, as I have shown, of the system generally, which derangements can be cured, only, by the perfect sexual blending of two perfectly or nearly related natures. Hence the young, who have never had sexual experience, are the foremost candidates for the new era of perpetuated life; while those who do not attain it, will continue to die and arrive at this condition from the opposite sphere by the opposite process, prolonged perhaps to hundreds of years....

By this new motive, given to sexuality, it is, at once and forever, lifted from the mire and filth, into which it has been cast by the debaucheries of the world, consequent upon mistaken sexual restrictions, and seated upon the throne, it cometh to judge the world in righteousness. It is indeed the Christ that is to come, by whom every person shall be justified of himself and to himself; by whom alone can any man be saved from the vices, superstitions and miseries of earth-life. It is by this gate by which alone the kingdom of heaven—happiness—can be entered; and whether we first lay the mortal body in the ground and enter it from the other sphere, having passed through the purgatory necessary to purge our sins; or been driven to the depths of the lowest hell by the tremendous weight of our iniquities, that they may be consumed by its quenchless fire; or whether we enter it by the direct and natural methods of regular growth—continuous evolution—without the descent into purgatory or hell, depends upon the use we shall make of this new-found salvation. This is not only to usher in the resurrection of the dead, and thus fulfill the Scripture, but also to unite the parts of the system of salvation, which are now scattered among the various religious beliefs, into one complete and perfect system for the whole world.

There has been personal experience sufficient to prove that what the spirits have told me about this matter, is true. Almost every woman, at some time in her life, has suffered from false sexual relations.[11] Many who by nature are eminently endowed, sexually, seldom or never know delight, thinking the while that they love their husbands with their whole souls; but they will some time learn, that this is custom and education rather than genuine affection on the part of either. For years these endure sexual starvation, since starvation means unconsummated sexual desire. They lose their health, not knowing the cause. They grow old before they are fully matured in form, and some disease sets in that ultimately proves fatal, and of which it is imagined they die, while the real cause lies back in these false sexual relations.

But all these long weary years, there is a void in the inner soul of every woman, which tells spiritually and prophetically—for all women are endowed in this way to a greater or less extent—of a lover with whom she shall traverse the infinitude of futurity. In spirit dream she wanders the woods and hills with him, and gathers flowers of sweetest fragrance; and when some sorrow presses her heavily, his Spirit comforts and soothes. And when she meets, as meet all shall, oh what a revelation. Words are insignificant to express it. A new life dawns. A low and thrilling melody breath[e]s transcendent strains of hope and fear, and the longing ear listens lest one sweet note escape, and the hope go by forever. The stars grow brighter; the moon fairer; the fields greener, and all nature roll onward in its mighty circuit, in an atmosphere of perfect joy. The heart beats faster; the eye sparkle[s] with a new lustre; the crimson deepens on cheek and lip, the voice grows low and deep and tremulous; and the whole being thrills with ecstasy as it recognizes and embraces, the companion so long watched and prayed for. The emaciated form assumes its rounded proportions; disease vanishes, and again she is a woman restored to her pristine beauty, vigor and life.

To sum up what I have to say on this most important of questions, and to generalize what I have said upon the subject of sexuality, I would repeat that the conditions under which progressive rejuvenation or immortality in the form may be attained, can only be secured under the auspices of absolute and entire freedom—a freedom not incompatible with perfect law, but its certain consequent and proper consummation. Let us hope that it may soon be established, notwithstanding the fact that it has taken ages to evolve the yet imperfect law which obtains among us. To the credit of our country, in our Revolutionary War we placed the keystone in the arch of man's spiritual freedom when we decreed in our Constitution, if not civil, at least religious liberty, and guaranteed it to our people by law. We must now advance upon that position and ordain Social Freedom, which is its natural ally, and its necessary aid and support.

And of all freedom that the spirit of man or woman can conceive, or the heart of woman or man can desire, the highest—Social Freedom—culminating in personal liberty, is the most valuable. It is the natural foundation, the true basis of all other liberties. We must affirm, and, as far as we are able, must secure for all human beings this most sacred of all rights—a right which belongs to every man and every woman (unconvicted of crime) at all times, in all places, and under all circumstances; and of all functions in the body of a man or woman to which this greatest of liberties most especially pertains, the sexual function is the most important: it must not and ought not to be disturbed in its offices by arbitrary laws, unless it unwarrantedly invades another's liberties; and the effort to reduce it to legal or religious bondage has resulted, and ever must result, in introducing into society misery, bestiality, anarchy and destruction. If we would change the present rotten state of the world with regard to our sexual horrors, all that we have to do is to acknowledge and inaugurate this grandest of all liberties; to recognize the right of woman to rule in the domain of the affections; to aid the full development of the natural love that yet exists between the sexes; and to guard our children from that ignorance in sexual matters which has decimated and is decimating the present generation of mankind.

Then, and not till then, when we have performed all the above-mentioned duties, may we look for our reward in that progressive and progressing life, which I believe is even now at our doors, waiting for admission. When that is obtained then we behold a light without a shadow, a morn without an eve, a day without a night. Then shall we be able to bridge over the gloomy chasm of death, and to build for ourselves a Jacob's ladder,[12] reaching from earth to heaven, on which spirits and mortals will be perpetually engaged ascending and descending in unending harmony and felicity. It may be that not one of us may witness this fulfillment of the prophecies of the past; but, if we do our duty, we have every reason to hope, and I, for one, believe, that we shall soon succeed. We are now like Bunyan's Pilgrims in Doubting Castle,[13] the den of the giant Despair; but, like them also, we have a key in our bosoms that will unlock the gate of it, and let us out into the flower-spangled fields of pleasure and delight, and the name of that key is—Liberty!

Yes—Liberty! Full and free in all matters pertaining to humanity; civil, political, religious, social and sexual liberty. When that is attained, then may we hope by right education to achieve for men and women, that improvement and exaltation which we have already accomplished, by arbitrary laws, based upon those of nature, for flowers, fruits and animals. Then may we look to bid adieu to the miserable and deformed specimens of humanity, which now meet us on every side, too often exposing their infirmities as a means of soliciting our charity. Then may we aspire to see nations doing their duty by their children, extending their fostering care over them in their infancy, and bringing them up tenderly to labor and to love. Then may we expect woman to throw off the chains of the barbarisms of the fashions, and prove *in propria persona*[14] that art cannot improve the charms which nature has lavished on her when following right counsels and obeying true laws. Then may we also find in man, not a pitiless tyrant absorbed in the pursuit of money, but a benign benefactor, the provider and careful distributor of the wealth of communities.

Oh! that these my earnest desires may speedily be realized! That the ghastly darkness in which the world is now involved with regard to sexual affairs may rapidly pass away! That, by the attainment of a better knowledge of ourselves we may be able to produce a very superior race of men and women to that at present existing! That the sexual miseries and bestialities of the present time may soon be annihilated forever! If I had the power I would unveil all the hidden horrors of the system which now are covered, to the scorn and loathing of the world; but I would do so, as the skillful surgeon dissects a rotten corpse, not to injure the dead—but to benefit the living: I hack to teach; not mangle to expose.[15] But the world charges me with taking delight in so nauseous an occupation. It is mistaken. I would that my lot had fallen in pleasanter places; but it has not. Sufficient for me, and for all of us, if, in our passage through life, we perform our duties therein.

Alas! who should envy me my position? Fortune, fame, a good name, even health itself, has been demanded from me in my work, and I have given—cheerfully given them all. I have been the sport of society—in many instances the rejected of the sex I have served and am serving so well. The debauched ruffian, tobacco-stained, and redolent with the fumes of whisky, points at me as something worse than himself. I have been for the past three years pitilessly lambasted and caricatured in lewd and impossible positions by execrable artists, in the public press; unjustly hounded out of my office by the minions of the law; my business destroyed without hope of renovation; torn from my family and illegally imprisoned for more than a month; excessive bail demanded from me, not for the purpose of security, but with intent to compass my further oppression; and all these for an act which has since been repeated by other journals, with additions—without punishment. Added to this, as a consequent of the intense mental anxiety arising from judgment deferred, I have been stricken almost to death, having been in a comatose state for many hours, so that my life was, for a long time, almost despaired of by my nearest friends and kindred. Yet—in spite of all this—I am here, unchanged, fighting the old, old battle for the liberty of woman, and the consequent exaltation of man....

And although, at the present time, in the industrial, civil, financial, intellectual and social world, every thing appears to be in chaotic confusion, I have the faith to believe, that the picture of the future I previously painted will soon be succeeded by a glorious and unending reality. Is it wicked for me to wish for the realization of such a vision? That human beings may speedily be relieved from their fetters, and men and women walk forth free in the light of perfect purity, holiness, liberty and love. Surely not! In the language of the ancient seer, then, let me conclude this lecture, calling upon all of you to aid in blinking forward so blessed a consummation. "And the Spirit and the Bride say—Come!—and let him that heareth, say—Come!—and let him that is athirst—Come! And whosoever drink of the 'Water of Life' freely."[16]

# Chapter Twenty

## *The Scare-Crows of Sexual Slavery*

*This speech was delivered at the Silver Lake Camp Meeting of the American Society of Spiritualists in August 1873, when Victoria Woodhull was still president of the organization. As Mary Gabriel notes, while some responded well to the speech, "there was a growing faction of dissenters in the crowd who were not sure that Victoria C. Woodhull and her radical social theories were what the spiritualists needed" (Gabriel,* Notorious Victoria, *215). The speech was published in* Woodhull and Claflin's Weekly *on September 27, 1873. The concluding paragraphs are omitted here.*

*My Brothers and Sisters.—*

I am going to tell you some plain truths to-night. I know I shall not please all your ears. I value the good opinion of you all, but I value the truth more, and if to gain the former I must withhold one iota of the latter I shall fail in securing it. Your good opinion I crave, for I feel that you are my friends—friends to the great human race, and he or she who is this, though they hate me with a deadly hatred, is my friend; but public opinion I stamp in the mud. It is a stench in the nostrils of truth, for which, if any care, he must say, "Get thee behind me, Satan!"[1] I will not so much as vary a single hair's breadth from what I conceive to be my duty, though public opinion should turn the faces of every man and woman against me. I will speak the truth, I will be heard; but you may kill me afterward if you will. I have but one sentiment in my soul, and that is to do what in me lies to lift up the down-trodden and enslaved of earth, and to inaugurate equality and happiness in the world. I have no kindred, less than the human race, who demand or can have service of me. My life is dedicated to this work, and I come to you to speak such words as will make your souls sink in horror and your curses to rest upon yourselves, that you have so long quietly permitted these things to go on unrebuked. I would, if it were possible, wring from you the declaration that you would know no rest again until these wrongs be righted. It must come to this. The world is to be made free and beautiful, and happy because so, and methinks I can see in the not distant future, a time when misery and heartaches and poverty and all unhappiness shall be banished the earth, and the entire human family, both in earth and spirit life, fully and harmoniously united, singing the glad songs of the redeemed. But before this can be, other and terrible things must be. So much suffering as the soul-sick sons and daughters of earth now suffer, cannot be transformed to bright and happy conditions, without the atoning blood of, I had almost said, millions of martyr souls. Let the sacrifice be what it may, however, it must be paid, and heaven help all of them, who love their brothers and sisters all over the world, to endure what must be endured. Having thus briefly alluded to what I shall say to you, I will proceed to speak upon

THE SCARE-CROWS OF SEXUAL SLAVERY

If a stranger visit the farming districts of the New England States in the month of June, he will observe in many newly-planted corn-fields the most hideous-looking objects, fashioned after the human form....

But now observe upon what the efficiency of these men of straw depends. There they stand motionless, with not so much as the power to raise a hand for harm or good; but the crows, having just sense enough to see in them the resemblance to their great enemy—man—carefully avoid coming within their domain; and thus through ignorance is the young corn saved.

But scare-crows are found in other than corn fields, and for other purposes than to save young corn. They are found in the religious field. Those who have commanded here, in order to save their realm, hold up a hell-fire and the Old Nick himself as scare-crows, to prevent the ignorant and the foolish from invading their possessions, or rather from exploring beyond them....

In the field of politics there are the same class who invent scare-crows with which to fool the people—their serfs—one of the most terrible of which, at the present, is that of a woman voting, and the idea of justice for industry. These are, indeed, terrific sights, enough to blanch the face of such as, all their lives, have lived under the rod of male domination and the money god, and the belief that man is the natural lord of creation altogether, when every sensible woman knows she belies herself by the admission, since she also should know that she may be the absolute monarch over man, able to compel him upon his knees to supplicate for, instead of presuming to grant favor. Oh! woman, hast thou not yet learned thy subtle yet potent power, that thou doth still grovel in mean servility at the feet of thy serf, if thou wouldst have him so!

This naturally introduces the social field, whose scare-crows it is our special province at this time to consider. I know them all to be "men of straw" merely, that the lightest puff, the slightest breath of truth will topple over and expose to the world, if it will but look on them as they fall.

Before we begin this destruction, to pull them in pieces to learn of what they are made, let us if we can, and may, what is the occasion that has called the pretended lords of this field to erect them, and also forestall the criticism that would otherwise be clutched from our simile of the corn field, the distinction to be made between which and the field of sexual freedom being this: While those who plant the corn and erect the straw men to preserve its growth in the former instance, in the latter, reverse the order. The enemy invade the fields where we have sown the seeds of social reform, which are just beginning to make its withered and whitened surface look green again, and on our ground erect these scare-crows to prevent the crows, the ignorant among people, from coming to partake of the feast of gladness that is hear spread. We trust the enemy will take this distinction home with him and carefully bestow it in his memory, so that he may not make himself doubly foolish after a while by the introduction of the criticism for which this is intended as an antidote.

THE SCARE-CROWS OF SEXUAL SLAVERY

But what is all this about? Well, it is a part of the contest between despotism and freedom. Absolutism on the one hand, representing the former, and individual sovereignty on the other hand representing the latter. This contest is not so much a strife between opposites, however, as it is an effort on the part of despots to prevent their subjects from becoming freemen. In the evolution of civilization the people walk in the path of progress, taking a departure from despotism toward freedom, which is at the other extreme of civilization....

Freedom, in general terms, means simply this: that each and every individual has the right in his or her own proper person to make such use of any or all his powers and capacities as he or she may elect to do. Anything less than this is not freedom—it is restriction, and restriction exercised by any person or aggregate of persons over another person is despotism, but the rule of social order must be either freedom or despotism: it cannot be a mixture of both.

SCARE-CROW NO. 1

Immediately this proposition is made, scare-crow No. 1 is presented to affright the inquirer, and this declares: If everybody be given the right to do just as they wish, anybody would not be safe a moment anywhere. Every saint will be robbed, outraged or murdered by some sinner, and anarchy itself would hold high carnival, while civilization would sink in the blackness of the dark ages.

Now let us not imitate the crow, and fight shy of the scare, but walk straight in its face, and pull off its mask, and tear down its pretense. In the first place the short-sighted wiseacres who pretend to be frightened out of their wits at the thought of freedom, do not see if the right of each individual to freedom be guaranteed, that this alone is perfect protection for everybody; since if everybody have this right secure, he is safe from every interference from another person. If, then, the freedom of any person whatever, is interfered with, it is the fault of the organization of society which causes it to fail to secure every individual of whom it is composed in the possession of his freedom, and not the fault in any sense or shape of the right of freedom itself....

### SCARE-CROW NO. 2

No sooner, however, than No. 1 is demolished, than instantly No. 2 is put forward. "Well," says the objector, "suppose it be admitted that it is right for every individual to have his or her freedom, it is not expedient that it should be exercised entirely free from restraint." Expediency is the great scare-crow No. 2, but it is even more fatally faulty than No. 1, though a deal more dangerous. Many a person will admit that it may be right for him or her to possess freedom and to exercise it, but they don't exactly know whether it will be quite safe to trust the neighbors with it....

It is simply none of your business what other people do; nor any of the business of society what any of its members do, unless they interfere with somebody else without his or her consent; and you and all like you might as well learn this fact here and now as later; since your system of meddling interference with that which is none of your business will not be longer tolerated. If freedom be a right possessed by all individuals, it cannot matter what use be made of it. It must be adopted as the basic principle, and be assured that the results will take care of themselves. Having adopted freedom as opposed to despotism, all its logical deductions are also adopted. It is impossible that anything founded on truth should result in error. If the foundation be right the structure built upon it will not fall from any basic defects.

"But," replies the objector, "I cannot understand about this business. If there be no law to compel people to live together, everything will be in confusion, the family will be broken up; and this is the safeguard of society, morality and everything else that is good and pure. Everything will go to the bad directly if it be not maintained by all the safeguards that can be thrown around it. No! no! It will never do to break up the family."

### SCARE-CROW NO. 3

And thus scare-crow No. 3 is elevated to be in turn demolished. To begin, we deny in toto everything you have said. The very safeguards that you have thrown around the family to make it pure and holy have made instead, a community of little hot hells, in which the two principals torment each other until one or the other gives up the contest, and by which the seeds of devilism are sown in all the children who may unfortunately for themselves and society, result. These safeguards to virtue and morality have made almost every wife a prostitute and every husband a sexual monster, and compels them both, against their better natures, to continually go from bad to worse.

Compel people to live together, would you? Of all the monstrous propositions, this is the most monstrous. As a theory, it is absurd enough; but as a practice it is simply revolting infernalism. Even the condition of prostitutes, of which there is so much pretended commiseration, is to be preferred to this! They have the right to refuse to cohabit when they choose; but the poor wife is denied even this. She must submit or take a thrashing, perhaps! Why, sir, your safeguards are the allies of hell, and are responsible for more misery, more sickness and more crime than all other causes combined; and humanity as a whole, perhaps as yet unconsciously, cries to its God for deliverance. Be assured this cry will be heard and answered. For the sake of consistency, sir, you would do well to take in your family scare-crow before you and your like become utterly obnoxious.

"But," says the objector, "suppose I do, what will become of the children? If the family be left free to be broken up, they will be at the mercy of the world, not knowing who are their fathers even—a terrible dilemma, surely!"

SCARE-CROW NO. 4

This is scare-crow No. 4. Wouldn't know their fathers! Ah! That would be bad; a fearful state of things, wouldn't it? Now, do you really mean that as an objection; do you wish it to be understood that you are in earnest? You must be attempting to play a joke upon somebody! Why, sir, there isn't a person in the world who knows absolutely who his father is! There may be many who perhaps *think* they know; but thought has deceived many a one in other things, and undoubtedly has in this one as well. It is not safe, only to think, in a matter where it is assumed that positive certainty is necessary....

What will become of the children, indeed? A pretty question to ask is this, when next to nothing is now done to prevent them from going to the bad! Look at the children! What are they but a scraggy, scrawny, half made up lot! And again at the way through which they grow to maturity! Which of them at that time is really worth calling a man or a woman? He is nothing but a poor excuse for a man; and she a worse one for a woman. He has spermatorrhea, and she leucorrhœa, and both are unfit to cohabit or to reproduce themselves; and yet you talk about the children. Why, sir, you must be beside yourself.

Why do you not, in place of asking what will become of the children, ask what is becoming of them now? Go ask the fifty thousand houseless, half starved, wholly untaught children of New York city, who live from the swill-barrels of the rich Christians, what is becoming of them, and they will tell you they don't know! But it will be plain to be seen that they are going to the bad, surely. I cannot understand how it is that the critics of social freedom should be so terribly concerned about the children who are to be, when they have no concern whatever for those who are. Solicitude for children, when there are five millions of people in the United States, one-eighth of the total population, over ten years of age, who can neither read nor write! Why, it is simply absurd! There is no such thing. This pretended solicitude is something pumped up in the imaginations of these idealists as a scare-crow to prevent inquirers after freedom from finding the direct road.

If there were any such thing as solicitude for children, it would show itself in having the conditions in which they are begotten of the most favorable character. The mother, during pregnancy, would be treated as if she were performing the divinest mission of nature, where now she is too often treated more like a slave. Thousands of poor weak women are to-day performing the task of maternity, who are also compelled to labor, to the utmost extent of their strength, for their daily bread, and perhaps also to feed a drunken tyrant to whom the law has made her slave, both sexually and industrially. Care for children! Again I repeat it, they who pretend this must be fools or insane, or else think that you are both, that they may play upon you such a pretense as this. . . .

The conditions under which children are begotten and raised, are certainly about as bad as they can well be. Since they are the results of the social system, their condition should not be taken as an indication of what children ought to be under an entirely opposite order; nor as an objection to the establishment of such an order. Inaugurate the new order, and the method of rearing children will be determined by the new conditions of that order.

In the first place, however, in the new social order of society, women will be individually independent of men for support. From the beginning it will be known that they are not to be educated as sexual slaves for man, merely. In place of this, it will be well understood that no man owes them anything, and that all their intercourse will be governed by a maxim of equivalents in love. It may be necessary to inform men, but it is not to inform women, that in such conditions there will be no undesired pregnancy; whereas, now, four-fifths of the children who are born are unwelcomed.

Next, when a woman becomes pregnant, it will be held immediately that she is laboring for society in the fact that she is to replenish its natural decrease. She will become the especial care of society and, while she is performing this sacred duty, be paid the highest wages received by any class, and be treated accordingly during the entire period of gestation and lactation, when the fruit of her labor will of right belong to society and she return to her common industrial pursuits.

I know that this by the thoughtless will be considered almost a heartless proposition, since there is no love like a mother's love for her child. It will, however, be found, if patience permit the full consideration, that what is proposed will give the very greatest scope for the exhibition of the mother's love. It must not be lost sight of that the first thing to be gained by a revolution in our present social system is better men and women; and if a mother's love can in any way interfere with this result, then it should not be permitted to do so.

But before going further, a grave error that exists almost universally should be corrected. It is thoughtlessly and inconsistently held that the children belong to their parents, and because it is so held, it is the most dangerous question with which the reformer has to deal; but at the same time, of the very first importance. To say that children do not belong to their parents, is to attack a supposed right that has existed from time immemorial, and to call down upon the head of the attacking party the reprobation even of radicals. I am after the truth, however, and let it be what it may and lead where it may I shall pursue it mercilessly, well knowing that when found it will doubly repay all the expense incurred, if that be even complete ostracism.

I would not, however, ruthlessly wound or shock any tender mother's heart. I would rather show her that her love, if it be really worthy of that divine name, will incline her to desire for her child that which will make it the best man or woman. Now I will ask every mother present if this is not what the love of every mother ought to desire; and also further, if, in desiring this, any selfish love that she bears merely for her own sake, regardless of the good of her child, ought not to be ignored in the higher consideration of its best interests and through it of society? Every true mother will answer, yes! without hesitation; only those who would sacrifice their children to their own selfish love will even hesitate.

A single question will, however, show the absurdity of the theory of ownership. If parents own their children, how does it come that they ever lose their title, as they do at adult age; or again, and still more forcibly, if the title of children is in the parents, how is it that society, by its laws, claims them when, before adult age, they commit some crime; or still again, to whom is this ownership transferred when the parents die; and again, how is it that society compels the education of children? If they belong to their parents, what right has society to meddle? Answer these and then say if you can that children do not belong to society.

It is well known that, as civilization progresses and education becomes more a question of public interest, society demands more and more the conduct of the instruction of children. Public schools are now imperative, where, but a hundred years ago, there was no such system.... It is but one step beyond compulsory education to the complete charge of children. If society have the right to say how and how much a child shall be educated mentally, it certainly has the right, also, to say what the other processes of education shall be....

We have not yet disposed of all the scare-crows, and the next one that is erected to frighten the people, of freedom, is license—a most terrible spectre indeed, one from which the multitude falls back in dismay, almost convinced that it is impossible to discover freedom where this monster stands guard over the way. This monster assumes, if all restriction to liberty be removed, that license is thereby granted to everybody to do all sorts of bad things, and that a great many people will immediately proceed to do all these bad things.

First of all, every woman, except those of our household, will incontinently go to the bad, indulging in the most outrageous extremes of all sorts of debauchery; while the men, everybody excepting "ourselves" of course, will also incontinently proceed to commit rape upon every woman who is so unfortunate as to fall in their way. Age of either extreme will fail to command respect when men are free, and terror and horror will reign triumphant. So much for the assumptions.

But hold, dear sir. Are you not making yourself just a little ridiculous? Did you not say that all the women would immediately rush into the arms of every man they should meet, let it be in the street, in the car or wherever else; that even negroes would not escape the mad debauch of white women? Now observe. If this be so, upon whom are these outrages, by men, to be committed? Do you not see if every woman is of her own accord to rush to debauchery, that it will be entirely unnecessary for men to resort to any sort of force whatever, or even to resort to persuasion. A splendid commentary on woman, indeed....

All the laws that can be made regarding sex, and be in harmony with the general theory, maintained in everything else, are such as would punish sexual intercourse obtained by force—in other words, rape; and this is the end of the whole question....

License in love where consent is made a necessary qualification, by the guarantee of freedom to women to refuse, if they will, is simply an absurdity....

Marriage licenses sexuality, while nothing else does; and the horrors that are practiced under this license, are simply demoniacal; almost too horrible to be even thought of without shuddering, how much more so to relate! There is nothing else but marriage that licenses a man to debauch a woman against her will. There is no sexual license except in marriage.

But those who would save this institution by force, having attempted to defend it, and thereby having invited us to the contest, we must not hesitate to drag from their hiding-places the terrific skeletons that marriage has left in almost every household; and it must be expected that it will be done mercilessly. This infamous system that murders one-half the children in babyhood and three-fourths of the mothers, and robs almost all the rest of all happiness in this life, shall not, if it can be helped, be tolerated any longer. I have declared relentless warfare against it, and by the help of heaven, it shall be waged until the last vestige of this remnant of savagery shall be wiped from the otherwise fair face of present civilization.

Going a little backward to the early days of abolitionism, it is found that the same system of warfare that is now proposed was waged by the heroes of that freedom. They not only attacked slavery upon the question of abstract right, but they also attacked it in the concrete, in its practices. Individual instances of cruelty, as well as the general tendency of the system, were pointed out and depicted with all the terrible effect of truth. Individual offenders were compelled into the light and held up to public detestation, and were made a by-word to the fullest possible extent. The public sensibilities were shocked by actual and vivid pictures of whatever atrocities the slaveholding system developed. Many people cried shame! and denounced it as scandalous, stopping their ears and eyes lest themselves should be shocked at the knowledge that such things could be in a civilized country, and pretended to share all their sympathy with the real offender for being driven to the light, just as if it were not a thousand times worse that such things should be enacted at all. But the brave warriors rushed on in spite of their criticisms and their sensibilities until at last the institution fell, and nobody now dare say they were wrong or that aught but good has resulted; but they repeat the error nevertheless.

Now through just such experiences have the holders of sexual slaves got to be compelled. All the horrors of this slavery will have to be dragged to the light, and whenever individual offenders can be caught they must be exposed. All this may be seemingly hard; nevertheless it is the only method by which the atrocities to which the system has given birth, can be unearthed, and its own foundation shattered. Many are the tales of horror and brutal violence that have been related of negro slavery, where the lash of the driver was depicted until their hearers almost felt its stings in their own flesh, and almost the red streams flowing down their own backs, and these appealed to the souls of men and women until they were ready to do whatever was needed to destroy a monster that could cause such suffering to a single human being. But I am fully convinced that all the suffering of all the negro slaves combined, is as nothing in comparison to that which women, as a whole, suffer. There were several millions of negro slaves. There are twenty millions of women slaves. The negroes were dependent upon their masters for all the comforts of life they enjoyed; but it was to the interest of their masters to give them all of these that health demanded. Women are as much dependent upon men for their sustenance as were the negroes upon their masters, lacking the interest that they had in the negroes as personal property.

It is an unpleasant thing to say that women, in many senses, are as much slaves as were the negroes, but if it be true, ought it not to be said? I say, a thousand times, yes! And when the slavery to which they are subjected is compared to that which the negro endured, the demand for its consideration increases again, still a thousand times more.

Perhaps it may be denied that women are slaves, sexually, sold and delivered to man. But I tell you, as a class, that they are, and the conclusion cannot be escaped. Let me convince all doubters of this. Stand before me, all ye married women, and tell me how many of you would remain mistresses of your husbands' homes if you should refuse to cohabit sexually with them? Answer ye this, and then tell me that ye are free, if ye can! I tell ye that you are the sexual slaves of your husbands, bound by as terrible bonds to serve them sexually as ever a negro was bound to serve his owner, physically; and if you don't quite believe it, go home and endeavor to assert your freedom, and see to what it will lead! You may not be made to feel the inevitable lash that followed rebellion on the part of the negro, but even this is not certain; yet lashes of some sort will surely be dealt. Refuse to yield to the sexual demands of your legal master, and ten to one he will turn you into the street, or in lieu of this, perhaps, give you personal violence, even to compelling you to submit by force. Tell me that wives are not slaves! As well might you have done the same of the negroes, who, as the women do not, did not realize their condition!

... For my part I would rather be the labor slave of a master, with his whip cracking continually about my ears, my whole life, than the forced sexual slave of any man a single hour; and I know that every woman who has freedom born in her soul will shout in deepest and earnest response to this—Amen! I know what it is to be both of these. I have traveled the icy pavements of New York in mid-winter, seeking employment, with nothing on my feet except an old pair of india-rubber shoes, and a common calico dress only to cover my body, while the man who called me wife and who made me his sexual slave, spent his money upon other women. I am not speaking whereof I know not. My case may be thought an extreme one, but I know of thousands even worse. Then tell me I shall not have the right to denounce this damned system! Tell me I shall be sent to Sing Sing if I dare expose these things! Open your Sing Sings a thousand times, but none of their terrors shall stop a single word. I will tell the world, so long as I have a tongue and the strength to move it, of all the infernal misery hidden behind this horrible thing called marriage, though the Young Men's Christian Association sentence me to prison a year for every word. I have seen horrors beside which stone walls and iron bars are heaven, and I will not hold my peace so long as a system, that can produce such damnation and by which, as its author, heaven is blasphemed, exists.

Would to Heaven I could thunder these facts forth until women should be moved by a comprehension of the low degradation to which they have fallen, to open rebellion; until they should rise *en masse* and declare themselves free, resisting all sexual subjection, and utterly refusing to yield their bodies up to man until they shall grant them perfect freedom. It was not the slaves themselves who obtained their own freedom.[2] It was their noble white brothers of the North, who, seeing their condition, and realizing that though they were black, still that they were brothers, sacrificed themselves for the time to emancipate them. So it will not be the most suffering slaves of this horrible slavery who will accomplish its abolition; but it must be those who know and appreciate the terrible condition, who must, for the time, sacrifice ourselves, that their sisters may come to themselves and to own themselves.

Go preach this doctrine, then, ye who have the strength and the moral courage: No more sexual intercourse for men who do not fully consent that all women shall be free, and who do not besides this, also join the standard of the rebellion. It matters not if you be wife or not, raise your voice for your suffering sex, let the consequences to yourself be what they may. They say I have come to break up the family; I say amen to that with all my heart. I hope I may break up every family in the world that exists by virtue of sexual slavery, and I feel that the smiles of angels, the smiles of those who have gone on before, who suffered here what I have suffered and what thousands are suffering, will give me strength to brave all opposition, and to stand even upon the scaffold, if need be, that my sisters all over the world may be emancipated, may rise from slavery to the full dignity of womanhood.

# Chapter Twenty-One

*Tried as by Fire;*
or, the True and the False, Socially

> This speech, which Victoria Woodhull gave at least 150 times, includes her most famous explanations of free love. The success of the speech helped alleviate her financial woes (Underhill, The Woman Who Ran for President, 259).

For what purpose has this audience assembled; and what does it expect of me? Consider this question well now, since I propose to perform my duty regardless alike of approval or disapproval. In this duty you may listen to speech, such as, perhaps, you never heard from a public platform before.

You have been invited to hear the social problem discussed; to see it placed in the crucible of analysis to be tried by the hot flames of truth, the fire meanwhile fed by stern facts, and stirred to intensest heat, until the dross shall rise to the surface and gradually disappear in fumes which may be unpleasant to the senses, but leaving behind the purified residuum gathered, indicating clearly what is true and what false in the tested subject—the sexual relations.

This is my task, not to be explained as it progresses in terms of glittering generalities, or of poetic fancy, or in gingerly words that may leave any in doubt as to what is intended, but plainly, honestly and earnestly, so that no one can misunderstand; but which will clearly set forth the conditions requisite to the health of these relations and the ignorance and abuse producing their diseases, and show what all knew, well enough, but few dare acknowledge to themselves, even: that there is much that is rotten in Denmark.

You are here as my guests, knowing in advance upon what subject I should speak; and I shall expect from you, individually and collectively, that courteous treatment which would be my due under any other circumstances than these, in which I might be your hostess, and you my guests. I shall not utter a word, phrase or sentence, except such as I conscientiously believe to be true, and that ought, for the good of the race, to be uttered. Nor shall I, in the course of my speech, plain, bold, even bald as it may be, use any expressions that, by the remotest construction, trench upon the boundaries of the vulgar. I shall, however, call things by their plain, Saxon names, holding that there is no part of the beautiful, human mechanism for which the pure in heart and thought ought be able to blush while it is under consideration. . . .

We now understand each other. It is not expected, it is not desired, that I withhold any fact I may have to offer, or advice I may have to give, regarding a subject which, more than any other, ought to command the attention of all enlightened people; but which, from falsely conceived ideas and a wrongly educated public opinion, is, more than any other, anathematized by almost the whole world.

People may pretend to blush, and the editors may write of me as indecent and vulgar, and say I have no shame to speak as I shall, what they will not dare to print. But, after all, ought not they and you and I rather to blush with real shame that such things as I shall mention, exist to be spoken about? I say, shame upon the newspapers, upon the preachers, teachers and doctors, that it is necessary for me to tell you what they ought long ago to have freely discussed, and have thus relieved me of this unpleasant task! I say, shame upon them all! and if the papers must perforce reproduce this word, let them be honest enough to properly apply it to the existing facts that of themselves are obscene and vulgar, and not to the speaker, who deals with them, not because it is either her nature or pleasure, but because she desires, like Boards of Health dealing with nuisances, to abate them.

Therefore if any vulgar or indecent thoughts arise in the mind of any person when these things are discussed, they do not attach to the speaker, but belong wholly to the individual; hence whatever may be thought now, or said hereafter, by any of you, or written about them at any time, is, by no possible, far-fetched construction, an insult or imputation offered me. On the contrary it is a degradation to their subjects or authors, indicating the moral standpoint from which they, and not I, view the subject; and an insult to their mothers, to be explained by bad rearing and worse moral teaching. So do not think that, when I pick up the paper and read the nasty things that are said of me, I feel insulted or hurt; but rather believe that I pity those who write them, and feel that they have need of a loving mother or a darling sister, to snatch them from a degradation in which they can see only vulgarity or vileness, where there is, really, nothing except purity and holiness.

If any of these mothers or sisters have such sons or brothers, let me beg of them to never let their yearning affections cease their efforts, nor their entreaties and tears to flow, until they are rescued—until they are restored to manhood.

No man who respects his mother or loves his sister, can speak disparagingly of any woman; however low she may seem to have sunk, she is still a woman. I want every man to remember this. Every woman is, or, at some time, has been a sister or daughter; and if she be now "out upon the cold world," do not forget that some son or brother helped, perhaps forced her there. Nor can it be amiss for men to ask: "Am I pure enough to make my judgments just?"

Let these thoughts check the rising frown and the cruel words you would bestow upon any unfortunate woman, in whatever condition, and call forth your love and sympathy instead, in some practical way for her rescue or assistance. . . .

The sexual relations of humanity are fundamental to its continuous existence, and are, therefore, the most important into which men and women enter. It is vital that they should be entered into properly, that they should be understood clearly, and, still more so, that they should be lived rightly. Nevertheless, the world has virtually declared that this shall not be. It denies all knowledge of them to the young, and permits the youth and the maiden to walk blindfolded into their exploration, ignorant even of their own functions, only taking special care that the journey, once begun, may never be retraced or stopped. It has left the travelers, as it were, in the mid-ocean of what may be their eternal happiness, if the course pursued be right; or their certain destruction if the chosen way be wrong, without chart or compass, subjected to winds which drive them, they know not where, and to currents and counter-currents, for which no haven of safety is provided; and, alas! they too often go down to untimely graves, victims to a willful ignorance. Such are the results of modern social regulations.

I am conducting a campaign against marriage, with the view of revolutionizing the present theory and practice. I have strong convictions that, as a bond or promise to love another until death, it is a fraud upon human happiness; and that it has outlived its day of usefulness. These convictions make me earnest, and I enter the fight, meaning to do the institution all possible harm in the shortest space of time; meaning to use whatever weapons may fall in my way with which to stab it to the heart, so that its decaying carcase may be buried, and clear the way for a higher and a better institution.

I speak only what I know, when I say that the most intelligent and really virtuous people of all classes have outgrown this institution; that they are constantly and systematically unfaithful to it; despise and revolt against it as a slavery; and only submit to a semblance of fidelity to it, from the dread of a falsely educated public opinion and a sham morality, which are based on the ideas of the past, but which no longer really represent the convictions of anybody.

Nor is this hypocritical allegiance the only or the greatest or gravest consideration that is capturing the opinions of the really intelligent. It is rapidly entering into the public thought, that there should be, at least, as much attention given to breeding and rearing children, as is given to horses, cattle, pigs, fowls and fruit. A little reflection shows that the scientific propagation of children is a thing of paramount importance; as much above and beyond that of personal property as children are above dogs and cats. And this conviction, practically considered, also shows that the union of the sexes, for propagation, should be consummated under the highest and best knowledge, and in such manner and by such methods as will produce the best results. These considerations are so palpable that they cannot be ignored; and they look to the early supercedure of the institution of marriage by some better system for the maintenance of women as mothers, and children as progeny. This is as much a foregone conclusion with all the best thinkers of today as was the approaching dissolution of slavery, no more than ten years before its final fall.

But in the meantime men and women tremble on the verge of the revolution, and hesitate to avow their convictions; but aware of their rights, and urged by the impulses of their natures, they act upon the new theories while professing allegiance to the old. In this way an organized hypocrisy has become a main feature of modern society, and poltroonery, cowardice and deception rule supreme in its domain. The continuation of such falsity for a generation, touching one of the most sacred interests of humanity, will eradicate the source of honesty from the human soul. Every consideration of expediency, therefore, demands that some one lead the van in a relentless warfare against marriage, so that its days may be made short.

This is my mission. I entered the contest, bringing forward, in addition to the wise and powerful words of others, such arguments as my own inspirations and reflections suggested. No sooner had I done this, however, than the howl of persecution sounded in my ears. Instead of replying to my arguments, I was assaulted with shameful abuse; and I was astonished to find that the most persistent and slanderous and foul-mouthed accusations came from precisely those whom I happened often to know should have been, from their practices, the last to raise their voices against any one, and whom, if I had felt so disposed, I could have easily silenced. But simply as personality or personal defense, or spiteful retort, I have almost wholly abstained during these years of sharp conflict from making use of the rich resources at my command for this kind of attack and defense, and, passing the vile abuse which has beset me, have steadfastly pressed on in the warfare.

In a single instance only have I departed from this course. Circumstances conspired to put me in possession of certain facts regarding the most prominent divine in the land, and from him I learned that he too was not only false to the old dispensation, but unfaithful to the new—a double hypocrisy, over which I hesitated many months, doubting if I should use it. It was not that I desired or had any right to personally attack this individual; but something had to be done to break down the partition walls of prejudice that prevented public consideration of the sexual problem, and fully to launch it upon the tide of popular discussion. This revolution, like every other that ever preceded it, and as every other that ever will follow it, must have its terrific cost, if not in blood and treasure, then still in the less tangible but equally real sentimental injury of thousands of sufferers. It was necessary that somebody should be hurt. I cast the thunderbolt into the very centre of the socio-religio-moralistic camp of the enemy and struck their chieftain, and the world trembled at the blow. In twenty years not anybody will say that I was wrong, any more than anybody now says that the old leaders of the anti-slavery revolution were wrong in attacking slavery in the concrete.

My purpose was accomplished. Whereas, before, none had dared to broach the sexual question, it is now on everybody's lips; and where it would have been impossible for a man, even, to address a public, promiscuous audience anywhere without being mobbed, a woman may now travel the country over, and from its best rostrums, speak the last truth about sexuality, and receive respectful attention, even enthusiastic encouragement. The world has come to its senses—has been roused to the real import and meaning of this terrible question, and to realize that only through its full and candid examination may we hope to save the future from utter demoralization.

But why do I war upon marriage? I reply frankly: First, because it stands directly in the way of any improvement in the race, insisting upon conditions under which improvement is impossible; and second, because it is, as I verily believe, the most terrible curse from which humanity now suffers, entailing more misery, sickness and premature death than all other causes combined. It is at once the bane of happiness to the present, and the demon of prophetic miseries to the future—miseries now concealed beneath its deceptive exterior, gilded over by priestcraft and law, to be inwrought in the constitutions of coming generations to mildew and poison their lives.

Of what in reality does this thing consist, which, while hanging like a pall over the world, is pretendedly the basis of its civilization? The union of the opposites in sex is an instinct inherent in the constitutions of mankind; but legal marriage is an invention of man, and so far as it performs anything, it defeats and perverts this natural instinct. Marriage is a license for sexual commerce to be carried on without regard to the consent or dissent of this instinct. Everything else that men and women may desire to do, except to have sexual commerce, may be and is done without marriage.

Marriage, then, is a license merely—a permission to do something that it is inferred or understood ought not to be done without it. In other words, marriage is an assumption by the community that it can regulate the sexual instincts of individuals better than they can themselves; and they have been so well regulated that there is scarcely such a thing known as a natural sexual instinct in the race; indeed, the regulations have been so at war with nature that this instinct has become a morbid disease, running rampant or riotous in one sex, and feeding its insatiable maw upon the vitality of the other, finally resulting in disgust or impotency in both.

Isn't this a pretty commentary on regulation? Talk of Social Evil bills![1] The marriage law is the most damnable Social Evil bill—the most consummate outrage on woman—that was ever conceived. Those who are called prostitutes, whom these bills assume to regulate, are free women, sexually, when compared to the slavery of the poor wife. They are at liberty, at least to refuse; but she knows no such escape. "Wives, submit yourselves to your husbands," is the spirit and the universal practice of marriage.

Of all the horrid brutalities of this age, I know of none so horrid as those that are sanctioned and defended by marriage. Night after night there are thousands of rapes committed, under cover of this accursed license; and millions—yes, I say it boldly, knowing whereof I speak—millions of poor, heart-broken, suffering wives are compelled to minister to the lechery of insatiable husbands, when every instinct of body and sentiment of soul revolts in loathing and disgust. All married persons know this is truth, although they may feign to shut their eyes and ears to the horrid thing, and pretend to believe it is not. The world has got to be startled from this pretense into realizing that there is nothing else now existing among pretendedly enlightened nations, except marriage, that invests men with the right to debauch women, sexually, against their wills. Yet marriage is held to be synonymous with morality! I say, eternal damnation sink such morality!

When I think of the indignities which women suffer in marriage, I cannot conceive how they are restrained from open rebellion. Compelled to submit their bodies to disgusting pollution! Oh, Shame! where hast thou fled, that the fair face of womanhood is not suffused with thy protesting blushes, stinging her, at least into self-respect, if not into freedom itself! Am I too severe? No, I am only just!

Prate of the abolition of slavery! There was never servitude in the world like this one of marriage. It not only holds the body to whatever polluting use—abstracting its vitality, prostituting its most sacred functions, and leaving them degraded, debauched and diseased—but utterly damning the soul for all aspiration, and sinking it in moral and spiritual torpor. Marriage not slavery! Who shall dare affirm it? Let woman practically assert her sexual freedom and see to what it will lead! It is useless to mince terms. We want the truth; and that which I have about this abomination I will continue to give, until it is abolished.

It is useless to cry, "Peace! Peace!" when there is no peace. It is worse than useless to cry, "Freedom! Freedom!" when there is nothing but slavery. Let those who will, however, in spite of the truth, go home and attempt to maintain it there, and they will wake up to find themselves sold, delivered and bound, legally, to serve their masters sexually, but, refusing to do which, there will be a penalty, if not the lash. Now, husbands! Now, wives! Isn't this true? You know it is. And isn't it shameful that it is true?

Is this too sweeping? What was it that condemned slavery! Was it that all slaves were cruelly treated? Not the most ultra-Abolitionist ever pretended it! They admitted that the majority were contented, comfortable and happy. Can the same be said, truly, of the slaves to marriage, now?

But it was claimed and proven, as I claim and shall prove of marriage, that the instances of extreme cruelty were sufficiently numerous to condemn the system, and to demand its abolition. Proportionally, the instances of extreme cruelty in marriage are double what they were in slavery, and cover a much broader field, involving all the known methods by which the body can be tortured and the heart crushed. I could narrate personal cases of various kinds, for a week, and not exhaust my stock; but I cannot pause to do so. Judged by the logic of the past, this institution stands condemned, and will be soon relegated to the limbo of the past.

But there is another picture of this holy institution, scarcely less to be deprecated than are its actual cruelties; and little, if any, less degrading to womanhood: All men and women now living together, who ought to continue to so live, would so continue were marriage laws repealed. Is this true or false? This depends upon the truth or falsity of the following further propositions: Marriage may be consummated by men and women who love mutually; or, marriage may be consummated by men and women who have no love. If it be said that the former is false and the latter true, it is denied that love has anything to do with marriage—an affirmation, virtually, that they who hate may marry rightly; but if, on the contrary, the former is true and the latter false, it is agreed, constructively, that all I ever said or ever can say is true.

Now which is it? Has love, or ought it to have anything to do with marriage? Who will dare say that love should not be a precedent to marriage? But when this is affirmed, the legitimate corollary is not seen: That, since marriage should not begin without love, it should cease when love is gone. To accept the former, is to declare the latter. And no logician, however subtle, can escape it. Nor can you escape it; nor could I, although I labored for years to do so.

But if there are any who are in doubt as to what is right and true, I offer a test that will decide it. Let the married who live together, who would separate were the law repealed, rise! Not any here of that stripe; or, if there are, they are ashamed to make a public confession of it. I should be so, too, were I sailing the voyage of life in such a ship. Ask any audience, or any individual, this question, and the result would be the same. What is the inference? Clearly that, if people really do live together who do not love, they are ashamed of it, and, consequently, of the law that holds them; and that they want the world to think that they love each other, and choose to live together on that account, regardless of the law.

Who is there in the community who would like to have it understood that there is no love at home? Isn't it the fact, on the contrary, that those whose homes are loveless, and who fight and wrangle and fuss continually take special pains to conceal these things from the world? Everybody knows it is. What more sweeping condemnation could there be than this, both of the law which compels it and the practice itself? None! It is the hot-bed of hypocrisy, deceit and lust, and is doing more to demoralize the world than all other practices combined.

I am justified, therefore, in concluding that all people who are not practical free lovers, living together for love, are theoretically so, and are ashamed to confess that their practices do not accord with their theories; or, in other words, are ashamed that their practice is enforced lust instead of free love. These are the alternatives, and the only ones, and I don't intend that the people shall escape them. Every one of you—every one of the people generally—either practices Free Love or enforced lust, and the world shall understand when people denounce me as a Free Lover they announce themselves as enforced lusters; and I'll placard their backs and they shall walk up and down the world with this mark of depravity, as they have intended that I should do for having the moral courage, which they lack, to make my theories and practices agree.

There is but one objection, then, to the abolition of this last and greatest of all the slaveries, that, from the popular standpoint, has any validity whatever. This one is the *dernier resort*[2] to which every opposing orator flies when driven from other positions: What will become of the children? Ah! That is the rub, is it? And it is asked with an air of *nonchalance* and self-complacency that seems to say, "Now I have you on the hip." This is the question that everybody asks; but it is not seen that it is answered when the other position is abandoned. The assumption is this: if there were no marriage "the family" would cease to exist, and children would be left on the world. But this preposterous proposition is refuted by the denial and proof that "the family" exists by virtue of law. If the law were abrogated, and men and women should generally live on as now, which they say they would by denying that they live together on account of the law, what would be the difficulty about the children? And yet this bugbear has been pumped up into the imaginations of the people until it is regarded almost universally as an antidote to all allegations against marriage.

But aside from all this there are direct proofs, equally fatal to the children antidote. Are there men and women here who, in the face of this audience, or anywhere else, who, in the face of any other audience, would dare stand up and confess that they would abandon their children if the law of marriage were repealed? I have never been able to find such a person. If there are such here I want to see them. Barnum would pay a big price for such animals. I shall never be able to accept the doctrine of total depravity as applicable to any person until I meet such a specimen. The Darwinian order of descent acknowledges no such connecting link.

Oh, no! Of course WE could never neglect our children under any circumstances, but we fear that our neighbors might, therefore it wouldn't be quite expedient to give them an opportunity. If I were to go to your neighbors they would say the same of you. So the world goes on—one-half of it submitting to a semblance of law which they really despise, pretending that it is necessary on their neighbors' account—the old pharisaical godliness, "I am holier than thou," and I thank God that "I am not as other men are."

If people are really honest, however, in this opinion of their neighbors they should settle the matter. Let them go to their neighbors and say, "Now, my friends, here is a law upon the statute books that is an expensive one to administer, which, so far as I am concerned, might as well be repealed; but I fear if it be done that you would abandon your children and perhaps do a great many other bad things that I, with my superior honor and manhood, could not stoop to do." My opinion is that neighbors would help them out of doors much more rapidly than they entered, especially if there should be heavy boots ready for service, with this advice gratis, if in the rapidity of the movement it shouldn't be forgotten: "You had better go home and take care of your own family, and you won't have so much time to worry yourself about mine."

It is this stuff that is the matter with the world. Everybody, individually, is ready for freedom, but regards everybody else, collectively, as being in danger. Everybody is afraid that everybody else's wife and daughters would go to the bad if social freedom were to obtain, and their children to the dogs if the leash of the law were to be loose. And these are what are offered as arguments against the introduction of freedom into the social relations.

It is an imputation that neither you, nor I, nor anybody else would submit to for a moment were we to consider its insolence. It is an insult alike to the manhood of man and the womanhood of woman, and an outrage upon good sense and common decency.

But I would not leave the children [in] question under the impression that I think their present conditions are by any means what they ought to be. Indeed I believe that they could not well be worse, and that an equally radical revolution is requir[ed] [in] the methods of rearing and educating the young as there is [in] begetting them.[3] But right begetting stands first in importance, hence the marriage questions the first one to be revolutionized.

Without going into details, such methods for rearing and educating children should obtain as will give to them the right to live to adult age, each having had equal advantages in all directions with every other child; that shall assure each the capacity and acquirements for good citizenship; and equal pecuniary endowments, so that all may begin adult life equal. Freedom without equality is a fraud; and both these, without justice, a snare. There is but one question to ask: How can children be born, reared and instructed to make them the best men and women, physically, mentally and morally. If the answer demand the abrogation of so-called parental rights and authority, they must go. The best interests of children, at whatever cost, is the proper motto. It's useless to waste time upon the present generation. Let it go; but its ignorance and stupid blundering should not be transmitted to the next.

Nor should one-half of all the children born continue to die before reaching the age of five years, sacrificed, as they now are, to the inexcusable ignorance of mothers—murdered, it ought rather to be said, by the popular barbarity which condones ignorance of sexual matters. This fact is a commentary upon our social relations that transforms them into horrid tragedies and stamps the mark of Cain upon every mother. When a ship founders at sea, with the loss of a few hundred lives, the whole world is shocked at the horror; but it sleeps quietly over the still greater horror of double that number of children—babes, almost—falling victims, daily, to these fell destroyers, the so-called safeguards of society, maintained by the canting hypocrisy of its fifty thousand ministerial frauds who know better, and the sham morality and mock-modesty of their willing dupes. . . .

Infancy and childhood ought to be the most healthy periods of life; but they are ten times more fatal than any other. Of this sickening fact there can be but one verdict: Cut off at the age of from one day to five years, by maternal ignorance. This is still more evident when we remember that, from the very moment children begin to take care of themselves, the death rate diminishes. Think of these things, and then let it be said, if it can, that the social question ought not to be discussed publicly! Why, there is nothing else worthy to be discussed, so long as this remains unsolved! It should be the topic of conversation at the breakfast table, at dinner, at supper—everywhere—until the whole matter is well understood by everybody.

Will the press dare, hereafter, to condemn me for pressing it upon the attention of parents—for showing them the fearful ignorance and its frightful results? No! not directly; but instead of reporting what I say, so that the public may learn, they will daub me with the feculence of their own thoughts, and say I am vulgar and indecent, and ought to be avoided by everybody; and the too-confiding people will repeat the villainous lies in good faith.

A step beyond marriage as a means to gain sexual relations reaches the relations themselves, their uses and abuses. Here a query arises: Which is the end to be gained? Is it marriage merely, regardless of the character of the relations which it legalizes; or is it proper, natural, healthful, useful relations, such as will bless the parties themselves and the children who result? In other words, is it happiness, and peace, and comfort, and health, and all the good which can follow; or is it the legal union regardless of results?

Let us see. There will scarcely be found in this late day any intelligent person who will maintain that marriage ought ever to be consummated by persons between whom there is no love. The argument is, that men and women who love each other may consummate that love after being legally married but not otherwise; and if either party refuse to consummate the marriage, it becomes void. This establishes the theory that the principal feature of marriage is legal. But this controverts the common consent that love is a necessary precedent. Almost the whole word is in a "mull" over the confusion of ideas caused by the attempt to make these contradictions harmonize—desiring to live out their interior convictions, but fearing to do so lest they incur the legal or social penalty; desiring that their natural instincts and sentiments should be their guides, but fearing to let them lest they be accounted followers of the baser passions.

The law, then, and the real convictions of the people are at variance; but since the latter are inherent in the constitution of man, while the former is a contrivance of his intellect, invented for specific purposes, it must be concluded that the latter ought to take precedence in determining the conduct of life. And when it is remembered that the law binds together only those people who otherwise would separate, this conclusion becomes inevitable.

After careful observation I have deliberately concluded that there are two classes only who have anything more than an imaginary interest in maintaining the marriage system: The hypocritical priests who get their fees for forging the chains and the blackguard lawyers who get bigger ones for breaking the fetters. The former have an average of ten dollars a job, and some of them a hundred jobs a year; while the latter, not quite up to the former in number, to keep even with them, raise their average price per job to two hundred and fifty dollars. A thousand dollars a year for the priests! How should people know whether they ought to marry or not without asking their consent? Of course marriage is divine! A thousand dollars a year for the lawyers! How could people be supposed to know whether they ought to separate or not until the lawyer has got his fee? Of course virtue must have a legal standard. How could morality and modesty be preserved unless the priest got his ten dollars; or how could husbands and wives be prevented from killing each other unless the lawyer got his two hundred and fifty? Will the priest ever cease his cant about the former, or the lawyer change the law about the latter so long as the people are fools enough to pay them fees? They who suppose they may, don't yet understand how much divinity there is in this marriage business.

The real question at issue then is one entirely apart from law, relating wholly to the conditions that make up the unity, whether they are such as judged by the results, warrant the unity that is sought. What are proper and what improper sexual relations is the problem to be solved, and it is that one which of all others is most fraught with the interests, the happiness and the real well-being of humanity. Upon these relations, as I shall show, depend not only the health, happiness and prosperity of the present generation, but the very existence of future generations.

That existence is involved in these relations. If they be pure and good and withal natural, which they must be to be pure and good, then the existence which they make possible will be of the same character; but if they be impure, bad, and withal unnatural, which if they are they must be impure and bad, then the existence which they make possible will be of like character. A pure fountain sends forth pure waters, but the stream flowing from an impure source will assuredly be unclean. To make the fountains of life—the sexual relations—pure, is the work of the reformer, so that the streams they send forth may flow through coming ages uncontaminated by any inherited contagion.

There are a few propositions necessary to be laid down that will become self-evident as the subject develops: 1. A man or woman who has perfect physical health, has natural and healthful sexual relations. 2. A man or woman, married or single, old or young, professional prostitute or *roue*, or a professed nun or celibate, who has bad general health—and suffers from any chronic disease—has unnatural and unhealthy sensual conditions. 3. A man and woman, living together, who have perfect physical health, have natural and healthful sexual relations, and will have healthy offspring. Such a union is God-ordained, if it do not have the approval of the law or the sanction of the priest; and no man can put it asunder. If either or both of the parties to a union have generally poor physical health—suffer from any chronic disease—such parties have unnatural and unhealthful sexual relations, and their progeny will be puling, weakly, miserable, damned. Such a union is God-condemned if it have the approval of all the laws, and the blessing of all the priests in the world; and as corollary to all these, this: All diseases not to be attributed to so-called accidental causes are the result of improper, or the want of proper, sexual, conditions; and this applies to all ages and to both sexes.

It may now be asked: What are proper sexual conditions? I reply: Sexual commerce that is based upon reciprocal love and mutual desire, and that ultimates in equal and mutual benefit, is proper and healthful; while improper sexual commerce is that which is not based upon reciprocal love and mutual desire, and that cannot, therefore, ultimate in equal or mutual benefit. Children begotten by the former commerce will never be bad children physically, mentally or morally; but such as are begotten by the latter commerce will inevitably be bad children, either physically, mentally or morally, or, which is more likely to be the case, partially bad throughout.

I desire to be fully understood upon this part of the subject. I have been generally denounced by the press as an advocate of promiscuousness in the sexual relations. I want you to fully comprehend the measure of truth there is in this charge. Hence I repeat that there is but one class of cases where commerce of the sexes is in strict accordance with nature, and that, in this class, there are always present, first, love of each by each of the parties; second, a desire for the commerce on the part of each, arising from the previous love; and third, mutual and reciprocal benefit.

Of improper sexual commerce there are several classes: First, that class where it is claimed by legal right, as in marriage; second, where the female, to please the male, accords it without any desire on her own part; third, where, for money, for a home, for any present, as a payment for any claim, whether pecuniary or of gratitude, or for any motive whatever other than love, the female yields it to the male; fourth, where there is mutual love and desire, but where, for any reason, there is such want of adaptation as to make mutual consummation impossible.

This is the promiscuousness that I advocate now, and that have, from the first, advocated.

Will the representatives of the press, who have covered me with their abuse until I am regarded with horror all over the land as a person whose presence is contamination and whose touch contagion, correct their foul lies by stating these propositions, and, so far as they can at this late day, do me justice? We shall see!

"But," said a prominent woman of this country, with whom I was recently discussing these maxims in sexuality, "how are you going to prevent all this intercourse of the sexes, which you condemn?"

"Ah!" said I, "that's the question. I have no right nor has anybody else any right to prevent it in any such sense as you infer."

This is a matter that must be remanded back from law, back from public interference, to individuals, who alone have the sovereignty over it. No person or set of persons, however learned and wise, have any right, power or capacity, to determine legally for another when commerce is proper or when it shall occur. It is not a matter of law to be administered by the public, but a question of education to be gained by individuals—a scientific problem to expound and elucidate which, should be one of the chief duties of all teachers and reformers. Every person in the world, before arriving at the age in which the sexual instinct is developed, should be taught all there is known about its uses and abuses, so that he or she shall not ignorantly drift upon the shoals whereon so many lives are wrecked.

I advocate complete freedom for sexuality the same as for religion. The charge of promiscuousness is laid in this fact, and some intelligent minds have thought it was a sound charge, until its inconsistency and utter absurdity have been pointed out to them. This is the proposition: I advocate sexual freedom for all people—freedom for the monogamist to practice monogamy, for the varietist to be a varietist still, for the promiscuous to remain promiscuous. Am I, therefore, an advocate of promiscuousness, variety or monogamy? Not necessarily either. I might do all this and be myself a celibate and an advocate of celibacy. To advocate freedom in sexual things and also the right of individuals to choose each for himself to which class to belong, is by no means synonymous with the advocacy of the class which he chooses. Advocating the right to do a thing and advocating the doing of that thing are two entirely separate and different matters.

Is not this too clear to be misunderstood? I will make it still clearer, lest some may not see it. As I said, I not only advocate sexual freedom, but also religious freedom. I claim that every individual has the right to be a Pagan, Christian, Jew, Mohammedan, Quaker, Oneida Perfectionist, Calvinist, Baptist, Methodist, Trinitarian, Unitarian, Universalist, or whatever else he has a mind or the will to be. Every person advocates the same right—the same freedom—and I am sure if an attempt were made to subvert this right in this country, every hand would be raised against it. I am, however, neither one nor any of these, but a Spiritualist, and I bend all my religious energies to the advocacy of Spiritualism.

Nobody would think of calling me a Romanist[4] because I say that everybody has the right to be a Catholic; but, transfer the question from religion to sexuality, and because I advocate the same theory for this that I do for religion, I am denounced as an advocate of promiscuousness. Did any of you ever hear that I ever said that the monogamist has no right to practice monogamy? Was I ever known to assert that all people should be promiscuous, or varietists? No! What am I, then? I cannot be all of them. Why then class me as promiscuous? I will tell you why: Simply to brand me with supposed infamy, and to frighten the people so that they shall not come to an understanding of these things. That's the reason, and the press knows it.

There is an honest difference of opinion among its advocates in regard to what will be the result of sexual freedom, but none in regard to freedom itself. Some thinkers of wide experience in social matters have concluded that ultimately there will be no constant sexual relation; that change will be the order of society. Others, equally honest and conscientious, believe that a select variety will be the order; while others, still, hold just as firmly that the perfected union of one man and one woman is the highest order. I do not remember ever to have made a speech on this subject in which I did not affirm my belief in the latter order. Not because I desired to soften the feeling against me by so doing, but because I conscientiously believe that in such conditions will be found the highest attainable happiness; and I urge education, discussion and enlightenment upon the subject, believing that they will tend to carry the people toward this condition. Therefore, while I advocate the right of the promiscuously inclined to be promiscuous if they will, I ought to be classed as a monogamist. But if freedom be right in the abstract it does not matter whether monogamy or promiscuousness be the ultimate, since let it be which it may it will be right.

I cannot illustrate the ridiculous ideas of promiscuousness better than by relating an incident that once happened to me while traveling from Washington to New York. I was approached by an intelligent woman, who, learning who I was, desired to hear my opinions for herself. In the conversation that ensued she remarked, "Oh, Mrs. Woodhull, is it true that you are a promiscuous woman?"

I replied, quietly, "Well, I do not know what you would call promiscuousness. Let me ask you a question, and then I may be able to determine."

Looking her in the face I saw the figure 4 appear upon her forehead. I said, "Madame, I believe you have known at least four different men sexually. Is that true?"

"Oh, yes! I am now living with my fourth husband."

Turning away from her with affected disdain I replied, "Madame, you are altogether too promiscuous for me."

Society permits a woman to have a dozen men, legally, in as many years, and she is all right. She's sound on the Goose Question.[5] But if a woman live with her sexual mate without the payment of the fee, she is all wrong; she is a prostitute. And this is called purity, called morality! I say damn such morals. Such purity stinks. Logically, there is room for no other conclusion than this: That let the highest order of sexuality be what it may, the monogamists have no more right to enforce monogamy by law, as the rule of society, than the promiscuous have to enforce promiscuousness as the order to be observed. Society does, however, attempt to enforce monogamy, but it makes a bad failure.

The Oneida Communists, on the contrary, do not permit monogamic attachments.[6] If they are found springing up, the parties are compelled to separate. If we are to judge which is the better rule by the results, nobody who has ever visited Oneida will hesitate a moment in the decision. Judged by its fruits—by its prosperity, its honesty, its morality, its health—Oneida is the best order of society now on the earth. Its enforced promiscuousness is preferable even to our enforced monogamy, and for very good reasons, which will become evident further on.

Suffice it, here, that promiscuous sexuality among people who have no love attachments, is not so debased a condition as is that which prevails so widely in marriage, where passion in the male, vents itself at the expense of disgust in the female. I know these are bitter pills for those to swallow who think that purity consists in fidelity to marriage. But whether bitter or sweet, they are true; and though I may be cursed now, if they purge the people of their false and absurd notions about sexual purity, I shall some day have their thanks for administering them. I offer you the remedy of Free Love as an antidote for enforced lust, and the world will have to take it before the disease can be cured.

So much for promiscuousness. But what of prostitution, what of love and what of lust? Terrible words are these in the vocabulary of modern society, but still more so in that of social reform! The question with it is, not as to what is the popular meaning of these terms, but what is their natural, their scientific significance as tested by exact analysis or the stern logic of experience?

Prostitution is popularly applied to certain kinds of sexual commerce but it has a much wider application, extending to every faculty, function and capacity of the body and mind. It means a perverted, unnatural or excessive use of a capacity. A person who overworks his body or brain is a prostitute. The unhealthy use of anything is its prostitution. They prostitute their stomachs who over-eat or over-drink. Therefore, prostitution, sexually, means a great deal more than intercourse obtained in houses of ill-fame for money. In a scientific sense, it means all sexual commerce that has not a proper basis in love and desire. There may be prostitution in marriage, and proper commerce in the bawdy house. It depends upon the specific conditions attending the act itself, and not where or how it is obtained.

In the exact sense, the woman who sells her body promiscuously is no more a prostitute than she is who sells herself in marriage without love. She is only a different kind of a prostitute. Nor are either of them any more prostitutes than are the countless wives who nightly yield their unwilling bodies to lecherous husbands, whose aim is sexual gratification without regard to the effect upon their victims. The difference is this: In the latter cases the men have legal permission to use the women whether they desire or object, while in the former the woman consults her own wishes—it is a slip of paper costing twenty-five cents and upward, good during life, that a man carries about with him to save the expense of purchasing, from time to time, elsewhere.

It's a sharp trick played by men upon women, by which they acquire the legal right to debauch them without cost, and to make it unnecessary for them to visit professional prostitutes, whose sexual services can only be obtained for money. Now, isn't this true? Men know it is. Those who haven't a wife know very well that they procure for money what they would otherwise have by law. And what is more disgraceful still, is that thousands of men marry because they cannot afford the cost of satisfying their sexual demands with prostitutes. You and I and everybody else know that what I say is true, and yet the sanctity of marriage—the holy sacrament—is talked of as if it had existence! Bosh! It's an insult to common honesty to trade in such stuff and call it holy. Holy! To me it is nastiness; or if there is any worse name, call it that.

I know hundreds of wives who confess privately that they would not live another day with their husbands if they had any other method of support; and yet pass the poor prostitute as though her touch were leprous. As between the two, the legal prostitute is the more depraved at heart. It is axiomatic, that only those women are really pure whose sympathies go out to the unfortunate whom society has driven to the street and brothel by its unjust anathema; who can visit them without contamination; whose virtue is so assured that it is above suspicion. If there is any sister in this place so low that no other woman will visit her, tell me; there will my feet wend their way. If there is any child so wretched that none will care for it, there will my mother's heart wander.

Why should Christian women shun the outcasts of society? The Master whom they profess, habitually made them His companions. What excuse can they offer for a departure from His example? None! But it adds to their long lists of crimes the sin of hypocrisy. Let them beware lest the harlots get into the Kingdom before them.

What a commentary upon the divinity of marriage are the watering places during the summer seasons! The mercenary "mammas" trot out their daughters on exhibition, as though they were so many stud of horses, to be hawked to the highest bidder. It's the man who can pay the most money who is sought; makes no difference how he got it, nor what are his antecedents. It doesn't matter if he is just from the hands of the physician, cured of a loathsome disease; if he have the cash he is the man. To him who bids highest, in the parlance of the auctioneer, the article is knocked down.

Everybody knows that this is the ruling spirit, not at watering places only, but in so-called best society everywhere. Marriages of love become rarer year after year, while those of convenience are proportionately on the increase. How much better is this than the actual exposure and sale, of Oriental practice?[7] Yet we boast of superior intelligence, purity and morals! And we prate of the holy marriage covenant! Verily, we "make clean the outside of the platter, but within are dead men's bones and all uncleanliness."[8]

I respect and honor the needy woman who, to procure food for herself and child, sells her body to some stranger for the necessary money; but for that legal virtue which sells itself for a lifetime for a home, with an abhorrence of the purchaser, and which at the same time says to the former, "I am holier than thou," I have only the supremest contempt. If there is anything that is vulgar it is a modern fashionable marriage. The long retinue, the church, the priest—all to do what? To give the bride, sexually, to the bridegroom. It is a public notice that these people, who have been everything else to each other, are now united sexually. Why, modesty itself should forbid such a parade!

But would you break up that which is called prostitution? The women can do it if they will. The virtuous women of an eastern city recently made an effort. They called secret meetings, and resolved to visit "the houses" and learn who it was that supported them, and then afterward to ostracize them. The visiting began. The New York papers were filled with the matter; day after day column after column was devoted to this crusade. After a week it suddenly stopped. The press was mystified. What was the matter? Had the women succeeded? Nothing could be learned. Finally one of the keenest of the metropolitan Bohemians determined to solve the matter. He visited this inland city; but not a word from the recently zealous women. They said they had abandoned the project; but would give no reason. At last he visited the keepers of the houses, and from them he got the key to the sudden closing of the campaign. "The women," they said, "pressed their investigations until they pressed themselves into the faces of the best men of the city, some of them their husbands and brothers; and considering that they could not ostracize this class of persons they went home and delivered 'Caudle Lectures'[9] instead."

Now I will tell you wherein they failed, and why they were not honest. When they found their best men—their husbands and brothers—were supporting these women—consorting with them of course—they should have taken them home and seated them at their tables beside their companion, and said: "If you are good enough for our husbands to consort with, you are good enough to sit at our tables with them, and to occupy their homes with us, and to visit where we visit, and generally to be our companions."

If the women, in every city where there are professional prostitutes, would organize, and agree to bring the women home to the men who visit them, prostitution, so called, would be abolished at once. It is the women who stand in the way. They, knowing that their husbands visit these women, continue to live on, doing their best to damn the women, but saying nothing about the men. They probably forget that the wife who consorts with the man whom she knows consorts with prostitutes, is just as bad as they are.

But where is prostitution in its greatest luxury? At Washington.

There are to be found the most elegant mansions, most sumptuously furnished. Why all this magnificence? Why, indeed! Because in Washington there are assembled the best, the most brilliant men in the nation—the men to whom the people have committed the national interests and who conduct the national affairs. Of course there should be all the elegance that wealth can furnish for the accommodation of such men. And there is; of course there [is].[10] And they know how to appreciate it, I can assure you.

Everybody knows what the "third house" in Washington is. It consists of the lobbyists who are there to obtain legislation—to push this little scheme, or that small appropriation. Large sums of money are expended by this lobby. When a particular scheme is to come up, its friends distribute ten, fifteen and even twenty thousand dollars among the mistresses of these houses. Why? To secure their influence with Representatives and Senators. You needn't take my word for this; anybody who will inquire can learn the truth. Of course none of these gentlemen ever visit these houses to get under this purchased influence. Oh no! It is exerted upon them by these women magnetically, from afar off, of course it is.

I say it boldly, that it is the best men of the country who support the houses of prostitution. It isn't your young men, but the husbands and fathers of the country, who occupy positions of honor and trust. It is not the hard-working, industrial masses at all, but those who have money and time to expend for such purposes, who are really the old hoary-headed villains of the country. The young haven't money enough to support themselves. So when you condemn the poor women, whom you have helped to drive to such a life, remember to visit your wrath upon the best men of the country as well.

And when legislators discuss Social Evil bills let the women demand equality for their outraged sisters. These bills are professedly to prevent the spread of venereal diseases, and they provide for the medical examination and registration of women to effect it. Now if they really wish to stop these diseases and make the business safe, why not register and examine every man who visits these houses before he is admitted. A house of prostitution, free from disease cannot be contaminated, except through the visits of diseased men. Examine the men, then, and deny admission to the diseased, and there will be an end of the business. How many Social Evil bills would be passed under such conditions? Echo answers, "How many?"

But we are told that prostitution is a "necessary evil," and long articles are published tending to establish this proposition. Necessary for what? So that men may satiate their sexual demands. This is the plain English of it! Mothers, what does this say to you? This, and it is a blotch of infamy upon womanhood that can never be effaced except by woman herself rising in the dignity and divinity of her maternal nature and making a falsity of the damning fact: that you must yearly contribute a certain percentage of your daughters to fill the infernal maw of prostitution; give them up to be sunk in infamy, to be abhorred of their sisters and despised of their brothers; in a word, to walk the prostitutes' road to hell.

Necessary evil! Necessary indeed! Isn't it rather your shame, and my shame, and the dishonor of womanhood and the disgrace of manhood that should make the stones weep to contemplate—a million of innocent, virgin girls of from twelve to sixteen years of age—your daughters, mine, perhaps sacrificed to this "necessary evil" every fifteen years! Think of it, mothers, and let the blush of shame never fade from your cheeks until this infamy is blotted from existence; or until you have made the victims of this "necessary evil" as respectable as its promoters and supporters.

Statistics inform us that there are two hundred and fifty thousand professional prostitutes in the country, nearly one-tenth of whom are in New York City; and that these are visited and supported by not less than two and a half millions of men—one-third of the voting population of the country. Think of it! A quarter of a million professional female prostitutes and two and a half millions of professional male prostitutes, or ten men to one woman. And yet Congress is wonderfully concerned about Utah.[11] Consistency is a jewel which Congressmen don't seem to carry about with them. They must be jealous of the Mormons. If the proportions were reversed so that there would be ten women to one man on their side of the question, they would probably let Brigham alone, and think it rather a nice thing to be a Mormon; but Brigham has got the better of them; 'twas very wicked of him to go and do such a thing; very, very wicked that he should, in a small way, presume to imitate both the meekest and the wisest of the Biblical fathers.

But love and lust are terms equally misapplied even by the most brilliant minds. Love is an universal principle. It is the life of the universe. It is that power called attraction which holds all things together. It is that force which unites the two elements from which water is formed and the two natures of which a sexual unit is composed. It uplifts the mountains and depresses the valleys; causes the water to flow and the clouds to float; the lily to blossom and the violet to bloom; the dew to fall and the storm to descend; it is the living and motive power of the world; it is God.

The Christian tells the same story, but he speaks in a language which he does not understand—God is Love. If this be so, then Love is God; then all the love there is, is God; but this love they tell us is free. I have been endeavoring to convince them of the truth of their own most cherished, though heretofore meaningless proverb, so that they may appreciate its beauty and bask in its glory, and for my pains I am dubbed "the Devil." I have tried to show that all love must be as they say that God is—Free; that love cannot be confined to the limits of a man-made law any more than God can be shut up in a creed. Attempt to put the limits of a written law about love, saying, thus far and no farther, and love is destroyed. It is no longer love, because it is limited, and love, being God, cannot be limited.

When a limit is placed upon anything that by nature is free, its action becomes perverted. All the various attractions in the world are but so many methods by which love manifests itself. The attraction which draws the opposites in sex together is sexual love. The perverted action of sexual love, when limited by law or otherwise, is lust. All sexual manifestations that are not free are the perverted action of love—are lust. So, logically, the methods enforced by man to ensure purity convert love into lust. Legal sexuality is enforced lust. All the D.D.'s and LL.D.'s[12] in the world, though they have all the mental gifts and the tongues of angels, cannot controvert the proposition.

This brings us to a still more serious part of my subject. Remember I am to withhold nothing—no fact, no advice. We are now face to face with the most startling and the most common fact connected with the miseries of marriage. But I know of no author, no speaker who has dared to call attention to, or to suggest a remedy for it, or even to hint at it as needing a remedy, or to recognize its existence in any manner.

It will be remembered that early in the evening I showed that marriage when analyzed, is a license to cohabit sexually. Now I am going to show that the enforcement of this method eventually defeats the original object. I state it without fear of contradiction by fact or of refutation by argument that it is the common experience among the married who have lived together strictly according to the marriage covenant, for from five to ten years, that they are sexually estranged. There may be, I know there are, exceptions to this rule, but they are the exceptions and not the rule. It is a lamentable fact that all over this country there is a prolonged wail going up on account of this condition. Sexual estrangement in from five to ten years! Think of it, men and women whom Nature has blessed with such possibilities for happiness as are conferred on no other order of creation—your God-ordained capacity blasted, prostituted to death, by enforced sexual relations where there is neither attraction or sexual adaptation: and by ignorance of sexual science!

Some may assert, as many do, that failure in sexual strength is intellectual and spiritual gain. Don't harbor the unnatural lie. Sexuality is the physiological basis of character and must be preserved as its balance and perfection. To kill out the sexual instinct by any unnatural practice or repression, is to emasculate character; is to take away that which makes what remains impotent for good—fruitless, not less intellectually and spiritually than sexually.

It is to do even more than this. From the moment that the sexual instinct is dead in any person, male or female, from that moment such person begins actually to die. It is the fountain from which life proceeds. Dry up the fountain and the stream will disappear. It is only a question of time, and of how much is obtained from other fountains, when the stream will discharge its last waters into the great ocean of life.

Others again seem to glory over the fact that they never had any sexual desire, and to think that this desire is vulgar. What! Vulgar! The instinct that creates immortal souls vulgar! Who dare stand up amid Nature, all prolific and beautiful, whose pulses are ever bounding with the creative desire, and utter such sacrilege! Vulgar, indeed! Vulgar, rather, must be the mind that can conceive such blasphemy. No sexual passion, say you? Say, rather, a sexual idiot, and confess that your life is a failure, your body an abortion, and no longer bind your shame upon your brow or herald it as purity. Call such stuff purity. Bah! Be honest, rather, and say it is depravity.

It is not the possession of strong sexual powers that is to be deprecated. They are that necessary part of human character which is never lacking in those who leave their names standing high in the historic roll. The intellect, largely developed, without a strong animal basis is never prolific of good in any direction. Evenly balanced natures, in which there are equal development and activity of all departments are those which move the world palpably forward for good; but if superiority of any kind is desirable at all, let it be in the animal, since with this right, the others may be cultivated to its standard. If this be wanting, however, all possible cultivation, intellectually, will only carry the individual further away from balance, and make the character still more "out of tune" with nature. These are physiological facts inherent in the constitution of mankind, and they cannot be ignored with impunity. No reliable theory of progressive civilization can ever be established that does not make them its chief corner stone, because they are the foundation upon which civilization rests.

It is the misuse, the abuse, the prostitution of the sexual instinct that is to be deprecated. Like all other capacities, it needs to be educated, cultivated, exercised rightly, and to do this is to live in accordance with nature and as commanded by the higher law, that law which every one finds deep-seated in his soul, and whose voice is the truest guide. When the world shall rise from its degradation into the sphere of this law, when the sexual act shall be the religion of the world, as it is now my religion, then, and then only, may we reasonably hope that its redemption is nigh.

What other religion so near alike to God—the all-loving, all-creating Father; or so much in harmony with Nature—the ever-receptive and ever-evolving Mother. Let your religious faith be what it may[,] if it do not include the sexual act it is impotent. Make that act the most divine of all your worship. Let it be unto you without spot or blemish. Let it rise unto God a continual incense of piety and holiness, and be henceforth resurrected from the debauch in which the ages have sunk it. This is my religion—the fundamental principles for the generation of the race. Let it be yours and all mankind's, and with no other, the salvation long sought, long prayed for, long prophesied and long sung will soon be found. Discard it, put its life and health-giving blessings aside, and all the other religions ever conceived or dreamed, or that may be conceived of dreamed, combined, will be impotent to usher in the glad time.

Oh! that my lips were smitten with the inspiration of an archangel, that I might reach your hearts and show you the better life; that I might pierce your understandings and force in upon them the mighty import of these truths. Oh! that I could so appeal to my brothers everywhere, that forever after they would regard women as of angelic order, to be approached only as they would approach the enthroned Goddess of Purity, upon whose presence none would dare presume, and whose favors it is theirs to merit and receive, rather than to command and appropriate. Look not upon her for selfish purposes, but rather to bless her, let that blessing depend upon what it may, even if to bless is not to possess. Other love than this is selfishness, and a profanation of the Holy Word. That is love which will bless the object, even if to do so is to yield it. Remember that it is a pretension and a fraud to think of ownership in, or control over, the person of a woman. This is her inheritance, never to be bartered, never to be sold, never to be given away, even; but only to be exchanged, blessing for blessing, when an all-absorbing, all-embracing, all-desiring love points out the way.

And my sisters. Oh! what shall I say to them; how awaken them to realize the awful responsibilities conferred through their maternal functions. How shall I arouse, how startle them into a comprehension of the divinity of maternity; how sting them, if nothing else will do it, into self-respect? How shall I show them the destruction they have sown broadcast over the earth; how exhibit the black damnation, the sin, misery, shame, crime, disgrace, that come home to them as mothers; how stab their hearts with the awful monstrosities with which they have desecrated the earth; how bring to their hearts, to wring them in bitter anguish, the wild ravings of the maniac, the senseless drivel of the chattering idiot, the horrid delirium of the drunkard, the desolate moans of the "outcasts," the heart-sobs of criminals, the dreaded spectacle of the murderer, face to face with death! Ah! how adequately shall I bring these things—all these—home to the mothers of humanity; how make them feel the horrid misery that they have wrought by the outrage and desecration of their divine maternal functions?

Oh! mothers, that I could make you feel these things as I know them. I do not appeal to you as a novice, ignorant of what I speak, merely to excite your sympathies, but as one having learned through long years of bitter experience. Go where I have been; visit the prisons, insane asylums and the glittering hells that I have visited; see the maniac mother at the cell door of her son, to be hanged in the morning, as I have seen her—cursing God, cursing man, cursing until nothing but curses filled the air, and until their fury flecked her face with foam, that her crime should be visited upon her poor, poor boy. Follow her home, and when the agony of the gallows has come and gone, ask her the meaning of all this, and she will tell you, as she has told me: "That boy was forced upon me; I did not want him; I was worn out by child-bearing; and I tried, in every way I knew, to kill him in my womb. I thought of nothing else until it was too late to think of that. I failed. He was born; and I have made him a murderer. He committed the deed, and has suffered an ignominious death; but I am the real criminal.

"But I did not do this willfully. I had never been taught any better— never been told the fearful effect of such acts and deeds upon the unborn child. I followed the common practices of my friends. I did not know I was stamping my child with the brand of Cain. But all this did not save him. He was hanged for my crime."

But look upon another scene. Go home with me and see desolation and devastation in another form. The cold, iron bolt has entered my heart and left my life a blank, in ashes upon my lips. Wherever I go I carry a living corpse in my breast, the vacant stare of whose living counterpart meets me at the door of my home. My boy, now nineteen years of age, who should have been my pride and my joy, has never been blessed by the dawning of reasoning. I was married at fourteen, ignorant of every thing that related to my maternal functions. For this ignorance, and because I knew no better than to surrender my maternal functions to a drunken man, I am cursed with this living death. Do you think my mother's heart does not yearn for the love of my boy? Do you think I do not realize the awful condition to which I have consigned him? Do you think I would not willingly give my life to make him what he has a right to be? Do you think his face is not ever before me pressing me on to declare these terrible social laws to the world? Do you think with this sorrow seated on my soul I can ever sit quietly down and permit women to go on ignorantly repeating my crime? Do you think I can ever cease to hurl the bitterest imprecations against the accursed thing that has made my life one long misery? Do you think I can ever hesitate to warn the young maidens against my fate, or to advise them never to surrender the control of their maternal functions to any man! Ah! if you do, you do not know the agony that rests here. Not to do less than I am doing were madness; it were worse than crime; it were the essence of ten thousand crimes concentrated in one soul to sink it in eternal infamy.

Nor is this all that urges me onward. A few months ago I laid a beautiful sister away in Greenwood.[13] Above her is written, "Cut off by marriage at thirty-one years." She had always opposed my social theories, though I knew her life was being sacrificed to a legal marriage. When on her death-bed she called me to her and said, "My darling sister, I am going to die. Oh! if I could have had the moral courage to have stood by you and to have broken loose from my thralldom I should not have been here. I knew you were right; but I could not endure the obloquy that the ungrateful world was heaping upon you. Knowing that I am to die I wanted to see you alone and ask your forgiveness for the anguish I have caused you by joining with the world to crush you out. It is meet that I should be sacrificed. I deserve it. It is just. But I shall soon be freed from the galling chains I dared not break myself, and will then be near you to make you bold and strong, and in so far as I can, repair the injury I have done."

My brothers and sisters, I never walk upon a platform without feeling the presence of that darling sister; and I now see her beautiful face flitting above me, hear her sweet voice encouraging me, and feel her magnetic power inspiring me to do my duty. "Cut off by marriage at thirty-one" rings in my ears, and I repeat it to the world as the mournful refrain of millions of wives, who, like her, were its victims; who, like her, after suffering untold miseries for years, went down to untimely graves murdered by the men to whom marriage sold them sexually.

When I review the conditions under which humanity is born I am surprised, not so much that it is so bad, but that it is so good. I do not wonder that there are all classes of criminals, that there are all sorts of diseases, that there are all grades of intellect; I do not wonder that debauchery and drunkenness meet us at every hand, and that lust in adults and sexual vice in children are sapping the life of the people; nor that in summing them all up and calculating their effects that the conclusion is reached that unless there soon come a change the American people will be blotted out. And then tell me that I shall not discuss the sexual question! I should like to see the power or law that can prevent me.

You remember that little game was tried in New York, and failed. When I published the biography of the American Pope, the United States authorities, urged on by the minions of the Church—the Y. M. C. Assassination Association[14]—swooped down upon me and carried me off to jail, not for libel on the Pope, but for obscenity. I remained there quietly enough for some weeks, trusting that the outrage upon the freedom of the press and free speech would rouse the people to my defense against such an unwarrantable act. But Beecher was bigger than a free press—of more consequence than free speech. His danger cowed the whole country into silence; and the people sneaked after the trail of the popular preacher, in abject submission. "It was well worth the while of the United States to protect the reputation of a revered citizen," said District-Attorney Noah Davis; and the whole country complacently repeated it.

What was a little woman, in jail, compared with Mr. Beecher! What if a free press and free speech were imprisoned with her—were struck down in her person! What were they to the American people when Mr. Beecher was in danger; and through him the whole rascally set of fifty thousand preachers; and through them, again, the Christian Church everywhere! If she were to rot in jail, what was that beside the necessity of "hushing things up"; of strangling the scandal before it should spread into other churches all over the country and show them all rotten? Simply nothing.

It was the United States that held me illegally imprisoned. It was the people everywhere, you among the rest. But you did not raise a single voice at the outrage. You left me powerless in the cell of the State while the Church carried the key. But if you were dead to the infamy, I was not. I saw it was useless to wait for the people to protest, so I gave battle alone. I went into the combat single-handed against both Church and State led on by all their minions, and with the aid of honest Judge Blatchford, I whipped the whole cowardly crowd. I will speak what I will; and I will publish the truth about any professional hypocrite when I think I can render the world a service by so doing. I have just come from a second fight with them. In the first it was free press and free speech, that triumphed. In the second it was Free Love, and the victory in both instances was complete. I don't think they will try it over again; but if they do, I'll fight them again, armed with truth and with justice, and have no fears for the result.

But to return from this digression, let us inquire the real end to be gained by reform. The pretense of every reform ever advanced has been to better the condition of the people. But first and last—one and all—they have dealt with existing conditions—with effects—endeavoring to mitigate and cure evils, instead of preventing them. No sooner is one evil cured than the causes that produced it send forth another that requires to be cured; and thus reform, traveling in circles, has made but little real advance, except in the direction of intellectual development, in which a different practice has prevailed. People are better, intellectually, than they were; but not so physically or morally.

There can be a better race only by having better children. If they are bad, good men and women are impossible. There can be better children only through better conditions of generation; a better understanding by women of the processes of gestation, and better methods of rearing and education. These propositions are self-evident, and point directly to the sexual relations as the place to begin the work of improving the race. All effects in other directions, however promising, will prove futile for permanent good. The necessity for regeneration must be replaced by proper generation. If all women in the country were to join the temperance crusaders they might, for the time, decrease drunkenness; but the moment they should cease their efforts it would return. Now let these women go home and breed no more drunkards, and the remedy will be effectual. And so of all other vices and crimes.

Not long ago, when passing through Janesville, Wisconsin, a young man who had heard me lecture about the pre-natal effect of the mother's conduct upon the child, came and asked me to look at his breast. I did so. It was covered with bottles. When his mother was carrying him she was in the habit of going into her uncle's liquor store and tasting his liquor. The result was she "marked" him with bottles. Of course this young man is a confirmed drunkard. He might be importuned into signing the pledge a hundred times, but he would always break it at the first opportunity. And what is true of him is also true of nearly every other drunkard. They are made so by their mothers, or else they inherit it from their fathers. The temperance crusade, then, must begin in the home, in the marriage bed, in begetting children, and in proper surroundings and influences for the mother during gestation. Nothing else will ever cure the world of drunkenness, or any other vice.[15]

The power of the mother over the unborn child, for evil, is too well attested by too many facts to need further elucidation. But it teaches a lesson of mighty import which ought to receive universal consideration. If her powers for ill are so marked, what must they be for good, when exercised under an enlightened understanding! Nothing is more certain than that mothers can make their children just what they want them to be, limited only by the inherited tendencies of the father.

There are, then, but two questions in this whole matter of reforming the world; but they are vital and inseparable. The first is, to discover and develop the science of proper generation, so that all the inherited tendencies may be good; and the second is, that the germ life, once properly begun, may not be subjected to any deleterious influences, either during the period of gestation or development on to adult age.

This is the meaning of social reform. It means better children, and it doesn't care how they are to be obtained—only to obtain them. Any methods that will secure them are good, are true, are pure, are virtuous methods. The question to be asked of the mothers of the future will not be, "Who is the father?" but, "How good is the child?" If it be not good it will be a disgrace to the mother, no matter if the father is her legal husband.

I say it, and I want the world to know that I say it, that a woman who bears a dozen or less scraggy, scrawny, puny, half-made-up children, by a legal father, is a disgrace to her sex and a curse to the community; while she who bears as many perfect specimens of humanity, no matter if it be by as many different fathers, is an honor to womanhood and a blessing to the world. And I defy both the priests and the law to prove this false. Every sensible man and woman will have to admit it. It is a self-evident proposition.

In August, 1873, at the Silver Lake camp meeting, I said, before fifteen thousand persons, that no one knows who his father is. Think of it for a moment, and you will see how impossible it is that he should know. Can any person make oath that he knows who it was who, in unity with his mother, was his father? He may swear that he has been told so, but that does not amount to knowledge. I made this statement, not specially to declare this fact, but to enforce the argument that it doesn't make any difference who may be the father of any child, if he is only a good child and an honor to his mother. I have repeated this statement a hundred times since, and never a hiss. Hasn't the sexual question grappled with the thoughts of the people? This is an evidence not to be misunderstood.

But among all the radical things I have never quite equaled one recently published in *Popular Science Monthly*, in an article written by Mr. Herbert Spencer,[16] the acknowledged philosopher of the age. Quoting from an eminent English surgeon, he says: "It is a lamentable truth that the troubles which respectable, hard-working married women undergo are more trying to the health[,] and detrimental to the looks[,] than any of the irregularities of the harlot's career."[17] What a commentary is this on the marriage institution! Much [of] the larger part of the married women of the world [are] in a worse condition, as to health and looks, than are the harlots! Take that home with you, and think of it, and see if you can come to any other conclusion than that an institution that produces such results in women, needs to be replaced by something better. Now don't forget that these are not my words, and say that I advocate prostitution; but remember that they are the words of the highest authority in philosophy and science now living, published in the most popular monthly in the country, and give them weight accordingly.

There are many popular fallacies about prostitution. Statistics inform us that the average life of prostitutes is about four years; but this does not show the real causes of such fatality. It leaves it to be inferred that it is in the fact of prostitution merely. It does not say that it is caused by dissolute living, and drinking, and by the diseases which usually accompany promiscuous intercourse.

The real truth about this is that those prostitutes who never drink, and who never permit themselves to become diseased are among the healthiest of women, and hold their beauty and vigor to an advanced age. Is this a startling assertion? Anybody who will take the trouble can easily confirm it. I do not make it without the most unmistakable proof, which is open to all inquirers, as it was to me, to obtain. It was necessary for me to know by personal investigation, and it shows me as it will everybody else that what Herbert Spencer writes in *Popular Science Monthly* is true: that the promiscuous life of the harlot is less detrimental to health and beauty than is the common life of the married slave. The reason is simple and clear. Promiscuous intercourse, when sexual conditions are imperfect, when the act is not based on mutual love and desire, is better than so-called monogamic intercourse under the same conditions, made more intolerable by a deep-seated disgust. But by no means is this an argument against monogamy. It is an argument against legal monogamy when the monogamy of nature is wanting; and, as such, is the most convincing that can be offered in favor of monogamy founded upon love. Free relations of any kind are better than any can be that are enforced. These are the logical deductions from the facts. I did not create the facts, so if you have fault to find, find it with them and not me. I merely offer them to you for consideration, so that you may think of and discuss this subject understandingly.

I have already said that the salvation of the world can come only through better children. This fact has been widely recognized by all so-called Christian denominations. Each is very anxious to get hold of the children. The Romanist says: "Give me the children for twenty-five years and I will make the world Catholic." True enough. They have taken a step in the right direction, but only a step. They say: give me the children, good or bad. The reformer, who shall really save the world, must go another step and see that there are none but good children born. Then the root of the matter will be reached.

But how to accomplish this is now the vital question. Many may think that I am too severe on my sex—on the mothers; but I wish I could be ten times more so, because, and I say it in sorrow, this is a work for the mothers, to the fearful importance of which I fear they cannot be roused. They have a terrible responsibility resting upon them and a fearful preliminary task to perform. They have got first to conquer their sexual liberty, so that their maternal functions shall be under their own control at all times; and next to guard them from contamination, so that their children may be pure.

I do not complain of women as willfully sending the race onward to destruction, I only wish to show them that they are doing it, and to urge them by every argument that my woman's nature can suggest, or my mother's heart conceive, to stop the desolation. What can I say? How shall I plead with them to reach their hearts and rouse them into consciousness upon this terrible theme? Shall I remind them again of the death of one half of their children? Shall I show them the still-born babes, strangled at birth because they are not wanted? Shall I tell them that the birth-rate among the more intelligent classes has decreased one-half in twenty years by abortions; and that, unless these things cease, the race will ultimately be blotted out?

Or shall I turn to the other side of the picture and show them the awful fact that nine women in ten are so diseased, sexually, as to make them unfit to become mothers, brought to this condition by their efforts to prevent pregnancy, or to procure abortions, or by continually submitting to undesired intercourse until the sexual instinct is dead; and that if these conditions go on for twenty years it will be impossible for women even to become pregnant?

Or, again, shall I ask them to look on the faces of their children and see the history of sexual vice indelibly written—their boys and their girls, the former in the first stages of self-abuse, or, having too late discovered their danger, in the last stages of spermatorrhea; and the latter, pale, yellow and dejected from irregularities, or, having too late discovered their cause, prostrated by leucorrhœa and prolapsus uteri?[18]

And having done this, shall I ask them if they wonder that these things are so, when they remember that they were constantly debauched by the insatiable lust of their husbands during the whole period in which they were bearing these children beneath their hearts? What else can be expected than premature and precocious development of the sexual passions in children when, during their gestation, the influence of this passion is continually forced upon them; or what else than that this passion should be vented in vicious ways which carry their victims down to certain destruction?

Or what other pictures can I bring to lay at the feet of mothers to show them the horrors they are working for humanity by this willing sexual slavery in which they slumber as if nothing were the matter? Oh! let me plead with mothers in the name of future generations to rescue your divinely ordered maternity from the horrid debauch in which it is plunged. Let me implore you for your own soul's future happiness to emancipate yourselves, at whatever cost, from the awful crime of sexual slavery, so that you may dedicate your lives to the good of future generations rather than to expend them in ministering to the lustful demands of legal masters. Let me urge upon you, for your own sakes, the strict observance of the laws of your sexual natures, and to never permit their divine instincts to be trifled with or debauched by any man, whether he be husband or lover. Let me beg of you, for humanity's sake, to rescue yourselves from this thralldom of license, snatch yourselves from the rude grasp of lust, and elevate yourselves from the quagmire of disgust into which license and lust have cast you, so that womanhood may once more become Queen of purity, nobility and virtue.

Instead of supporting churches and sending missionaries to the heathen; of praying and singing to convert the liquor-sellers; of building and supporting hospitals for foundlings and for women about to become illegal mothers; of erecting penitentiaries, insane asylums, alms-houses and gallows, let the women come together in solemn conclave and register an eternal vow that they will never bear any more children to fill these places. Let them swear by the God of humanity that they will never again become pregnant of an undesired child. Let them enter a solemn oath that they will never again surrender their sexual or maternal functions to be outraged by undesired commerce. Let the women come together and do these things in earnest and the world will be saved from that time.

I repeat that I do not complain of women as willful perpetrators of all these crimes; but I charge it home upon the intelligent men, upon the teachers, preachers, and doctors especially, that they willfully keep the rest of the world in ignorance of the truths about sexual debauchery. But still more specially do I hurl this indictment against the editors. They know these truths, but they know also if women generally come to a knowledge of them that the sexual domination of man will cease. Hence by blackguarding me they hope to frighten the women away, so that I may not reach their ears. But, thank heaven, they cannot entirely shut them out. Some there are who, having suffered, and knowing there is something wrong somewhere, have the moral courage to come for the facts, and they go away and repeat them to others, until there is a general inquiry among women all over the country to offset this attempt at suppression on the part of men. Some papers also dare sometimes to hint at the facts; sometimes publishing what I say, but taking care to condemn me editorially, so as to make the editorial censure wash the reportorial facts.

The scientific journals and monthlies are filled with articles leading directly to the solution of this question where ten years ago there was not so much as a word to be seen in any publication about sexual subjects, even hinting in the remotest manner that there was anything rotten sexually. If I do nothing else I know that I have awakened investigation on this subject. If all I have said is error; if the truth lie in altogether different directions from those in which I point, out of the discussion now going on the truth will be evolved. . . .

Now can you understand for what I have been made the victim of such vile abuse? The truths which I have presented to you are those I have always sought to enforce. I have always contended that, if there is to be any ostracism for prostitution, the men should suffer equally with the women; that the seducer should be held up to the same scorn and contempt that is visited upon the seduced. I have asked for equality— nothing more; and I will accept nothing less for my sex, let them heap whatever contumely they may upon me.

It would appear from their opposition that women do not want the ostracism of male prostitutes, or to be deprived of them as companions; that they do not want the seducer debarred from their society, and he is usually a "lion" among them; that they do not want to own and control their maternal functions and sexual instincts; that they do not want to have the right to say when they shall bear children and when not; but, on the contrary, that they want to be owned, want to be supported by men, in return for the sexual favors which they can confer. They don't want reform; they want things to remain as they are.

Isn't this a legitimate conclusion? Think of it, women of the nineteenth century! Shall your names go down to posterity in such connection? Let me warn you this is where they are going. In September, 1872, I said, before a convention in Boston: I believed that, in twenty years, the daughters of to-day, then grown, would regard their mothers as having been the real prostitutes of this time. If what I have presented are facts, wouldn't it be a just verdict?

A popular objection against Free Love is, that it breaks up families. My answer to this indictment is, that a family which falls in pieces when Free Love strikes it, is already broken up, and waiting for a loophole out of which to escape; and as the press have coupled my name with this *role*, the discontented think it a good thing to shift whatever opprobrium there may be connected with their cases, upon Woodhull. Thus I become the pack-horse for thousands who have no more conception of Free Love than a donkey has of mathematics.

But I'll tell you what I do. If a husband or a wife get discontented and uneasy, and chafe in their bonds, I advise such to seek out the ulcers, come to a mutual understanding, talk out the hidden and corroding cause, sum up the difficulties and grievances and see if they are of such character and magnitude as to preclude all hope for peace and happiness, and not under any circumstances call in the services of a blackguard lawyer.

I ask men and women to be honest with each other. If any find their attachments growing cold—their love waning—say so, and not continue the pretense while the real love is lavished elsewhere. I ask men and women to be thoughtful of each other's needs and desires. If a wife find her husband spending his evenings away from home, let her be sure there is something wrong; and when he goes again, put on hat and shawl and accompany him. If it is to the club, the bar-room, the billiard table, the theatre, the opera or the house of ill-fame, tell him that any place which he frequents is good enough for you to visit. Face him in his discontent, and say: "What is the matter, my darling? What is it in which I fail that you must spend your evenings away from me? Has your love for me gone, or what is the matter? Tell me! It is useless to continue an unhappy life when there is so easy a remedy. If you do not love me any longer, take me into your confidence; let me be your friend and adviser."

If there is any basis of hope left, this course will develop it; and there are hundreds of families who owe their present unity and happiness to having followed it. It is an error into which people naturally fall who think that my supporters are among the dissatisfied families. It is precisely the reverse of this. It is the families which cannot be separated or broken up which believe in the efficacy of freedom as a regulative element. My most bitter opponents among my own sex, are the professional prostitutes who know I am going to break up their business, and the ignorant wives who read little and think less, and who are in constant fear of losing their "Paw," over whom they have none except a legal control; and among the opposite sex, those who are habitually unfaithful to marriage, and the ministers who know their nice arrangements will be spoiled, and the lawyers, whose divorce business will be ruined by freedom. Ask any of these, when found denouncing Mrs. Woodhull, if they ever heard her speak, or ever read her paper or speeches, the reply will be, "No! and I don't want to."

But I would remind these exceedingly virtuous people that the Catholic says, that every one who was not married by the Catholic method is living in prostitution. So please remember when they cast their epithets about so freely, that there is a greater authority than they are, which denounces them in equally opprobrious terms. This class say that those living together who are not married as they are, are prostitutes; the Catholic Church looks at them, and, because they are not married as it marries, calls them by the same name.

For my part I look beyond the ceremony and the law, and observe the facts; and if I find people living together in hate and disgust, whether married after the Protestant fashion or the Catholic style, I say they are prostituting their sexual functions, and in sight of the God of Nature are prostitutes....

I make the claim boldly, that from the very moment woman is emancipated from the necessity of yielding the control of her sexual organs to man to insure a home, food and clothing, the doom of sexual demoralization will be sealed. From that moment there will be no sexual intercourse except such as is desired by women. It will be a complete revolution in sexual matters, in which men will have to take a back seat and be content to be servants where they have been masters so long. The present system is at variance with everything in nature. Everywhere, except among men and women, the female has supreme authority in the domain of sex, and the male never pretends to oppose it, nor to appeal from its decisions. Compare men and women with the animals and see how far below them they have fallen in this regard. Yet among animals the principle of freedom is thoroughly exemplified. Why are they not degraded, debauched and diseased? Simply because the female is the dominant power in sex. What would be the result among animals were the barbarous rule of marriage enforced; were the female to be compelled to submit herself without reserve to the lecherous instincts of the male? It would be the same that has obtained among women—disease everywhere, until there is scarcely a sexually healthy woman past the age of puberty to be found. This is the parity, this the morality, this the divinity of marriage. Oh, God! is there no power that can restore woman to the level of the brutes? Is there nothing that can rescue her from this shameless condition, from this pollution, this nastiness?

To woman, by nature, belongs the right of sexual determination. When the instinct is aroused in her, then and then only should commerce follow. When woman rises from sexual slavery into freedom, into the ownership and control of her sexual organs, and man is obliged to respect this freedom, then will this instinct become pure and holy; then will woman be raised from the iniquity and morbidness in which she now wallows for existence, and the intensity and glory of her creative functions be increased a hundred-fold; then may men and women, like the beasts or the birds, if they will, herd together, and the instinct in woman, by the law of natural attraction and adaptation, rouse in man its answering counterpart, and its counterpart only.

This is the purity at which I aim; this is the holiness to which I would have woman and, through her functions, the sexual relations elevated; this is the glory with which I would have woman crowned; this is what it means to be virtuous; this is what it means to be pure. Again I ask, is there a man or woman who hears me who will ever dare hereafter to associate this doctrine with the debased and the low, and call it an attempt to descend further into lust and license?

Oh, woman! would that the beautiful, the shining, the redeemed of heaven could come to you in their white-robed purity and sing in your ears the blessed song of the angels who "neither marry nor are given in marriage,"[19] and who live in their own natural element of freedom. Oh! that they could come to you as they have to me, and show how, through you, as represented by Eve—through your sexual slavery to men—has sin, and misery and crime been introduced into the world; and how through the assertion and maintenance of your sexual freedom and purity only, can "the seed of the woman bruise the serpent's head,"[20] and humanity be restored to its original sexual purity, the Scripture fulfilled and the millennium ushered in.

Instead of opposing this doctrine, the Churches should see that through its propagation only can their sacred prophecies be realized. Instead of denouncing me the ministers ought to be my most earnest advocates, not merely because through the theory of Free Love only can their lives be justified, but because by its practice alone can salvation come to the world. They have been working at the wrong end of salvation; they have been trying to save souls while their bodies were damned. Now let them save bodies, and the souls will take care of themselves. I should be glad to believe that these clerical persons are honest, but I cannot. They know the sad lives of thousands of women, suffering and yearning for comfort and sympathy; these women go to their pastors for relief, and I have the very best of reasons for believing, indeed, I know that in numerous instances, they not only get that for which they yearn, but also that further comfort and sympathy to which the others naturally lead, and which the ministers know they can so safely administer. This is another reason to be added to the matter of fees, which I have already mentioned, why this class do not wish the marriage relations disturbed. The ministers, lawyers and doctors have a monopoly of this field, and they intend to keep it.

The world will have a genuine surprise some day when it shall awaken to the truth, as I know it, about the churches; to a knowledge of the kind of currency in which lawyers often receive their divorce fees. As this, however, is none of my business, I shall let the world take its own time about it. But I sometimes think it would be only a just reward for their stupidity were husbands to be shown why it is that their wives are so earnest in religious matters. Everybody knows that the churches would totter and tumble if it were not for the women. Men have mostly grown out of churches, and attend them because their families wish it, so that the "pew rent" may be paid. There are many churches besides Plymouth in which half the women are in love with their pastors; and in these cases I think it safe to say, as it is in that of Plymouth, it is usually reciprocated.[21]

But as to the difficulty of freedom for woman: There is but one, and that is pecuniary independence. I know that opposers refer to the condition of women in Greece and Rome, when there were few restrictions sexually, and use it as an argument against freedom now. But it doesn't apply, and I will show you why. In those times it mattered not whether there were marriage laws or not. In either case woman was dependent upon her sex for support; if married, then upon her husband; if not married, then upon her lover.

So the mere abolition of marriage does not necessarily mean sexual freedom for woman. I do not hesitate to admit that marriage has played its necessary part in the evolution of society; nor that among a people where women have a very limited position in the industrial organization, that it provides them a support. I will go so far even as to say that, so long as women prefer to depend upon the sale of their sexual favors rather than upon their industrial capacities for support, that marriage may be deemed a sort of protection. But I also hold that, to a woman who prefers rather to rely upon her own talent for support, marriage is intolerable.

This is the same argument that was used by the slaveholders. "Slaves," they said, "were better off as slaves than they could be, free. They need to be taken care of; and until they are capable of self-support it is best that slavery continue." The slaves themselves generally coincided with this idea. Only a few of the more intelligent saw that the argument was a deceit.

So now do most women coincide with the same argument as applied to marriage. Only a few who have solved the question for themselves, see that it is fallacious. In spite of the argument the anti-slavery revolution came, and violently cast the slaves upon their own resources. Who is there who now dare say their condition is not improved? So will it be with women. They will hesitate to take the responsibility of freedom. They will say: "I prefer to rely upon my sex a little longer." But the revolution will come eventually, and thrust them upon their own resources; and in ten years nobody will be found to doubt that their condition has been improved.

But the old argument as applied to women is fallacious in still another way, as I will show. Suppose that all the women in the land, on a given day, should rise and throw off the yoke of marriage, and declare and hold themselves free, how long would it be before the men would accede to any terms? Do you think it would be a month—three weeks—two weeks? I haven't the slightest idea that they would hold out a single week. Women are entirely unaware of their power. Like an elephant led by a string, they are subordinated by a writing, drawn up by just those who are most interested in holding them in slavery. I am sometimes almost out of patience at the servility with which women fawn upon their masters, when they might lead them by the nose wherever they please.

It is sometimes asked: "If what you say is true, and that marriage is a curse, why did not the deprecated results obtain years ago?" I will show you why. It will be remembered that it used to be said by the slaveholders, that the moment a slave got the freedom crotchet[22] into his head he was no longer of any account. A negro was a good slave so long as the idea of freedom was not born in his soul. Whenever this birth occurred he began to feel the galling of his chains.

It is the same with women. So long as they entertain the idea that their natural destiny is to be owned and cared for by some man, whom they are to repay by the surrender of their person, they are good, legal wives; but from the moment the notion that they have an individual right to themselves—to the control of their bodies and maternal functions—has birth in their souls, they become bad wives. They rebel in their souls, if not in words and deeds; and the legal claims of their husbands become a constant source of annoyance, and the enforcement of their legal rights an unbearable thing.

It is this repugnance, this sexual rebellion, that is causing the degradation and widespread disease among women, sexually; and this reacts upon man, and degrades him. The mind, in rebellion at the enslaved condition, has such an effect upon the sexual act that it becomes impossible for its subject to respond or reciprocate; and the organs suffer the natural penalty.

In speaking of this almost anomalous condition in woman, Dr. John M. Scudder,[23] Professor of the Diseases of Women in the Cincinnati

Medical College, says: "If the act is complete, so that both body and mind are satisfied, no disease arises, though there be frequent repetitions; but if the act be incomplete, the organs being irritated merely, and the mind not satisfied, then disease will surely follow. There is no doubt that the proper gratification of the function is conducive to health and longevity; or that its abuse leads to disease and shortens life. Therefore," he adds, "the wife should not lose control of her person in marriage. It is hers to rule supreme in this regard. This is a law of life, and is violated in no species except in man."

What better confirmation could there be of all that I have been trying to enforce upon you, than these words from this large-hearted man and widely-experienced physician? Every wife should obtain the book from which I quote these words, and study it carefully. It is entitled, "The Reproductive Organs," and has just been published by Wilstach, Baldwin & Co., of Cincinnati, Ohio.

I said at the outset that I am endeavoring to effect a revolution in marriage, or rather to replace the institution by a better method of providing for women as mothers and children as progeny. Everybody admits that our social system is far from perfect. Society, like everything else in the universe, evolves by natural laws. Marriage is not the perfect condition. It will be replaced by another and more perfect, which will be a legitimate outcome of the old. As republicanism in politics is a legitimate child of constitutional monarchy, so in socialism shall personal freedom be the offspring of legal limitation; and when it shall come, not anybody will doubt its parentage or question its legitimacy.

Sexual freedom, then, means the abolition of prostitution both in and out of marriage; means the emancipation of woman from sexual slavery and her coming into ownership and control of her own body; means the end of her pecuniary dependence upon man, so that she may never even seemingly, have to procure whatever she may desire or need by sexual favors; means the abrogation of forced pregnancy, of antenatal murder,[24] of undesired children; means the birth of love-children only, endowed by every inherited virtue that the highest exaltation can confer at conception, by every influence for good to be obtained during gestation, and by the wisest guidance and instruction on to manhood, industrially, intellectually and sexually.

It means no more sickness, no more poverty, no more crime: it means peace, plenty and security, health, purity and virtue; it means the replacement of money-getting as the aim of life by the desire to do good; the closing of hospitals and asylums, and the transformation of prisons, jails and penitentiaries into workshops and scientific schools; and of lawyers, doctors and ministers into industrial artizans; it means equality, fraternity and justice raised from the existence which they now have in name only, into practical life; it means individual happiness, national prosperity and universal good.

Ultimately, it means more than this even. It means the establishment of co-operative homes, in which thousands who now suffer in every sense shall enjoy all the comforts and luxuries of life, in the place of the isolated households which have no care for the misery and destitution of their neighbors. It means for our cities, the conversion of innumerable huts into immense hotels, as residences; and the combination of all industrial enterprises upon the same plan; and for the country, the co-operative conduct of agriculture by the maximum of improvements for labor-saving, and the consequent reduction of muscular toil to the minimum. And it means the inter-co-operation of all these in a grand industrial organization to take the places of the present governments of the world, whose social basis shall be all people united in the great human family as brothers and sisters.

So after all I am a very promiscuous Free Lover. I want the love of you all, promiscuously. It makes no difference who or what you are, old or young, black or white, Pagan, Jew, or Christian, I want to love you all and be loved by you all; and I mean to have your love. If you will not give it to me now, these young, for whom I plead, will in after years bless Victoria Woodhull for daring to speak for their salvation. It requires a strong and a pure woman to go before the world and attack its most cherished institution. No one who has not passed through the fiery furnace of affliction, and been purged of selfishness by the stern hand of adversity, and become emancipated from public opinion, could stand the load of opprobrium that I have been forced to carry. I sometimes grow weary under its weight and sigh for rest, but my duty to my sex spurs me on. Therefore I want your sympathy, your sustaining love, to go with me and bless me; and when I leave you for other fields of labor and stand upon other rostrums, fearing I may not be able to do my duty, I want to feel the yearnings of your hearts following me with prayers that my efforts may be blessed. I want the blessings of these fathers, the affections of these sons, the benedictions of these mothers and the prayers of these daughters to follow me everywhere, to give me strength to endure the labor, courage to speak the truth and a continued faith that the right will triumph.

And may the guardian angels who are hovering over you carry the benign light of freedom home to your souls to bless each sorrowing heart, to relieve each suffering body, and to comfort each distressed spirit as it hath need, is the blessing which I leave with you.

# Chapter Twenty-Two

## *The Garden of Eden;*
or, Paradise Lost and Found

*Mary Gabriel describes this as one of Victoria Woodhull's most popular speeches (Gabriel,* Notorious Victoria, *241); Woodhull herself called it "the chief work of her life" (quoted in Frisken,* Victoria Woodhull's Sexual Revolution, *186n57). She delivered it in 1876. It was later published in* The Human Body the Temple of God. *The latter version begins with a statement by Woodhull and a lengthy passage from Genesis.[1] The following is a brief excerpt from the essay.*

People talk of purity without the least conception of the real meaning of the term. They imagine those are pure who restrict themselves to commerce sanctioned by the law, and when not under law, abstain altogether. Now, this is not the test of natural virtue—you may call it legal virtue if you like—it is the legal kind, but the genuine sort is of the heart. Those who are virtuous simply because there is a law to make them so, belong to the class of whom Jesus said, "They make clean the outside of the platter, but within are full of dead men's bones, and all uncleanness."[2] The people who do no evil because they have no desire to do it, are infinitely more virtuous than are they who refrain because there is a legal or any other kind of penalty attached thereto. So it is with the relations of the sexes. They are the really pure who need no law to compel them to do the right. I do not say that the law has not been useful, nor that it is not useful still. It is better to be restrained by law from doing wrong than not to be restrained at all; but it is those who need restraint who ought to be ashamed, and not those who have grown beyond the need of law and wish for freedom from its force....

Jesus said, that "He that looketh on a woman to lust after her, hath committed adultery with her already in his heart."[3] Judged by this standard at purity, who are not adulterers? I will tell you who, and who only. Only those are not who can stand the test of natural virtue; and this test is never to do an act for which, under any circumstances, there is cause to be ashamed. Adam and Eve were not ashamed until they had eaten the forbidden fruit—the fruit of the tree which stood in "the midst of the garden," "whose seed is within itself;"[4] but the moment they had done what they knew to be a wrong; when they had learned of good, by knowing evil as its contrast, by reason of having done the evil, then they were ashamed and made covers for themselves. They are sexually pure and virtuous who enter into the most sacred and intimate relations of life, just as they would go before their God, and by being drawn to them by the Spirit of God, which is ever present in His temple, and ready to respond when called upon aright.

This is to have natural virtue, of which when once possessed there is no need to have the other sort. This is to have natural, in place of artificial purity. People who are pure and virtuous in this way may be brought into intimate physical relations, and never think of commerce; they may not only live in the same house, and eat at the same table, but they may even sleep in the same bed, and never have a lustful thought come into their souls, or a passion fire their bodies. Now, this is the kind of virtue, purity and morality that I would have established; it is the kind I advocate as the highest condition to which the race can rise. Those who censure me for what I teach and live, had better know that they can stand the test, which I present, before condemning either me or what I advocate. Suppose that the world were in the condition of which I speak, do you not know that it would be a thousand times more pure than what it is? Answer this to your souls before condemning Mrs. Woodhull again, and when you hear her defamed by others, have the manhood or the womanhood, as the case may be, to ask her defamers if they know what it is that they condemn?

THE GARDEN OF EDEN

But do you say that all this is too far in the future to be of any use now? This plea is often made. But it would not be made at all by those who offer it if they would stop to see its bearing. If the objections have any rightful force against my teachings they have a four-fold force against what Jesus taught. The only new commandment that he gave is scarcely kept by any human being yet. But shall it be said that the doctrine of that command ought not to have been broached upon the earth by Jesus at that time—ought not to have been given to the people till they were ready to receive and live it? None of you, I think, will say so much as that. The people begin to have a little comprehension of that doctrine now, because it was given to them at that time. He taught the people that they ought to love each other well enough to have all things in common. Are any of you ready, even now, almost 2,000 years since Jesus taught, to live that teaching? And if so, how many? but if not, who shall dare presume to question the propriety of teaching what I do? I cannot have a more complete endorsement than to have it said that the people are not yet good enough to live the doctrines that I teach.

I know that there are many who think, or who pretend to think, or who pretend to think that they think that, if my social theories were to be made the rule of life and the law of social intercourse, there would be anarchy and confusion in the social realm. But if they really do imagine this, I can assure them that they do not give the people credit enough for goodness. Bad as they are, they are not half so bad as some would make them out to be. Place men and women on their honor, and most of them would do better than they now do under the restraints of law. A law forbidding anything is a direct challenge to all who possess the capacity, to do the thing forbidden. You are all familiar with this principle, but you never think of applying it to the social relations, while it is really more applicable to them than it is to almost anything else. But, if the people are not good enough to live under the law of individual honor, then it is quite time that some one should have the courage to go before the world and begin to advocate the things that are needed to make them so; and, instead of throwing all possible obstacles in my path, the world ought to help me on my way, and thank God that I have the inclination and the strength to do what I am doing.

Before leaving this part of my subject, I wish again to impress it upon you that when there is purity in the heart, it cannot be obscene to consider the natural functions of any part of the body, whether male or female. I am aware that this is a terrible truth to tell to the world, but it is a truth that the world needs to be told in thunder tones nevertheless; one which it must fully realize before the people will give that care and attention to their creative functions which must precede salvation from impending death. In the eyes of the Creator, the reproductive system performs the highest and divinest functions of the body. It is the holy of holies, from whence God's highest purposes have been evolved. Can such functions, or the organs that perform them, be vulgar? Can that, by the use of which man is created only "a little lower than the angels,"[5] be obscene? Nay, charge not such degradation upon God. Let man rather acknowledge that what God has most preferred has been debased in vulgar thoughts and acts. What can be more sublimely beautiful, more entrancingly sublime than the thought that within ourselves—in our bodies—there is the power to create an immortal soul, and an immortal residence for that soul, if we will but learn aright—if we will but learn the truth, which, by being known, shall make us free indeed.

Then who shall dare blaspheme a place where such perfections dwell by daubing it all over with his own vulgarity and his filth? Who shall dare look God in the face and say that the place where he performs His noblest works; nay, that is His holy temple—the kingdom of God—is obscene? Perish the thought, I say, and perish the vulgarity that makes such thoughts possible, and let those who have them take heed lest they die, not only past the hope of resurrection, but also past the hope of escaping death eternal.

If all this be true of the creative parts of the human body, if they be God's perfectest and divinest exemplifications of His power, why should they not be the Garden of Eden? Where should the land of pleasure and delight be found if not within the human body? This, God created not only "a little lower than the angels," but "crowned it with glory and honor,"[6] that glory and honor being the power which it has to create as God creates. Is there any other place or thing in the universe more worthy to be called an Eden? called the happy land? called the paradise? Is it not in this garden where man and woman find their greatest source of happiness? Then why degrade it below the level of the brute? Why attempt to make it what it never was, save in the impure thoughts of the people, and what it was never intended to be by God? No! . . .

Then let who may, esteeming himself a better judge than God, condemn this Garden as impure. We shall prefer rather to give it the worship and the honor that so wonderful a thing ought to command, and to treat it reverently as if we were in the presence of our God. Let those who can join in this reverential sentiment take home what we are now about to say of this Garden of Eden, and give it that thought and study which the gravity and grandeur of the subject demand most clearly. Let me assure you if you will do this you will never again think meanly of, or do meanly by, your own bodies, nor wish to do meanly by the body of anybody else; but that, instead, you will do what Paul commanded (1st Corinthians vi. 20): "Glorify God in your body."

Any one who will read the second chapter of Genesis, divorced from the idea that it relates to a spot of ground, anywhere on the face of the earth, must, it seems to me, come to, or near, the truth. We have shown, conclusively, that it is not a Garden in the common acceptance of that term; indeed that the Garden of Eden, according to Moses, is a physical absurdity, if it be interpreted to mean what it is commonly held to mean by the Christian world. We believe that many of its best scholars have long since seen this but have not dared to express it. They have not been willing to accept the modifications of their religious theories which a rejection of the propositions upon which they are based would make inevitable, and so between the two alternatives they have clung fast to the old and ignored the new, so that it should not be necessary for them to make a change that would lead to, they knew not where.

We are now prepared to assert that the Garden of Eden is the human body, that every body is a Garden of Eden, and that the second chapter of Genesis was written by Moses to mean the body; and that it cannot mean anything else. Furthermore, that Moses chose the language used because it describes the functions and uses of the body better than any other that he could choose without using the plain terms. The first words: "And the Lord God planted a Garden eastward in Eden"[7] demonstrate what I wish to impress; for Eden is the land of pleasure and delight. Could there have been a more poetic statement of what really did occur? The spiritual sight of Moses revealed to him that the first reasoning human beings were the product of the land of pleasure and delight, as such beings still continue to be. All mankind were created in that Garden, in pleasure and delight. This method of expression is in perfect keeping with the times in which Moses wrote; indeed, it is in perfect keeping with a much later period of time than that of Moses. What more complete idea could there be formed of paradise than a perfect human body—such as there must have been before there had been corruption and degradation in the relation of the sexes? Therefore the Garden of Eden, in which the Lord God put the man whom he had formed, "to keep it and to dress it,"[8] and in which He created Adam and Eve—universal thinking man—was the human body.

But now let us go on with the application of our former inquiries into this garden of pleasure and delight. "And a river went out of Eden to water the Garden, and it was parted and became into four heads."[9] The name of the first river is Pison, as we have seen. It will be remembered that this term signifies changing and extension of the mouth. Now, apply this rendering to the body and see if we cannot find River Pison in this Havilah, which we failed to find in the Arabian land. How is the body watered and fed? Is it not by a stream which is the extension of the mouth, and that changes constantly as it encircles the system? Does not the support of the body enter it by the mouth, and by the river which is the extension of the mouth, run to the stomach? "And from thence it was parted and became into four heads."[10] Now, this is precisely what is going on in the body all the time. From the stomach, or rather from the small intestines, where the separating process in the chyle, which is the digested contents of the stomach, begins, this River Pison has four principal heads; that is, it divides and becomes into four heads, giving off three branches, while the main current continues on its course to compass the whole land of Havilah. This current—this River Pison—empties itself into the heart, and then into the lungs, where it is de-carbonized and oxygenized, and returned to the heart to be distributed over the entire system by the arterial circulation. In its course toward the extremities it gives to the various parts through which it passes their necessary supplies. This constant giving-off changes the character of the current as constantly, until the circumference of the body is reached. From thence it is returned to the heart through the veinous circulation, gathering up the worn-out matter to expel it from the body. This is the process by which the River Pison compasseth the whole land of Havilah, which is the land "that suffers pain and brings forth," and in which there are precious things, besides the bdellium and the onyx-stone. This land that suffers pain and brings forth is the land of Havilah, which is compassed by the River Pison. Can any one conceive a more graphic description of the process by which the body is nourished and fed? A river, to water the land of pleasure and delight, enters by the mouth, and extending by the way of the stomach, intestines, heart, lungs, arteries and veins, waters the whole land that suffers pain and brings forth. What is there in the world to which this description of the River Pison and the land of Havilah could be applied, save to the body? It cannot be found. I challenge the world to find it. It would be absurd, simply, to say that the district south-east of Sanaa,[11] in Arabia, which is called Havilah, suffers pain in bringing forth. Nevertheless, this is the Christian's land of Havilah.

"And the name of the second river is Gihon: the same is it that compasseth the whole land of Ethiopia."[12] The first branch that divides from the main river of the body is that which drains the body by the way of the intestines. This is the River Gihon, which is the valley of grace. Could there be a more appropriate name than that of "grace" for the process by which the refuse from the River Pison is discharged from the body? or than the valley of grace for the operations that are performed within the abdomen for the elimination from the body of the refuse that is gathered there, and which bursts forth from the valley as from a fountain. Is not this a process of grace?—a process of natural and involuntary purification? If it were not for this process of grace we should be lost through the debris of which the system is relieved by this bursting forth of the River Gihon from this valley of grace.

And this is the river that compasseth the whole land of Ethiopia—the land of blackness (darkness), and where there is heat. That is to say, the intestines occupy the abdominal cavity which is the land of darkness in Eden. All of the movements that are made therein are made in darkness, and therein also is the heat, which signifies the warmth that gives and maintains life; that maintains the old and that produces the new; that sustains the temperature of the body, and that gives it the power to reproduce. Physiologically this is absolutely true, just as are all the other descriptions and allegories that are given by Moses of the Garden.

"And the name of the third river is Hiddekel, that is it which goeth toward the east of Assyria."[13] Next in importance to the maintenance of the human economy, is the river that drains the system of another class of impurities, running by the way of the kidneys, uretus, bladder and urethra. This is the river Hiddekel; or the stream that runs with a "swift current" and a "sharp sound." Search the language through and through for a more appropriate description for the elimination of the waste matter by the means of the urinary organs than this one given by Moses, and find it if you can[.] And this river of Eden runs toward the east of Assyria, which is the happy land of the Garden. Those who dwell in this land are in the happy land of the Garden of Eden, in the midst of which is the tree of life—are in the land of pleasure and delight. That this may be still more evident, it is proper to remark there, that it is the female human body which is referred to by Moses, because it is her body that suffers pain in bringing forth, while that of the male stands as representative for the Lord God, who planted the Garden that has produced universal man; and it was the producing part of the Garden—the reproductive female power—that was the land which was cursed in Eden by the transgressions, by eating of the fruit of the tree of life improperly. It was this curse that woman's "sorrows and conceptions were multiplied," as stated by Moses.[14] So the happy land of the Garden of Eden—its Assyria—is the producing land of the human family into which the Lord God put the man whom he had formed, "to keep it and to dress it," so that it might lie fruitful. Don't you see how perfect the allegorical statement is, which Moses made?

"And the fourth river is Euphrates." The last river of the Garden of Eden is that one which renders it fruitful; that makes it yield its fruit and that flows through the reproductive system. Euphrates means fruitfulness, and this river, the last one in the order of physiological sequence, is the fruit or the result of the perfected action of all the others combined. This river, as seen by Moses, was in its natural, healthful, primitive state of purity, from which purity, from which physical purity, Adam and Eve fell by the improper use of the functions of the Garden, which were committed to their care, the same as people still continue to do, and are cursed—die in Adam—as Adam and Eve were cursed. All this is peculiarly feminine, since it is from the waters of the river Euphrates, that the fruit of the tree of life (whose seed, as Moses said, is within itself) is developed and perfected. In the female system, the water of this fourth river Euphrates is being separated constantly from the great river Pison—the blood—and made into the matter of life, out of which the body of the child in the womb is constructed. But this stream of life was turned to blood by the transgressions of primitive man, and has been entirely wasted to the race, save that small portion which is utilized during gestation. The supposition that this river is something of which the female system ought to be relieved; that it is lifeless, disgusting and corrupt, is false and wrong. It is precisely the same matter of which the body of the child, its flesh, bone, nerve and brain is formed, and when it is not used in this way, it is the hidden manna of the Revelations by which your bodies and my body ought to be constantly replenished, so that they would never grow old and die; for do you not see, if it be from this river that the body of the child, is formed; if its waters can be utilized in the bodies in which they are manufactured, that they would have a well of water in them springing up into everlasting life, as Jesus explained to the Samaritan woman? It is the method, the process, by which this utilization, this appropriation is to be effected, which is the great hidden mystery of the Bible, which, when revealed and understood and practised, will redeem the body from the power of death and hell, which is the devil of the Bible. I mean just this—I mean that the salvation which Jesus came to bring to light, and which he did bring to light, is the salvation from death; and that it is to come through a proper life in the much despised Garden of Eden.

But this river of life has been left to waste the health and strength—the vigor and vitality—of the race away, and no efforts have been made to remedy the destruction which it threatens, which is a no less disaster than the fruitfulness of the Garden itself, and the consequent wiping out of the race. This wasteful process is considered to be a natural function and necessary to health and life, and so indeed it is, all in the unnatural conditions in which we live, and in which the world has lived since this river was turned to waste, as described by Moses, allegorically, in the 4th and 7th chapters of Exodus. This wasting away of the life of the race is the vicarious atonement by which death is averted for the time. Oh! that I could tell the world, that you would let me tell you what I know about this terrible, terrible fact! But the fullness of time is not yet, and I must be content to see the race still, for a time, rush madly onward toward destruction and extinction; but when the New Jerusalem[15] (which is the purified woman) shall come in the new heaven and the new earth, as seen by John on Patmos Isle,[16] then this river of waste will return again to be "A pure river of life proceeding out of the throne of God"[17]—proceeding out of His highest creative place—out of the happy land of the Garden of Eden—the land of pleasure and delight, through which flows the beautiful and fruitful river Euphrates. In the midst of the waters of this river there shall be also the tree of life, the leaves of which are for the healing of the nations.

The Garden of Eden, then, is the human body, and its four rivers, which have their source in the extension of the mouth, are the Pison, the blood; the Gihon, the bowels; the Hiddekel, the urinary organs; and the Euphrates, the reproductive functions. By these four rivers the whole Garden is watered and or nourished and supported, drained of refuse matter, and its fruit produced. It was in this Garden that mankind was planted by the Lord God after the same manner in which He performs all his other works—through the agency of law and order, as exemplified in evolution. It was the ground of this Garden that was cursed, so that in sorrow man should "eat of it all the days of his life," and that it should bring forth "thorns and thistles,"[18] as Moses said it should, instead of the pleasant and agreeable fruit of perfect and beautiful children. Has not this allegorical picture been literally verified? Has there not been sorrow upon sorrow for man; and have not woman's "sorrows and conceptions been multiplied" until the whole earth is groaning, as Paul said, for the redemption of the body. Paul said even himself was also groaning, having but "the first fruits of the spirit;"[19] that is to say, having the intellectual comprehension of the means for redemption of his body, but not its physical realization, because he had no counterparting life through which to receive it. But John saw that these fruits were to be fully realized in the new heaven and the new earth, meaning the new man and the new woman, when "to him that overcometh"[20] and is able to pass the cherubims and the flaming sword set at the gates of the Garden of Eden—the sentries guarding the approaches to the Holy City—shall be given to eat of the "hidden Manna";[21] and this hidden manna is the pure water of life of the fruitful river Euphrates, and the fruit of the tree of life, mingling their divine essences, under the blessings of Almighty God. When this shall come then "there shall be no more death, neither sorrow nor crying, neither any more pain."[22] The new Jerusalem, the new woman, "shall then come down from God out of heaven,"[23] as the new Man Jesus came down, "adorned as a bride prepared for her husband,"[24] the new woman being the bride and the new man being the husband, through which marriage of the bride and the Lamb, the union of the worlds, so long separated, will be re-established, the resurrection day inaugurated, and the judgment day begun.

"Adorned as a bride prepared for her husband." Can there be any mistaking the significance of this figure? Can it mean anything save the perfected union of the sexes in the reopened Garden of Eden? returned to its primitive and pristine beauty and purity? And in the understanding that this perfection is coming to the world, hear the sounding of the seventh angel who comes to herald forth the doom of death, and realize the prophecy of Paul, who said: "The last enemy that shall be destroyed is death,"[25] and reveal the mystery of God hid from the foundation of the world in Christ.

Welcome! Thrice welcome!! Thou messenger of God! And welcome! Thrice welcome! Thrice welcome!! Thou regenerated Garden of Eden, which God's messenger doth herald! In thy grateful shades, beneath thy life-giving trees, and in the health-restoring waters of thy pure rivers do we long to cleanse ourselves from all impurities. Welcome! thrice welcome!! Thou rebuilt Temple of God!!! In thy magnificent splendors we fain would worship the Great High Priest and King, and pour out our souls in holiest praise and song! Welcome! thrice welcome!! Thou Kingdom of God!!! Eagerly and earnestly we seek to renew our long-lost allegiance before the throne whereon sitteth Him who hath prepared all these glories for his children from the foundation of the world, to be realized in these last days by the way which our elder brother hath opened up to us. Welcome! thrice welcome all!!! Dost thou, three in one, come as the fulfillment of all the prophecies, of all the wise and good of olden time, on which the children of this world have hung in the sublimest hope and faith so long—a faith and hope which saw no way to consummation, but yet, which never wavered even in the darkest hour! Art thou the realization of that for which the gentle Jesus suffered, died and lived again; art thou the life eternal which he came to offer us? When we catch glimpses of thy perfections, we do indeed see them through the door by which he entered once into the holiest place, and is set down forever at the right hand of God, to invite us all to seats beside him! Shall we enter through the gates into the holy city, by "The straight and narrow way," and find eternal life in the sunshine thy everlasting glories, O, enchanting Garden!

Yes! This is what the great and loving Father hath prepared for all his children from the beginning, to all of whom it shall be realized in God's own good time, as He shall be able to draw Himself, and enter them into their rest to know no sorrow more forever; but in glad anthems of never-ending progress, expand their souls, until they shall be one with God, and see Him face to face. This is what it is to enter once more into the Garden of Eden and to live bathed in the glory of its pleasures and delights.

# Chapter Twenty-Three

*Stirpiculture;*
or, the Scientific Propagation
of the Human Race

*This essay was published in London in February 1888. The first paragraph is omitted here.*

Sociology may be compared to the construction of a building: the myriads of poor are the foundation; the rest of the structure corresponds to the different grades of society. The last could not exist without the first named. It is the struggling masses who are the foundation; and if the foundation be rotten or insecure, the rest of the structure must eventually crumble. We must not consider the durability of the structure from the upper portion, that is, the upper classes, to whom the existing social condition is well enough; but we must look to the foundation of the structure, or, in other words, the millions of wretched humanity who are daily increasing and whose condition is becoming inevitably more miserable. The architect of this building corresponds to the Government; and, before he commences to build, he must be quite sure that the foundations are all right, so as to give strength and support to the whole....

We shall always find people devoting their lives to perfecting beautiful orchids or some other rare plant; astronomers are searching the sidereal universe to find some new star; amateur breeders in the highest circles of society are devoting their time and their money to perfect their horses and cattle; farmers employ different food for the different effects they wish to have in their sheep,—fine wool, or excessive fat, &c.; all the influences of temperature, air, food, and external surroundings, are brought to bear to perfect the animal and vegetable organisms: but to waste a moment's reflection over the solution of perfecting so miserable a creature as man, what he may become, to what standard he may attain—impossible, the discussion is vulgar. The consequence is that people are not shocked to read and discuss the terrible crimes which may be committed by so low and vulgar a creature as man, or the horrible descriptions of want and misery accumulating on every side among the poor; but they are shocked at anyone's daring to talk of the causes that made this crime and misery possible.

Even the discussion of these social evils can scarcely mitigate the degraded condition of the people whom it is most necessary to reach. Among the poor, to all that appeals to the worst side of man's nature is given full scope. In the terrible fight for existence, they are obliged to work hard all day, and sometimes far into the night, having no time to pause, to consider the terrible evil that they are daily making greater by this crime of reproducing in their offspring their own debilitated condition both of body and of mind. They are perpetuating the hereditary curse from which they are daily praying that death may release them; but from which they are too weak, morally and physically, to abstain from cursing their children with. And these children have not only the hereditary instincts of crime to contend against, but are made familiar from their infancy with vice of every description. And when we read in the daily papers, that crime among children is becoming more prevalent, who is responsible? When our cities are counting their outcasts and paupers by the tens of thousands, to whom are we to look for relief; when those in authority, who represent the people, remain apathetic, or say, when appealed to, that they are powerless to offer a remedy?

In the pulpit, and in every department of life, leaders and teachers are shutting their eyes to this growing evil; but still they say that there has been no suffering like the present; and they make charitable appeals for countless starving, ignorant people, regardless of the causes that make these charities possible. And yet they insist that the people are not prepared for the discussion of the scientific propagation of the race. *The time never was nor ever will be ready for the cowards who fear to be included among the agitators of an unpopular subject.*

It is man who requires to be perfected; and in order to do this we must first understand the laws operating upon his social and physical condition. First, that condition of sociology which made certain human laws compulsory, and which created the necessity for the erection of public buildings to enforce them.

Moses studied for thirty years at the court of Pharaoh, and was initiated by the priests into those laws governing human society which preceded them. With this knowledge, he constructed laws and institutions which have been more or less modified and adapted by each succeeding government according to the degree of civilization that each nation has attained. The Ten Commandments have become an integral part of the codified laws. The Government does not leave these commandments as optional moral laws, but makes them obligatory. For example, the law says:—

Thou shalt not kill.

Thou shalt not commit adultery.

Thou shalt not steal.

Thou shalt not bear false witness against thy neighbour—that is, thou shalt not perjure thyself. If you break these laws you must suffer the penalty. The Government has the authority to enforce obedience, and therefore immense capabilities of forming the character of its subjects. By the very fact of punishing these offences, it creates a repugnance in the minds of people; and in successive generations, it is not so much the law which is the restraint, as the association that has been engendered with these crimes. It has created a horror in the human *mind* of murder, of adultery, of theft, of perjury. Why cannot it go further and add something towards perfecting the human *body*? Let the Government incorporate as part of its laws the following commandments:—

Thou shalt not marry when malformed or diseased.

Thou shalt not produce His image in ignorance.

Thou shalt not defile His Temple.

Let it make it a crime against the nation, as it is against God's Divine laws, to break these commandments, to thrust the results of their ignorance on the body social to be supported at the expense of the nation. Then in successive generations these crimes, too, may be regarded with horror and repugnance. It is no longer a question of expediency, but one of absolute necessity, which the Government will be obliged to deal with.

What is the commonweal of the public? It is to inaugurate such laws as will react with beneficial effects on its subjects. And as population increases and intellectual growth advances these laws should not remain stationary, so as to retard progress, but should be revised to keep pace with the times. The laws which were made to legislate for our forefathers, should not be allowed to become our legislators. Inertia is not progress. It is owing to the ever advancing nations that civilization has reached its present altitude. The most conservative throughout nature are ever the slowest in development.

We build institutions in order to incarcerate the insane, the idiots, the epileptics, the drunkards, the criminals, &c. If the lower organism of animals were subject to such infirmities and propensities, we should soon exterminate them; and yet we have not thought it needful to take measures to eradicate them from the highest organism, man. All such propensities have been contracted or acquired by the parental organism, or during the life of the individual itself, and have become hereditary in the offspring, reproducing itself so exactly as to develop itself at the same age in the offspring as when acquired by the parent.

What will the future enlightened ages think of the women who are calmly looking on, oblivious of the fact that their husbands are at work erecting the very edifices in which they, in their ignorance as human architects, may see their offspring incarcerated; or if not their own children, some other mother's child? And in after years, in visiting these buildings, they will see the result of their ignorance in the brutish faces of the inmates with the legible stamp of hereditary sensuality and vice. Every building erected to meet the exigencies of this ignorance will be a reproach to all womanhood. Do people realize, that nowhere on the face of the earth is there a building erected to teach people how to perfect the human body? The sooner mankind awaken to the all-important truth, that you cannot force people into moral conduct, into a better social condition—that you must educate them—the sooner we shall have emptied the buildings erected to contain those monstrosities.

The phase of civilization which envelops in mystery the origin of life conceals within itself the greatest incentive to the very crimes that intelligence would dissipate. Well did Sokrates define virtue as knowledge, and vice as ignorance. This truth should be brought home to every woman, and she should be made to feel that she is criminally responsible for all the misery from which the human race is suffering through her ignorance of the vital subject of proper generation. The vulgar prejudices of a narrow-minded people have, in woman, cloaked with ignorance the fundamental principles of life in which our mothers should be most educated—an ignorance which is powerless to inspire in their husbands and sons that chivalry and respect due to every other mother's daughter. The mothers are incapable of teaching their children what they themselves have not been taught, leave their sons and daughters in ignorance of those dangers which await them at the very threshold of the struggle for existence, leave them to take their chance in this unsympathetic, pitiless world, leaving them to weep tears of blood over the dying embers of a misspent life!

Mankind has forgotten the lesson taught by the Hindus five thousand years ago—that to degrade or to oppress woman involves the physical and moral degradation of man; that the assumption of superiority and tyranny of the master, which for ages man has assumed over woman, has almost extinguished that Divine spark in her which alone has the power to regenerate humanity.

We cannot over-estimate the influence for good or evil that the mother has over her child. Who can train with such loving tenderness the shooting tendrils of the young inquiring mind? Who can with such unerring judgment instruct the child in those dangers which surround the developing manhood and womanhood? Who is so capable of awakening the soul to a higher life? And when this is realized, and superstition and ignorance give way to a reign of intelligence, and the full comprehension that there is nothing so vulgar as ignorance, then medical statistics will not have to tell us that one half of our sons on reaching manhood are unfit to become fathers, and that one half of our daughters on reaching maturity are unfit to become mothers. For it is this class of the unfit, who, on becoming parents, engender in their children the hereditary consequences of their thoughtless marriages, thereby sealing the doom of unborn generations. The marriages of such individuals produce epileptics, idiots, neurotics, insane inebriates; and by far the larger number become criminals. Nearly all the crime committed is the result of the inherited weak blood, or a malformation, or disease of the brain. It is familiar to everyone that when the brain is injured a corresponding loss of intellectual activity supervenes, causing in some cases a total lapse of memory, or hallucinations which occasion the most extraordinary actions on the part of its victim. If we know the cause producing this effect, we regard them as irresponsible beings and try to alleviate their sufferings; but where the cause producing this effect is unknown to us, where these hallucinations and extraordinary actions are the result of an hereditary diseased formation of the brain, or injurious conditions of life reacting on the brain, we regard them as hardened criminals and hold them as responsible citizens. It only proves to us how little the psychical as well as the physical part of man is understood. We should not treat these unfortunates as criminals, as responsible beings; we should treat them as having a diseased mental condition. For it is the cooperation of the different parts of the body which insure the organization of the whole; injure one part, and the whole suffers; debauch the stomach, and the whole is debauched; disease the mind, and the whole is diseased; outrage nature, and monstrosities are the result. By the magnitude of these social evils we are overwhelmed, but of their origin we have been neglectful....

SOME THOUGHTS ABOUT AMERICA

While they promise them liberty, they themselves are the servants of corruption.
—2 *Peter ii.* 19

This is pre-eminently an age of progress. A restless dissatisfaction with the old order of things pervades every heart. The needs of the people grow daily greater, and they will not submit to being ignored. If there be a cesspool in a street, the neighbours do not hastily cover it up so that it may be hidden from the public view. No; they have the very bottom dredged that their loved ones may not sicken and die from the malaria. But the social and political cesspools may go on gathering in the germs of deadly miasma, while each human soul vies with the other to ignore the fatal effects, until the nation is ready to faint under its own corruption. I say social and political cesspools, because one is the outcome of the other.

The government of a nation indicates more than anything else the character of its people. The laws that are needed and enforced determine the degree of civilization which that nation has attained, and the extent to which the people are capable of governing themselves. The laws demonstrate whether the people are the slaves of their own passions, or whether they feel the true dignity of manhood, and are conscious that they have control over a kingdom that they within themselves can make or mar. We have nowhere on the face of the globe a government which aims at perfecting its people. Upon the slightest provocation nations and individuals alike are ready to resort to brute force which was the government of the lowest type of civilization, and from which we to-day are not educated enough to free ourselves.

The best land if left uncultivated grows the rankest weeds, so the country with the greatest possibilities, if governed unwisely, may commit the most fatal errors.

More than a hundred years have come and gone since that momentous day when our Declaration of Independence was signed. What a promise of future achievement! No shackles of autocratic despotism to weigh down the American people! They were free—free to mould their own future greatness.

Let us see how this promise has been fulfilled. The century has seen many Presidents in office; men who have had glorious opportunities to show the world that our Government was the highest type of human advancement—that they were self-made men, an example of indomitable courage and perseverance, and that through these qualities they had attained the highest office America had to bestow; that they were worthy of the nation's confidence, and would work for that nation's greatness to the best of their ability—to realize, in fact, an ideal republican government. Have we in any one respect attained this? Has any European country any confidence in our officials? Have we ourselves any reliance on the integrity of our representatives? Is it the best man to whom is entrusted the highest office? Is he put in office by the voice of the people, or by the political wire-pullers who have their own self-aggrandisement in view? We call ours a republican government. Does that mean that it is framed for and by the people, or for and by the select few? We see in every department diplomacy and trickery indifferent to the cry of the great mass of starving individuals. We shall have to give an answer to their demands before many years elapse. But unless this problem be met and grappled with soon, America will have one of the most terrible revolutions that has ever shaken the world. A political, social, and moral earthquake is concentrating its force beneath the very foundations of our so-called free country.

The laws of the United States are constructed to deal with effects only, and do not take into consideration the causes.

Good care is taken that each State shall have its prisons, lunatic, idiotic, inebriate, foundling, and other asylums; but not one building is erected nor one law enforced that would teach the people how not to contribute to these over-crowded receptacles of human misery. And yet the American Government can boast of the surplus in the United States treasury with which it is at a loss what to do.

Never a consideration or thought for the thousands of human beasts of burden who live from hand to mouth, to whom justice, nature, and God are dead letters.

But they are regaled by the Press with a description of what the President has had for breakfast, luncheon, or dinner, how many calls he has had, how many times he has shaken hands, &c. To what great uses is put the highest office that America can confer for the organizing of peace, prosperity, and good will to all!

Let us review the situation. Paupers, tramps, and professional beggars are largely on the increase. Statistics show that the same name will constantly recur among the diseased and criminal classes, and that pauperism is hereditary. Say that one criminal may be the ancestor of a thousand criminals, and one pauper the ancestor of a thousand paupers. Are these not questions that are seriously connected from an economical and social point of view with our Government? Have any of our Presidents tried to meet this question, or in any way tried to alleviate the anxiety of the people?

The social question has reached an acute stage. We may arrest the disease for a short time, but all the more terrible will be the malady when grappled with. We see thousands and thousands of parasites born every year who have no means of subsistence, who are destined to fasten upon their fellow-creatures, draining the vitality and strength of the nation, and precipitating its downfall.

It is not so much to political power that a country owes its greatness, but to that social fabric upon which all laws are based. All of our politicians are ready to deal with the effects, but not one of them is brave enough to penetrate the substratum of society and deal with the cause. A weak and vacillating leader does more to destroy a nation's greatness than does a really bad man. Our Government should be the example to the world, but above its doors of State are written in letters of blood, "*Mene, Mene, Tekel, Upharsin.*"[1] The people want the leader capable of grappling with this hydra-headed social monster and one who understands the terrible urgency of this question. For they will no longer tolerate in power the men who assert that the masses are too ignorant to comprehend the true cause of these social upheavals. The Government should make it possible for the masses to be educated on these vital subjects, that they may no longer in ignorance thrust upon the body social the myriads of paupers, and those who, to eke out a miserable existence, are forced through incompetency for labour to accept the smallest pittance. They thereby exhaust the demand for the skilled artisan, they lower the standard of labour, but above all they curse humanity by doubling their kind every few years, until all our large towns are over-populated. Education and the proper understanding of the procreative principle of life are the only checks to over-population. And this was the curse, not the blessing, which was put upon woman when she was driven out of Eden: *Unto the woman he said, I will greatly multiply thy sorrow and thy conception; in sorrow thou shalt bring forth children; and thy desire shall be to thy husband, and he shall rule over thee.* (Gen. iii. 17.)

Yes, read your Bible again, not with the understanding dwarfed and blinded by the bigotry and darkness of centuries, but with the true comprehension that we to-day are suffering from the very curse that was put upon Eve in the Eden of her body. Go anywhere among the most miserable of any community, and you will find there the largest number of improvident marriages. Mere girls and boys, married and not married, become parents before complete maturity. And herein lies the germ of the world's discontent; and the disease is not in the crust which covers the ulcer, but in the core of the ulcer itself. Until that is probed with a daring and skilful hand, socialism and poverty will go on increasing, for the people who will not, or do not know how to, work, are the superfluous, or, in other words, ought never to have been born. . . .

We have agricultural fairs all over the civilized world; each one is competing with the other to breed the finest horses and cattle, and prizes are awarded for so doing. In the animal kingdom in a few years we shall have none but domestic animals, and those in a higher state of perfection. All wandering herds will have been exterminated. But in the human kingdom, vagabondage is on the increase; and even the children of these vagabonds, when taken to reformatories or put into schools, sooner or later find their way back to swell the ranks of that rapidly increasing pauper class, who are lower than animals, having no instinct of domesticity. If the animal kingdom were subject to the debauchery, the foul air, the unwholesome food, the filthy abodes, the prevalent diseases that the human race has to contend with, in five years it would be extinct.

A man could not put on again the clothes of his childhood, he has outgrown them. The laws which clothed our constitution over a hundred years ago, when the American nation was in its infancy, are too small and too narrow in their limits for the intellectual demands of her people at the present day. The people have grown beyond them. To-day is as pregnant with revolution for independence, and as laden with as mighty import as was that memorable day in Philadelphia, when Tom Paine rose to the situation and said: "What this country wants is independence, and I mean revolution"; what the people want now is independence of thought and action and a revolution of old systems and ideas.

The Constitution of America, tattered and torn, has been hallowed by the blood of her noblest sons fighting for freedom. And that same spirit of freedom is only slumbering in the breasts of her sons and daughters to-day. And when she realizes that she is the leading nation of the world, she will rise to the occasion, and shake off the shackles of the Old World's diseased and worn-out social systems which are gradually creeping in and destroying her young life.

Victoria Woodhull Martin
*February*, 1888

# Chapter Twenty-Four

## *The Rapid Multiplication of the Unfit*

*This essay was published in London and New York in 1891. The first paragraph is omitted here.*

There are often greater differences between individuals of the same race than between individuals of different races. Some are more richly endowed with more highly evolved nervous systems. If we wish to understand the basis of a superior faculty, we study how the nervous system of the individual has become specialized. In the same way if we wish to understand the inferiority of individuals we study in what way their nervous systems are defective. It is this differentiation of the nervous system which separates man from man more effectually than geographical isolation in our modern civilization. The period of reaction to tactual, to auditory, to visual sensations, depends upon the physiological condition of the central nervous system....

In the same way that we build insane asylums to house our insane because they have lost their mental balance, so we build pauper institutions for those who have lost their physical balance. The vagabond, the pauper, is as much born and made one as the man of insane temperament under stress demonstrates his neurotic heredity and the criminal his pathological condition. The terrible effects on posterity of depleting our workers and then allowing them in ignorance to breed is the burning question for humanity. The physical condition of the population of a manufacturing town is proverbial.

It is said that in a new country where the land has not yet been appropriated, there is no such thing as the unemployed or the pauper. When colonists first settle upon a piece of land there is plenty of outdoor exercise, manly pursuits, work which does not cause physical deterioration. But after a time as population increases and sedentary occupations take the place of active pursuits, crowded enclosed workrooms supplant work in the open air, the energy of the workers is gradually sapped by artificial life in cities, and they become the progenitors of a class physically enfeebled, spiritless, incapable of sustained effort. Work is carried on by means of the contractions of muscular fibres.[1] ... The pallid faces and stunted growth of some of our town-bred workers tell their own tales. If exhaustion be carried too far in the living organism fatigue ensues, and in fatigue the muscles are slow to respond to stimuli. Individuals who are tired move and think more slowly and are less energetic. It can be imagined how terrible are the physical results that ensue to those whose normal condition is one of fatigue.

Power of endurance in individuals is not equal; so that we could not say that eight hours' work or that less or more is beneficial to all alike. One may work eight hours continuously and not be exhausted, whereas another may be totally exhausted in six. Physicians warn us that if we do not allow sufficient rest to a tired organ to recuperate, waste products accumulate producing poisons which are a fruitful source of disease. The most active agent in generating the unfit is fatigue poison.[2] If a large percentage of histories of family degeneration can be traced in the offspring of parents who have passed the prime of life, how much larger must the percentage of family degeneration be that is due to physical exhaustion from overwork or the lack of sufficient light and fresh air. ...

It is said that one in every five of the population of London does die or is destined to die in a hospital, the workhouse, or pauper lunatic asylum. *Pari passu*[3] with this statistical statement the cry is growing louder for more public institutions to house the incapable, and it is urged that all stigma should be removed from them.

In visiting one of these institutions a short time since, in one of the wards I saw a little child moving about with the aid of a chair, its body being too big and heavy for its legs; in another ward a nurse, who was carrying a baby covered with scrofulous sores, asked me if I would adopt it. The baby had no one to claim it and they were only waiting to find someone who would take charge of it. There were cases of hip disease, some had been successfully operated upon. There was one with spina bifida. The doctor took great pride in showing me a child on whom he had just operated for hare-lip; my attention was drawn to the success he had had in delivering a mother of an idiotic baby. What is the destiny of these children? They require able-bodied nurses from their birth, and able-bodied physicians to spend their valuable time over them. They are scarcely ever able to shift for themselves, they are a care all their lives, and at last swell the ranks of the one in five who die in the hospital, the workhouse, or pauper lunatic asylum....

The following extract I copied from a paper: "A woman named Abigail Cochrane, who has just died at Kilmalcolm at 84 years of age, was a pauper from the cradle to the grave. She was born in Greenock in 1807, and was imbecile from her earliest youth. It is estimated that she cost the public purse between £2000 and £3000."

As in the case of Abigail Cochrane, each one of our human failures adds a considerable item to the burden, already large, put upon the healthy useful citizens. And if our present industrial workers are overtaxed, overburdened, and under the strain their health is undermined, what benefit will their progeny be to future generations? How are superior qualities to be transmitted to the offspring, if for generations the economic pressure has been so great as to deteriorate the physical constitution of their progenitors?...

Many are so deficient in sensibility that although afferent impulses may be started by the most beautiful pictures, sculpture, divine strains of music, noble and humane examples, in fact the most sublime combinations of nature and art, they will awaken no response, they will arouse no afferent processes of noble thoughts and actions. This accounts for the fact that certain persons only take pleasure in vulgar low resorts and the companionship of coarse people. They seek their affinities. The saying is, that a man is known by the company he keeps; in other words, his nervous system is similarly developed.

If we study the nervous system of the pauper class, we find that instead of their nervous energy being economically expended, there is lavish, uneven and wasteful expenditure which is of no great benefit to the individual nor to society. They are organically deficient: they inherit defective, ill-regulated nervous systems, or their nervous systems become badly adjusted through irregular habits, bad training, or diseases. They are incapable of sustained effort. They prefer jobs to regular work, spasmodic efforts to work for a few hours or days, and these efforts are followed by a reaction of utter inability to make further exertion. They can assign no reason why any sustained effort is wearisome to the last degree. These characteristics are symptomatic of retrogression, or they are the reappearance of a more primitive type.

There are savages who will work hard to collect material things, and then will debauch and idle away weeks and months until the pangs of hunger compel them to make another effort to work. In this we have the simplest condition of economic pressure. It is said that the special characteristic of the savage is that he has no thought for the morrow. He eats until he can eat no more, then goes hungry until he finds more food. These very characteristics we see exhibited among our own savages. I saw a poor man, who said he was hungry and had been given some bread and cheese, eat until his hunger was appeased and then throw the bread and cheese which remained into the street; he could not or did not realize that in a few hours he would be hungry again. I have frequently seen bread thrown away by such and lying in the street. To them bread had been given once, it would be given again, or they would go hungry until the pangs of hunger compelled them to make a further effort to procure more. It is a waste of words to say that these individuals are paupers because they have not been careful, thrifty, and temperate. We might lecture for hours to them on the advantages of industry, we might urge our plea with the fervour of a divine oracle, the afferent impulses we give rise to arouse no response in those torpid brains. For our plea to have an effect they must be given new nervous systems and healthy rich blood, in other words, they must not be bred. It is characteristic of those organically defective that it is the voluntary part of their nature which is most affected. They have not the *will* to make any exertion, they fall into the conditions which circumstances place them. With the offspring of parents suffering from fatigue or other poison, compulsory education may be enforced, but our efforts will not be repaid by healthy useful individuals unless they spring from a healthy source.

Political economists have said that the conscientious, the right-minded, will not marry until they are in a position to do so, and herein is the *crux* of the social problem. The more highly developed human beings yield less and less readily to the dictates of sexual passion alone. They judge and consider consequences. They profit by the experiences of others and therefore avoid doing that which will bring sorrow to those whom they love. High motives deter the fit from marrying until they are in a position to do so. Among the better classes marriage is being deferred more and more, the standard of living is becoming higher among them, and more time is given to education, whereas the unfit who are not deterred by any qualms of conscience or apprehension of consequences go on multiplying. And as the more highly developed are not perpetuated, or if perpetuated it is in fewer numbers, the thoughtless, improvident, degenerate, and diseased, multiply upon us.

An educated man made the remark a short time ago, "The cause of so much misery among the poor to-day is over-population, it is their reckless indulgence in large families. I am too poor to marry, I can't afford to have a family, I wish I could, and yet I am called upon to pay taxes to educate and help to support others' paupers." Here is a man who was accustomed to a certain standard of living, and who therefore did not care to have offspring who would not have the same advantages as he had had, or to have a family who might become a burden on others. An example of the conscientious not marrying until he could afford it, a result which is most disastrous in its effects on the quality of the human race.

A man may possess a noble character and have a magnificent physique, but if he do not perpetuate these qualities they do not survive. A man may be diseased, stupid or reckless, but withal he marries and raises a large family: his qualities are perpetuated, but it is not the survival of the fittest. Many men break their health down by overwork, and the terrible strain is seen in the physical condition of their children. Many men have not over exerted themselves, and have had no scruples about living on the charity of their relations or friends, and hence their children do not suffer from the depleted physical condition of their fathers; but are these children the survival of fittest? Moral checks which would appeal to the superior intellectual mind, do not influence the unfit. In the majority of cases they have not a nervous system sufficiently developed to appreciate these motives.

A great many seem to think that interference with marriages of the unfit will only give greater opportunities to races, lower in the scale of development who are multiplying so fast, to overcome and conquer the more advanced races. We have an example of this in the rapid multiplication of the negroes in America, who at some not far distant day will outnumber and overrun the whites if the rapid increase be not checked. Eventually, if America is owned and governed by negroes, would it be the survival of the fittest? The outlook is as ominous in Europe.

Mr. Raines[4] states in his census of the population of India, that the returns show an increase of thirty millions in the population in ten years, the total being 285,000,000. Add to this number 400,000,000, or probably more in China, and it looks as if these vast hordes may yet overrun and wipe out Western civilization. With this spectre looming up in the distance it is considered a dangerous policy to advocate any theory which would tend to limit the population of Western nations. The argument holds good if we wish simply to limit the numbers of the population of the fit, but has no application with regard to the marriages of the unfit. An American child brought up in China, if it had a defective nervous system, will demonstrate it in China; and a Chinese child brought up in Europe, if born of diseased parents, will demonstrate its hereditary condition here. We find often that physical causes, not numbers, determine whether races shall be conquerors or conquered. Stamina often gives the victory to a race. Generalship indicates superior development of the general.

But in any attempt to raise the standard of humanity, to aid evolution, we must take into consideration that it is not the survival of the fittest, but the survival of the unfit by means of their rapid multiplication in societies as presently organized.

Any cause which determines the mating of individuals has a direct influence on the quality of the human race. All artificial social inducements for the mating of unsuitable individuals are instruments for the multiplication of the unfit. To prove how detrimental our present social life is to the human race, we have only to ask how many of the marriages which take place would be consummated if there were no social inducements, no fear of public opinion, no regard for the law, if there were no other inducement but the fact that he is male and she female, and that they are physiologically mated. How many who to-day are not mated would under such a state come together and propagate, and how many who to-day propagate from other inducements than love would no longer not do so? One great cause of the rapid multiplication of the unfit over the fit, is our false social system which places so many obstacles to prevent the coming together of our best men and women.

How many opportunities has a girl to find her physiological mate in her little set—even if she were free to choose? Sexual selection has very little scope in our conventional system. Take the many instances of women who marry for a home, very often the only choice between that and starvation, and ask if there could be a greater perversion of the sexual instinct. I have heard it said, "What a good marriage Mr. ——— has made, he married a girl with fifty thousand pounds, more or less; *she* is ugly and unattractive, but what a windfall for him." A suitable marriage is often considered the one which will relieve the man from his debts or the marriage which will raise him or her up in the social or financial world. Money bags are highly valued in the marriage mart, and the, at present, artificial sign indicating that you, the vulgar, might not know the value of this piece of human flesh, so we tabulate him Lord or Prince.

Thousands of examples might here be given of the *marriages de convenance* of old men and young girls, and of young men and aged women which are so frequent nowadays. When these marriages are fruitful they too often produce idiots, murderers, or otherwise unfit. There are many social barriers which prevent the respectable poor from making physiologically suitable marriages. A respectable working woman said, "I work with a great many men, but after business hours I do not dare go about with any of them, for immediately all kinds of reports would be circulated which would ruin my reputation." The reckless or unfit not being deterred by any false restrictions go on multiplying. . . .

To sum up some of the principal causes in the rapid multiplication of the unfit, we may class them under two heads, namely, Physiological and Psychological.

Among the probable Psychological causes are:—

(1.) The more intelligent the individuals the more they think of consequences and the less likely are they to be influenced by sexual passion alone. Later marriages among the upper classes with the result of having fewer children, and if too long deferred the marriages are infertile. The improvident therefore would marry first and would rear the largest number of offspring. The sense of responsibility develops with age, but the very poor marry at very early ages.

(2.) Among the unfit easier modes of becoming acquainted, less prudery, more freedom in the intercourse of the sexes.

(3.) The mystery and secresy which envelopes these natural functions, too often create a morbid desire which often leads to masturbation and other practices.

(4.) Marriages among the upper classes for money and position, or the marriages of those who have not sufficient opportunities under our present social decrees to seek and find a more suitable partner.

(5.) The sexual passion excited by the intermingling of the sexes in overcrowded tenements; whole families often sleeping in one room. A lady who has a home for girls to help them through their first confinement, and to save first offenders, if possible, said: "It is appalling the number of girls who come here who have been seduced by their own brothers."

Among the probable Physiological causes are:—

(1.) Marriages of the immature, those who have passed the prime of life, or the physically exhausted, which produce offspring lacking in vigour and mental power, and only too often absolute idiocy is the result.

(2.) Inbreeding, especially if the parents are very similar, which intensifies morbid tendencies, the offspring from these marriages suffer from impaired mental power and lack of vigour; although close inbreeding gives a tendency towards idiocy, it also inclines towards insanity. It is said that insanity is one of the scourges of Newfoundland where intermarriage obtains. This also may be the result of the parents having been subjected to the same conditions of life.

(3.) Too great a difference between parents, for instance, cross-marriage, which give a tendency to reversion, as Darwin has so clearly demonstrated. Disease affecting the reproductive system also favours a tendency to reversion. It is said that cross-breeding is analogous to disease by producing an abnormal condition of ovum and sperm. From these marriages are supplied our criminals and the monstrosities....

(4.) Artificial preventive checks, which are more within the reach of the well-to-do classes than the very poor. Especially as these would affect the reproductive organs unfavourably and by this means gives a tendency to reversion.

(5.) The extreme susceptibility of the reproductive organs to changed or unnatural conditions, whether these be psychical or physical. The perversion of the sexual instinct often destroys all natural feeling, instance ancient and modern infanticide, fœticide, overlaying,[5] suffocating infants, slow starvation, the frequent falls which are only too often premeditated, and many other instances of perverted natural feelings. The accounts of the perverted sexual instinct among certain tribes and even among modern nations may be due to unnatural conditions affecting the reproductive system; and to this fact also may be attributed prehistoric cannibalism, anthropophagy. Darwin remarks under the heading sterility from changed conditions, showing the extreme susceptibility of the reproductive organs to these changes: "When conception takes place under confinement, the young are often born dead, or die soon, or are ill-formed. This frequently occurs in the Zoological Gardens, and, according to Rengger,[6] with native animals confined in Paraguay. The mother's milk often fails. We may also attribute to the disturbance of the sexual functions the frequent occurrence of that monstrous instinct which leads the mother to devour her own offspring."

(7.)[7] Disease, unless it directly affects the reproductive organs, seems to have no direct influence in lessening fertility. Diseased animals if left to nature would in all probability die off. Medical science, however, keeps them alive in order that they may propagate their kind.

(8.) The evident correlation between the brain and generative organs, the more the brain is exercised or when the female is given abundant rich food; in fact, the more the vegetative organs are developed in the female, especially where this is excessive, sterility is often the result. We have analagous cases in rich seedless fruit and double flowers.

The extreme delicacy of the females of the upper classes from their artificial life is also a cause of lessened fertility. Also the sowing of the wild oats of the young men of the upper classes, is too often the cause of the sterility of the females whom they marry.

To disease in the parents may be attributed the largest share in generating the unfit. I read some time ago an article on Hydrocephalus, written by a doctor, who states that hydrocephalus occurs in about one in three thousand confinements, and that if syphilis, which is *such a common disease*, were the cause of hydrocephalus, why hydrocephalus would be more common still. To look up the family history of a patient is now a common practice. I had a girl in my employ whose conduct was very strange; I found on enquiry that her father and brother were in an insane asylum, and it will only be a short time when she will have to be placed under restraint.

The best minds of to-day have accepted the fact that if superior people are desired, they must be bred; and if imbeciles, criminals, paupers, and otherwise unfit are undesirable citizens they must not be bred.

The first principle of the breeder's art is to weed out the inferior animals to avoid conditions which give a tendency to reversion and then to bring together superior animals under the most favourable conditions. We can produce numerous modifications of structure by careful selection of different animals, and there is no reason why, if society were differently organized, that we should not be able to modify and improve the human species to the same extent. In order to do this we must make a religion of the procreative principle. Our girls and boys must be taught how sacred is the life-giving principle. The most wonderful of all the forces at work throughout nature.

Our young men and women should realize the purpose for which they are uniting in the holiest bond of physical life. And by this means we would have inaugurated the upper million and the lower ten.[8] Any social conditions which tend to transpose these terms are subversive of the true interests of humanity.

Victoria C. Woodhull Martin

# Chapter Twenty-Five

## *I Am the Daughter of Time*

*This manuscript is in the Victoria Woodhull-Martin Papers, Special Collections Research Center, Morris Library, Southern Illinois University–Carbondale. It is dated July 1895. While the subject of the manuscript is not clear, it may be a fragment of the uncompleted autobiography she began that year. The document is a typescript with several handwritten edits inserted above the line, which are shown by a superscripted caret.*

"I am the daughter of Time," said Truth, "and I get everything from my Father."[1]

If a story comes from the heart it will contrive to reach the heart.[2]
 —Carlyle

I regret having to inflict on my friends any account of the sorrow and anxiety I am passing through, owing to the duplicity and treachery of those who should have stood fast by me. I need not say how deeply humiliating to me is the course of action I am forced to take, both privately and publicly, in this matter; but I feel that the position I have occupied, and am now occupying before the public, demands from me an explanation of conduct seemingly inconsistent ~~with past professions~~. Not until the long struggle that I have made in the old world since my worn heart and weary feet first touched its soil in August, 1877, is known in its entirety, shall or can I be judged justly.

The truth cannot possibly be told in these few lines: it would have to be told seriatim,[3] with all the circumstances which led to that or this ~~action~~, ^affair and when all the causes that made possible such chaotic actions shall be laid bare, for my enemies as well as my friends to judge me by, my heart at least may find an hour's rest before it is laid by the gentle hand of Nature in old Mother Earth's receptive bosom. I unhesitatingly say and I feel I shall be believed, that during all these long years of exile from the land which gave the casket which holds all there is of me, I have never known one moment's real rest. Often during these days and months of ceaseless conflict, I have prayed and wished for release suddenly; but it came not, nor will it come until the little fevered part it was destined to play here has run its course.

Link after link of a busy life has been snapped by malevolence and hatred, until there have been moments of such fierce rebellion in my woman's outraged spirit that I would have ended the unnatural condition violently, had it not been for those I must have left behind me to struggle on and on.

If the story of all these persecutions were told in the simplest way, it would not be believed, and if it were depicted in the cold light of actuality, it would be deemed the wildest fiction.

When I left New York City on July 26th, 1877, with my mother, sister, and little daughter, I did not know that I should live to reach our destination; but the Gods who have, ^watched and do, watch over me, silently led me on, sometimes blindly, as it seemed to me, but oftener with strength and faith, which, in a figurative sense, did remove mountains of opposition. I do not believe that I should have retained my reason during many of these volcanic outbursts of malevolence if my brain had not been illumined by divine wisdom to penetrate the causes which produced them. Often, in tracing such phenomena to their source, I was given an insight into Nature's laws, which inspired me with an intense love for study on scientific lines of thought, leading to grand results.

But at last I begi^an to realize that if I was to be of any real service to mankind, I must put it out of the power of the undeveloped brains of those by whom I was assailed to keep me in a constant tumult, whereby unable to concentrate my whole will-power on the subject before me; thus often causing me to lose the light and shade of an important problem, which may have been months or even years in maturing.

Nature performs her great works in silence, and it is in our most tranquil moments the divinest thoughts are brought into activity, which, if undisturbed at the moment of reflection, may leave on the retina of our brain, the outlines of a truth never to be prejudice or ignorance. Those whose souls are attuned to the music of the spheres know how slight a jar may destroy divine harmony, leaving the physical sometimes prostrate and unable for long periods to pick up the line of thought or action thus wantonly disturbed.

~~As Schopenhauer says: "A great intellect sinks to the level of an ordinary one, as soon as it is interrupted and disturbed, its attention distracted and drawn off from the matter in hand; for its superiority depends upon the power of concentration, of bringing all its strength to bear upon one theme, in the same way as a concave mirror collects into one point all the rays of light that strike upon it."~~

The deeper I delve for a sure footing, the higher I reach for light, the more convinced am I that only here and there do we find an instrument capable of responding to the hungry heart's desire for Truth.

Whittier had a glimpse of this subtle truth, and leaves it as a memory for those who understand:

**(My soul and I)**
Like warp and woof, all destinies
  are woven fast,
Linked in sympathy like the keys
  of an organ vast:

Pluck one thread and the web ye
  mar,
Break but one of a thousand keys,
And the paining jar
  through all will run.

O, restless spirit, wherefore strain
  beyond, thy sphere,
Heaven and hell, with their joy and
  pain,
Are now and here.[4]

Therefore I feel well assured that whatever be the misrepresentations to which I may be subject at present, the event must be committed to Time, who relentlessly unravels all distortions and rights all wrongs.

Victoria Woodhull Martin
New York, July, 1895

# Chapter Twenty-Six

## *Woman Suffrage in the United States*

*This essay was published in the* Humanitarian *in July 1896.*

The cause which is bringing woman suffrage in America to the front with a rush is the forthcoming Presidential election, and more particularly the fact that the women of the State of Colorado will be permitted by Colorado to vote for the Presidential electors of that State.[1] Thus, for the first time in the history of the United States, women will have a direct voice in the election of the President. If the Presidential election be a close one, and there is every possibility of its becoming so, the votes of the women of Colorado may suffice to turn the balance of power, and then, the President would owe his election to women.* This then is the situation; one unparalleled in the history of America, and in a wider sense in the history of humanity.

If it be conceded that the women of the State of Colorado should vote for the President at the Presidential election of 1896, on what grounds of reason or justice shall the women of the other States of the Union be debarred from voting too? To permit the women of Colorado to vote at the Presidential Election and to exclude the women of the remaining States will be an illogical and invidious position which cannot be maintained. The cause of woman suffrage in America is virtually won. And it has been won on the ground which I have all along urged was the only one which could lead to victory, namely, on the plea that the Federal Constitution of the United States, as it stands, permits the suffrage of women. The plea put forward by the women of Colorado to-day is no new plea. It is the same which I put before the Judicial Committee of Congress at Washington in 1870—now more than a quarter of a century ago.

In 1870 not only was it unpopular, but it was dormant. The Women's Suffrage Convention had been in existence for twenty years, it had held many meetings and presented many petitions, but it had achieved nothing except from the educational point of view. Countless resolutions had been passed.

The object of the Women's Suffrage Convention had been to obtain the franchise by amending the Constitution. The whole gist of my contention from the first was, and is, that no amendment is necessary since the suffrage was already granted to both sexes by the written Constitution. We were not pleading for a privilege, but demanding a right. This is the identical position of the women of Colorado to-day.

In the autumn of 1870, acting on my own initiative, I prepared a Memorial setting forth the Constitutional view and went to Washington to get it presented to Congress. It was not an easy task. However, all difficulties were overcome by the 22nd December, when the Memorial was duly presented to Congress; in the Senate by Senator Harris, in the House of Representatives by the Hon. W. P. Julian,[2] an early friend of the woman's cause. In this Memorial I set forth clearly my claim to vote as a citizen of the United States, not basing the demand upon any legal opinion or suffragist's essay, but on the written words of the Constitution itself, and especially upon Section I of Article XIV, which runs as follows:

> All persons born or naturalized in the United States, and subject to the jurisdiction thereof, are citizens of the United States and of the State wherein they reside. No State shall make or enforce any law which shall abridge the privileges or immunities of citizens of the United States; nor shall any State deprive any person of life, liberty or property, without due process of law; nor deny to any person within its jurisdiction the equal protection of the laws.

This article, it will be seen, expressly defines who are citizens of the United States, and makes no restriction as to sex, for the word "persons" cannot by any legal or verbal sophistry be twisted to exclude women.

I also supported my case on the 15th Amendment of the Constitution, which decrees that:

> The right of citizens of the United States to vote shall not be denied or abridged by the United States or by any State on account of race, color, or previous condition of servitude.

The Memorial was a brief one, but it opened up an entirely new point of constitutional law, and one which had not struck anyone before. It impressed both Houses of Congress so much that it was carefully considered, referred to the Judiciary Committee, and ordered to be printed in the official *Globe*. The sensation which followed upon its publication outside Congress was immense, and I at once followed up the advantage by demanding a personal hearing before the Judiciary Committee, when the Memorial should come up for consideration. Such a demand had never before been made by a woman, but it was granted, and the hearing was fixed for the 11th January, 1871. Upon this being known, the Woman's Suffrage Convention, then sitting at Washington, resolved to support me. To quote from the Secretary's report: "Hearing this important step taken by Victoria Woodhull, a stranger to the Convention, a conference was held between the parties, resulting in a friendly agreement that with the consent of the Chairman of the Committee, Mrs. Isabella Beecher Hooker, on the part of the Convention, should at the same time, through a constitutional lawyer, the Hon. H. G. Riddle, ex-Member of Congress, defend the Memorialists (30,000 women) whose names were already before Congress, asking also to exercise the right of ballot."**

I shall never forget the 11th January, 1871; it will always remain as one of the most memorable days of my life. And it was also a memorable day in the history of the woman's movement in America, for it was the first time that a woman's voice was heard in the Judiciary Chamber. The Chamber was thronged when I rose to address the Committee, and around the table were seated some of the most eminent jurists of America, and by me were all the best known among the woman suffragists of the day. My argument took some time to deliver, for it was lengthy and I had fortified it by frequent reference to the great Constitutional authorities. It was in the main an amplification of the plea put forward in the Memorial, and supported by every consideration which I could think of as likely to advance the cause and influence the judges. But the dominant note running through the whole was that women demanded the vote as a right under the existing Constitution; in short the very ground on which the women of Colorado are now claiming the vote. The argument which I advanced then is the one which has led to their victory to-day.

The Committee heard me with careful attention, and at the end announced that they would take time to consider their decision. Three weeks later, on January 30th, 1871, Mr. Bingham submitted the Majority Report to the House of Representatives. It admitted all the basic proposition, of my Memorial, yet recommended that the petition should not be granted. On the following day, Judge Loughbridge and General B. F. Butler, two of the acutest legal intellects of America, presented the Minority Report. They reviewed and upheld all my contentions and fortified them by copious quotations from constitutional lawyers. They recommended that Congress should pass a Declaratory Act for ever settling the disputed question of woman suffrage.

This Minority Report and the agitation which had preceded it gave an immediate impetus to the movement. A Special Committee of the Woman's Convention at Washington was formed, consisting of Mrs. Isabella Beecher Hooker, Mrs. J. S. Grilling, Mrs. M. B. Bowen, Susan B. Anthony, Paulina Wright Davis, and Ruth Carr Denison (prominent women suffragists of the day), and a special effort was made to advance the cause.

I entered upon my Presidential Campaign, by announcing myself as a candidate for the Presidential Election of 1872. This I did chiefly for the purpose of bringing home to the mind of the community woman's right to fill any office in America, from the Presidency down. The storm of ridicule and abuse which followed this move may be imagined, nevertheless I addressed meetings in almost every town and city of the Union in pursuit of my candidature, and was nominated for the

Presidency at an immense gathering at Apollo Hall, New York. Also to drive home another object lesson, my sister and I presented ourselves at the ballot to record our votes. They were refused amid a scene of great excitement.

It was at this time (1870–1871) that the movement reached its flood in America. It has now come forward with a rush again, and if taken at the flood, will assuredly lead to victory. The victory will be achieved on the constitutional plea which I advanced at Washington twenty-five years ago.

In a characteristic letter to the London *Times* recently, Professor Goldwin Smith from his Canadian coign of vantage, reviewed the position of woman suffrage in America (of course unfavourably), and came to the conclusion that the movement was retrogressing.[3] I do not propose to answer the points raised by Professor Goldwin Smith—some minor inaccuracies in his letter were ably dealt with by Mrs. Fawcett. I prefer to take a wider view. The woman's movement generally has gained ground, but the suffrage phase of it has not kept pace with the general advance. I am aware that certain points have been gained here and there, but with the exception of Colorado, the progress of the cause generally is very far short of what we confidently hoped and anticipated it would be twenty-five years ago. The reasons of this are not far to seek. I stated them in a recent letter to the London *Times* in answer to Professor Goldwin Smith, and I again assert them here. The first reason is to be found in the internal dissensions, divisions and jealousies which have been the bane of the suffrage movement from the beginning. Those who would govern others must first learn to govern themselves. Soon after I raised the constitutional question in 1870–71, the woman suffragists drifted away from it and back again to the old and discredited methods and worn-out cries. Yet it is on the constitutional plea alone that they can win—the fact that the Federal Constitution as it stands admits women to every political right—and the ultimate triumph of the movement in America will be secured in this way alone.

In England while other aspects of the woman's movement have gained ground, this has moved slowly. Little has been achieved beyond a "monster petition," despite the platitudes of vote-catching Ministers, the bill was relinquished in the last Parliament amid ribald laughter, and this Session it has been dropped with a silence which is almost more contemptuous. Clearly then the question is not in the forefront of practical politics, and a great deal remains to be accomplished before it can arrive there.

Suffrage is only one phase of the larger question of woman's emancipation. More important is the question of her social and economic position. Her financial independence underlies all the rest.

*Victoria Woodhull Martin*†

\*See "North American Review," May, 1896, p. 632, where my original argument of 1871 is re-stated in a letter, signed W. S. Harwood.
\*\*Letter of Mrs. Griffing, Secretary of the Committee of the Woman's Suffrage Convention. Appendix to the history of the Decade Meeting of Oct. 20, 1870.
†The illustrations inserted in the foregoing article are reproduced from plates which appeared in the contemporary press.—Editor[4]

# Notes

INTRODUCTION

1. Woodhull's relationship with other suffragists was not helped by her alleged or actual blackmail of such figures (Gabriel 175).

2. The line about "a Church's creed" is in her article "The Spirit World" (chap. 18, this vol.), located in the Victoria Woodhull-Martin Papers, PP20 (old MSS 15) Box 1 Folder 2, Special Collections Research Center, Morris Library, Southern Illinois University Carbondale (hereafter referred to as Woodhull-Martin Papers, SIUC).

3. Woodhull includes this cartoon in her 1890 book *The Human Body the Temple of God*, perhaps out of pride for her effect on Wall Street.

4. Woodhull was not, of course, the only white woman with such allegiances; Elizabeth Cady Stanton and Susan B. Anthony also voiced racist sentiments about the Fifteenth Amendment and accepted Train's funds to support their newspaper, the *Revolution*.

5. Frisken suggests that Douglass's lack of response was encouraged by abolitionists who feared any association with the disreputable Woodhull. Douglass publicly supported President Grant. None of the African American newspapers that Frisken consulted mention Douglass's nomination to the Equal Rights ticket (see 55–84). William McFeely's biography of Douglass notes that he did not actually meet Woodhull until a visit to Europe in 1866: in his words, "'a lady of very fine appearance who introduced herself as Mrs. John Beddulph Martin, of 17 Hyde Park Gate SW. She frankly—and I thought somewhat proudly told me that she was formerly Mrs. Victoria Woodhull—I am not sure that I quite concealed my surprise.' All that he had heard about the most flamboyant and controversial American woman of his century flashed through Douglass's mind. 'I however soon began to think, what do I know about this lady—that I should think her otherwise, than merely holding strange . . . opinions.' . . . Douglass for his part concluded, 'I do not know that she is not in her life as pure as she seems to be. I treated her politely and respectfully—and she departed apparently not displeased with her call'" (McFeely 332–33). I thank Lori Askeland for posting this quotation to the Society for the Study of American Women Writers listserv on April 16, 2008.

A small number of African American readers of the *Weekly* have been identified: Passet points to a black man who wrote to the paper to announce the formation of a club of readers (58).

6. Although she never attained the name recognition her sister enjoyed, Tennie also wrote and delivered speeches such as "The Ethics of Sexual Equality."

7. It is widely believed that Tilton wrote *Victoria C. Woodhull, a Biographical Sketch* in an effort to buy Woodhull's silence on the Beecher-Tilton affair. For more analysis of her relationship with Tilton, see Underhill; Gabriel.

8. See Boggis, Raimon, and White, eds., *Harriet Wilson's New England: Race, Writing, and Region*.

9. This letter is included in the Woodhull-Martin Papers, Box 1 Folder 2, SIUC. The citation included with the letter is incomplete; no page number is indicated.

10. The word "anarchy" had increasingly negative connotations with the unrest of events like the Haymarket bombing of 1886 and the later assassination of President McKinley (Marsh 6–8). In "And the Truth Shall Make You Free," Woodhull distances herself from the term, distinguishing individual rights from an "anarchy" in which "each individual is a law unto himself . . . at the mercy of all such who are bent on conquest" (chap. 10, this vol.).

11. Woodhull applied for divorce in September of 1876; it was granted the next month. Underhill notes that "since adultery was the only grounds for divorce in New York at this time, the charge was probably arranged to meet legal requirements" (271). According to court transcripts, Blood said he and Woodhull had filed for an earlier divorce in Chicago in 1868 (Gabriel 101). If they did so, it was a symbolic act to protest the institution of marriage.

12. Martin's letters are located in the Victoria Martin (Woodhull) Collection (1883–1927), Boston Public Library, Rare Books and Manuscripts.

13. This document is located in the Woodhull-Martin Papers, Box 2 Folder 9, SIUC.

14. The will can be found in the Woodhull-Martin Papers, Box 2 Folder 9, SIUC.

15. These documents are in the Victoria Martin (Woodhull) Collection (1883–1927), Boston Public Library, Rare Books and Manuscripts.

16. The Missionary Society of St. Paul the Apostle (known as the Paulists) was founded by Isaac Thomas Hecker in 1858. Hecker came to be well known for his faith in the compatibility of Catholicism and American ideals. He was involved with Brook Farm, the experimental community of the 1840s that was heavily influenced by the ideas of Charles Fourier.

17. This letter is in the Woodhull-Martin Papers, Box 1 Folder 2, SIUC. The citation included with the letter is incomplete; no precise date or page number is indicated.

18. This letter is in the Woodhull-Martin Papers, Box 2 Folder 5, SIUC. While Sue Davis in *The Political Thought of Elizabeth Cady Stanton* speculates that Stanton may not have been familiar with Woodhull's writing on eugenics at the turn of the century, this letter demonstrates her familiarity at least with the *Humanitarian*.

1. THE WOODHULL MANIFESTO

1. Hiram Rhodes Revels served in the Senate from February 1870 to March 1871. He was one of only two African American senators elected during the nineteenth century.

2. Such revolutionary calls for social welfare and a more even distribution of wealth resemble those from "A Page of American History: Constitution of the United States of the World" (1870) (chap. 3, this vol.).

5. CONSTITUTIONAL EQUALITY

1. Naturalization Laws give citizenship status to those not born in the country. Although naturalization was first mentioned in the U.S. Constitution, it was key to the Fourteenth Amendment, which was ratified in 1868. As the first section of the Fourteenth Amendment reads, "All persons born or naturalized in the United States, and subject to the jurisdiction thereof, are citizens of the United States and of the State wherein they reside. No State shall make or enforce any law which shall abridge the privileges or immunities of citizens of the United States; nor shall any State deprive any person of life, liberty, or property, without due process of law; nor deny to any person within its jurisdiction the equal protection of the laws." In the Naturalization Act of 1870, Congress extended citizenship to those of African descent.

2. The Married Women's Property Act, passed in New York in 1848, became a model for other states. The act provided married women with rights to property and inheritance that they had previously been denied. See Basch for further information.

3. Romans 13:12–13. All scripture is taken from the King James edition of the Bible.

4. *Ita lex scripta est* translates as "such is the written law." Woodhull is saying that we must abide by the law of the Constitution as it is written, and since the Constitution does not place limitations upon who has the right to vote, no one should be allowed to do so.

5. 3 Dall., 382; 6 Wheaton, 405; 9 Id., 868; 3d Cure., Pa., 1832. The first case mentioned, *Bingham v. Cabot* (1798), found that an individual's change in residency from one state to another did not necessarily warrant federal rather than state jurisdiction. The second, *Cohens v. Virginia* (1821), found that two men from the District of Columbia who sold lottery tickets in Virginia, where such sales were not permitted, had violated state law and could be prosecuted by Virginia. At the same time, Justice John Marshall held that Congress could "review criminal as well as civil cases arising out of state courts, to assure national uniformity" (Rosen 64). The third case, *Osborn v. Bank of the United States* (1824), found in favor of the bank, concluding that a state did not have the right to tax a federal corporation. The last citation is incomplete. Woodhull uses these cases to argue that states do not have a right to limit women's suffrage as it was promised in the Constitution. I thank David Krech for assistance with interpreting these cases.

6. S.C., 1847: Fox vs. Ohio, 5 Howard, 410: In *Malinda Fox v. the State of Ohio* (1847), the Supreme Court found that the Constitution does not prevent a state from passing a law penalizing counterfeiting.

7. *Ad inconvenienti*: Woodhull probably meant *ab* ("from" in Latin) instead of *ad* ("to"). *Ab inconvenienti* is a legal term of art that means "from an inconvenient" or "from hardship." *Argumentum ab inconvenienti* refers to a rule in law that the degree of inconvenience an argument causes should be accounted for. Here, the difficulties would be the expense and time it would take for the parties to enter into the "needless litigation" discussed above. Woodhull asks the court to make a decision that would limit such time and expense.

6. THE NEW REBELLION

1. "Overslough," a version of "overslaugh," means "to pass over (a person) in favor of someone else, esp. in the case of a promotion or appointment." *Oxford English Dictionary*, http://www.oed.com (accessed July 5, 2009).

7. MY DEAR MRS. BLADEN

1. Woodhull refers to accusations of her immorality made by Harriet Beecher Stowe in the *Christian Union*, a periodical owned in part by Henry Ward Beecher. Stowe was an ardent defender of her brother and a harsh critic of free love.

2. Vice versa.

3. This should be *sub rosa*, a Latin term meaning "under the rose"; secretly.

4. Cape May was a popular vacation retreat in New Jersey during the nineteenth century.

8. CORRESPONDENCE BETWEEN VICTORIA LEAGUE AND VICTORIA WOODHULL

1. *De facto* is a legal term defined as existing in fact, regardless of the law. It is usually opposed to *de jure*, which means existing because of and according to law.

2. The Declaratory Act was passed by the House of Commons on March 18, 1766, on the same day the Stamp Act was repealed. It allowed for British governance of the colonies and was one of the acts that led to the American Revolution. In making this reference, Woodhull seeks to associate women's suffrage with the American Revolution.

3. A withe is a band or tie used for binding.

4. The National Labor Union (1866–1873) was the first of its kind; one of its primary goals was the eight-hour-day legislation.

5. In the Bible, Miriam was a religious leader and the sister of Moses. See Exodus 15:20–21.

10. "AND THE TRUTH SHALL MAKE YOU FREE"

1. The Pharisees were members of a separatist Jewish group (536 BC to AD 70) known for being strict about following doctrine. In the New Testament, they are frequently

described as self-righteous, so that the word itself has come to mean hypocritical, rigid, and arrogant, a definition many find antisemitic.

2. Luke 23:34.

3. A reference to the *Tribune*, a New York paper established by Horace Greeley in 1841. According to Gabriel, it was "'often avant garde and a trifle snobbish,' but it was also the most influential newspaper in the country" (58).

4. In November 1870 Laura Fair shot Alexander Crittenden after an extended extramarital affair that Crittenden was trying to end. Crittenden later died from his injuries; Fair was first sentenced to death but was later acquitted because of a mistreatment of evidence. In 1869 Daniel McFarland, outraged that his estranged wife, Abby, planned to divorce him for journalist Albert Richardson, shot Richardson at his *Tribune* office. Henry Ward Beecher married Albert and Abby at Richardson's deathbed.

5. "Tombs" refers to Manhattan's Ludlow Street Jail, where executions were conducted.

6. By midcentury, Greene Street (today part of Manhattan's SoHo District) was associated with prostitution.

7. Matthew 4:19 and Mark 1:17.

8. Psalm 8:2.

9. A reference to the Latter-day Saints movement that was established by Joseph Smith in the mid–nineteenth century. Mormons were the subject of much media attention in the following decades.

10. Influenced by Herbert Spencer, American sociologist Lester Frank Ward organized human development into three categories: "the chaotic and anarchical stage of primitive man; second, forced organization into loose communities for protection; third, the formation of rudimentary forms of government and eventually nation-states for further protection of the social order" (Rafferty 112).

11. Matthew 26:39.

11. SPEECH ON THE IMPENDING REVOLUTION

1. The Vanderbilts, Stewarts, and Astors were three famously wealthy families in New York. Tennie and Victoria depended on Commodore Vanderbilt, the railroad magnate, for much of their wealth early on, and it was in part her public criticism of him that ultimately led him to cease this support. Alexander Turney Stewart made his fortune as a retailer. The German immigrant John Jacob Astor found his wealth in the eighteenth-century fur trade.

2. Blackwell's Island, now known as Roosevelt Island, was the site of correctional institutions in the nineteenth century.

3. Charles Sumner (1811–1874) was an abolitionist senator from Massachusetts who supported Horace Greeley over Ulysses Grant in 1872. Because of this support, he lost the favor of Grant's administration. He included controversial school integration in his Civil Rights bill; the bill only passed when he omitted it.

## 12. CORRESPONDENCE OF THE EQUAL RIGHTS PARTY

1. Matthew 20:16.
2. The word "phalanx" comes from Fourier's conception of the social commune; a literal "phalanx" was an arable site with an administrative center, a residential area, and a parade ground that commemorated the harvest. Here Woodhull uses it in a more metaphoric sense to endorse a space for social reform.
3. James 5:4.
4. Horace Greeley (1811–1872) was the influential editor of the *New York Tribune*. He ran against Grant in the 1872 election and lost by a landslide.
5. Woodhull refers to the stockholders of railroad companies, who had tremendous economic and political power.
6. According to the *Oxford English Dictionary*, "builded" is an archaic form of "built." http://www.oed.com (accessed July 5, 2009).

## 13. SPEECH OF VICTORIA C. WOODHULL

1. The law Woodhull refers to was passed on April 26, 1870. A *New York Times* article from February 4, 1884, entitled "Some Inoperative Laws; Passed by the 'Friends of Working Men'" (1), indicates that the law was not well enforced and was ultimately replaced with other legislation.
2. "Euchre" was used as a verb in the nineteenth century; it meant to gain the advantage over someone. "Also, *to euchre* (a person) *out of* (a thing)." "Euchre," *Oxford English Dictionary*, http://www.oed.com (accessed September 12, 2008).

## 14. THE BEECHER-TILTON SCANDAL CASE

1. William Lloyd Garrison (1805–1879) was one of the most prominent abolitionists of the nineteenth century.
2. Otto von Bismarck (1815–1898) was prime minister of Prussia from 1871 to 1890; his greatest achievement was the unification of Germany. Woodhull would have been particularly aware of him because of France's loss to Prussia in 1870, which frustrated the Paris workers with whom she aligned herself.
3. Woodhull refers to the war between the Paris Commune, a short-lived government in 1871, and the old-guard French government. It resulted in the execution of thousands of communists.
4. Strongly criticizing.
5. In June of 1872, Woodhull collapsed from an unexplained illness and was thought to be near death; several newspapers reported her imminent demise. She recovered a few days later. The obscenity trial was postponed as a result of her illness, leading some cynics to speculate that she had faked the illness.
6. According to Gabriel, this is a mock dialogue; Woodhull wrote both the reporter's questions and her responses.

7. "Enceinte" was a term used in the seventeenth through nineteenth centuries for pregnancy. *Oxford English Dictionary*, http://www.oed.com (accessed July 9, 2009).

8. As Theodore Tilton's closest friend, Frank Moulton became a main figure in the Beecher-Tilton scandal. He came to be known in the press as "The Mutual Friend" (Shaplen 92).

9. "Suzz" was a phrase for "sirs" common in New England (Bartlett 345).

15. THE NAKED TRUTH

1. "American Bastille" was a colloquialism for the building that became a prison during the Civil War. Inmates included Confederate prisoners, President Lincoln's assassins, and several notorious female spies from the south.

2. Woodhull is referring to 17 Stat. L. 302, passed June 8, 1872, which stated that "no obscene book, pamphlet, picture, print, or other publication of a vulgar, or indecent character . . . shall be carried in the mail." For the full statute, see John Lilburn Thomas, *Law of Lotteries, Frauds, and Obscenities in the Mails* (Littleton CO: Rothman, 1980), 271.

3. Woodhull probably meant the word "procedure."

4. Anthony Comstock (1844–1915) was a notorious moral crusader of the nineteenth century. It was his crusade for anti-obscenity legislation that led to Woodhull's imprisonment.

5. *Nolle prosequi* is a legal term meaning "unwilling to follow through." It refers to a prosecutor's statement to a judge that she or he is dropping the case.

6. In November of 1872, *Woodhull and Claflin's Weekly* ran an article about Luther Challis, a businessman who had bragged about his sexual conquest of young women. Challis responded by charging James Harvey Blood and the sisters with libel, of which they were acquitted in 1874.

7. Woodhull alludes to a Latin phrase that means representing in writing "point for point," or verbatim. In this case, Woodhull means the entire case was spelled out in the paper.

8. Better known as the temple of Artemis, the temple of Diana was dedicated to the Greek goddess around 550 BC.

9. In addition to being Woodhull's financial supporter, George Francis Train published the *Train Ligue* in 1872 in a protest of Comstock's obscenity laws. His arrest followed.

10. James Gordon Bennett (1795–1872) was the founder and editor of the *New York Herald*.

11. George H. Williams was Grant's attorney general from 1872 to 1875.

12. It was John Creswell who appointed Comstock to the position of special agent for anti-obscenity efforts.

13. See "The Capital," *New York Times*, December 5, 1872, 1.

14. "In chancery" is a term used in boxing or wrestling to refer to a maneuver in which the opponent's head is held under the contestant's arm.

15. According to *Cassell's Dictionary of Slang*, "joss" was a derogatory term in the late nineteenth and early twentieth centuries for a Chinese person or god (813). An article using this term appeared in the *New York Times*, August 31, 1877, 3.

16. Commodus followed Marcus Aurelius as emperor of Rome. Caligula was the nickname of Gaius Julius Caesar Germanicus.

17. Mrs. Grundy is a character in *Speed the Plough* (1798), a play by Thomas Morton. Mrs. Grundy reappeared in other works of literature as a symbol of conventionality.

18. Nero and Tarquin were leaders of ancient Rome.

19. Genesis 4:9.

20. Thomas Cogswell Upham (1799–1872) was a theologian influenced by the Scottish Common Sense movement and mysticism. Madame Guyon (1648–1717) was a famous French mystic. Woodhull uses an incorrect spelling of her name.

21. Woodhull refers to the popular belief that Jesus would return to reign for a thousand years. Liberals, or postmillennialists, tended to believe that people can improve the world in preparation for his arrival; conservatives believed the only thing people could do was to convert nonbelievers. I thank Jane Donovan for explaining this distinction. See Passet for further explanation.

## 17. REFORMATION OR REVOLUTION, WHICH?

1. Woodhull modifies a line from Thomas Hutchinson's well-known account of the Boston Tea Party: "That worst of plagues, the detested tea, shipped for this port by the East India Company, is now arrived in this harbour—the hour of destruction, or manly opposition to the machinations of tyranny stare you in the face." See Thomas Hutchinson, *The History of the Province of Massachusetts Bay: From 1749 to 1774* (London: Murray, 1828), 429.

2. Woodhull refers to the 1872 scandal involving the Credit Mobilier construction company and the Union Pacific Railroad. Members of Congress who supported the company were given cheap shares. The *New York Sun* blamed the Grant administration for the scandal, and vice presidential candidate Schuyler Colfax was ultimately replaced by Henry Wilson.

3. In 1873 Treasury secretary William Adams Richardson issued greenbacks in an attempt to curb bankers' growing unease. He also made arrangements with a tax collector who was able to keep a portion of the unpaid taxes he had garnered, which became known as the Sanborn Incident.

4. Tammany Hall (or Ring) was the name of a New York City political organization that controlled much of local government in the nineteenth century.

5. James 5:1–4.

6. Matthew 7:1.
7. A tocsin is a signal, usually of alarm, indicated by bells.
8. Oliver Goldsmith's *Miscellaneous Works* (1820) describes Hypatia as a beautiful Greek orator. Semiramis was a legendary Babylonian queen who has been portrayed alternatively as a harlot or a goddess. Boadicea, queen of the Iceni people, was a British heroine who rebelled in c. AD 60 against the Romans. She committed suicide once captured.

18. THE SPIRIT WORLD

1. Woodhull refers to Napoleon I of France (1769–1821) and his first wife, Josephine de Beauharnais. Napoleon remained a celebrated symbol of military might and imperialism long after his death. Demosthenes was a Greek orator whom Woodhull viewed as a muse.

19. THE ELIXIR OF LIFE

1. John Stuart Mill, *Principles of Political Economy*, ed. William J. Ashley, 7th ed. (1848; London: Longman's, Greens and Co., 1909), 374.
2. Spiritual materialization was the embodiment, rather than the mere suggestion, of spirits. Belief in materialization became more popular in the 1870s. As McGarry notes, "These séances were enough of a rage—or popular titillation—to warrant coverage in the tabloid press almost every week, and often every day, through summer and fall 1874" (14).
3. Animal magnetism, the belief in magnetic fluid in beings, dates back to the theory of Franz Anton Mesmer (1734–1815). It was particularly popular in the nineteenth-century United States. Mills describes it as the belief that "unseen causes exist behind observable—effects—that bodies can act upon each other from a distance" (22). He argues that magnetism should be understood as "evolving conceptions of the unconscious," which in turn were communicated in the literature of the time (22).
4. Notice how Woodhull describes sexuality in financial terms.
5. Spermatorrhea was a medical term popular in the nineteenth century for an ejaculation that was thought to be involuntary and excessive.
6. Sodomy was thought to be an "unnatural" form of sexual intercourse, usually referring to homosexuality. This is one of Woodhull's few references to same-sex relations. Horowitz notes that the sporting publications of the nineteenth century, of which Woodhull would have been familiar, frequently blasted "sodomites" (172).
7. Lines 75–76 of Alexander Pope's "Eloisa to Abelard" (1717), a popular love poem of the time.
8. Moses Hull was a sex radical who wrote about "prostitution, the abolition of marriage, the single sexual standard, and dress reform" (Frisken 26). He was active in the Woodhull-Douglass nomination. He disclosed his open marriage in 1874 and

was criticized for it. He later criticized Woodhull for abandoning her principles and marrying John Martin (Frisken 147).

9. The Upas tree was a "fabulous tree alleged to have existed in Java, at some distance from Batavia, with properties so poisonous as to destroy all animal and vegetable life to a distance of fifteen or sixteen miles around it." *Oxford English Dictionary*, http://www.dictionary.oed.com (accessed June 12, 2008).

10. Woodhull refers to nineteenth-century beliefs that magnetism could cure many bodily disorders. Woodhull's statement is reminiscent of Margaret Fuller's gendered take on magnetism: "Male and female represent the two sides of the great radical dualism. But, in fact, they are perpetually passing into one another. Fluid hardens to solid, solid rushes to fluid. There is no wholly masculine man, no purely feminine woman" (115–16). In most cases, men were positioned as the "active" mesmerist of negative energy whereas women were the "passive," "positive" recipients. Harriet Martineau also describes being healed by mesmerism in *Life in the Sick-Room* (London: Moxon, 1844).

11. Woodhull and other sex radicals used the term "false sexual relations" to refer to relationships in which love does not exist, usually held together only by the legal tie of marriage.

12. Genesis 28:12.

13. This is a reference to John Bunyan's extremely popular allegory, *Pilgrim's Progress* (1678). In this section, the main character—"Christian" and his companion "Hopeful"—are captured by a giant and forced to spend a brutalizing night in Doubting Castle. They escape with a key called "Promise."

14. A legal term meaning "in one's own person"; representing oneself in court.

15. Woodhull takes this line from Robert Burns's poem "To Robert Graham of Fintry, Esq."

16. Revelation 22:1.

20. THE SCARE-CROWS OF SEXUAL SLAVERY

1. Matthew 16:23, Mark 8:33, Luke 4:8.

2. Here Woodhull makes a common, deeply flawed argument that whites were the only ones involved in abolition.

21. TRIED AS BY FIRE

1. Social evil bills were laws regulating prostitution.

2. *Dernier ressort* is a legal term meaning "last resort." It usually refers to the U.S. Supreme Court, the final court to hear an appeal of a case. With the court of last resort comes finality and closure, as there is no higher court to appeal to for reversal of a decision. Woodhull is saying that when someone critiques free love and an antimarriage stance, the question they save for last, the strongest tool they have hidden away

in their arsenal for a final swift refutation of free love, is this question of reproductive futurity.

3. The original is illegible.

4. "Romanist" was a sometimes derogatory term for a Catholic.

5. The "Goose Question" referred to the issue of whether or not Kansas would enter the Union as a slave state. Anti-abolitionists were "pronounced 'S. G. Q.,' that is to say 'sound on the goose question,' and all others were abolitionists" (Blackmar 765). The precise origins of the term are not known. Here, Woodhull means a woman who is married, regardless of the circumstances, has passed muster.

6. The Oneidas believed in communal rather than individual property, a belief that made many outsiders suspicious; a *New York Times* article used their communism as evidence for their status as "lunatics." This communism was associated with the "weird delusion of perfectionism," the belief that humans could avoid sin. See "Father Noyes' Fanatics," *New York Times*, August 9, 1878, 1.

7. The nineteenth century witnessed an American intrigue with "the Orient" in the popular press. For extensive discussions of such exoticism, see for example Said; Arac.

8. Matthew 23:25–27.

9. *Mrs. Caudle's Curtain Lectures*, by Douglas William Jerrold (1803–1857), was published first in *Punch* and then in book form. After the death of his wife, who always delivered lectures to him in bed, Mr. Caudle records them in print. They are considered a window into Victorian middle-class culture.

10. Illegible in original; based on the context, the word "is" should be here.

11. In the 1870s the *New York Herald* ran a series of interviews with Mormon leader Brigham Young (1801–1877). Much of the coverage dealt with his controversial role in the Mountain Meadows Massacre of 1857, in which over one hundred emigrants were killed when passing through Utah.

12. LL.D. stands for *Legum Doctor* (Doctor of Laws); D.D. is short for *Divinitatis Doctor* (Doctor of Divinity).

13. Green-Wood Cemetery in Brooklyn NY was "the fashionable resting place of the time" (Underhill 249). Utica Brooker, who died of Bright's disease in July 1873, was buried there. Woodhull also paid to move Canning Woodhull's body to Green-Wood (Gabriel 213). A *New York Times* article from November 30, 2008, quotes an item of its own from 1866: "Green-Wood is as permanently associated with the fame of our city as the Fifth Avenue or the Central Park." See Seth Kugel, "You Can Come and Go. They're Staying Awhile," *New York Times*, November 30, 2008, TR5.

14. Woodhull's slang for the YMCA, the organization through which anti-obscenity crusader Anthony Comstock came to power. Beecher was the "American Pope."

15. Like many feminist reformers of the time, Woodhull advocated temperance as part of the larger women's movement.

16. Herbert Spencer was an English philosopher (1820–1903) who was heavily influenced by Darwin's theory of evolution. He coined the phrase "survival of the fittest" in *Principles of Biology* (1864).

17. These words were written by the British physician Holmes Coote. He is cited in "The Study of Sociology" (455–82), an article by Herbert Spencer, republished in *Contemporary Review* (London: King, 1872), 463.

18. Leucorrhœa is a medical term for vaginal discharge. A prolapsed uterus is a condition in which the uterus collapses into the vaginal canal.

19. Matthew 22:30, Mark 12:25, Luke 20:35.

20. Genesis 3:15.

21. A reference to Henry Ward Beecher's affair with Elizabeth Tilton.

22. A peculiar idea.

23. John Milton Scudder (1829–1894) was a physician specializing in homeopathic and other unconventional methods. He wrote, among other things, *On the Reproductive Organs, and the Venereal* (Cincinnati: Wilstach and Baldwin, 1874.)

24. "Ante-natal murder" was a term for abortion. Until early in the nineteenth century, abortion was permissible until "quickening" (the movement of the fetus). Anti-abortion laws began to emerge early in the century. Horowitz notes that sporting publications were loudly opposed to abortion (194). See also Smith-Rosenberg; Brodie.

## 22. THE GARDEN OF EDEN

1. See Genesis 2:1–25; 3:1–24. In the nineteenth century, "higher critics" began to analyze the Bible as any other text. Higher criticism, Darwinian theory, and German liberation theology, which appear in Woodhull's speech, often converged in such studies.

2. Matthew 23:25–27.

3. Matthew 5:28.

4. Genesis 2:9; Genesis 1:11.

5. Psalm 8:5.

6. Psalm 8:5.

7. Genesis 2:8.

8. Genesis 2:15.

9. Genesis 2:10.

10. Much of this comes from John Quarry's *Genesis and Its Authorship: Two Dissertations* (1873), which refers to River Phison, Havilah, Bdellium, and the onyx-stone. It also comes from Genesis 2:8–17: "⁸And the LORD God planted a garden eastward in Eden; and there he put the man whom he had formed. ⁹And out of the ground made the LORD God to grow every tree that is pleasant to the sight, and good for food; the tree of life also in the midst of the garden, and the tree of knowledge of good and evil.

¹⁰And a river went out of Eden to water the garden; and from thence it was parted, and became into four heads. ¹¹The name of the first is Pison: that is it which compasseth the whole land of Havilah, where there is gold; ¹²And the gold of that land is good: there is bdellium and the onyx stone. ¹³And the name of the second river is Gihon: the same is it that compasseth the whole land of Ethiopia. ¹⁴And the name of the third river is Hiddekel: that is it which goeth toward the east of Assyria. And the fourth river is Euphrates. ¹⁵And the LORD God took the man, and put him into the garden of Eden to dress it and to keep it." The essay stems from the popular idea of the body as a temple (1 Corinthians 6:19).

11. Sanaa is the capital of Yemen; Many believed Havilah was near Sanaa.

12. Genesis 2:13

13. Hiddekel is an ancient name for the Tigris River (see Genesis 2:14 and Daniel 10:4). Assyria was a Mesopotamian empire lasting until 612 BC (see Genesis 2:14).

14. Genesis 3:16. It was commonly believed in the nineteenth century that Moses wrote the first five books of the Old Testament.

15. New Jerusalem was the literal or figurative city for saints that was particularly important to Emanuel Swedenborg and the followers of the New Church. See Revelation 21. Fuller references it in *Woman in the Nineteenth Century*: "[Swedenborg] announces the New Church that is to prepare the way for the New Jerusalem, a city built of precious stones, hardened and purified by secret processes in the veins of the earth through the ages" (122).

16. Patmos was the island to which the apostle John was banished. See Revelation 1:9 (NIV): "I, John, your brother and companion in the suffering and kingdom and patient endurance that are ours in Jesus, was on the island of Patmos because of the word of God and the testimony of Jesus."

17. Revelation 22:1.
18. Genesis 3:17–18.
19. Romans 8:23.
20. Revelation 2:17.
21. Revelation 2:17.
22. Revelation 21:4.
23. Revelation 3:12.
24. Revelation 21:2.
25. 1 Corinthians 15:26.

23. STIRPICULTURE

1. Daniel 5:25–27. Translated from Aramaic as "It has been counted and weighed, weighed and divided." Daniel interprets this as a sign of the weakness of the kingdom.

24. RAPID MULTIPLICATION OF THE UNFIT

1. Woodhull quotes loosely from Michael Foster's *Text Book on Physiology* (1876), a popular medical text.

2. "Fatigue poison" was a nineteenth-century term for exhaustion resulting from industrial labor. The term was used by reformers who sought protective labor laws.

3. *Pari passu* means "hand in hand" or "in equal step." Woodhull probably draws this term from her experience in the business world. Here she is referring to the public outcry to change the circumstances that are responsible for these dire statistics. Today, the term is used most frequently in finance to mean that multiple loans, stocks, and other monetary forms have an equal standing; one does not have seniority over another.

4. Woodhull is likely referring to India census commissioner Jervoise Athelstane Baines, who published *Census of India, 1891: A General Report*.

5. Fœticide referred to abortion; overlaying was a synonym for the suffocation of infants.

6. J. R. Rengger's *The Reign of Doctor Joseph Gaspard Roderick De Francia, in Paraguay* (London: Hurst, 1827). Woodhull is citing Darwin's *The Variation of Animals and Plants Under Domestication*, which first appeared in 1868.

7. Woodhull appears to have accidentally skipped over number six.

8. Woodhull refers to George Lippard's influential book, *New York: Its Upper Ten and Lower Million* (Cincinnati: Rulison, 1853).

25. I AM THE DAUGHTER OF TIME

1. A slightly modified quotation from Voltaire's *The Man of Forty Crowns* (1768).

2. The actual line is, "If a book comes from the heart, it will contrive to reach other hearts." Thomas Carlyle, *On Heroes, Hero-Worship, and the Heroic in History* (1871; New York: Houghton Mifflin, 1907), 90.

3. One after another, or serially.

4. A slightly modified version of Whittier's poem "My Soul and I."

26. WOMAN SUFFRAGE IN THE UNITED STATES

1. Colorado was the second state to give women the right to vote (1893); Wyoming was the first (1869).

2. Indiana representative George Julian (1817–1899) was suggested as an alternative to Frederick Douglass as the vice presidential candidate on the 1872 Equal Rights Party ticket.

3. Goldwin Smith was a British Canadian writer who was known for his educational reform and abolitionist policies. He moved to the United States in 1864 and become a professor at Cornell University. Tension existed between the *London Times*, a powerful publication of English elites who tended to side with the South, and abolitionist Englishmen like Smith.

4. This issue of the *Humanitarian* included a photograph of Woodhull along with several woodcuts representing her memorial, her acceptance of the presidential nomination, and her attempt to vote. The caption to the latter reads "VICTORIA VICTA!—VICTORIA WOODHULL AND TENNIE C. CLAFLIN AT THE POLLS IN THE CITY OF NEW YORK, ON ELECTION DAY, NOV. 7TH.—THEY PRESENT THEIR BALLOTS, BUT ARE DENIED THE EXERCISE OF THE ELECTIVE FRANCHISE."

# Bibliography

Andrews, Stephen Pearl, ed. *Love, Marriage, and Divorce and the Sovereignty of the Individual: A Discussion by Henry James, Horace Greeley, and Stephen Pearl Andrews.* New York: Stringer and Townsend, 1853.

Arac, Jonathan, and Harriet Ritvo, ed. *Macropolitics of Nineteenth-Century American Literature: Nationalism, Exoticism, Imperialism.* New Americanists. Durham NC: Duke University Press, 1995.

Bartlett, John Russell. *Dictionary of Americanisms: A Glossary of Words and Phrases, Usually Regarded as Peculiar to the United States.* New York: Bartlett and Welford, 1848.

Basch, Norma. *In the Eyes of the Law: Women, Marriage, and Property in Nineteenth-Century New York.* Ithaca NY: Cornell University Press, 1982.

Blackmar, Frank W. *Kansas: A Cyclopedia of State History,* vol. 1. Chicago: Standard, 1912.

Boggis, JerriAnne, Eve Allegra Raimon, and Barbara A. White, eds. *Harriet Wilson's New England: Race, Writing, and Region.* Durham: University of New Hampshire Press, 2007.

Braude, Ann. *Radical Spirits: Spiritualism and Women's Rights in Nineteenth-Century America.* Boston: Beacon, 1989.

Brodie, Janet Farrell. *Contraception and Abortion in Nineteenth-Century America.* Ithaca NY: Cornell University Press, 1994.

Buhle, Mari Jo, and Paul Buhle, ed. *The Concise History of Woman Suffrage.* Urbana: University of Illinois Press, 1978.

Claflin, Tennie. "The Ethics of Sexual Equality." New York: Woodhull and Claflin, 1873.

Comstock, Andrew. 1883. *Traps for the Young.* Ed. Robert H. Bremner. Cambridge MA: Harvard University Press, 1967.

Davis, Sue. *The Political Thought of Elizabeth Cady Stanton: Women's Rights and the American Political Traditions.* New York: New York University Press, 2008.

Falk, Erika. *Women for President: Media Bias in Eight Campaigns.* Urbana: University of Illinois Press, 2008.

Frisken, Amanda. *Victoria Woodhull's Sexual Revolution: Political Theater and the Popular Press in Nineteenth-Century America.* Philadelphia: University of Pennsylvania Press, 2004.

Fuller, Margaret. 1845. *Woman in the Nineteenth Century*. New York: Norton, 1971.
Gabriel, Mary. *Notorious Victoria: The Life of Victoria Woodhull, Uncensored*. Chapel Hill NC: Algonquin, 1998.
Graham, Sylvester. *A Lecture to Young Men on Chastity*. 1837. 4th ed. Boston: Light, 1838.
Green, Jonathon. *Cassell's Dictionary of Slang*. London: Cassell, 1998.
Hatch, Nathan O. *The Democratization of American Christianity*. New Haven CT: Yale University Press, 1989.
Hofstadter, Richard. 1944. *Social Darwinism in American Thought*. Rev. ed. Boston: Beacon, 1955.
Horowitz, Helen Lefkowitz. *Rereading Sex: Battles over Sexual Knowledge and Suppression in Nineteenth-Century America*. New York: Knopf, 2002.
Kent, Austin. "Mrs. Woodhull and Her 'Social Freedom.'" Clinton MA: Independent Radical Tract Society, 1873.
Klaw, Spencer. *Without Sin: The Life and Death of the Oneida Community*. New York: Penguin, 1993.
Leslie, Eliza. *Miss Leslie's Behavior Book: A Guide and Manual for Ladies*. Philadelphia: Peterson, 1859.
Marsh, Margaret S. *Anarchist Women, 1870–1920*. Philadelphia: Temple University Press, 1981.
McFeely, William S. *Frederick Douglass*. New York: Norton, 1991.
McGarry, Molly. "Spectral Sexualities: Nineteenth-Century Spiritualism, Moral Panics, and the Making of U.S. Obscenity Law." *Journal of Women's History* 12, no. 2 (Summer 2000): 8–29.
Mills, Bruce. *Poe, Fuller, and the Mesmeric Arts: Transition States in the American Renaissance*. Columbia: University of Missouri Press, 2006.
Passet, Joanne Ellen. *Sex Radicals and the Quest for Women's Equality*. Urbana: University of Illinois Press, 2003.
Rafferty, Edward C. *Apostle of Human Progress: Lester Frank Ward and American Political Thought, 1841–1913*. Lanham MD: Rowman and Littlefield, 2003.
Rosen, Jeffrey. *The Supreme Court: The Personalities and Rivalries that Defined America*. New York: Macmillan, 2007.
Sachs, Emanie. *The Terrible Siren: Victoria Woodhull*. New York: Harper, 1928.
Said, Edward. *Orientalism*. New York: Pantheon, 1978.
Sanchez-Eppler, Karen. "Bodily Bonds: The Intersecting Rhetorics of Feminism and Abolition." *Representations* 24 (Fall 1988): 28–59.
Shaplen, Robert. *Free Love and Heavenly Sinners: The Story of the Great Henry Ward Beecher Scandal*. New York: Knopf, 1954.
Smith-Rosenberg, Carroll. *Disorderly Conduct: Visions of Gender in Victorian America*. 1985. New York: Oxford University Press, 1986.

Solomon, Martha M. *A Voice of Their Own: The Woman Suffrage Press, 1840–1910*. Tuscaloosa: University of Alabama Press, 1991.

Stern, Madeleine B. *The Pantarch: A Biography of Stephen Pearl Andrews*. Austin: University of Texas Press, 1968.

———. *The Victoria Woodhull Reader*. Weston MA: M&S, 1974.

Tilton, Theodore. *Victoria C. Woodhull, a Biographical Sketch*. New York: Golden Age, 1871.

Underhill, Lois Beachy. *The Woman Who Ran for President: The Many Lives of Victoria Woodhull*. New York: Bridge Works, 1995.

Waller, Altina L. *Reverend Beecher and Mrs. Tilton: Sex and Class in Victorian America*. Amherst: University of Massachusetts Press, 1982.

OTHER PUBLICATIONS BY VICTORIA WOODHULL

*The Alchemy of Maternity*. Cheltenham: Sawyer, 1889.

*The Argument for Women's Electoral Rights, Under Amendments XIV and XV of the Constitution of the United States: A Review of My Work at Washington, D.C., in 1870–1871*. London: Norman, 1887.

*Breaking the Seals; or, The Key to the Hidden Mystery*. New York: Woodhull and Claflin, 1875.

*Congressional Reports on Women Suffrage*. New York: Woodhull, Claflin, and Co., 1871.

*Constitutional Equality the Logical Result of the XIV and XV Amendments*. New York: Journeymen Printers' Co-operative Association, 1871.

*The Human Body the Temple of God; or, The Philosophy of Sociology*. London: n.p., 1890. With Tennessee C. Claflin.

*Humanitarian* (1892–1901). With Zula Maud Woodhull.

*Humanitarian Government*. London: n.p., 1890.

*A New Constitution for the United States of the World Proposed for the Consideration of the Constructors of Our Future Government*. New York: Woodhull, Claflin, and Co., 1872.

*The Origin, Tendencies, and Principles of Government*. New York: Woodhull, Claflin, and Co., 1871.

*Paradise Found*. London: Culliford, n.d.

*Victoria C. Woodhull's Complete and Detailed Version of the Beecher-Tilton Affair*. Washington DC: Bradley Adams, 1876.

# Index

*Note: Victoria Woodhull's name has been shortened to the initials VW.*

Abbott, Lyman, xxxii
abolition, 210–11, 314ch20n2; rhetoric of, 100, 115, 129, 148, 153, 208, 217, 219–20, 256–57; and spiritualism, xxxi
abortion, xxi–xxii, xxii, 316n24, 318n5; and fear of race extinction, 248–49; T. Claflin on, xxi–xxii
Adam and Eve, 262, 266–69
adultery: Jesus on, 262. *See also* Beecher-Tilton scandal; extramarital affairs
alcoholism: developed in utero, 245; of first husband, 242
Allen, George R., 79
American Association of Spiritualists, xxx–xxxi, xxxv, 104, 172
American Bastille, 125, 311n1
American Bible Society, 134
American Revolution: labor reform compared to, 94; social freedom compared to, 194; social revolution compared to, 151, 312n1; women's suffrage compared to, 44, 308ch8n2
American Society of Spiritualists, disaffection with VW, 198
American Woman Suffrage Association, break with VW, 147
anarchy, xxxii, 306n10; and spiritualism, xxxi

Andrews, Stephen Pearl, xxii, xxiv, xxv–xxvi, 135; and free love resolution, 29; religious research of, 142; and VW's writings, xlii–xliii
animal magnetism, 313n3; and sex, 175–76
antenatal murder. *See* abortion
Anthony, Susan B., xi, xiii, xliii, 37, 147, 302, 305n4
anti-obscenity movement, xxvii–xxviii
armed forces, universal, 13
"A Speech on the Principles of Social Freedom" (Woodhull), xxvi
Assyria, 268
Astor, John Jacob, 69, 72, 95, 309n1

Baines, Jervoise Athelstane, 289, 318ch24n4
Beecher, Henry Ward, xxvi–xxvii, 118–20, 120–24, 216–17, 243–44, 306n7, 308ch7n1, 309n4; and Beecher-Tilton scandal, 98, 101–2, 108–10, 135–36, 140; and evolutionary theory, xxxii; excused after scandal, 140–41; "Gospel of Love," xxxviii
Beecher-Tilton scandal, xxvi–xxvii, 98–124, 135, 243–44, 255, 306n7, 316n21; public exposure of, 105–6, 128–29, 216–17
Bennett, James Gordon, xviii, 131
Bible, obscene material in, 134, 143
biblical scripture, VW's use of, xiii,

biblical scripture (*cont.*)
xxxviii; example, 27, 53, 59, 63, 80, 82, 139, 140, 159, 161, 197, 233, 254–55, 261, 265, 266, 267, 268, 270, 272, 278, 307ch5n3, 309ch10n2, 309n11, 309nn7–8, 310ch12n1, 310ch12n3, 312n5, 312n19, 313ch17n6, 314n16, 315n8, 316nn1–9, 317n11, 317n12, 317nn17–25; paraphrase of, 264. *See also* Christian rhetoric
*Bingham v. Cabot* (1798), 307ch5n5
birth control, 292
birth rates, 248; of negroes, 289; of the unfit, 290–91
Bismarck, Otto von, 100–101, 310ch14n2
Blackwell's Island, 69, 309ch11n2
Bladen, Elizabeth, 37
Blatchford, Samuel, xxvii, 244
Blood, James Harvey (second husband), xv, 129; arrested for obscenity, xxvii–xxviii; and vw's writings, xlii–xliii
Boadicea (early British heroine), 164, 313ch17n8
Bonaparte, Napoleon, spirit of, 169, 313ch18n1
bondholders, 95–96
*Boston Herald*, 103
Bowen, Henry C., 101, 126
Bowen, Mrs. M. B., 302
Braude, Ann, xxix–xxxi
Briggs, Ruth W. S., 79
Bunyan, John, 314n13
Burton, Harriet, 79
Butler, Benjamin, xviii, 43, 302

Caligula (Roman emperor), 139
cannibalism, 292
Cape May, 39
capitalism, indictment of, 68–72, 91–93
Carlyle, Thomas, 295, 318ch25n2

Carpenter, Matthew, 102
Catholic Church, 229, 248, 315n4; and marriage, 253
"Caudle Lectures," 234, 315n9
Cervantes, Miguel de, 116
Challis, Luther, xxviii, 126, 128, 129
children: breeding and raising of, 215–16, 223–24, 244–45, 248; crime and, 274; damaged by parents' false sexual relations, 186, 226–27, 241–42, 249; and dependency on fathers, 158; disease in, 285–86; education of, 206; fate of without marriage, 221–22, 314ch21n2; masturbation and, 180–81; as oppressed class, 156, 158; as products of true sexual relations, 248; raised by society, not parents, 205–6; sexual impulses in, 183; society's neglect of, 203–5; unwanted, 179–80, 241, 248; and in utero development of character, 245–46, 249. *See also* stirpiculture
child welfare, national system of, 10–11
China, population of, 289
Christ. *See* Jesus
Christianity: conservatism of, 265; and free love, 172–73; hypocrisy of as practiced by society, 158–60
Christian rhetoric: example, 48, 58–59, 63, 68, 70, 73, 75, 308ch8n5; vw's use of, xxxv–xxxvi, xxxvii–xxxviii, 123, 133–34, 165. *See also* biblical scripture
Christian Scientists, xxxi
*Christian Union* (magazine), 38, 308ch7n1
churches, hypocrisy of, 155
citizenship: qualifications for, 16; women's, 30
Civil War, 153
Claflin, Buck (father), xv

Claflin, Rose (mother), xiv, xxx
Claflin, Tennessee "Tennie" (sister), xiii, 131; on abortion, xxi–xxii; arrested for obscenity, xxvii–xxviii, 127; and attempt to vote, 303, 319n4; as lecturer, 306n6; sexualization of in press, xvi; as stockbroker, xv–xvii
class system: and conditions of lower classes, 273–74, 282; improving conditions of working class, 3, 307ch1n2; and oppression of lower classes, 156–57
class warfare, 76–77, 82, 92, 150–53
clergy: hypocrisy of, 255; mercenary objectives of, 225–26, 253, 255; preaching conservative values, 144; scandals of, 145; women's crushes on, 255. *See also* Beecher-Tilton scandal
Cochrane, Abigail, 286
cohabitation, compulsory, 202–3
*Cohen v. Virginia* (1821), 307ch5n5
Colorado, women's suffrage in, 299–300, 302, 318ch26n1
Commodus (Roman emperor), 139, 312n16
communal living, 259
communism, VW's support for, 73
*Communist Manifesto* (Marx), xiii
companies operating illegally, nationalization of, 14
"Complete and Detailed Version of the Beecher-Tilton Affair" (Woodhull), 98–124
Comstock, Anthony, xix, xxvii–xxviii, 126, 130, 311n4; accused of implicating VW, 133
conception, 277
Congress, U.S., 30; VW's address to, xvii–xviii, 21, 300–302
"Congressional Reports on Women's Suffrage" (Woodhull), 23

Constitution, U.S., 151, 283; Fifteenth Amendment, 21–22, 31, 36, 40–41, 43–44, 47; Fourteenth Amendment, 21, 31, 36, 40–41, 43–44, 307ch5n1; and women's suffrage, 21–22, 23–27, 299–300, 300–303, 307ch5nn4–5
Constitutional amendments, and direct vote, 20
"Constitution of the United States of the World" (Woodhull), 7–20; imperialism in, xli–xlii; racism in, 8. *See also* universal government
contracts, protection and enforcement of, 18, 20
cooperative businesses, 12–13, 86
cooperative homes, 259
cooperative labor, 259
copyright laws, 10
corporate earnings, limits to, 14
Credit Mobilier, 154, 312n2
Creswell, John, 132–33, 311n12
crime: and government, 275; inherited tendency toward, 274–78
criminality as mental illness, 278
criminal justice system, reform of, 87–88, 160–62
criminals, as oppressed class, 156
Crittenden, Alexander, 54–55, 309n4
cross-marriage (interracial marriage), 292

Darwin, Charles, 318n6
Darwinian theory, xxxii, 316n1. *See also* evolution
Davis, Noah, 126–27, 130–33, 243
Davis, Paulina Wright, 43, 109–11, 302; and Beecher-Tilton scandal, 135
Dawes Act (1887), xli–xlii
*The Days' Doings* (newspaper), xvi
Declaration of Independence, 150–51

Declaratory Act, 44, 308ch8n2
degeneracy, hereditary, 274, 276–77, 281, 286–87; and *marriages de convenance*, 290
Democratic party, 40; criticism of, 33; and labor issues, 47; and suffrage, 30
demonstrations, violent, 81
Demosthenes, spirit of, 169, 170–71, 313ch18n1
Denison, Ruth Carr, 302
*Detroit Union*, xxxviii
direct trade, 12, 71
direct vote, 19–20, 85
disease: in children, 285–86; and false sexual relations, 249, 257–58; and fertility, 293; and sex, 177–78
Dividends Takers. See stock companies
domestic violence, 5–6; and Beecher-Tilton scandal, 110
Douglass, Frederick, xx, 77, 79, 90, 305n5, 318ch26n2
Dundore, Lavinia C., 78

education: compulsory, 206; guaranteed right to, 180; national system of, 10–11, 88; wasted on the degenerate, 288
eight-hour workday, 87, 94; in New York state, 92, 310ch13n1
elected officials, 17–18, 88
election fraud, 154
election procedures, 16–17
"The Elixir of Life" (Woodhull), xiv, xxxv
Elliot, John T., 78
employment guaranteed by government, 87, 160
Enforcement Act (1870), 31
equality, government to maintain, 68
Equal Rights Party, xix–xx, 40–42, 104; correspondence of, 78–89; platform of, 83–84, 91; ratification meeting of, 90–91

Ethiopia, as abdominal cavity, 268
eugenics, xiv, xxxii–xxxiii, xxxviii–xl, 248, 287, 289, 294; and conflict with free will, xxxviii–xxxix; and government, 275–76; and women's rights, xxxv, xl
Euphrates River, as human reproductive system, 269–70
Evangelical Alliance, 159–60
*Evening Telegram*, 103
evolution, xxxii, 271; and population growth, 289
extramarital affairs, 190; ubiquity of, 145–46, 173, 176, 177. See also Beecher-Tilton scandal

Fair, Laura, 309n4
Falk, Erika, xviii
false sexual relations. See sexual relations, false
family life, society's damage of, 202–3
fatigue poison, 285, 318ch24n2
federal power, limits to, 19
fertility, and disease, 293
Fifteenth Amendment. See Constitution, U.S.
financial bailouts, and U.S. Government, 154
financial speculation, 74, 154
fœticide (abortion), 292. See also abortion
Foster, Michael, xl, 285, 318ch24n1
Fourier, Charles, xxix, 135, 310ch12n2
Fourteenth Amendment. See Constitution, U.S.
Frazier, Isaac, 78
freedom: individual, 66–67, 81, 117, 122–23; as moral truth, 137
freedom of religion, 136–37, 186–87, 229; free love compared to, 63
freedom of the press, 131

free love, xix, xxi–xxii, xxv, xxxv, 29, 38, 61–64, 99, 135, 173–74, 221, 237, 248; as alternative to masturbation, 181; and child rearing, 246; and Christianity, 172–73; common but hidden, 187; compared to freedom of religion, 63, 138; defense of, 51–53, 65, 139–41, 251–52, 253–55; defined, 139, 186; endorsed by spirit world, 174–75; and Equal Rights Party, 78; explanation of, 214–15; not licentiousness, 138; and organized religion, 255; and superior children, 182–83
free speech, 172
free will, and conflict with eugenics, xxxviii–xxxix
Frisken, Amanda, xi, xvi, xx, xxvi, xlii, 51, 149

Gabriel, Mary, xxxviii, 198, 261
Galton, Francis, xxxii–xxxiii
Garden of Eden, 262, 264–65, 316–17n10; as the human body, 265–68, 270–71; as the human family, 268–69; restored, 271
"The Garden of Eden" (Woodhull), xxxvii–xxxviii
Garrison, William Lloyd, xxix, 76–77, 100, 129, 310ch14n1
*Genesis and Its Authorship* (Quarry), 316–17n10
George, Henry, xxiv
German liberation theology, 316n1
Gihon River, as intestinal system, 267–68, 270
*Globe*, 301
God: love as, 237; and sex, 262–65
*The Golden Age* (magazine), 102
"The Good Gray Poet" (O'Connor), 144
Goose Question, 230, 315n5

government: and corruption, 153–55, 312n2; and crime control, 275; and eugenics, 275–76; and guaranteeing employment, 87, 160; and maintaining equality, 68; universal, 88; uses of, 84, 91, 150–51, 180
Government, U.S.: criticism of, 279–81; and financial bailouts, 154
Graham, Sylvester (*A Lecture to Young Men*), xiv
Grant administration, and government corruption, 154, 312n2
Greeley, Horace, 88, 102, 310ch12n4; criticism of, 82–83
Greene Street, 58, 157, 309n6
Greenwood Cemetery, 242, 315n13
Grilling, Mrs. J. S., 302
Grimké sisters, xxix
Grundy, Mrs. (fictional character), 139, 312n17
Guion, Madam. *See* Guyon, Madam
Guyon, Madam, 142, 312n20

handicapped, as oppressed class, 156
Harlan, James, 143
*Harper's Monthly Magazine*, 82
*Harper's Weekly*, xxii
Harwood, W. S., 304
Hatch, Nathan O., xxx
Havilah, land of, as the human body, 266–67, 316–17n10
health: and magnetism, 174–76; and sex, 175–77, 226–27, 258
Henry, Patrick, vw's paraphrasing of, 146, 219
*Hereditary Genius* (Galton), xxxii
*On Heroes, Hero-Worship, and the Heroic in History* (Carlyle), 295, 318ch25n2
Hiddekel River, as elimination system, 268, 270, 317n13
higher criticism, 316n1; example of, 265

Hindu religion, 277
Hofstadter, Richard, xxxii
Hooker, Isabella Beecher, 23, 37, 43, 109, 138, 301, 302
Horowitz, Helen Lefkowitz, xxiv, xxvii
House Judiciary Committee, 30
House of Representatives, 20
Hull, Elvira, 187, 190
Hull, Moses, 187–88, 190, 313–14ch19n8
"The Human Body the Temple of God" (Woodhull), xxi
*The Human Body the Temple of God* (Woodhull), 21, 23, 305n3
*Humanitarian* (magazine), xxxix
human rights, 84
hydrocephalus, 293
hygiene movement, xiii–xiv, xl
Hypatia, 164, 313ch17n8
hypocrisy: and marriage, 221, 232; of society, 113, 115–16, 135, 158, 216, 233

"The Impending Revolution" (Woodhull), xvii
imperialism, xli–xlii
inbreeding, 292
*The Independent* (newspaper), 101
India, population of, 289
infanticide, 292
*Inquiries into Human Faculty* (Galton), xxxii–xxxiii
insane, as oppressed class, 156
institutions for the dysfunctional, 276, 280, 284–86
International Workingmen's Association, xxiv
interview, fabricated, 106–22, 310ch14n6

Jesus, 272; on love, 263; as model of social freedom, 142, 158–59, 233; on virtue, 261; and the woman at the well, 269

Josephine, spirit of, 169, 313ch18n1
judges. *See* elected officials
Julian, W. P., 300, 318ch26n2

labor issues, 92–94; strikes, 93; VW and, xxiv, 47
land grants, 15
land ownership, nationalization of, 11
land redistribution, 73
land speculation, and railroads, 72, 86
laws: and effect on behavior, 263; federalization of, 85; reasons for, 67; revision of, 276, 282–83; state and local, 27–28
lawyers, mercenary objectives of, 225–26, 252, 253
*A Lecture to Young Men* (Graham), xiv
leucorrhœa (vaginal discharge), 204, 249, 316n18
Lippard, George, 294, 318n8
literature, obscenity in, 143–44
lobbyists, 235
*London Times*, 303
Loughbridge, William, xviii, 43, 302
love, 137–38, 184–85; as God, 237; Jesus on, 263; lust as antithesis of, 63; and marriage, 220, 225
*Love, Marriage, and Divorce* (Andrews), xxiv
lust: as antithesis of love, 63; defined, 186, 237

magnetism, 191, 314n10; and health, 174–76
male-dominated institutions, criticism of, xvi, 149–50
*Malinda Fox v. the State of Ohio* (1847), 28, 308n6
*The Man of Forty Crowns* (Voltaire), 295, 318ch25n1
markets, public, 71

marriage, 98–99; compared to prostitution, 60–61, 203, 230–36, 232, 253; compared to slavery, 99, 107, 116–17, 204, 207–11, 218–19, 247, 256–57; contradictions of, 225; criticism of, 56–57, 64–65; deferred, 288, 291; deterrents to, 290–91; as economic necessity, 157, 256; evils of, 180–81, 207–8, 215–16, 217–19, 247; and false sexual relations, 178; and forced sex, 181, 232; honesty in, 252; and hypocrisy, 221, 232; limits to, 289; and love, 220, 225; as potentially lethal, 242–43; reasons for, 290; sexual estrangement in, 238; as sexual slavery, 186, 249–50; and true sexual relations, 176
"Marriage and Maternity" (Woodhull), xxxix
marriage market, 233
*marriages de convenance*, 290
Married Women's Property Act, 307ch5n2
Martin, John (third husband), xxxiii
martyrdom theme, 162
Marx, Karl (*Communist Manifesto*), xiii
masturbation, xiii–xiv, xl, 183, 186, 291; children and, 180–81
materialization, spiritual, 168, 174, 188–89, 313n2; and sex, 189–91. *See also* spiritualism
McFarland, Daniel, 54–55, 309n4
McGarry, Molly, xxviii–xxix
medical books, obscene material in, 143
medicine, and sex, 174–75
*Mene, Mene, Tekel, Upharsin*, 281, 317n11
mesmerism, 314n10
Middlebrook, Anna M., 78
middle-men, elimination of, 71. *See also* direct trade
Mill, John Stuart, 172, 313ch19n1

millennialism, 142, 312n21
*Miss Leslie's Behaviour Book* (Leslie), xxxvi
money-lenders, elimination of, 86–87
money system, national, 10
monogamy, 247–48
monopolies, 86; criticism of, 72, 74
Mormons/Mormonism, 60, 236–37, 309n9, 315n11
Moses, 265–66, 268–69, 270, 271, 275, 317n14
motherhood, xxxii; importance of, 277–78; rhetoric of, xxxvi–xxxvii, 240–41
Mott, Lucretia, 29, 50, 147–48
Moulton, Frank, 114–15, 118, 311ch14n8
"My Soul and I" (Whittier), 297, 318ch25n4

Nast, Thomas, xxii; cartoon by, *xxiii*, 305n3
National Association of Spiritualists, 103–6
National Convention of Spiritualists, 163–64
National Labor Union, 47, 308ch8n4
National Woman Suffrage Association, xiii, 29, 147
nativism, xli
*Natural Inheritance* (Galton), xxxiii
Naturalization Laws, 25, 307ch5n1
natural resources, nationalization of, 13
negroes, birth rates of, 289
Nero (Roman Emperor), 139, 312n18
New England Revivalism, 142
New Jerusalem, 270, 317n15; the new woman as, 271
New York City, 158; condition of children in, 204; prostitution in, 236
New York College of Physicians, 179
*New York Courier*, xvi

*New York Evening Post*, 125
*New York Herald*, xvi, xviii, 1, 129, 130
*New York: Its Upper Ten and Lower Million* (Lippard), 294, 318n8
*New York Times*, xvi, 130; and Beecher-Tilton scandal, 112
*New York Tribune*, 31, 54, 126, 130, 309ch10n3
*New York World*, and Beecher-Tilton scandal, 112
*nolle prosequi*, 127, 311n5
*North American Review*, 304
Noyes, John Humphrey, xxv, xxxiii, 142

oaths of office, elimination of, 17, 19
obscenity: defined, 143; in literature, 143–44; in medical books, 143; and Postal Service, 126–27, 132–33, 311n2
O'Connor, William, 144
Oneida Community, xxv, xxxiii, 142, 231
"The Orations of Demosthenes," 170–71
Orient, popular fascination with, 233, 315n7
*On the Origin of Species* (Darwin), xxxii
*The Origin, Tendencies, and Principles of Government* (Woodhull), xvii–xviii
*Osborn v. Bank of the United States*, 307ch5n5
overpopulation, 281, 285; of the poor, 288

Paine, Thomas, 283
Paris Commune, 101, 310ch14n3
Passet, Joanne E., xxi, xxxviii
passports, elimination of, 135
paternity, uncertainty of, 203, 246
Patmos Isle, 270, 317n16
Paulist socialism, xxxviii, 306n16
persecution, feelings of, 162–64, 196, 198, 216, 259–60, 262, 295–97; by church and state, 244; by Comstock, 126, 133; endurance with help of spirits, 170; by the press, 106, 224, 228–29, 250–51; by the YMCA, 210
personal freedom, 194–95; defined, 201; and socialism, 258; society's fear of, 201–2
personal rights, protection of, 8–9, 18
*Pilgrim's Progress* (Bunyan), 195, 314n13
Pison River, 269; as circulatory system, 266–67, 270
*Pittsburgh Leader*, xxx, xxxi
Plymouth Church, 126, 255
political reform, 151
political secession, 35–36
"Poor Comstock" (Woodhull), xxvii
Pope, Alexander, 185, 313ch19n7
*Popular Science Monthly*, 246–47, 316n16
Postal Service, U.S., 132–33
pregnancy: ideal treatment of mothers during, 204, 205, 311ch14n7; unplanned, 179; unwanted, 205, 248; and in utero character development, 245–46, 249
the press: censorship of, 129; and fabricated interview, 106–22, 310ch14n6; freedom of, 131; and perceived bad treatment of reform movement, 104–5; and persecution feelings, 106, 224, 228–29, 250–51; and suppression of truth about sex, 250–51; and women's suffrage, 30–31
"The Principles of Social Freedom" (Woodhull), xxi
prison reform, 3, 11, 161
privacy, right to, 123, 138–39
prolapsus uteri, 249, 316n18
promiscuity, 231–32; accusations of, 227–31
property rights, 84–85, 87, 91
prostitution, 58, 59–60, 190, 218, 309n6;

INDEX

defined, 231; as economic last resort, 156–58; and life span of prostitutes, 247; marriage compared to, 60–61, 203, 230–36, 232, 253

"Qualification for the Franchise" (Woodhull), xxxviii
Quarry, John, 316–17n10

race, 284; as issue in women's suffrage, xviii–xx, 305n4; rhetoric of, 2–3, 25, 79
race extinction, 270; and abortion, 248–49
racism: in society, xl–xli; VW's, xviii–xx, xxxi, xl–xli, xli, 8, 207, 256
railroads: and land speculation, 72, 86; nationalization of, 12, 74
Raines, Mr. *See* Baines, Jervoise Athelstane
rape, within marriage, 218–19
"The Rapid Multiplication of the Unfit" (Woodhull), xv, xxxix, 253, 284–94; racism in, xli. *See also* eugenics
redistribution of wealth, 11–12, 73, 96, 163; through taxation, 95
referendum, 85. *See also* direct vote
Reformatory Workshops, 161. *See also* prison reform
reform movement, 80–81, 104–5, 244–45, 310ch12n2
*The Reign of Doctor Joseph Gaspard Roderick De Francia* (Rengger), 318n6
religion: freedom of, 63, 136–37, 138, 186–87, 229; sexual desire as, 239–40; and spiritualism, 166–67. *See also* Christianity; Christian rhetoric; churches; Hindu religion
Rengger, J. R., 293, 318n6
representatives. *See* elected officials
*The Reproductive Organs* (Scudder), 258

reproductive system, 264; delicacy of, 292; relationship with brain, 293; and true sexual relations, 258
Republican Party, 40, 69; criticism of, 32–33; and labor issues, 47
resurrection (of spirits), 188–89, 192–93. *See also* spiritualism
retrogression in humans, 287. *See also* reversion in humans
revenue system, nationalization of, 13–14
reversion in humans, 292. *See also* retrogression in humans
Reymert, J. D., 78
Richardson, Albert, 54–55, 309n4
Riddle, H. G., 301
right to privacy, 123, 138–39
right to publish, and sexual discrimination, 130
Rochester Knockings, 166

Sage, Abby, 54
Sanaa (capital of Yemen), 267
Sánchez-Eppler, Karen, xxxi
"The Scare-Crows of Sexual Slavery" (Woodhull), xviii–xix, xxv, 198–211
Schopenhauer, Arthur, 297
scientific socialism, 99
Scudder, John, 257–58, 316n23
Second Great Awakening, xiv, xxx
Semiramis (Assyrian queen), 164, 313ch17n8
Senate, abolishment of, 20
sex: and animal magnetism, 175–76; and disease, 177–78; forced, 178, 232; and God, 262–65; and health, 175–77, 226–27, 258; and materialized spirits, 189–91; and medicine, 174–75; and need for mutual fulfillment, 177–79; as woman's primary fiscal asset, 256. *See also* sexual relations

| 333

INDEX

sex education, xiii–xiv, 183, 195, 228
sexual demoralization, 181
sexual desire: as natural religion, 239–40; as necessary for life, 238–39
sexual discrimination, 131; and right to publish, 130
sexual dissatisfaction, and women, 178–79
sexual estrangement, in marriage, 238
sexual freedom, 228–29, 230–31; benefits of, 258
sexual passion, as the voice of God, 146
sexual relations: legitimate reasons for, 182; when unadvisable, 178; women's control over, 253–54
sexual relations, false, 177–78, 192, 227–28, 314n11; as cause of disease and death, 193, 249; children of, 186, 226–27, 241–42, 249
sexual relations, true, 193–94; children of, 248; defined, 227–28; and marriage, 176
"sexual science," xxxi–xxxii, xxxv–xxxvi
sexual selection, 290
sexual slavery, marriage as, 249–50
shame, rhetoric of, xxxvi
slavery: male-female sexual relations as, 61, 199–200; marriage compared to, 99, 107, 116–17, 204, 207–11, 218–19, 247, 256–57; sexual hypocrisy as, 190; wage labor compared to, 70, 76, 91, 153; women's situation compared to, 25, 45, 83, 141–43, 157
Smith, Goldwin, 303, 318ch26n3
Social and Industrial Palace (France), 82
social aristocracy, 163
social commune, 310ch12n2
Social Evil bills, 218, 235–36, 314ch21n1
social freedom, 53–54, 123, 194–95; compared to American Revolution, 194. *See also* free love

socialism, 67–68, 74–75, 141; French, 142; and personal freedom, 258; scientific, 99
social license, 206–7
social norms, tyranny of, 145–46
social organization, stages of, 62, 309n10
social reorganization, 81–82, 123–24, 143
social revolution, 75–76, 127, 150–52, 155, 160, 162; compared to American Revolution, 151, 312n1; prediction of, 68, 280
social welfare, 3, 10, 134, 180, 307ch1n2; as role of government, 160
society, conservatism of, 123, 134; as despotism, 139; and hypocrisy, 113, 115–16, 135, 158, 216, 233
sociology, 89, 164–65, 273
sodomy, 181, 186, 313ch19n6
Sokrates (Socrates), 277
Solomon, Martha M., xiii
Spear, John M., 78
Spencer, Herbert, 246–47, 316n16
spermatorrhea, 181, 204, 249, 313n5
spiritualism, xiv, xxviii–xxxi, 166–67, 188–89; and abolition movement, xxxi; and anarchy, xxxi; and Beecher-Tilton scandal, 105; and deception, 167–68; and Equal Rights Party, 78; and religion, 166–67; and sex, xxviii–xxix; and vw, xv, xxviii–xxxi, 56, 103–4, 168–70, 229; and women's rights, xxix–xxx
spirit world: endorses free love, 174–75; vw's visit to, 169
Stanton, Elizabeth Cady, 29, 37; and Beecher-Tilton scandal, 111, 135; and vw, xliii, 147, 306n18
state and local laws: prohibiting women's suffrage, 21–22, 27–28; replaced by federal law, 85

state governments, 19
states, admission to union, 15
sterility, causes of, 293
Stern, Madeleine B., xli–xlii
Stewart, Alexander Turney, 69, 71, 95, 309n1
stirpiculture, xxxiii, xxxix–xl, 99, 287, 293–94; Beecher's supposed support for, 118; and free love, 182–83. *See also* children, breeding and raising of; eugenics
"Stirpiculture" (Woodhull), xv, xxxix–xl
St. John, 270, 271, 317n16
*St Joseph (MO) Herald*, 149
stock companies: and railroads, 86; taxation of, 14–15
Stockham, Alice, xxxi–xxxii
stock speculation, 74
Stowe, Harriet Beecher, 38, 308ch7n1
St. Paul, 159, 265, 271–72
suffrage, women's, 2–3, 23–27, 30–36, 40–41, 299; appeal for men's support of, 45–46; in Colorado, 299–300, 302, 318ch26n1; movement associated with American Revolution, 44, 308ch8n2; movement compared to early Christianity, 53, 308–9ch10n1; race as issue in, xviii–xx, 305n4; and state and local election laws, 21–22, 27–28; VW's appeal to Congress for, 21–22
Sumner, Charles, 76–77, 102, 309ch11n3
Supreme Court, and women's suffrage, 31
Swedenborg, Emanuel, xxix, 317n15
Swedenborgism, xxix
syphilis, 293

Tammany Hall (or Ring), 153, 155, 312n4
tariffs, 9–10, 12
Tarquin (Roman king), 139, 312n18
taxation: as argument for suffrage, 25–26; limits to, 13; redistribution of wealth through, 95; reform of, 11–12
temperance, 245, 315n15; rhetoric of, 5–6
Ten Commandments, 275
territories, establishment and government of, 15–16
*Text Book on Physiology* (Foster), xl, 285, 318ch24n1
Tilton, Elizabeth, xxvi–xxvii, 123, 306n7; and Beecher-Tilton scandal, 109–10, 114–16
Tilton, Theodore, 76–77, 101, 121, 123; and Beecher-Tilton scandal, 110–13, 115, 117–18, 135; and free love movement, 102
Tombs (prison), 57, 69, 309n5
Train, George Francis, xix, 131–34, 305n4
*Train Ligue*, 131, 134, 311ch15n9
"Tried as by Fire" (Woodhull), xix, 212–60
true sexual relations. *See* sexual relations, true

unemployed, as oppressed class, 159–60
United States, social condition of, 280–81
universal government, 3, 7–8, 13, 88
"The Unsolved Riddle" (Woodhull), xxxiv
Upas tree, 190, 314n9
Upham, Thomas Cogswell, 142, 312n20
Utah, polygamy in, 236–37

Vanderbilt, Cornelius, xv–xvii, 66, 69, 95, 309n1
Vanderbilt, Scott & Co., 74
*The Variation of Animals and Plants Under Domestication* (Darwin), 318n6

venereal disease, 235–36, 293
Victoria League, 40–49
*Victoria Woodhull's Sexual Revolution* (Frisken), xiii
virtue: Jesus on, 261; Socrates on, 277; VW on, 261
Voltaire, 295, 318ch25n1
voting rights, 16–17, 19

wage labor: abolishment of, 87; compared to slavery, 70, 76, 91, 153
wages, guaranteed by government, 160
Waller, Altina, xxxviii
Warren, Josiah, xxii, 135
*Washington Chronicle*, xxxviii
Washington DC, prostitution in, 234–35
wealth: inherited, 73; redistribution of, 11–12, 73, 95, 96, 163
*Weekly Times and Echo*, xxxix
Whitman, Walt, 143–44
Whittier, John Greenleaf, 297, 318ch25n4
Williams, George H., 132, 311n11
Wilson, Harriet, xxx
women: condition in Classical Greece and Rome, 256; and crushes on ministers, 255; and economic dependency on men, 60–61, 156–58, 232, 256; and financial independence, 304; as oppressed class, 156; and sexual dissatisfaction, 178–79; situation of compared to slavery, 25, 45, 83, 141–43, 157; unrecognized power of, 200, 257
women's rights, xxxii–xxxiii; and eugenics, xxxv, xl; and spiritualism, xxix–xxx. *See also* suffrage, women's
Women's Suffrage Convention, 300–301
"To Women Who Have an Interest in Humanity" (Woodhull), xxxvii
Woodhull, Byron (son), xv; mental handicap of, 242

Woodhull, Channing (first husband), xv; alcoholism of, 242
Woodhull, Victoria, *xii*; accused of ambition, 36; accused of immorality, 38; addresses Congress, xvii–xviii, 21, 300–302; arrest for obscenity, xxvii–xxviii, 125, 127–29; attempt to vote, 303, 319n4; birth, xiv; blackmail allegations against, 113, 305n1; and Blood, xv; call for worker's revolution, 66; cartoon of by Nast, *xxiii*; Cooper Institute address, xxviii; death of, xxxiv–xxxv; defense against promiscuity accusations, 227–31; divorce of, xxxiii, 306n11; illness of, 105, 196, 310ch14n5; as lecturer, xx–xxi, 105–6; lose of support from less radical suffragists, 66; marriage to C. Woodhull, xv; marriage to Martin, xxxiii; as presidential candidate, xix–xx, 1–4, 36, 41–49, 78–89, 302–3; prints *Communist Manifesto*, xiii; sexualization of in press, xvi; and spiritualism, xv, xxviii–xxxi, 56, 103–4, 168–70; as stockbroker, xv–xvii; and theme of victimhood, xxxiv; visit to spirit world by, 169; wearing male clothing, xx
Woodhull, Zula Maud (daughter), xv, xxxv
*Woodhull and Claflin's Weekly*, xiii, xvi–xvii, xxiv, 101, 104, 198; and Beecher-Tilton scandal, 112, 128–29; scandalizing young Christian men, 133–34
Woodhullism, 187–88
worker's revolution, 66. *See also* labor issues
working class, blamed for political support of capitalism, 94–95. *See also* labor issues

Young, Brigham, 236–37
Young Men's Christian Assassination Association, 154, 243, 315n14. *See also* Young Men's Christian Association (YMCA)

Young Men's Christian Association (YMCA), 126, 133–34, 143, 159; and persecution feelings, 210

In the LEGACIES OF NINETEENTH-CENTURY
AMERICAN WOMEN WRITERS series

*The Hermaphrodite*
By Julia Ward Howe
Edited and with an introduction by Gary Williams

*In the "Stranger People's" Country*
By Mary Noailles Murfree
Edited and with an introduction by Marjorie Pryse

*Two Men*
By Elizabeth Stoddard
Edited and with an introduction by Jennifer Putzi

*Emily Hamilton and Other Writings*
By Sukey Vickery
Edited and with an introduction by Scott Slawinski

*Nature's Aristocracy: A Plea for the Oppressed*
By Jennie Collins
Edited and with an introduction by Judith A. Ranta

*Selected Writings of Victoria Woodhull: Suffrage, Free Love, and Eugenics*
By Victoria C. Woodhull
Edited and with an introduction by Cari M. Carpenter

To order or obtain more information on these or other University of Nebraska Press titles, visit www.nebraskapress.unl.edu.

www.ingramcontent.com/pod-product-compliance
Lightning Source LLC
Chambersburg PA
CBHW030332240426
**43661CB00052B/1606**